D0346441

A Vital National Interest – Ireland in Europe 1973–1998

A VITAL NATIONAL INTEREST – IRELAND IN EUROPE 1973–1998

Edited by Jim Dooge and Ruth Barrington

First published 1999
Institute of Public Administration
57–61 Lansdowne Road
Dublin 4
Ireland
for
The European Movement
32 Nassau Street
Dublin 2

© Authors of their respective chapters 1999

All rights reserved. No part of this publication may be reproduced or transmitted in any form or by any means, electronic or mechanical, including photocopying, recording or any information storage and retrieval system, without permission in writing from the publisher.

ISBN 1 902448 22 7

British Library Cataloguing-in-Publication Data
A catalogue record for this book is available from the British Library.

Cover design by Butler Claffey, Dún Laoghaire
Typeset in 10/12.5 Goudy by Peanntrónaic Teo., Dublin
Printed by Smurfit Print, Dublin

Contents

Contributors

Donal Barrington was born in 1929, and educated at Belvedere College, University College Dublin and King's Inns. He married Eileen O'Donovan, and has two sons and two daughters. He was called to the Bar in 1951 and served until 1979; senior counsel 1968–79; Judge of the High Court 1979–89; Judge at the Court of First Instance of the European Communities 1989–94. He was appointed to the Supreme Court on 12 January 1995.

Ruth Barrington is a graduate of University College Dublin and the College of Europe, Bruges. She was awarded a doctorate by the University of London in 1986. She is the author of *Health, Medicine and Politics in Ireland, 1900–1970* (IPA, 1987) and, with John Cooney, of *Inside the EEC – An Irish Guide* (O'Brien Press, 1984). She joined the Department of Health and Children in 1975 and was appointed Assistant Secretary in 1996. She took up her present position of Chief Executive of the Health Research Board in 1998. Dr Barrington has been a member of the executive committee of the European Movement since 1986.

Tony Brown is Alternate Director for Ireland and Denmark at the European Bank for Reconstruction and Development. He was an economist and policy adviser in the Irish Sugar Company 1961–86; an independent European affairs consultant 1986–97; a special adviser to Frank Cluskey in the Office of the Tanaiste and Minister for Social Welfare 1973–77; and special adviser in the Department of Tourism and Trade 1994–97. He has been a member of the European Movement since the mid-1960s and a member of its National Council for over 20 years. He was a co-founder of the Institute of European Affairs, and Project Leader on EU Enlargement 1991–97. He is Editor of the IEA European Document Series. He was honorary International Secretary of the Labour Party and a member of the Bureau of the Confederation of Socialist Parties of the European Community 1977–97.

Richard Burke was born in the USA and educated by the Christian Brothers in Thurles and Dublin, at University College Dublin and in King's Inns. He was elected to Dáil Éireann in 1969, and was Chief Whip of Fine Gael. As Minister for Education he initiated reorganisation of the Irish university system and introduced degree status for primary teachers, management boards for schools and the transition year programme. He founded Dublin City University in 1976. As Commissioner for Taxation he introduced the Sixth Value Added Tax Directive; as Commissioner for Transport he relaunched the Channel Tunnel as part of the major European infrastructure plan, and initiated the deregulation of air transport and the UN Code of

Conduct for Liner Conferences. As Commissioner for Consumer Affairs he legislated for the First Programme for Consumer Affairs, and as Commissioner for Relations with the European Parliament he prepared the first direct elections in 1979. He returned to Brussels from Harvard to become Vice-President of the Commission until his retirement in 1987.

Thomas Byrne is a Director of the South-East Regional Authority since 1994. From 1974 to 1990 he was Town Clerk of the Urban District Councils of New Ross, Cashel, Wicklow and Arklow. He has also worked in Wexford and Tipperary South Riding County Councils. He holds a BA in Public Management from the Institute of Public Administration and an M.Phil in European Studies from the National University of Ireland, Cork. He has a special interest in local and regional development and European Affairs. He has been a member of the European Movement in Ireland for many years.

William G. Carroll is the Director of Community and Enterprise in Kildare County Council. He has a BA in public administration from the Institute of Public Administration and a master's degree in rural development. He was the Community Officer in Dublin County Council 1982–93, and Director of the Dublin Regional Authority 1994–99. Since 1995 he has been Secretary of the Irish Delegation to the EU Committee of the Regions. He was Chairman of the National Youth Federation 1980–82, and was given the Robert Schumann Award for Involvement of Young People in Europe in 1983; he was President of the European Confederation of Youth Clubs 1984–90. He is a longstanding member of the European Movement and has been a member of its National Executive since 1994.

Liam Connellan is a chartered engineer; he graduated from University College Dublin in 1957. He is currently Chairman of the National Roads Authority, Generale des Eaux Ireland, and Smurfit Venture Investments. He was Director General of the Confederation of Irish Industry and a member of the Executive Committee of UNICE (Confederation of European Industry and Employer Organisations) 1972–92; he was a member of the Economic and Social Committee of the European Communities 1991–96 and was Chairman of the Industry Section of the committee 1994–96. He was President of the Royal Dublin Society 1995–98. He is currently Vice-President of the Institution of Engineers of Ireland. He was awarded the Knight Commander's Cross of the Order of Merit of the Federal Republic of Germany in 1998.

Barry Desmond is a Member of the European Court of Auditors. He has held public office in many capacities in Ireland and in the European institutions; from 1969 to 1989 he was the first Labour deputy for the Dún Laoghaire constituency; member of Dublin County Council 1974–81; member of Council of State 1973–91; delegate, Council of Europe 1973–81; Minister of State, Department of Finance 1981–82; Minister for Health and Social Welfare 1982–87; member of the European Parliament 1989–94 and deputy leader of the Labour Party 1982–89. He has been involved in the European Movement in Ireland since 1967 and served as an officer and executive member.

Jim Dooge is Honorary President of the European Movement, Ireland, and a long-time member of the European Association of Teachers and of the Irish Council for the European Movement. He was a member of the Seanad between 1961 and 1987; Chairman of the Seanad 1973–74; Minister for Foreign Affairs 1981–82; leader of the Seanad 1983–87. He was chairman of the Ad Hoc Committee of Representatives of Heads of Government on Institutional Reform 1985–86; a consultant to the Commission on Environmental Research and Programme Policy Implications; and a member of the statutory committee to assess the five-year Framework Programme on Research and Development (Davignon Group), 1998.

Joe Fahy was Head of Information in Ireland for the European Parliament 1973–90. He was educated at Gorey CBS and at Mungret College, Limerick. He was a journalist with the *Connacht Tribune*; in 1959 he was on the editorial staff of Independent Newspapers in Dublin. He joined the reporting staff of RTE news in 1963 and was appointed Deputy News Editor in 1966. In 1967 he became a political correspondent for RTE, a post he held until his appointment to the European Parliament in September 1973.

Brendan Finucane is the Director of Technology Services in Enterprise Ireland and a member of the Board of the National Standards Authority of Ireland. A science graduate of UCD, he worked in the Departments of Finance and Industry & Commerce before joining the National Board for Science & Technology in 1978. He has been an Irish delegate to various European policy and technology programmes, such as CREST and COST, and the European Space Agency. In 1989 he was chairman of TAFTIE (the Association for Technology Implementation in Europe).

Garret FitzGerald is a graduate in history, French and Spanish, a barrister, and a PhD in economics. A former Taoiseach, he is a lecturer, writer, occasional consultant and company director, and Chancellor of the National University of Ireland since 1997. He worked for Aer Lingus 1946–58. He was a consultant to the Federation of Irish Industries 1959–63; in the 1960s he was Managing Director of the Economist Intelligence Unit, Ireland. He was

Chairman of the Irish Council of the European Movement, and is now an Honorary President. He entered politics in 1965; Minister for Foreign Affairs 1973–77; elected leader of the Fine Gael Party 1977; Taoiseach June 1981–March 1982 and December 1982 to 1987.

Pádraig Flynn was born in 1939. A former national school teacher and publican, he was a member of Mayo County Council 1967–86 (Vice-Chairman 1975–77) and a member of Galway Regional Development Council 1973–80; he was a Fianna Fáil TD until 1995. He was Minister of State at the Department of Transport and Power 1980–81, Minister for the Gaeltacht March–October 1982, for Trade, Commerce and Tourism October–December 1982; for the Environment 1987–91. He was a front-bench spokesman on Trade, Commerce and Tourism 1983–87. During 1992 he was Minister for Justice and Minister for Industry and Commerce. In 1993–94 he was European Commissioner for Social Affairs and Employment, Immigration, Home Affairs and Justice. In 1994–99 he was Commissioner for Employment, Industrial Relations and Social Affairs, and was Acting Commissioner from March to September 1999.

Tom Garvey is a Visiting Lecturer at the Graduate School of Public and International Affairs, University of Pittsburgh; Vice-Chairman of the Irish Institute of European Affairs in Louvain; and Director of the Regional Environment Centre, Budapest. He is a graduate of UCD in economics and political science. In 1969 he became Chief Executive of Coras Tráchtála/The Irish Export Board; in 1977 he became European Commission Delegate to the Federal Republic of Nigeria; in 1980–84 he was involved in setting up An Post; in 1984–90 he worked as Director General Adjoint for Environment and Nuclear Safety in the European Commission.

Joan Hart is a former National Secretary of the European Movement (1993–96) and has been an active member since the early 1980s. She is a management and organisation consultant with extensive experience in the public and the financial sectors in Ireland and overseas. In the past year she returned to Ireland following a management development assignment for chief executives of local authorities in Tanzania. A graduate of the University of Limerick and the College of Europe with a masters by thesis from Limerick, she also holds a certified diploma in accounting and finance.

Miriam Hederman O'Brien is Chancellor of the University of Limerick, Honorary President of the European Movement, and Chairman of the Irish Committee and of the International Executive Committee of the European Cultural Foundation. A graduate in languages from UCD, she is a barrister-at-law and holds a Ph.D in political science from Dublin University. She was

Chairman of the Irish Council of the European Movement 1977–80. She chaired the Commission of Taxation 1980–85 and the Commission on the Funding of the Health Services 1987–89. She held the Killeen Research Fellowship 1990–92 (impact of exchange, education, training and professional formation between Ireland and Czechoslovakia, Hungry and Poland). She has written and broadcast widely on European affairs.

Patrick Hillery was born in 1923 and educated in Rockwell College and at University College Dublin, where he qualified as a medical practitioner in 1943. He was a Fianna Fáil TD 1951–73 and Minister for Education 1959–65; Minister for Industry and Commerce 1965–66; Minister of Labour 1966–69; Minister for External Affairs 1969–72. He was Vice-President of the Commission of the European Communities 1973–76, with responsibility for social affairs; he was President of Ireland 1976–90. Dr Hillery is an Honorary President of the European Movement.

John Hume was a leader of the Civil Rights Movement 1968–69, and a founder of Derry Credit Union and Derry Housing Association. In February 1969 he was elected as an Independent to Stormont for the Foyle constituency. He co-founded the SDLP in 1970; he was its deputy leader 1970–79 and has been its leader since 1979. He was a member of the Northern Ireland Assembly 1973–74 and Minister of Commerce in the Power-Sharing Executive 1974; elected as MEP to the European Parliament 1970 (re-elected 1983, 1987, 1992, 1997, 1999). He was Special Adviser to EC Commissioner Richard Burke 1977–79. Mr Hume was involved in the New Ireland Forum Talks, 1983; the Brooke Talks, 1992; the Forum for Peace and Reconciliation, 1994; and the Good Friday Agreement, 1998. In 1994 he was awarded the International League for Human Rights' award for Peace and Human Rights; in 1998 he was jointly awarded the Nobel Peace Prize.

Brigid Laffan is Jean Monnet Professor of European Politics and Director of European Studies, University College Dublin, and Visiting Professor at the European College, Bruges. She is the author of *Integration and Co-operation in Europe* (Routledge, 1992) and *The Finances of the Union* (Macmillan, 1997), the editor of *Constitution-building in the European Union* (Institute of European Affairs, 1996), and co-author with R. O'Donnell and M. Smith of *Europe's Experimental Union: Rethinking Integration* (Routledge, 1999).

Ray MacSharry is Chairman of Bord Telecom Éireann plc, London City Airport, Coillte Teoranta, Green Property plc, and the Irish Equine Centre. He is a director of the Bank of Ireland Group, Jefferson Smurfit Group plc, and Ryanair. He was a Fianna Fáil TD for Sligo–Leitrim 1969–89; Minister for State, Department of Finance and Public Service 1977–79; Minister for

Agriculture 1979–81; Tánaiste and Minister for Finance 1982 and 1987–88; Governor, European Investment Bank 1982; MEP for Connacht/Ulster 1984–87; member of the Commission of the European Communities for Agriculture and Rural Development 1989 to 6 January 1993. He has an Honorary Doctorate from the National University of Ireland, and an Honorary Doctorate of Economic Science from the University of Limerick. He is a longstanding member of the European Movement and was elected honorary President of the Movement for 1998–99.

Katherine Meenan is Internal Consultant with Bord na Móna. A graduate of the College of Europe, Bruges and NUI Maynooth, she is a former chair of the Irish Council of the European Movement and is currently vice-chair of the Institute of European Affairs and chair of the Public Affairs Committee. She is also a Council Member, National Council for Educational Awards, and has worked for the European People's Party and as Technical Adviser to the Group of the European People's Party. She worked as Special Adviser to the Taoiseach, Dr Garret FitzGerald 1981–87; in 1984–85 she was Head of Secretariat of the Ad Hoc Committee on Institutional Affairs (Dooge Committee).

Jim Murray is Director of BEUC, the European Consumers' Organisation. He was the first Director of Consumer Affairs in Ireland 1979–90. He was also the first director of the National Social Service Council (now the National Social Service Board) from 1972. Prior to that, he was an engineer in the Department of Post and Telegraphs and an active member of the Dublin Simon Community in its early years. He is currently European chairman of the Transatlantic Consumer Dialogue in Brussels. A graduate of UCD in physics and mathematics, he was called to the Bar in 1976.

David Neligan has been a director general in the EU Council Secretariat in Brussels since 1983. His DG covers the work of the Council in the areas of research, energy and transport, and until 1995 also environment and consumer protection. He is an official of the Department of Foreign Affairs, and served in Brussels (including negotiations for Ireland's accession to the Communities) 1963–83, in Paris (Deputy Head of Mission), and as Ambassador of Ireland to Japan (1976–78). He was subsequently Assistant Secretary in the Department heading the Anglo-Irish Division, including external cultural relations, information and press. He is a graduate of Trinity College Dublin.

Patricia O'Donovan is Deputy General Secretary of the Irish Congress of Trade Unions. A graduate of UCC and Harvard Law School, she was called to the Irish Bar in 1975. In 1977 she was European Information Officer with the Irish Congress of Trade Unions. She was also Legislative Officer, Equality Officer and Assistant General Secretary in Congress; in 1998 she was appointed Deputy General Secretary. She is responsible for economic and social policy, and represents Congress on the National Economic and Social Council, the National Competitiveness Council, the Euro Changeover Board of Ireland, and the Social and Employment Policy Committee of the European Trade Union Confederation (ETUC). She is a member of the governing body of the International Labour Organisation (ILO). In 1991 she was appointed a member of the Council of State; she has been a member of the European Movement since the mid-1970s, is currently on the Executive Committee of the Institute of European Affairs, and is a member of the Board of Directors of the Irish Centre of European Law.

Tom O'Higgins was called to the Bar in 1938 and took silk in 1954. In 1967 he was elected a bencher of the Honourable Society of King's Inns; in 1973 he was appointed to the High Court. He was Chief Justice of Ireland 1974–85 and a member of the Court of Justice of the European Union 1985–91. In 1999 he was awarded an Honorary Doctorate by the National University of Ireland. He is a member of the Council of State.

Michael O'Kennedy is currently co-chairman of the British–Irish Parliamentary Body. He has a master's degree in classics from UCD. He was called to the Bar in 1961 and made Senior Counsel in 1973. He is currently a bencher in the King's Inns. He has been a member of Oireachtas Éireann since 1965 and a Minister for Education, Transport and Power, Foreign Affairs, Finance, Agriculture and Labour in various governments. He has been President in Office of the Council of Foreign Ministers, Finance Ministers and Agriculture Ministers of the European Union at various times since the late 1970s. He was a member of the Commission of the European Community 1981–82, and has been a member of the European Movement in Ireland since the 1960s.

Seamus J. Sheehy is Professor of Agricultural Economics in University College Dublin. He is a former board member of Allied Irish Banks plc and of Greencore plc, and is well known in the agricultural industry for research and his press, radio and television contributions on farm and food issues. He is an expert on the impact of EU membership on agriculture. In the early 1980s he was a leading advocate of quotas as the means of controlling EU surpluses least harmful to Irish farmers and the Irish economy. More recently he has highlighted the shifting balance of advantage against quotas as the Uruguay Round Trade Agreement progresses, as the Millennium Trade Round gets under way and as EU enlargement approaches. Professor Sheehy is a strong supporter of the MacSharry and Agenda 2000 reforms.

Peter D. Sutherland is Chairman and Managing Director of Goldman Sachs International and Co-Chairman of BP Amoco plc. Educated at Gonzaga College, University College Dublin and the King's Inns, he graduated in civil law. He was Attorney General of Ireland 1981–84; EC Commissioner for Competition Policy 1985–89; Chairman of Allied Irish Banks 1989–93; Director General of The World Trade Organisation 1993–95; Chairman of the European Institute of Public Administration 1991–96. He has received numerous awards and honorary doctorates. His publications include the book *Premier Janvier 1993 ce qui va changer en Europe* (1989) and numerous articles in law journals. He chaired the EEC Commission Committee on the Internal Market post-1992 which led to the Sutherland Report.

Frank A. Wall has been a director in the Council of Ministers since 1991 and is responsible for parliamentary and institutional affairs. A graduate of UCC and the Free University of Brussels, he is also a solicitor. Following a brief period in the Commission in 1973, he worked as Adviser to the Group of European Progressive Democrats in the European Parliament until 1979. In 1980 he was Special Adviser to Ray MacSharry TD, Minister for Agriculture; from 1981 to 1991 he served as General Secretary of Fianna Fáil. He was appointed a Senator in 1982. A long-time member of the European Movement, he was chairman from 1987 to 1991; a founding director of the Institute of European Affairs, he is currently chairman of its Brussels branch.

Foreword

BERTIE AHERN
Taoiseach

As President of the European Movement, Ireland, I am very honoured to have this opportunity to make a contribution to this unique publication, *A Vital National Interest – Ireland in Europe 1973-1998.*

This publication serves as a testimony, in many cases from those directly involved, to the enormous benefits which membership of the European Union has bestowed on the Irish people and also to the significant contribution which Ireland has made to that Union. Never before has an Irish publication on a European subject matter attempted such an ambitious project – covering as it does the negotiation of Ireland's entry as outlined in such fine detail by former President Hillery, to our present day experiences as discussed by the numerous other authors. This is the first time that the involvement of key Irish people in the development of the Union has been compiled in one publication and will ensure a greater understanding of the role we have played in the shaping of Europe.

The European Movement, Ireland, by pulling together such an outstanding list of authors, has demonstrated once again the high profile of the people involved in its activities and the role of the Movement, not just in Ireland, but on the international stage also.

This book serves as an 'A to Z' of Ireland in the European Union. The last 25 years in the EU have allowed Ireland to reach the point today where we now have a more mature perception of our position in the Union and not just a perception couched in economic terms.

Whatever course Europe takes in the next 25 years, I believe that Irish governments will continue to play a significant role which takes account of our own national identity, economic needs and our, now more mature, place in Europe. I hope that this will be reflected by the European Movement, Ireland, when Volume II of this publication is published in 25 years' time.

Preface

ALAN DUKES

The European Movement in Ireland had much to celebrate in 1998, the 50th anniversary of the setting-up of the International European Movement at the Congress of the Hague. It marked 25 years of Ireland's membership of the European Union, and was also the year in which the Irish people ratified the Treaty of Amsterdam by referendum.

A *Vital National Interest – Ireland in Europe 1973–1998* commemorates these achievements. It is a fitting tribute to the many Irish people who played such an important role in the development of the Europe we know today. It is a very personal account of the authors' experience in this process.

From the accession talks in the 1960s to the role that Europe has played in the economic growth in Ireland in the 1990s, this book chronicles Ireland's membership of, and contribution to, the European Union. It offers an insightful account of the development of European policy and its impact on Ireland over the years, while also outlining the role and constant development of the European institutions.

This book is a must-read for any student or observer of European affairs and politics in general. It will serve as a very valuable guide to those countries preparing for accession to the European Union. Written by former Commissioners, a former Taoiseach, a former President of Ireland, ministers, officials, civil servants, academics, legal experts and a host of other interested parties, *A Vital National Interest – Ireland in Europe 1973–1998* is an unrivalled account of Ireland's relationship with, and involvement in, the European Union.

On behalf of the European Movement I offer thanks to all those who contributed to the success of this book: to the authors for their valuable contributions; to editors Jim Dooge and Ruth Barrington and their Editorial Committee; to our publishers, the IPA; and to the staff of the European Movement for seeing this publication through to its completion.

Introduction

JIM DOOGE AND RUTH BARRINGTON

The project that resulted in the present book of essays was prompted by the near coincidence of three anniversaries – the 50th anniversary of the Congress of the Hague, the 45th anniversary of the foundation of the Irish Council of the European Movement, and the 25th anniversary of the accession of Ireland to the European Community. This publication does not purport to be either a comprehensive history of developments over this period or a systematic analysis of the interaction between this country and the Community. Rather it is a collection of individual accounts by people from widely varying backgrounds of either their personal involvement or the role of key groups in the development of a new relationship between Ireland and the rest of Europe in the second half of the 20th century. The views expressed are their own and do not necessarily represent the official views of the groups with which they are associated or the stated views of the European Movement.

The structure of the book was not predetermined but was developed after receipt of the first draft of essays in order to facilitate readers interested in particular aspects of the general topic. The six essays in Part I deal with different aspects of the historical context of Irish involvement in the European venture. The six essays in Part II deal with the institutional dimension of the Community other than the Commission, and the relationships between the institutions. Part III deals with eight aspects of European policy and the choice of topics is, of necessity, relative. To avoid any controversy about the relative importance of the different policy areas, the essays in this part are ordered alphabetically by author. The essay by Paddy Hillery (Chapter 2) is supplemented by essays in Part IV giving personal accounts by all the other former Irish Commissioners of some aspect of their time in office. It was because of the unique nature of this set of essays that it was considered unnecessary to include a descriptive essay on the work of the Commission in Part II of the book. The final essay, by John Hume, looks to the future of Ireland in Europe and the key problems of economic and social cohesion, institutional development, and relationships with the rest of the world.

The editors acknowledge with gratitude the co-operation of the authors, which made their task less onerous than it might have been. They commend the authors' work to the reader. They are also grateful to Deirdre Healy, Sean Ó Riordáin, Patricia Lawler and Anna Rose O'Dwyer who shared the work of planning and of editing the volume.

Part I
History

1

The role of the European Movement in referenda

MIRIAM HEDERMAN O'BRIEN

Introduction

Historians tend to be overconfident about the accuracy of documents and the wisdom that their scrutiny confers. The extent to which an event is documented is considered an indication of its importance, not just at the time or to its chroniclers, but as a proof of the thesis of the historian who assesses the 'evidence'. While oral narration is also subject to human fallibility, contemporary judgements tend to enter the collective memory, whether they are true or false. So how is posterity to judge what influences shaped the destiny of its forebears and, consequently, its own destiny? A historian who combines passion and scepticism, accuracy and insight, and is prepared to comb through the evidence would be the ideal solution.

The evolution of the Irish people's view of themselves as Irish *and* European has not been charted. Despite the poetic rhetoric of James Clarence Mangan, memorised by generations of Irish schoolchildren, 'European' was not an instinctive aspect of the self-definition of Irish people in the first half of the 20th century. Today, those who are Irish and those who observe them would claim that the European dimension is an essential ingredient of modern Ireland. How did this change come about?

This essay is a brief outline of the various occasions on which Irish citizens were directly involved in voting on issues that affected both the Irish constitution and European integration, and of the role played by the Irish Council of the European Movement (ICEM) in the process. The constraints of space preclude an adequate evaluation of the part played by many people, from the 1950s to the present day, in creating and maintaining a 'movement' which was heterogeneous in membership, remarkably united in purpose and quite distinctive from other national councils of the European Movement, large or small. Almost all those involved were also members of other groups such as student, farmer, political, trade union, business, educational, professional and cultural organisations. They therefore cross-pollinated the ICEM with the concerns of their other activities, and their own organisations with the ideas being explored in Europe.

3

In 1999 it is not easy to understand how idealistic, Utopian and apparently irrelevant it seemed in 1958 to suggest that Ireland should seriously consider the possibility of aligning itself with 'the Six' that had created the revolutionary structure of the European Coal and Steel Community. Yet this is what the Irish Council did. It encouraged members of the political parties to overcome the criticism made in the Dáil that 'Deputies know nothing whatever about the difference between the Common Market and the Free Trade Area. I am sure 99 per cent of Deputies and Senators are not properly informed of the issues and arguments involved.'[1]

To those who consider the 1950s in Ireland to have been a bleaker version of the Dark Ages, it may come as a surprise to learn that the Irish Council hosted a well-attended meeting in the Shelbourne Hotel in Dublin in 1956 at which the audience heard the exiled Spanish liberal, Salvador de Madariaga, call on the 'peripheries of Europe to revitalise the soul of Europe'.

The ICEM became more focused on economic matters when it was reconstructed in 1959. Its diversity, however, has ensured that it has always been able to ask the fundamental questions, e.g. 'What is Europe, what form should co-operation take within it and what should be the role and place of Ireland in the process?'.

In common with most voluntary organisations, the ICEM had its valleys as well as its peaks. Some of the setbacks arose from within, but most came from external events as agendas changed and Irish participation in the 'European experiment' was delayed again and again. The experience of the eleven years from the date of Ireland's first application for membership of the European Communities in 1961 until its admission in 1972 is something that the ICEM has later discussed with Councils from the applicants to the European Union. In some respects it is easier to play a role when there is a battle to be fought for the minds and hearts of the electorate than when there is widespread consensus.

Political pundits tend to equate voting patterns with allegiance and enthusiasm. They are misled by their special interest and expert knowledge. City-dwellers who do not vote for their elected representatives do not thereby reject their city – but they may be sending some messages to the candidates. Citizens who ignore national elections do not thereby consider themselves undemocratic, or, still less, unpatriotic, however much their behaviour may affect the quality of the civic life of their country. A decline in the number of votes cast in elections for the European Parliament may be due to many factors and, like the decrease of citizens' involvement in other elections, it is

Notes corresponding to superior numbers in the text are given at the end of the chapter.

dangerous to ignore such a signal. It may send messages about the people's perception of the European Parliament and of the political parties that vie for election to it. It is not, however, a rejection of the sense of the European identity that has given Irish people so much confidence in themselves and in their future.

One of the main European debates – a perceived conflict between nationalism and European integration – has caused little serious dissension in Ireland. This is because membership of the wider European community has been seen as supporting rather than undermining Irish identity. It is for its contribution to that sense of being, at the same time, both Irish and European that the ICEM deserves credit. But the historian who will write the story of how, why and in what ways this disparate group of people influenced the outcome has yet to come forward.

The Irish Council of the European Movement

The European Movement is an umbrella body, created by political and social groups in order to promote a progressive, democratic Europe in the aftermath of the devastation caused by the Second World War and the dictatorships that preceded it. New institutions were needed in order to accommodate a diversity of political philosophies and national priorities and to build a coherent structure in which Europe could develop in a dynamic way. The first major manifestation of the Movement was a Congress in The Hague in 1948, organised by the 'International Committee of United European Movements', which became the European Movement. It launched a programme of action for the unification of democratic Europe.

The European Movement was an important political element in the creation of successive European Communities, progressing from the European Coal and Steel Community to the European Union. In order to increase its effectiveness it created a network of national councils. These councils varied in their predominant political philosophy and also in their approach (some being much more federalist than others), but all subscribed to the goal of European co-operation and development.

Ireland was represented at the European Congress of The Hague in 1948. The three Irish delegates to the Congress were Eleanor Butler, Senator James Douglas and Professor Michael Tierney. Archdeacon Gordon Hannon and Frederick Thompson from Northern Ireland were also invited, but it was subsequently decided, probably by the organisers, that they should not be part of the Irish delegation. Several efforts were subsequently made to establish an Irish Council. Indeed, the international European Movement contacted a number of political figures in Ireland, without success.[2]

A meeting was convened in the Shelbourne Hotel, Dublin, in January

1954 as a result of which the ICEM was created and officers and an executive were elected.[3]

The ICEM held occasional meetings and endeavoured to include a wide cross-section of Irish political and sectoral opinion among its members. It was not dominated by any single approach to European integration, as was the case in countries where some particular political group provided the driving force. Neither was it characterised by any violent difference of opinion, as also occurred in councils where European issues impinged on matters of strong national party-political disagreement.

In 1959 the ICEM was relaunched, specifically to prepare for both the European Free Trade Area (of which Ireland was never a member) and the European Economic Community, membership of which Ireland would eventually achieve. Dr Donal O'Sullivan, the first chairman, was appointed president; Dr Garret FitzGerald became chairman and Denis Corboy, secretary. The executive committee was strengthened and the support of the Department of Industry and Commerce was acknowledged. This development marked some change of direction for the organisation from its original political and cultural standpoint. Some members withdrew; others lost influence; but most accepted the need for change. Corporate membership was introduced, a newsletter produced and the council put on a firmer financial footing. During the next two years, economic issues became dominant and a broad coalition was forged between the National Farmers' Association and business interests on the one hand and between economists and the two main political parties on the other.[4]

In 1960 the ICEM, at the request of Sean MacBride, facilitated the creation of an Irish section of the European League for Economic Cooperation. ELEC was designed to interest financial institutions (in particular) in the potential advantages of European integration. This willingness to support European organisations, particularly in their initial stages, was to become a feature of the ICEM. Irish branches of European associations of teachers, students, federalists and others were facilitated by the ICEM.

In 1962 Ireland applied for full membership of the European Communities, a step that had been strongly supported by the ICEM in its literature and in meetings held throughout the country.

The rejection of Ireland's 1962 application by France (in 1963) inevitably led to a slackening of activity by the ICEM itself. None the less, its core of supporters remained larger than it had been initially. The maintenance of interest in eventual membership of the European Communities became its ultimate goal. It was registered as a company limited by guarantee in 1963.[5] It continued to operate quite successfully within the limitations of the means at its disposal, and it enjoyed good relations with successive governments. It had also become better known as a result of its efforts to inform the Irish people about the relevance to Ireland of what was happening in Europe.

In 1967 another application to join the Communities was made by the four applicant states – and rejected.

The first president of the ICEM, Dr Donal O'Sullivan, died in 1965. In 1967 the practice of filling the office with the leader or former leader of either Fianna Fáil or Fine Gael and providing a chairman from the other party, or an independent chairman, with sufficient political representation on the executive committee to achieve a political equilibrium, was begun. (Sean Lemass was the first such president and T.F. O'Higgins, subsequently Chief Justice and Judge of the European Court, was chairman from 1967 to 1973; see the appendix on the European Movement 1954–99).

During the years of waiting, the ICEM continued to stimulate Irish interest in what was happening on the European institutional scene, promoted some research into its implications for Ireland and maintained links with the international European Movement. The emphasis on providing full and accurate information was to stand it in good stead when political opinions about Europe became more definite and more divided and, to an even greater extent, when Irish politicians had to compete with each other for seats in the European Parliament.

The ICEM and the accession referendum, 1972

In 1970 the governments of Ireland, Denmark, Norway and the United Kingdom decided to re-apply for membership of the European Communities. Negotiations were immediately opened and it became clear that they would succeed, so great was the desire to bring the UK, in particular, into the European Communities.

It was evident that Bunreacht na hÉireann, the Irish constitution, would require amendment to allow the Court of the European Communities to exercise jurisdiction *vis-à-vis* the Irish courts. A debate took place on the extent of the amendments that would be put to the electorate for approval at referendum. Should they be so extensive as to allow for future institutional changes in the Communities, or should they go only so far as was immediately necessary for membership? The ICEM, which had begun preparations for such a referendum as soon as the application was relaunched, seems to have taken very little part in this aspect of the debate.

The British and Irish Labour Parties and the majority of the trade union movement in the UK opposed membership of the European Communities. The impact of this opposition is well described by Brendan Halligan in his recent paper to the Institute of European Affairs.[6] It particularly affected those members of the Irish labour and trade union movement who were members of the ICEM and openly committed to Ireland's participation in the European Communities. They resigned from the executive of the ICEM but did not personally campaign actively against accession. After the referendum they rejoined the ICEM and were subsequently joined by others from the trade union movement.

The nature of the ICEM, which, unlike most of its sister councils in Europe, was run on a totally voluntary basis, posed problems. Its meagre financial resources and the absence of full-time staff would preclude it from mounting a satisfactory campaign in favour of accession. The Federation of Irish Industry therefore seconded one of its most able staff members, Michael Sweetman, to become the director of the ICEM in 1971. Funds were subscribed by the corporate sector and a grant of £10,000 was given by the Department of External Affairs. Michael Sweetman developed the office of the ICEM into a dynamic centre, which would make a considerable contribution to the campaign and disseminate information and literature on the issues before the electorate. The existence of a wide cross-section of members, with different social and political views on the future shape of Europe, preserved the independence of the ICEM and prevented it from becoming a 'business lobby'.

Radio and television were effectively used. The popular *Late Late Show* ran a marathon 'trial' of the issues, under the chairmanship of Mr Justice Kingsmill Moore (a retired member of the Supreme Court) in which several members of the ICEM executive argued the case for membership. The national press supported entry.

One of the difficulties experienced by those who campaigned actively for membership was a perception that, if the UK joined, Ireland had no realistic alternative to following the British lead. Such an approach would result in a low poll, and more seriously, would leave the electorate ignorant of the fundamental issues that membership would entail. The farming organisations deserve credit for highlighting the distinction between the European Communities and the Free Trade Area and between the interests of Britain and Ireland. Furthermore, they did not confine the analysis to agriculture.

The referendum was held in May. On a 77 per cent poll, 83.1 per cent of the votes were in favour and 16.9 per cent were against.

Tragically, a plane crash in June 1972 at Staines, Middlesex killed Michael Sweetman, Ned Gray, Guy Jackson and Con Smith, members of the ICEM executive committee, former member Michael Rigby Jackson and a member of the panel of speakers, Fergus Mooney, who were *en route* to a meeting of the international European Movement. The Chairman, Garret FitzGerald, rallied the Council and pledged to continue its work. The ICEM established the Michael Sweetman Trust to promote knowledge of Europe in vocational education committee second-level schools, in memory of the man who had done so much to bring Ireland into the European mainstream.

After 1973 the membership of the Irish Council continued to reflect good cross-party political support. Through its meetings and publications it also promoted inter-sectoral discussions of the implications of membership of the Community.

In a development unconnected with events in Europe, the issue of abortion had become a matter of political division in Ireland. During the negotiations on the Maastricht Treaty, the government negotiated a protocol safeguarding the constitutional protection for the unborn. In the intense public debate that followed the decision of the Supreme Court in the 'X' case in 1992, a question arose as to whether the protocol could be used to deprive Irish women of freedom to travel and to information on services legally available in other member states. The government attempted to have the protocol to the Treaty amended, but the other EU governments would only agree to a solemn declaration which confirmed the freedom to travel and the right to information. The task of the European Movement in explaining the complexity of the Treaty was not made any easier by the added complication of the abortion issue.

The first direct elections to the European Parliament, 1979

The first direct elections to the European Parliament in 1979 arose from the Treaty of Accession and marked a watershed in the approach of the political parties to the institutions of the EEC. They must, therefore, be noted in any account of major European institutional change. In some respects the preparation for these elections gave the ICEM a new impetus.

Many of the candidates were members of the European Parliament (EP) who had been nominated under the old system and appeared to enjoy a consequent advantage. The political parties, however, now had to field candidates who could win seats in constituencies, that were up to ten times larger than those for the Dáil. There was also a view that in selecting 15 members of a European Parliament totalling 410, the electorate might decide to use criteria that would diminish 'party' appeal or allegiance. The relevance of the European Parliament to the concerns of the population in general was far from evident.

It was important for the future of the ICEM that it should retain its cross-party support. It therefore used every effort to emphasise its independence and was able to involve the leaders of the main political parties in the launch of the election campaign.[7]

Apart from Dublin, the ICEM had only two branches, in Cork and Galway, which had not been consistently active. However, the help of members from all parts of the country was mobilised to organise meetings at which contending candidates could speak to groups representing local interests. Those members of the ICEM, including the chairman (the present writer), who were not attached to any particular party, were used throughout the country to chair such meetings. Despite increased public access to the media, particularly television, these meetings generally attracted an audience of at least 100. Occasionally, the audience appeared to be more *au fait* with current issues than some of the candidates. Indeed, some candidates referred to matters that had been used as arguments for or against joining the European Communities in the referendum campaign seven years earlier, without much evident grasp of the changed situation.

The ICEM, in co-operation with the European Parliament and Commission offices, ran a campaign to encourage the electorate to vote. Information on any particular aspect of the EP or on its role as a European institution was also provided for those who sought it.

There were two distinct aspects of the ICEM campaign. The first, which was to publicise the importance of the elections, was undertaken in collaboration with all the political parties and sectors, such as farming, voluntary and business organisations. The second, which was to highlight the issues that would be relevant to the European parliamentarians, had to be effected with an appropriate balance of contending candidates or by non-party protagonists.

Subsequent elections involved the ICEM to a lesser extent, although the role of providing an independent forum for meetings and disseminating information about the European Parliament and the elections remained.

The ICEM moved offices from Merrion Square to Nassau Street in 1981. During the 1980s it maintained a solid programme of activities, including a specific project aimed at schools which was organised by Rhoda O'Connor. Allied Irish Banks and Bank of Ireland had supported the ICEM for several years by seconding members of their staff for one to two years to assist its work. Patricia Lawler, later to become the prime mover in many initiatives, joined the organisation in 1984 and became director in 1988.

The referendum on the Single European Act, 1987

The European Parliament, under the leadership of Altiero Spinelli, prepared a Draft Treaty of European Union in 1984. Within a few months, the European Council, meeting at Fontainebleau, agreed to set up an *ad hoc* committee on institutional affairs, which was chaired by Senator James Dooge. To some extent, it could be said that the ICEM enjoyed a reflection of the honour that had been paid to one of its most prominent members. The committee reported to an Intergovernmental Conference in Luxembourg, and the text of the Single European Act was agreed in January 1986.

In 1987 Dr Raymond Crotty challenged the right of the government to ratify the Treaty without holding a referendum, and the Supreme Court upheld his challenge. The ICEM again sought to increase the resources at its disposal in order to campaign for the approval of the Treaty. It was strengthened by the secondment of Michael Hoey from the Department of Foreign Affairs in 1985, and was given support by corporate and individual members.

A press statement from ICEM in November 1986 calling on all political parties to support the campaign for the Single European Act shows the careful equilibrium that the executive had to achieve. It includes the following, with regard to political co-operation (EPC):

> The Irish Council of the European Movement welcomes the inclusion in the Single European Act of Title III on political co-operation, which for the first time in an international agreement acknowledges and safeguards the neutrality of Ireland by excluding military and defence aspects of security from debate within EPC.

Other members of the European Community might see this as an unusual emphasis on an effort to promote a more closely integrated Europe, but the ICEM had no difficulty in reconciling it with a final, resounding declaration:

> The Irish Council of the European Movement believes that the Single European Act will provide the basis for reviving the momentum necessary to construct a closer, more integrated Europe in which this country has its rightful place and from which it can draw for its economic development and prosperity.

The Chairman of the ICEM, Brendan Halligan, in his foreword to the brief but comprehensive review of the Act that accompanied that press release, sought to 'reassure those people who have misgivings about the Act'. He argued also that: '…it is our belief that membership of the European Community is of such central importance to the economic and political wellbeing of this country that it must not be turned into a vehicle for inter-party recrimination'.

The extension of Community powers for the European Commission and the Parliament was debated at a serious level, but most of the popular discussion centred on two issues: whether this extension of political co-operation would affect Irish neutrality, and the extent to which social issues would impact on questions of public morality. The ICEM had to address both issues, and the paper referred to includes the following:

> There is no legal basis for legislation relating to divorce, abortion or
> other matters concerning public morality and there is therefore no
> way in which the Community can affect legal provisions on these
> matters presently in force in Ireland.

The Labour Party was still divided in its approach to the European
Communities. Fine Gael, on the whole, was in favour. There was concern that
the Fianna Fáil party would not rally its troops for the referendum, but a
double approach by the Taoiseach, Charles Haughey and the Minister for
Foreign Affairs, Brian Lenihan improved the party's efforts. The ICEM
operated a sustained campaign, particularly in the week leading up to the vote.

The referendum was carried by almost 70 per cent to 30 per cent, but a
warning had been given against taking for granted Irish support for
institutional change in Europe.[8]

The expected lull in the activities of the ICEM following the referendum
was counteracted by some high-profile events, such as the creation of
'European of the Year', an award sponsored by Irish business, in 1988 and an
active celebration of 'Europe Day' on 1 May each year since 1986. The ICEM
called for an Oireachtas committee on foreign affairs, and appealed to the
political parties to appoint a minister for European affairs.

The impact of developments in Europe in 1989 and 1990 created new
areas of interest. The collapse of the Soviet Union, the reunification of
Germany and the dramatic changes in countries of central and eastern
Europe widened the horizons of all Europeans. The ICEM became more
involved in studying policy issues, particularly those relating to the new
conditions in Europe. Its members also met parliamentarians and others from
the central and eastern european states who wished to study aspects of Irish
'civil society' and to learn from Ireland's experience in applying for
membership of the European Communities.

The creation of the Institute for European Affairs in 1991 introduced a
new organisation into the field of European affairs in Ireland, but increasing
demands for a range of research and activities relating to Europe ensured the
viability of both organisations. There was a degree of common membership
of the two bodies. The ICEM retained (and probably increased) its role as
political advocate of European unity. The Institute provided a venue for
visiting delegations, symposia on aspects of European developments and a
centre for research.

The referendum on the Maastricht Treaty, 1992

The Treaty on European Unity agreed by the member states at Maastricht,
under the Dutch Presidency, was a most unsatisfactory document on which

to base a political campaign in a popular referendum. It was long, complex, couched in legal terms and contained potential contradictions within the text.

It was designed to allow the member states to:

- advance the convergence of their economies and to establish an economic and monetary union including, in accordance with the provisions of this Treaty, a single and stable currency
- establish a citizenship common to nationals of their countries
- implement a common defence, thereby reinforcing the European identity.

It also contained 17 protocols, most of which related to the misgivings or reservations of national governments on different issues. It represented a compromise which, it was hoped, would keep the UK on board, enable the Danish government to persuade its electorate to support the Treaty, and forge greater political and economic cohesion between the member states.

Preparation by the ICEM for the referendum campaign began in 1991. The number of branches was increased, extended to the south-east and north-west and given greater support. This increase was a major step towards achieving the Movement's objective to promote knowledge and debate on European affairs throughout Ireland. This was reinforced by the later extensions which covered Cork, Dublin, Galway, Kerry, Midwest, Northeast, Northwest and Southeast, so branches now exist in all these regions. Martin Mackin, who became the co-ordinator in 1992, was involved in the preparation, by various policy groups of the Council, of documentation on the Treaty. Popular promotional material, such as car stickers, badges and T-shirts with the ICEM campaign slogan (GO WITH EUROPE – GROW WITH EUROPE) were produced and distributed.

The Maastricht Treaty presented the ICEM with a difficult task. On the one hand, the Irish media were now producing a great deal of information, which in earlier days had not been available to the electorate. On the other, the political campaigning in favour of European unity had become interwoven with numerous other issues, many of which provoked strong reactions independently of the European situation. Such confusion was probably inevitable, as the reality of European integration impinged on more issues and affected people more directly.

Furthermore, the Treaty itself, including its major protocols, provided a significant challenge for anyone trying to explain it. Despite the quantity of information supplied by the media, the ICEM had to grapple with the task of clarifying the extent to which matters would or would not be changed by the passing of the Treaty.

The Maastricht Treaty provided for a European monetary union in order to bring about completion of the European internal market. It also provided for a widening of the competence of the EU in areas from which it had been excluded.

Unfortunately, one premise which speakers for the ICEM (and others throughout Europe) had accepted, i.e. that a rejection of the Treaty by any one member state would signify the demise of the Treaty (as had happened in 1954 when France, alone of the original Six, did not ratify the Treaty for a European Defence and Political Community), was subsequently shown to be incorrect. Ireland, which was the first country to hold a referendum, passed it by 69 per cent to 31 per cent.[9] Shortly afterwards, however, Denmark rejected the Treaty in a national referendum but, following the addition of a new protocol, a second referendum was held. The Danish electorate then approved the Treaty, which subsequently came into effect.

Immediately after the passage of the referendum on the Treaty of Maastricht in 1992, the ICEM began planning for the next stage of European institutional change. The scenario for European monetary union had been set and the issues of enlargement of the Union, common foreign and security policy and further reform of the institutions had to be faced.

The ICEM issued a policy document in 1993 on 'European Union and the Challenge of Enlargement'. It also relaunched its branches in Cork and Galway, which had become moribund, and began to establish others throughout the country.

The referendum on the Treaty of Amsterdam, 1998

The 'unfinished business' of the Treaty of Maastricht hung over the development of Europe throughout most of the 1990s. In 1997, the Dutch Presidency, once again, had the honour of providing the venue, in Amsterdam, for the Treaty designed to amend and complete the Treaty of European Unity. This amending Treaty unfortunately suffered from some of the same problems as had affected its predecessor. It was even more legalistic in tone, but was less inconsistent in content.

This time there was no feeling of complacency; there was, however, a real concern that the Irish electorate might pass the Treaty by only a very slim majority. There were even fears that it might not be approved. The Green Party in Ireland opposed each step towards further European integration. One of its members, Patricia McKenna MEP, sought a ruling by the courts that the government should be precluded from using state funds in seeking to persuade the electorate to vote in favour of either outcome of the referendum. The Supreme Court held in her favour and, as a result, an independent commission was established to set out the arguments in favour of and against the Treaty. The commission was not entitled to evaluate the respective merits of the arguments. No state-funded government information was to be issued on the advantages of the Treaty. Various bodies, including the ICEM, made representations to the commission as to which arguments in favour should be published. The onus of campaigning for acceptance, however, would have to fall more heavily on the protagonists, including the political parties and the ICEM. Furthermore, the ICEM had to maintain a clear distinction between its information role and its role as advocate of closer European co-operation. Because of its approach in previous campaigns, this was not too difficult to ensure.

The executive committee of the ICEM had set up a number of groups to prepare policy documents in 1991. These were reorganised and, in some instances, renamed in 1996, and Deirdre Healy was appointed as policy and research co-ordinator.

The campaign that ensued followed the professional approach which the Irish Council had adopted in relation to Maastricht. As well as publishing 'Questions and Answers' on the various aspects of the Treaty, similar to those produced in 1992, the ICEM introduced a freephone information service for the public and opened its own web-site. It ran a nationwide series of meetings, in close collaboration with the political parties, its eight branches and various member groups. Its slogan was KEEP EUROPE WORKING FOR YOU.

The main problem for campaigners for or against the Amsterdam Treaty was the lack of a single focal issue. Some of the public thought it was to establish a single currency, although this had already been decided. Others believed it was to integrate European foreign and security policy at last, even though it did not go that far. There was a considerable lack of interest, which was not helped by uncertainty, for a considerable time, about the actual date of the referendum. (March and later April had been suggested; the eventual date was 22 May.)

The ICEM launched its policy document on the Amsterdam Treaty in January 1998. Its common foreign and security policy document was published on 23 April, by which time the issue of Irish neutrality and independence had, once again, become a major point for the opponents of the Treaty. The chairman, Alan Dukes, who took a very active part in the campaign, also launched the Amsterdam Conradh na nDaoine and the Irish-language version of the Amsterdam Treaty questions and answers booklet.

The inclusion of the issue of employment in the Treaty, which had been a priority of the Irish Presidency, made somewhat less impact than might have been expected because of the fall in the Irish unemployment figures and the buoyant state of the Irish economy. On the other hand, dissatisfaction with changes in the Common Agricultural Policy caused the farming organisations to reserve their positions, and they did not express the same level of support as they had for previous campaigns. The larger political parties supported the Treaty but found it difficult to inspire enthusiasm for a Treaty that did not involve issues of party political relevance.

The Treaty was approved by 61.7 per cent to 38.3 per cent of the votes.[10]

It is always difficult to identify the extent to which any one factor affects a political outcome. The ICEM undoubtedly played a considerable role in successive campaigns. Its advocacy, however, has led to a certain confusion of identity between it and the European Commission and even, more rarely, the office of the European Parliament. In rebutting the charge that it was a mouthpiece for the institutions of the EU, the ICEM would point to its policy documents, which are analytical and sometimes critical of current EU policies and institutions, but such documents are not widely read by the electorate. It has certainly influenced its own members (who may have become involved for a variety of reasons) and improved their appreciation of the complexity of the issues facing Ireland and Europe. Its system of rotation of senior officers has extended its political and sectoral impact. Its educational activities, including its use of stagiaires (short-term graduate interns) in its administration, must have contributed to a greater understanding of the philosophy and *raison d'être* which underlie the Treaties for which it has campaigned.

It is typical, and indeed laudable, that in 1998 the ICEM should already have begun to consider the issues that will be fought in the next referendum, to complete the steps left unfinished in the Treaty of Amsterdam and make the adjustments necessary for enlargement, whenever that will happen. Circumstances have changed since its creation in 1954, but its role as advocate of Ireland's contribution to European integration, stability and social progress remains.

NOTES

1   John A. Costello, Dáil Report 163: 633–677.
2   Joseph Retinger, the Secretary General of the European Movement wrote to, among others, the Archbishop, John Charles MacQuaid, to ask him to use his good offices to get political and other Irish leaders involved. Retinger also corresponded with Sean MacBride and with the delegates who had been present, particularly Senator Douglas. In 1949 Senator Douglas wrote that an 'Irish parliamentary group' had been formed and that they would like to attend meetings, finances permitting.
3   Chairman, Dr Donal O'Sullivan; vice-chairman, General Liam Archer; honorary secretary, Brendan Malin; honorary treasurer, Geoffrey Coyle; members of the executive committee, Sean MacBride, Brian O'Connor and Michael Yeats.

4   An account of the period is given in *The Road to Europe – Irish Attitudes 1948–61* by Miriam Hederman, Institute of Public Administration, Dublin, 1983.
5   The directors were: Dr Donal O'Sullivan, university lecturer; Garret FitzGerald, economist; Louis P.F. Smith, economist; Denis Corboy, barrister-at-law; George J. Colley, solicitor; Declan Costello, barrister-at-law; Sean J. Healy, secretary.
6   Brendan Halligan, 'Before the dawn', *Europe: The Irish Experience*, Institute of European Affairs, 1999.
7   The leaders present were: the Taoiseach, Jack Lynch TD; Garret FitzGerald TD; and Frank Cluskey TD.
8   The turn-out at the referendum on the Single European Act was 45%.
9   The turn-out at the Maastricht Treaty referendum was 57%.
10 The turn-out at the Amsterdam Treaty referendum was 56.2%.

=== 2 ===

Negotiating Ireland's entry

PATRICK HILLERY

Introduction

In 1959 Sean Lemass was elected Taoiseach and invited me to join the Cabinet. That was when the 'grey paper' of Ken Whitaker was being acted upon and economic development was a high priority of the government. This involved a major change from protection policy to the policy of free trade. Developments in Europe were being followed with keen interest by the government. It was clear that everything that would happen in Europe would have immense potentialities for good or ill affecting our future, and we wished to have our voice in the determination of what would happen.

Ireland had need for economic expansion and escape from political isolation. In spite of political independence, there was still in 1960 an almost exclusive bilateral relationship with the United Kingdom. Ireland needed wider contacts, new markets, other trading partners. European membership could, as Emile Nöel said in a lecture in 1993, 'look like a second declaration of independence'.[1]

The reservations about Ireland's capacity to compete with the strong European economies expressed by Tánaiste Sean Lemass in the Dáil in 1957[2] were now less strong and replaced by more confident aspirations. Similarly, a note of doubt about our economy in an *aide-mémoire* to the foreign ministers of the EEC was absent from Ireland's application for membership in 1961. Great Britain, Norway and Denmark applied for membership at the same time. However, Ireland's application was in before the others.

The Council of the member states communicated a positive reply to the applications of Britain, Denmark and Norway. There was a delay in the reply to Ireland's application, and when queried the Council expressed reservations about Ireland's economy and very definite doubts about Ireland's commitment to the political aims of the Community.

The Taoiseach responded by communicating through the media of the EEC countries[3] and by travelling Europe to hold direct meetings with the governments of Germany, France, Belgium, the Netherlands, Italy and Luxembourg, making clear our acceptance of the political implications of membership and faith in our economic capacity as the growth rates following on the development programme were higher than ever before experienced in Ireland.

During this period the Taoiseach made it clear at home and abroad that the government was committed to the ideals of the founders of the community and accepted fully the political objectives. As a result there was agreement at a meeting of the Council in October 1962 to open negotiations with a view to Ireland's membership of the Community. No date was set for the start of the negotiations. Since the negotiations with the other applicant states collapsed following on a press conference given by President de Gaulle of France in January 1963,[4] the promised negotiations with Ireland did not begin.

The applications were reactivated in 1967. This time the European Commission in its formal opinion raised no problems in relation to Ireland's application. There were no questions now about our willingness to accept the political implications of membership, but again negotiations did not take place. President de Gaulle forestalled them again. The disappointments of 1961 and 1967 did not in any way reduce our active, determined interest in membership of the EEC. Membership of the EEC continued to be government policy. Sean Lemass expressed our intention of doing everything to promote membership and of 'avoiding any step that would make it more difficult to attain'.

Visits to European capitals were mainly undertaken by the Taoiseach and the Minister for Finance, but other ministers were active also. In Rome for a meeting of education ministers, I joined Sean Lemass at a meeting with Minister Colombo of Italy.[5] Lemass was in Rome for the ceremonies attending the installation of Pope John XXIII. Later, as Minister for Labour, I visited the Commission in Brussels. I have records of speeches delivered in my constituency during the 1960s on the subject of Ireland's membership of the community. The Minister for Agriculture, Neil Blaney, also visited the Commission in Brussels, as did other members of the government. The Anglo Irish Free Trade Agreement, signed on 14 December 1965, was regarded as a step on the road to EEC membership.

In 1969, President de Gaulle vacated the office of President of France and enlargement of the EEC was thought to be more likely than it had been.[6] As I had been appointed after the general election of 1969 to the post of Minister for External Affairs, I now set out to seek better information on the matter. I met the Minister for Foreign Affairs of France, Maurice Schumann, in New York, and in private discussion with me he was very positive that there would be progress in the development of the Community. While the functionnaire with him seemed to wish to warn him to be more careful, it was clear that Maurice Schumann thought there would be a decision on enlargement soon. My task now was to get Ireland to the negotiating table.

The Monnet Committee

While the Commission opinion was favourable to Ireland and no obstacles were expected from the Council, the Monnet Committee had pushed a proposal that the Council of the EEC deal with the United Kingdom's application for membership first and delay negotiating with the other applicant countries. Both Sean Lemass as President of the Irish section of the European Movement and Jack Lynch, his successor as Taoiseach, had expressed to Monnet the unacceptable nature of this proposal for Ireland. Jack Lynch said in his letter to Monnet that separation from the British market would be 'disastrous for Ireland'. Monnet persisted in his conviction that the negotiations should be with Britain first.

I visited the President of the Commission, Jean Rey, and he confirmed that the proposal was being taken seriously. President Rey advised me to meet the President of the Council before the planned upcoming meeting of the Council of Ministers. I arranged a meeting with the foreign minister of the Netherlands, J.M. Luns, who was President of the Council. We met in London. Luns listened to my arguments. I spoke of the damage it would do to Ireland and the disruption it would cause if they followed the Monnet proposal, and I suggested that the Community would not wish to do such harm to a small country. The proposed mode of action would not only delay our membership, but would also separate Ireland from its main market. He undertook to bring my views before the foreign ministers at the impending Council of Ministers meeting. The summit meeting of heads of state and government at The Hague made the big decision to proceed to the second stage of Europe. This included the decision to proceed to enlargement of the Community.

Our preparations for negotiations began with the publication of a government white paper. On the morning after the publication of the white paper, as I was leaving for the meeting of the government, Hugh McCann, the Secretary of the Department of External Affairs, came to my office to say that a request had come from RTE for a minister to take part in a programme about the white paper on television. I mentioned this request from RTE before the start of the government meeting. The Taoiseach, after a pause, said to me 'you do it'. The white paper of April 1970, dealing especially with the economic implications of membership, dealt also in detail with the constitutional, legal and political implications of membership. Three articles of the constitution would be affected by membership because of the supranational powers conferred on the institutions of the EEC.

Preparation for negotiations meant preparation of a detailed negotiating position, deciding our aim for the form of the negotiations, and preparatory work to make the governments of the member states fully informed of Irish interests before they prepared the Community negotiating positions. On a tour of the governments of the member states, once again I stressed the government's wish that Ireland become a member of the EEC and made clear our acceptance of the responsibilities of membership and of the political implications. We repeated the absolute need to avoid disruption in our trading relations with Britain: this could be dealt with by starting negotiations at the same time as the United Kingdom, finishing negotiations at the same time and acceding to membership at the same time as Britain. I also sought agreement to consult with the Irish delegation if matters affecting Ireland came up in the negotiations of the other applicant countries. In regard to the last item, consultation, I had asked George Thomson (who was responsible in the Wilson government for EEC matters and for their preparation for negotiations), during one of our meetings reviewing the Anglo Irish agreement, if the British government would agree to inform us of matters of concern to Ireland arising in his negotiations with the community. He agreed.

As a result of losing the British general election, the Labour Party was not in office for the negotiations. George Thomson's place as negotiator was taken by the Conservative minister, Anthony Barber. I sought a meeting with Barber, told him of George Thomson's undertaking and asked if he would honour it. Barber agreed. A further change took place when, on the death of Ian McLeod, Anthony Barber became Chancellor of the Exchequer and was replaced as head of the UK negotiating team by Geoffrey Rippon, who led the UK negotiating team for the rest of the negotiations. All through the negotiations, Rippon arranged meetings *à deux* with me after their sessions of negotiation with the Six to inform me of matters with which they had dealt.

The aims at this stage were membership of the Community and to protect Ireland's interests during the negotiations and the transitional period. Our aims in relation to the negotiations were the procedures that I had sought on visits to individual capitals, i.e. start together, negotiations at the same time, parallelism and consultation procedures in the course of the negotiations, and, of course, simultaneous accession to membership of the EEC. Sometime in the course of the negotiations we would have to seek measures to provide for our special needs after entry. In spite of unprecedented growth rates in the economy, Ireland would find it difficult to reach the level already attained by the stronger, more developed economies of Europe. We were fit to join, but much more effort was required to develop our economy. We needed to be allowed to continue with special measures to catch up.

It was clear that membership depended also on the acceptance by the Irish electorate of the proposed changes in the constitution, for which a referendum would have to be held if negotiations succeeded. Continuous information to the public on all matters involved in membership became an essential part of the programme of work. On 22 May the Taoiseach informed the Dáil that the delegation to conduct the negotiations would be led by the present writer, and in addition would include officials. He said on that occasion that other ministers would participate from time to time to deal with matters affecting their respective departments, but as time went on, I continued to be the sole ministerial representative on the Irish delegation during all the negotiations. The officials on the delegation (referred to at the meetings as deputies) were:

- Mr Sean Morrissey, Assistant Secretary, Department of External Affairs[7]
- Mr D.J. Maher, Assistant Secretary, Department of Finance
- Mr J. O'Mahoney, Assistant Secretary, Department of Agriculture
- Mr D. Culligan, Assistant Secretary, Department of Industry and Commerce
- Ambassador S. Kennan, head of the Irish mission to the European Communities.

Each of these officials had back-up from his own department and, when required, senior officials from other departments of state took part in the negotiations. Sean Morrissey was chairman of the deputies. The negotiations were organised around conferences attended by the Council of Ministers and the delegations of the applicant states. The chairman of each conference was the president in office of the Council. The first conference was presided over by Pierre Harmel, foreign minister of Belgium; the next one by Walter Scheel, foreign minister of West Germany; followed by Maurice Schumann, foreign minister of France and then Aldo Moro, foreign minister of Italy. The first conference laid down the ground rules for the negotiations. The Community stipulated that the applicants accept *l'acquis communautaire*. Negotiation was not intended on matters already achieved by the EEC. The applicant states must accept the Treaties of Rome and Paris and their political objectives, all the decisions that had been taken by the Community since the Treaties came into force, including decisions that would be taken during the period of the negotiations, and the choices made by the Community in the field of development to come. The solution to any problems of adjustment must be sought in transitional measures and not in changes in the existing rules. The applicant states were accepted into negotiations for membership only on the basis that any difficulty arising for them would have to be solved by a period of transition. The heart of the negotiations would be the Community global approach to transitional measures in industry and agriculture and the contributions of the applicants to financing the Community during the transitional period. There must be adequate parallelism between progress in the free movement of goods and the achievement of the common market in agriculture. In the trade sector, the transitional period would be the same for all applicants. In other sectors it might be varied according to the subject matter concerned and according to the country. The chairman stated also that the Community side would put forward proposals for giving information to negotiators in relation to any interest of theirs arising in the negotiations between the EEC and the other applicant states.

President Rey of the Commission spoke of, among other things, the need to make sure that the negotiations would not arrest or slow down the progress being made by the Community in a large number of areas which he listed. He also spoke of the need to keep the national parliaments informed of the progress of the negotiations, as the agreements reached after the negotiations would have to be submitted to the national parliaments. For me, the voting in the referendum was always ahead, and information to the Dáil and public had been early decided upon. The applicant countries declared their acceptance of the Treaties and their political finality, the economic objectives of the Communities and the decisions taken to implement them.

Work programme

Ministerial conferences would take place once every three months and the deputies would meet at their level once a month.[8] Briefing of the applicants would be arranged by the EEC after meetings with each negotiating team, and the decisions would remain provisional until multilateral meetings. The Community undertook to be available to consult on request and the Commission would provide all the applicants with a constant supply of detailed information.

There now started a great informing period. The Commission did a fact-finding operation on behalf of the Community, and, on our part, we communicated information aimed at giving the Community negotiators a very clear picture of our economic situation. Confidential documents presented to the Community became theirs. I had a problem with secrecy on our part and leaks in Brussels. Christopher Aliaga Kelly, the President of the Confederation of Irish Industry, asked to meet me and complained on behalf of his organisation that it was being given no information from the appropriate department. He said that the farmers' representatives had the same problem. To deal with this important problem and to get around secrecy imposed by the Commission and Council, I decided to have leaks. I instructed an officer of the Department of External Affairs to give all information of concern to them to these organisations. At the same time, I decided to give full information to the accredited Irish journalists. I told the official that I would be responsible for his doing this. He did it well.

Detailed memoranda from us were prepared and presented. Statements in support of our positions were given at officials' meetings. Visits to Ireland by foreign ministers of the Six as well as by members of the Commission were arranged. As well as being occasions for exchange of information, these were focal moments for media attention on the move towards membership and so contributed to the information of the public.

The conference and Council staff were the negotiators, but in the detailed engagements I had, it was the Commission representatives, Wellenstien and Deniau, that were most involved. Sometimes there were senior officials of the Commission. There was M. Rabot of the agriculture section to argue the merits of its system of doing things where we sought to retain another system. There were also cameo appearances by such as Malfatti, President of the Commission, to try to move me by a bit of bluster. The ministers often had to stay late at night or through the night at the ministerial conferences as we spent long hours seeking an agreed position during adjournments of the conference to find solutions.

There were no direct flights, as now, to Brussels. Sometimes I flew on Sunday on an early flight putting down in Brussels on its way to the snow with ski enthusiasts. This meant having all day Sunday and most of Monday waiting for the meeting. The 3.00 p.m. Monday meeting never started on time. Most times I went through a London airport. All-night sessions meant sometimes leaving for the hotel and, without going to bed, eating and flying to London. The memories of the night sessions are of poor sandwiches and disgusting coffee. In preparing for pressure nights I wrote down points that I would not yield on but might be at risk of yielding on at the 2 a.m. fatigue level, and pressures like a visit from President Malfatti of the Commission to try to convince me that I was holding everything up. Perhaps my early training as a house doctor in the Mater Hospital in Dublin was good preparation for this.

The list of matters to come up in the conferences was long, and included transitional measures – industry and agriculture, fisheries, contribution to Community budget, Anglo-Irish trading relations during the transitional period, economic and monetary union, regional and structural policies, the Irish language. The agreed transitional period was what the government had decided would be a desirable balance of benefits to Ireland. Some items required negotiating to protect our interests during the transitional period. This was particularly true of our trading relations with Britain under the Anglo Irish Free Trade Agreement. For others we had to seek derogation from Community practice after joining the Community, as in animal health policy. To protect other markets, e.g. Japan and the US, we had to keep our disease-free method of dealing with foot and mouth disease, fowl pest, etc., as distinct from the Community method of inoculation. For this we needed to be able to prevent the import of livestock and meat from any part of the Community, except Northern Ireland which was also disease-free.

Similar controls were required by us to maintain our disease-free status for plant health. The Community resisted both very strongly. In the end we were allowed to keep the practice, which suited our needs. This was after a long night during which I had to argue with Commissioner Mansholt; when Mansholt tired, he was replaced by the senior official in the Directorate General for Agriculture, M. Rabot, a Frenchman. They seemed not to understand the effectiveness and desirability of our system of control nor why we would not accept their system. It took a long night, but at the end they accepted that it was a matter of great importance to me to continue with our system.

Some matters to be dealt with in the negotiations required protection after membership, such as industrial development aids, and special arrangements for the motor assembly industry which was important for employment. Some of the matters were functions of the Commission, and the new Commission or later Commissions would decide what Community practice would be in relation to them. For example, we wished to continue with tax incentives because they were very important to our industrial development, but their position in the long term could not be concluded or guaranteed by the negotiators as such matters within the Community were a function of the Commission. For now, the immediate time, they were allowed to continue, but a future Commission could make rules governing such aids.

The motor assembly industry was an example of our seeking a longer time of continued protection than the transition period. This was part of the Anglo Irish Free Trade Agreement and had held up matters in the 1965 agreement. A solution devised by J.C.B. McCarthy of the Department of Industry and Commerce, agreed to by the governments and accepted by the motor traders of the United Kingdom, had saved the employment in the motor assembly industry. With some effort we settled on 1985 as the date for ending this protection.

Fisheries

Fisheries brought into action the ground rule in relation to the applicant nations having to accept the *acquis communautaire* and not seek to change it. During the negotiating period, the Council of Ministers decided two regulations on fisheries. The structural one caused us trouble. It meant that now there was Community law providing for common access to the fishing grounds of each member state by the fishing fleets of other member states. Ireland's fishermen were to a large extent dependent on our exclusive fishing limits. Our valuable inshore shell-fisheries could be damaged, as could our salmon stocks, by opening up the waters to other countries. At the same time, Ireland had no deep-sea fishing fleet that could benefit from access to the waters of the other member states.[9] *L'acquis communautaire* had been one of the conditions accepted by the applicant countries as a condition of the Community agreeing to open negotiations for membership. This included any progress made by the Six during the period of the negotiations. I raised the problem many times, and there was very strong reaction in Ireland to the Community structural proposal. This reaction was widespread and not confined to the fishermen. There was now an obstacle to the success of the negotiations.

After much pressure by us, the negotiators of the applicant states, 'political' will manifested itself and it was indicated that a derogation would be negotiated. This was a great relief and achievement, as it meant the Community putting aside one of the ground rules. However, it gave the negotiators a task that would normally be performed by the full Council of fisheries ministers after the enlargement, with the ministers of the applicant states present as full members dealing with the balance of national interest. It caused much difficulty for the negotiators on both sides.

Before the proposed regulation, the position in Ireland was that exclusive fishery limits extended twelve miles seawards from base-lines. In an arrangement covered by the London fishery convention relating to traditional fishing rights, six countries were permitted to fish in the outer six-mile zone (specific parts for specific species). These six countries were Belgium, the Netherlands, France, Great Britain, West Germany and Spain.

After prolonged and difficult negotiations involving repeated proposals by the Community negotiators, none of which I would accept, we agreed that the coastal member states of the enlarged Community be authorised to restrict fishing within a six-mile limit from their base-line, and that for Ireland this be extended to twelve miles on the north and west coasts from Lough Foyle to Cork for all species of fish and on the east coast from Carlingford Lough to Carnsore Point for fisheries of crustaceans and molluscs (shell fish). The Council of Ministers (fisheries) of the enlarged Community would decide on the arrangements for fisheries after 1982, when ten years were up. This was the absolute maximum that could be achieved if Ireland were to progress towards membership of the EEC, and was regarded as a notable achievement by those who understood. It was substantially what the government had asked for.

Beet

The application of national production quotas to qualify for support payments to mid-1975 was announced in December 1971. The proposed quota for Ireland's beet was 135,000 tons. The farmers' association in Ireland expressed great discontent, and named a figure of 240,000 as desirable. There was an immediate public display, including marches in towns where there were sugar factories. Again there was a possible bad effect on the prospects of the referendum.

At a ministerial conference in January 1972, which took the whole night, we persuaded the Council to move its figure to 140,000 tons. Later through the night I persisted in a personal contact with M. Deniau, the negotiating member of the Commission, and ultimately got him to agree to a further 10,000 tons. The commissioner was out of his bed anyhow, because that night there was a last-ditch effort by the Norwegians to gain a further concession in fisheries as they feared for the result of their referendum.

With the extra 10,000 tons that I had wrung out of Deniau, the Commission said that this was its final position. It was not prepared to consider any more. There was no more to be got. But the public display had to be considered for its damage to the vote in the referendum. I did not close the deal that morning, as there was quite a deal of publicity for the 240,000 tons. I went from the negotiations to the plane for London. I went home to discuss the situation with the government. We had consulted with the Irish sugar company officials, who advised that they could not process the figure being asked for and that there was serious doubt that the growers would produce more than the proposed quota. I put the position to the president of the Irish Farmers' Association (IFA). The president of the IFA made a positive statement and the government, after a short delay, instructed Sean Morrissey, who was in Brussels, to convey our acceptance of the 150,000 tons basic quota for Ireland.

Regional and structural imbalances

We foresaw difficulties on membership for our economy which, while it had been proved to be fit for membership, was not then quite strong enough to deal with the stresses and demands created by membership. While regional and structural policies of the Community were not a matter for negotiations, due to the role of such policies in an economic and monetary union, I took the opportunity to speak of the regional development problems which we faced and the need for the Community to supplement our national measures. In the development of Community regional policy there would have to be consideration of our special problems. We had had in mind for some time the need for a special protocol annexed to the Treaty to allow for necessary measures to be taken for the promotion of the economic and industrial development of Ireland. It was considered wise to hold this item back until the negotiations were well established.

I first mentioned the word 'protocol' at a dinner welcoming Altiero Spinelli to Ireland. In the negotiations, I dealt with Ireland's special needs in

terms of regional and structural disparities at a conference at ministerial level
in July 1971. At this time I had a special negotiating difficulty in dealing with
Ireland's industrial incentives. These were financial incentives in the form of
grants and fiscal incentives which relieved attracted manufacturing
enterprises of income and corporation profits tax on exports. There was
anxiety about how long these would be allowed to exist in the enlarged
Community. In the negotiations we were able to keep them. At the same
time, this was a European Commission function: the Council and the
negotiators with whom I was dealing could not tie the hands of the future
Commission. Our incentives were allowed to continue, but we knew that
they would be studied by a future Commission.

To solve my anxiety about future Irish governments' freedom to continue
policies for industrial development, it was agreed to annex to the Treaty of
Accession a protocol which declared that the high contracting parties,
desiring to settle certain special problems of concern to Ireland, recalling that
the fundamental objectives of the EEC included 'the harmonious
development of their economies by reducing the differences existing between
the various regions and the backwardness of the less favoured regions'
recognised that it was in the common interest that the objectives of the
policy of industrialisation and economic development embarked upon by the
government of Ireland be retained, and recommended that 'the community
institutions make adequate use of the community resources to realise these
objectives'.

At the end of the negotiations we were accepted as members of the EEC.

The length of the transitional period was what the government had
decided to seek. Our trade relations with Britain were not disturbed, so there
was no disruption to our economy during the transitional period. The
government's plans to develop the economy and remove imbalances were
intact, with a protocol to the Treaty to provide for future structural
investment and incentives. The Irish language was an official language of the
EEC.

At every stage of the negotiations I circulated to the Dáil a report of the
conferences with the Council. Parliamentary questions were also an
opportunity to supply information.

The referendum

The referendum to decide the third amendment of the constitution was set
for 10 May. The outcome of the referendum in retrospect seems to have been
assured with the President of Fianna Fáil, Jack Lynch and the President of
Fine Gael, Liam Cosgrave leading politically in favour of membership. Yet

the stakes were so high and the prospects for the country and its citizens outside of membership so bleak that there was anxiety. The government set out to reply to all the sensitive questions raised by the opponents of membership, and to supply all the information necessary for those who wished to know everything about Europe and the likely effect of membership on many aspects of national life. I was involved in this information campaign as Minister for Foreign Affairs, as we set up a special extra information section at the Department of Foreign Affairs.[10]

As well as this, Jack Lynch asked me to be responsible for the organisation of the Fianna Fáil party's campaign. This was the same as being director of elections. It involved meeting with the constituency organisations involved and meant ceaseless addresses to interested groups, associations, etc. In the headquarters we had a telephone reply system for people seeking information, and the volunteers there were kept very busy and played an important role in communicating their knowledge and commitment in their conversations with the public. We sought and got many volunteer speakers from outside the political party.

At a ceremony in the Palais d'Egmont in Brussels, the prime ministers and foreign ministers signed the Treaty of Accession. The Taoiseach Jack Lynch and I signed on behalf of Ireland. An Irish delegation was invited to attend the summit conference in Paris in October 1972 even though our membership did not begin until January 1973. There were delegations also from Denmark and the United Kingdom. Norway had decided against membership in its referendum, so it was not present.

Jack Lynch asked me to deal with the necessary legislation which now had to be considered by the Dáil and Seanad. The European Communities Bill was enacted in the autumn of 1972. The government nominated me to be a member of the new Commission, and the appointment was made by the governments of the nine member states. I was also named Vice-President of the new Commission, which meant occasionally chairing meetings when the President was absent. Francois Ortoli of France was appointed President of the Commission. We met in January 1973 to discuss the distribution of portfolios. I asked for social affairs. The summit meeting in Paris had called on the Commission to develop a social action programme, and it had also been decided at that summit to restructure the social fund. Both of these considerations were in my mind in choosing that portfolio. Chief Justice Cearbhall Ó Dálaigh was nominated to be judge of the European court, and appointments were made to the European Parliament and to the social and economic committee.

When I was President of Ireland, the Secretary of the Department of Finance on his appointment made a courtesy call on me. During our conversation I suggested that a record should be made of the accession negotiations. He undertook to have this done, and the task was put in the very competent hands of D.J. Maher, who had been the department of finance representative on the negotiating team. The result is a book, *The Tortuous Path*, which is an excellent reference for persons interested in a full account of the negotiations and all that went before, of the enormous amount of expertise, dedication and sheer hard work demanded of our civil service from the late 1950s when Ken Whitaker produced his 'grey paper' on the economy, to the actual negotiations in 1972 for Ireland's entry into this great enterprise in Europe.[11] The Taoiseach, as a gesture of recognition, presented each civil servant immediately involved in the final negotiations with a solid silver medallion to commemorate their individual contributions.

NOTES

1   Lecture to the Institute of European Affairs in 1993.

2   'The obligations involved in membership of the Community are of a character which I believe would be impossible for us to accept at the present stage of our development.'

3   At a meeting with the press invited from the member countries and Britain by the Irish branch of the European Movement.

4   Which showed his doubts as to the consequences to the Community if Britain were accepted as a member.

5   At different times during our acquaintance Colombo was foreign and prime minister of Italy.

6   This was not certain, as President de Gaulle had on each occasion given reasons why he thought Britain was not fit for membership. Britain had serious economic problems in 1961.

7   Sean Morrissey had been our ambassador to the EEC in the years before the opening of negotiations. A lawyer, he had entered the department of external affairs in the legal section and had represented Ireland in the law of the sea negotiations.

8   The meetings with the UK were arranged to take place twice every three months for ministers and twice a month for deputies.

9   There has been a significant change in profile of the fleet since the 1970s. In 1975 all vessels were under 24.4 metres (most were under 13.7 metres). 24 large (over 25 metres) pelagic vessels were added in the 1980s. The Irish pelagic fleet is among the most modern in Europe now, and a significant investment programme with EU support is under way. The volume of sea fish (excluding shell fish) landings at Irish ports in 1976 was 80,000 tonnes (£12.8 million); in 1997 it was 269,000 tonnes (£100 million).

10 The name of the department was changed at my suggestion by the government, so I refer to it at different times by the former name, 'external affairs', and by the present name, 'foreign affairs'.

11 D.J. Maher, *The Tortuous Path*, IPA, Dublin, 1986.

3

The impact of the EU
on the Irish constitution

DONAL BARRINGTON

Introduction

Our membership of the European Community has had a significant influence on the Irish constitution. In some ways this influence has been direct and obvious, but in other very important ways it has been subtle and pervasive. To understand this it is necessary to understand how the Irish constitution was developing as the constitution of an independent democratic nation state prior to our entry into the EEC.

Position on the eve of entering the European Community

It used to be said that the Irish constitution was the British constitution reduced to writing. This was a statement that revealed something and concealed a lot. In a broad way one can say that Ireland has borrowed from the United Kingdom the idea of a nominal head of state, the system of cabinet government, the whole system of the common law, and that many of Dicey's famous 'conventions' of the British constitution are to be found reduced to writing in Articles 28 and 29 of the constitution of Ireland.

But the ideology underlying the constitution is very different. Here we can find French notions of popular sovereignty brought into Ireland by the various nationalist and republican movements. Article 6 provides that:

> all powers of government, legislative, executive and judicial, derive, under God, from the people whose right it is to designate the rulers of the state and, in final appeal to decide all questions of national policy, according to the requirements of the common good.

The constitution accordingly provides that it may not be amended except by referendum of the people held in accordance with the provisions of Article 46.

Again one can see French influence in the separation of powers. Article 15 Section 2 provides that:

the sole and exclusive power of making laws for the state is hereby
vested in the Oireachtas: no other legislative authority has power to
make laws for the state.

Articles 28 and 29 provide for the exercise of the executive power by or
on the authority of the government. Article 35 provides that all judges are to
be independent in the exercise of their judicial functions and subject only to
the constitution and to the law. Article 34 s.4 ss.6 provides that 'the decision
of the Supreme Court shall in all cases be final and conclusive'.

The constitution also contains (at Articles 40–44 inclusive) a charter of
rights which shows many influences derived from French, English and
Catholic traditions. There is the right to individual liberty backed by a
powerful constitutional system of habeas corpus, the right to freedom of
speech, free association and assembly, the inviolability of the dwellinghouse
and freedom of religion. Alongside these are three guarantees clearly deriving
from Catholic social teaching and dealing with the family, education, and
private property in a social context.

This charter of rights, when read in the light of the preamble, probably
entitles the constitution to claim to be, in form, the first Christian
democratic constitution in Europe.

But there is one other element in the constitution that it is necessary to
mention. This is the judicial review of legislation. This comes to our present
constitution (via the constitution of the Irish Free State) from the
constitution of the United States of America. But the position in Ireland
varies from that in the United States of America. The American constitution
does not mention judicial review of legislation. The doctrine has been
developed by the judges of the American Supreme Court themselves from
their oath to uphold the constitution. In Ireland the constitution itself
provides for judicial review of legislation in two forms. First Article 34 s.3.2
provides that:

> ...the jurisdiction of the High Court shall extend to the question of
> the validity of any law having regard to the provisions of this
> constitution...

And, of course, an appeal lies from the decision of the High Court to the
Supreme Court. This decision is final.

A second form of judicial review exists which allows the President, in
certain circumstances, to refer a Bill passed by both houses of Parliament to
the Supreme Court for an advisory opinion as to whether the Bill or any
provision thereof is repugnant to the constitution. I shall return to this later.

But the normal form of judicial review arises where a plaintiff (or a defendant) against whom a particular piece of legislation is invoked and who feels aggrieved by it, raises a challenge to its constitutional validity. At first such challenges were very rare, perhaps because litigants were not fully conversant with their constitutional rights, or perhaps because judges who had been brought up in the British theory of parliamentary sovereignty found it unacceptable that a judge should attempt to frustrate the will of parliament. I remember an elderly judge saying to me on one occasion that surely the constitutional guarantees were merely intended as guidelines for parliament in enacting legislation.

All that changed with the Ó Dálaigh Supreme Court in the 1960s and 1970s. Soon the Irish bar and bench found themselves confronted with the problem of construing a common law system which had superimposed upon it a written constitution with a charter of rights. The obvious model was the United States of America, which was also a common law country, and which had gone through a similar process.

The Irish Courts found themselves wrestling not only with the finer points presented by the common or statute law, but also with the question of whether the prima facie solution thereby presented could be reconciled with abstract standards laid down in the constitution.

Soon Counsel appearing before our Supreme Court in constitutional law cases found that they were expected to be familiar with relevant decisions of the American Federal Supreme Court and even with the debates in the Courts of the individual states. While the decisions of the English Courts or of the former Irish Courts of common law remained of great importance in the daily interpretation of the common law, the American experience, or that of certain commonwealth countries, often appeared more relevant when the question at issue was the scope or significance of some constitutional guarantee. Thus in the State (Healy) v. Donoghue,[1] dealing with constitutional right to an effective system of legal aid in criminal cases, the influence of the decision of the American Federal Supreme Court in Gideon v. Wainwright[2] was obvious. In others, such as the origin of the constitutional right to privacy in McGee v. Attorney General,[3] the influence of the American Federal Supreme Court, while not so obvious, was still significant. In yet another class of case, such as the right to sue the state for the torts of its servants, the Irish Supreme Court took a much more radical line than its American counterpart, holding that while the state was sovereign, in the sense of being independent internally, it was subject to the constitution and the law and liable for the torts of its agents in much the same way as any other corporation.[4]

Perhaps one can also see American influence in the approach of the Irish Courts to 'unspecified' constitutional rights. Mr Justice Kenny, in his seminal judgment in Ryan v. Attorney General,[5] pointed out that the constitution, in

Article 40 Section 3, guaranteed that the state would in its laws respect, and as far as practicable by its laws defend and vindicate, the personal rights of the citizen but then went on to provide that:

> The State shall, *in particular*, by its laws protect as best it may from unjust attack and, in the case of in justice done, vindicate the life person good name and property rights of every citizen.

Mr Justice Kenny drew from the fact that the state was pledged to protect the personal rights of the citizen generally but in particular to protect four named rights, that there must be other *'unspecified personal rights which the State was also pledged to defend and vindicate'*. In the Ryan case Mr Justice Kenny identified the right to bodily integrity. But more importantly he sent lawyers and judges on a search, as occasion required, for other unspecified rights guaranteed by the constitution. To date they have identified the right to earn a livelihood; the right to privacy; the right of access to the Courts; the right to justice and fair procedures; the right to travel within the state; the right to travel outside the state; the right to marry; the rights of an unmarried mother in relation to her child; the right to communicate; and many others.

More important, for the purposes of the present essay, is the method of identifying such rights. For while neither the United Nations declaration of human rights nor the European convention on human rights is part of the domestic law of Ireland, it is permissible for a lawyer seeking to establish a particular personal right as a right protected by the constitution of Ireland to refer to rights which have been recognised by other countries or by the international community of constitutional states.

Presumption of constitutionality

The Courts presume that parliament carries out its legislative duties in accordance with the separation of powers. Unless, therefore, an Act or a Bill expressly violates, or would, if enacted into law, expressly violate, some provision of the constitution the Court will assume that the Act or the Bill is constitutional and the onus of proof will rest on the party attempting to challenge it. But this very presumption has far-reaching implications so far as administrative law is concerned. For if a legislative measure grants powers or discretions to administrative bodies, the Court will assume that the legislature intended that these powers or discretions were to be exercised in accordance with the provisions of the constitution and not otherwise.[6] As a result, constitutional law has had a dramatic impact on our whole system of administrative law and indeed it might be true to say that there is no branch of our law which the constitution has not touched.

Finally, it may well be that the great mass of our law is still common law or statute law, which was in force in the Irish Free State immediately prior to the coming into operation of the constitution. This law cannot be presumed to be constitutional. One cannot presume that legislatures in the nineteenth century or in the early part of the present century, in enacting their legislation, attempted to conform to the provisions of a constitution which did not then exist. Such laws are carried forward by the provision of Article 50 of the constitution *'To the extent to which they are not inconsistent therewith'*.

Take for example an Act of the imperial parliament. It is the Act of a sovereign parliament and it means what it says. Initially the Supreme Court took the view that you look at such an Act and you ask yourself what it meant on the day of its enactment. What was *intra vires* the Act? If something could legally be done under the Act and that something was inconsistent with the constitution, then the relevant provision of the Act was not consistent with the constitution and was not carried forward by Article 50. This was a fairly ruthless approach to the problem, but it had the advantage of what European Community lawyers would call legal certainty.

The Supreme Court does not appear, however, to have adhered rigorously to the *intra vires* test. For instance, in Garvey v. Ireland[7] the Court was dealing with a pre-constitutional Statute but, nevertheless, applied a different rule. In the course of his judgment, O'Higgins C.J. said:

> The Act of 1925 is a pre-constitution Statute. However, regard must be had to the fact that this Statute falls to be administered under different circumstances and under an entirely different constitution.

One of the problems with this kind of reasoning is that if one administers a Statute in a manner different from that contemplated by the legislature which enacted it, one may be accused of legislating. Moreover, it may be difficult to reconcile such an approach with the Community law principle of legal certainty: I shall return to this subject later.

I have mentioned these various points to emphasise the position of Ireland on the eve of entry into the EEC as a small independent sovereign state attempting to work out its own constitutional destiny in the context of its own peculiar institutions but in the context also of certain constitutional values and a certain respect for human rights which, if not universal, were common to many countries where the rule of law prevailed.

Entry to the European Economic Community

In 1972 the people voted by a huge majority to amend the constitution to permit Ireland to join the European Communities. Ireland formally became a member on 1 January 1973 and, by virtue of the European Communities Act 1972, the Oireachtas provided that:

> The Treaties governing the European Communities and the existing and *future* Acts adopted by the institutions of those communities shall be binding on the state and part of the domestic law thereof.

The nature of the Community Ireland joined

The European Community was created by a number of international treaties. Once the various member states had purported to ratify these treaties in accordance with their own particular constitutional procedures, the status of the various treaties became a question of international law. But the treaties also are, or may be, part of the domestic law of each member state. The treaties have created certain institutions such as the Council, the Commission, the Court and the Parliament which may also exercise powers over and in the various member states and for which the treaties are their roots of title. For those who, as it were, work under the common roof of the treaties, the treaties constitute a new form of constitution binding on the member states and their citizens.

It is important to remember that the nature of the community legal order had been worked out before Ireland became a member. The European Community is a community governed by law and within the area where Community law operates, Community law is supreme both as between member states and within them. It overrides pre-existing national law whether statutory or constitutional, and no subsequent national law can be invoked to challenge it.

This has been stated by the European Court of Justice on many occasions, but as early as 1964, in the case of Costa v. Enel,[8] the Court put the matter as follows:

> By contrast with ordinary international treaties, the EEC treaty has created its own legal system which, on the entry into force of the treaty, became an integral part of the legal systems of the member states *and which their Courts are bound to apply.*
>
> By creating a community of unlimited duration, having its own institutions, its own personality, its own legal capacity and capacity of representation on the international plain and, more particularly, real powers stemming from a limitation of sovereignty or a transfer of powers from the state to the community, the member states have limited their sovereign rights, albeit within limited fields, and have

thus created a body of law which binds both their nationals and themselves.

The integration into the laws of each member state of provisions which derive from the community, and more generally the terms and spirit of the treaty, make it impossible for states, as a corollary, to accord precedence to a unilateral and subsequent measure over a legal system accepted by them as a basis of reciprocity. Such a measure cannot therefore be inconsistent with that legal system. The executive force of community law cannot vary from one state to another in deference to subsequent domestic laws, without jeopardising the attainment of the objectives of the treaty set out in Article 5.2 and giving rise to the discrimination prohibited by Article 7.

The obligations undertaken under the treaty establishing the community would not be unconditional, but merely contingent, if they could be called to question by subsequent legislative acts of the signatories....

The precedence of community law is confirmed by Article 189 whereby a regulation 'shall be binding' and 'directly applicable in all member states'. This provision, which is subject to no reservation, would be quite meaningless if a state could unilaterally nullify its effects by means of the legislative measure, which could prevail over community law.

It follows from all these observations that the law stemming from the treaty, an independent source of law, could not, because of its special and original nature, be overridden by domestic legal provisions, however framed, without being deprived of its character as community law and without the legal basis of the community itself being called into question.

The transfer by the states from their domestic legal system to the community legal system of the rights and obligations arising under the treaty carries with it a permanent limitation of the sovereign rights, against which a subsequent unilateral act incompatible with the concept of the community cannot prevail....

This description of the community legal order underlines the significance of the amendments which were made to Article 29 of the constitution on entering the European Community and in particular the significance of what is now Article 29 s.4 paragraph 5 and which reads as follows:

No provision of this constitution invalidates laws enacted, acts done and measures adopted by the state which are necessitated by the obligations of membership of the European Union or of the

> communities, or prevents laws enacted, acts done and measures adopted by the European Union or by the communities or by institutions thereof, or by bodies competent under the treaties establishing the communities, from having the force of law in the state.

This means in effect that large portions of the constitution have been bypassed. Article 5 may still declare that Ireland is a 'sovereign, independent, democratic state' but, while Articles 5, 6, 15, 28, 29, and 34 are still in place, they no longer mean what they appear to say. They may be overridden not only by provisions of the treaties but by regulations, directives and decisions of the various European institutions. The European Community is undoubtedly a community governed by law. But there has been a significant loss of sovereignty. In Ireland's case that may not be very important. We probably have greater freedom of economic action and greater political influence than we had as a formally sovereign nation state, but there has been a significant loss in democratic control in that power in the community is no longer effectively controlled at the level at which it is exercised. This 'democratic deficit' is real, but rectifying it is primarily a matter for politicians rather than for lawyers.

The position of the national judge as Community judge

The European Community is an inchoate federal system. The federal aspect of the community is perhaps more fully developed in its legal system than anywhere else. Yet, apart from the European Court of Justice and Court of First Instance, it is not easy to identify a separate federal structure. This is because of the dual role of the national judge as a Community judge. His or her position results logically from the fact that Community law may be part of the domestic law each member state and that, where it applies, it takes precedence over national law. While therefore the national judge may seek guidance from the European Court of Justice in accordance, say, with Article 177 of the Treaty of Rome as to the correct interpretation of Community law, it is for the national judge, and the national judge alone, to apply Community law to the facts of the case before him or her. There is always the possibility that this situation could give rise to tensions, some of which are discussed by Diarmuid Rossa Phelan in a remarkable book on the constitutional boundaries of the European Community entitled *Revolt or Revolution*.[9]

Constitutional experience of Irish lawyers

There is a sense in which the problems of adapting a traditional system of law to a set of standards imposed from above are similar irrespective of what those standards may be. The fact that Irish lawyers had grown accustomed to the judicial review of legislation at the national level and to the fact that the national parliament was not internally sovereign made it easier for Irish lawyers – and indeed Irish politicians – to accept the discipline of the European Court.

A second comment can be made. The European Court of Justice, while primarily concerned with commercial and administrative problems, has had to accept that the doctrine of the primacy of Community law would not prove acceptable in the member states if the Court ignored the question of human rights. It therefore invented the doctrine that when a group of constitutional states came together and conferred powers on certain Community institutions they intended that those powers should be exercised in a manner which respected human rights and not otherwise. But as there was no express charter of rights in the treaties, the Court had to embark, as occasion required, upon an inquiry as to what were the human rights that the member states accepted. This inquiry was not altogether dissimilar from that embarked on, at an earlier stage, by the Irish Courts in attempting to identify the 'unspecified' human rights protected by the Irish constitution.

Thirdly, the European Court of Justice has been quite clear in stating that the national judge, in his or her capacity as a Community judge, must not let any provision of national law, whether enacted before or after the Community measure, defeat the Community law provision. He or she may have to set aside the national measure or, where possible, construe it in such a way as to make it reconcilable with Community law. But in this respect the European Court has been somewhat short on specific advice to the national judge. Perhaps it was inevitable that in a community where the local law and practice varied from state to state, the European Court should confine itself to generalities and leave the application of these general principles to the individual national judges. But it does not appear to have solved for us problems such as the *intra vires* test or the adaptations of individual discretions to make them consistent with the European law or with requirements of legal certainty.

Influence of the higher principles of Community law

Some of what are called the higher principles of European Community law, such as proportionality, legitimate expectation, legal certainty and equality before the law, have become part of the intellectual equipment of Irish lawyers, and it is probably just a matter of time until they have a significant effect on the development of Irish law.

The effect of the principle of proportionality is already apparent, although it is probably true that Irish constitutional lawyers use it in a manner somewhat different from that in which it is used in European Community law. In Community law the principle of proportionality requires that measures taken by the European institutions to achieve a community objective must not be out of proportion to the objective to be achieved. In Irish constitutional law, on the other hand, it is sometimes used as an aid to an inquiry as to whether parliament, in a particular piece of legislation, has struck the correct balance in attempting to reconcile the rights of the citizen with the exigencies of the common good. Thus in the case of Heany v. Ireland[10] Mr Justice Costello expressly made use of the principle of proportionality in considering the constitutional validity of section 52 of the Offences against the State Act 1939. He made use, however, of a formulation of the principle by the Canadian Supreme Court in Chaulk v. R.[11] This formulation was as follows:

> The objective of the impugned provision must be of sufficient importance to warrant overriding a constitutionally protected right. It must relate to concerns pressing and substantial in a free and democratic society. The means chosen must pass a proportionality test. They must:
>
> a   be rationally connected to the objective and not arbitrary, unfair or based on irrational considerations
> b   impair the right as little as possible, and
> c   be such that their effects on rights are proportional to the objective.

The Supreme Court, in its decision upholding Mr Justice Costello, did not deal expressly with this particular test but it did say that the Court was:

> of the opinion that the matter calling for resolution on this appeal is whether the power given to the Garda Síochána... by the section is proportionate to the objects to be achieved by the legislation.[12]

The principle of *legitimate expectation* is even more widely referred to in our Courts, though at times in parallel with promissory estoppel and more often in relation to matters of procedure than to constitutional right.[13]

The principle of equality before the law is enshrined in the Irish constitution, though at times the Irish Courts appear to have diminished the importance of the principle by stressing that the equality referred to in the Irish constitution was the equality of the citizens *'as human persons'*. The effect of European Community law on the question of equality has undoubtedly been to strengthen the position of those lawyers who believe that man is a social animal and that a guarantee of the citizens' equality as human beings is necessarily a guarantee that citizens shall not be discriminated against in their social or political or commercial activities because of any of their human attributes.

Reference under Article 26

Finally I should like to refer to an area where European Community law poses a fairly immediate problem. Under Article 26 of the constitution the President may, after consultation with the council of state, refer any Bill to which the article applies, to the Supreme Court for a decision on the question of whether the Bill or any specified provision or provisions thereof is/are repugnant to the constitution. The President may not sign the Bill until the Supreme Court has pronounced its judgment.

The Supreme Court, having received the Bill from the President, must assign solicitor and counsel to examine the Bill and must hear the arguments of such counsel and must also hear the attorney general or his counsel in support of the Bill. Usually it will require written submissions from both sets of counsel and, having considered the written submissions, will fix a date for oral argument after which it will usually reserve its decision and, later, pronounce its judgment.

The difficulty is that pursuant to the provisions of Article 26 Section 2 ss.1 all of this must be done not later than 60 days from the date on which the Bill was referred by the President to the Supreme Court. This is an extremely short period of time if one considers all that has to be done. But suppose it emerges in the course of the submissions that provisions of the Bill appear to be repugnant to some article of the constitution, but the attorney general relies upon the immunity from constitutional challenge conferred by Article 29 on the basis that the provisions in question are necessitated by our membership of the European Community; and suppose, moreover, that this question is disputed between the parties and one of them demands a reference to the European Court of Justice pursuant to the provision of Article 177 of the Treaty of Rome. What is the Court to do then? Clearly to refuse such a reference would be a very serious matter and might place Ireland in breach of its obligations under the Treaty. On the other hand, if the Court were to grant such a reference there would be no way it could fulfil its constitutional duty under Article 26 Section 2 ss.1 to pronounce its decision on the constitutionality of the bill not later than 60 days from the date of the reference.

NOTES

1   1976 Irish Reports p. 325.
2   1963 372 US p. 325.
3   1974 Irish Reports p. 285.
4   See Byrne v. Ireland 1972 Irish Reports p. 241.
5   1965 Irish Reports p. 294.
6   See East Donegal Co-operative v. Attorney General 1970 Irish Reports p. 317.
7   1981 Irish Court Reports p. 75.
8   1964 ECR p. 585 at p. 593.
9   D. Rossa Phelan, *Revolt or Revolution – Constitutional Building in the European Union*, Roundhall Sweet and Maxwell, 1997.
10 1994 2ILRM p. 420.
11 1990 3SCR p. 1303.
12 See Heany v. Ireland 1996 Irish Reports p. 589.
13 See Webb v. Ireland 1988 Irish Reports p. 353, Abrahamson v. Law Society of Ireland 1996 2ILRM p. 481, and Wiley v. Revenue Commisssioners 1993 ILRM p. 482.

4

Irish trade unions and the EU

PATRICIA O'DONOVAN

Trade union opposition to EEC membership

When the 465 delegates to the annual delegate conference of the Irish Congress of Trade Unions (Congress) gathered in Limerick in July 1971, one of the most contentious and important subjects for debate was the question of Ireland's proposed membership of the European Economic Community (EEC). Six motions on this topic had been placed on the agenda for debate. Some of them advocated outright opposition to EEC membership; others expressed qualified support. In spite of the contradictory terms of these motions, all six were successfully composited into one comprehensive motion, which was debated and adopted by the conference. This followed an earlier decision by the conference to reject a proposal that the six motions would just be discussed and referred to the Executive Council without the delegates having an opportunity to vote on them.

The decision to debate and vote on the composite motion was taken against the background of an announcement that day by the executive council of Congress of a special delegate conference on the question of the trade union attitude to EEC membership. Such a conference would consider this question in detail and enable trade unions to debate fully all the implications of membership and decide on whether or not the trade union movement should support, or oppose, Ireland's joining the EEC. Some delegates were clearly suspicious that this was a ploy on the part of the pro-European members of the executive council of Congress to defer a decision on this crucial policy question. Nevertheless, the conference delegates entered into the debate on the composite motion with gusto and conviction, enhancing their speeches with references to economic research and data and international authorities on political and economic theory, and quoting poets and writers in support of their arguments.

The composite motion expressed serious concern with 'all aspects of the proposed accession of Ireland to the EEC'. It was critical of the government's failure to survey and quantify adequately the effects of membership on employment and workers' living standards and its failure to get the EEC to recognise the special industrial and regional development needs of Ireland; it expressed concern about loss of effective control of political and economic policy and possible involvement in military commitments; and it concluded by stating that the conference could not express any support for the proposed entry of Ireland given the inadequacy of the information available. Adoption of this motion would not therefore amount to a clear-cut decision to oppose EEC membership *per se*, but would be an interim decision to withhold support for EEC membership at that stage because of the dearth of information and the perceived weakness of the Irish negotiating position.

The debate was opened by Ruadhri Roberts, General Secretary of Congress. He made a comprehensive statement to the conference which analysed the main economic threats posed by membership of the EEC, identified vulnerable sectors, and pointed to the potential negative impact on agriculture, regional development and employment. Summing up at the end of his speech, he said:

> the position at the present time is we have not enough information to justify an expression of support for EEC membership and such information as does exist would appear to lead toward the conclusion that the government of Ireland has not done its job in presenting the special position of Ireland to the EEC and in making the necessary plans and taking the necessary steps to secure the development of industry in Ireland.

The General Secretary was followed by 16 speakers representing a broad cross-section of the unions affiliated to Congress. Most of these contributions continued the negative tone set in the introductory speech, expressing serious reservations about job security, industrial development and economic independence. The contributors to the debate included Brendan Corish TD (then leader of the Labour Party and an ITGWU delegate to the conference), who expressed a fear of Ireland 'becoming the Alabama of the EEC'. Barry Desmond TD (also a delegate from the ITGWU) described the EEC as 'a Western European, neo-colonial trading block'. Another delegate (T. Foley from the AUEW) described the EEC as 'a rich man's club in a world where the widening gap between the rich and poor nations is an indictment of modern humanity'.

Even though the debate was overwhelmingly negative, a number of delegates courageously came to the rostrum to put forward a contrary view. Among them was Professor Charlie McCarthy from TCD (a delegate from the Vocational Teachers' Association), who concluded his speech by saying that 'the answer lies in looking vigorously outward, not in putting up the shutters and withering away inside'. D. Nolan (a delegate from the ASTI) posed the following question:

Do we remain a small country as we are with a small mind and isolate ourselves from mankind, or do we see ourselves in a new role with a large mind and a large influence? This can only be achieved within the ambit of the Common Market, and there is where our true role lies.

The composite motion was passed on a vote, and the debate concluded on the understanding that the issue would be fully aired again at the promised special delegate conference. That conference was held on 27–28 January 1972. Four motions were before it. The first motion simply called for special safeguards for employment in the event of EEC membership; the second motion was pro-EEC membership, recognising that it was in Ireland's interest; the third motion explicitly opposed EEC membership on social, economic and political grounds; and the fourth motion called on Congress to organise a trade union campaign of opposition to membership. The first motion was adopted; the second motion supporting EEC membership was defeated; and the third and fourth motions opposing membership were adopted. The underlying division on this issue among trade unions was reflected in the votes on the third and fourth motions. The third motion was adopted by a majority of only 45 votes; the fourth motion was adopted by a majority of only 51 votes. The significant minority voting against these was a clear signal that a substantial number of unions were in favour of EEC membership, a fact that is often overlooked.

Following this conference, a campaign committee was established which was chaired by Senator Fintan Kennedy (president, ITGWU and treasurer of Congress). The campaign committee concentrated on the publication and dissemination of an eight-page broadsheet paper entitled *Economic Freedom*, which comprehensively analysed the economic implications of EEC membership; presented detailed data on production and employment in individual sectors; vigorously promoted the view that there were viable alternatives to EEC membership; and focused on the cost-of-living increases that EEC membership would inevitably bring. This last aspect was reinforced by reference to a *Financial Times* survey which compared prices across a number of European cities, including Dublin. For example, it showed that women's clothing was 124 per cent more expensive in Brussels than in Dublin. The women's clothing priced included 'two medium-priced summer dresses off-the-peg from a multiple store, a pair of medium-priced nylons and a pair of day shoes'. Readers of *Economic Freedom* were assured that 'we are not considering high fashion wear here' and the article went so far as to acknowledge that 'it may not be surprising that Parisians paid even more' – a staggering 255 per cent above the Dublin price!

The first print run of *Economic Freedom* was 500,000 copies. Due to unexpectedly heavy demand, a second printing of 250,000 copies was necessary. The 1972 executive council report states that 'the physical distribution of some 60 tonnes of printed matter throughout the country itself posed problems which were, however, resolved by the excellent co-operation received from CIE'. The report also records dissatisfaction with the level of media coverage given to important statements from Congress, and complains bitterly that 'no publicity or wholly inadequate publicity' had been given to the views of Congress during the referendum campaign.

Given the outcome of the referendum held in early May 1972, which recorded overwhelming support for EEC membership based on an exceptionally high electorate turn-out of 70 per cent, it is clear that the trade union campaign had very limited impact and had spectacularly failed to convince workers and their families to vote 'no'. Congress accepted that the campaign was not successful. In its report to the 1972 annual delegate conference, it identified a number of factors that it believed contributed to this failure. These included the support of all the national newspapers, of the two largest political parties and of the farmers' organisations for EEC membership, and 'other irrelevant, political considerations'. On that desultory note, the executive council concluded its report on the campaign, thus closing this contentious chapter in the first phase of its relationship with the EEC. In sharp contrast to the 1971 annual delegate conference in Limerick, there were no motions on the EEC on the agenda of the 1972 annual delegate conference and no debate on the outcome of the referendum or the Congress campaign. The brief section of the executive council report on the EEC was agreed without discussion.

Adapting to EEC membership

Throughout 1972 and 1973 the trade union movement set about coming to terms with the practical implications of membership of the EEC. In September 1972, Congress appointed an EEC information officer to deal with the demand for information on matters relating to the EEC, including the organisation of seminars and courses and 'the general establishment of a line of communication and information on EEC matters of particular trade union interest.' The appointment was initially made for only a six-month period, but at the end of that period it was confirmed as a permanent post. By the end of 1972, Congress had submitted trade union nominations to a number of important EEC advisory and consultative committees and had participated in a number of briefing sessions on a wide range of issues. At that time, there were twelve committees/commissions at European level that provided for trade union representation: by the end of 1973, Congress had ensured its participation in all of these.

There is no doubt that the involvement of a substantial number of senior trade union leaders in European-level activities had a major impact on their thinking and attitude towards the EEC. Apart from participation in formal EEC structures, Congress had also moved to affiliate to the European Trade Union Confederation (ETUC) and this was formally accepted in March 1974. This broadened significantly the perspective of Irish trade unions beyond the traditional close links with the British trade union movement, which, for historical and practical reasons, had a very strong influence on Irish trade unions. The significance of this development was acknowledged by Denis Larkin (Workers' Union of Ireland) when he addressed delegates to the 1976 annual delegate conference of Congress and described his experience of participation in ETUC activities as follows:

> We see in this confederation the beginning of an attempt to meet the employers on an international basis, throughout all Europe. We have been heartened by attending these meetings and conferences and by an increasing realisation that the problems of trade unionists in Germany, France, Italy, Holland, Norway, Sweden, Britain and this country are common problems and need common action on many occasions. We believe that this confederation in Europe will be of benefit to all workers.

But it was the equal pay debate which erupted in 1974 that brought the Irish trade union movement face to face with the procedures and institutions of the EEC in an effort to secure the basic right to equal pay for equal work for women. This would be the first test of the practical value to Irish workers of the lofty principles of the Treaty of Rome, and the first real opportunity since joining the EEC to determine whether or not this so-called 'rich man's club' was interested in and committed to securing basic rights for workers.

Discussions on the implementation of equal pay in Ireland got off to an inauspicious start in Brussels in October 1973. A tripartite meeting was held on the proposal for a Council Directive on Equal Pay, which would provide for implementation of the right to equal pay no later than 31 December 1975. An Irish government representative at the meeting implied that the date set in the Directive might not be acceptable to the Irish government. The Treaty of Accession of Ireland did not provide for any exemption or for any transitional period for the implementation of equal pay, although it emerged that the government in the course of entry negotiations had requested a transitional period but later withdrew the request.

The Anti-Discrimination (Pay) Bill, 1974 was published in February 1974 to transpose the European Directive into Irish law. Even though Congress had serious reservations about many of the provisions of the Bill, which did not go as far as similar legislation in Northern Ireland, the Act was passed in July 1974 and provided for full implementation of equal pay by 31 December

1975, in accordance with the European deadline. However, on 17 December 1975, the Taoiseach, Liam Cosgrave TD, announced in the Dáil that the government had decided that amendments were necessary to the Act before it came into force. Congress immediately notified the government that in the event of the non-implementation of the Act, it would lodge a formal complaint to the European Commission. The government persisted in deferring implementation and sought a derogation from the Commission. Congress forwarded a comprehensive submission to the European Commission in February 1976 opposing the application by the government for a derogation. A bitter war of words broke out between Congress and the Minister for Labour, Michael O'Leary TD, who publicly criticised the European Commission, contrasting the speed with which the Commission had responded on the question of equal pay to what he described as 'their more leisurely approach' to attempts to enlarge the EEC social fund and regional fund. Congress waded in on the side of the Commission, vigorously defending its integrity and pointing out that 'attacks on members of the European Commission must not be allowed to obscure the fact that the Commission has upheld the right of women to have equal pay against the government's attempt to defer the application of this right'.

On 5 May 1976, the Minister for Labour informed the Dáil that the government had received a formal communication from the European Commission rejecting the government's application for a derogation from the provision of the Equal Pay Directive and that, in consequence, the government would not now be proceeding with the proposed amending legislation.

This represented an outright victory for the trade unions with the European Commission as a strong ally. It was a very public engagement, which pitched the trade unions and the European Commission together against the Irish government. The outcome guaranteed the timely enactment of one of the most significant pieces of employment legislation, which transformed the Irish workplace for women and still reverberates today – 25 years on. The stereotype of the EEC as being only the voice of big business and capital was shattered.

The Equal Pay Act was the first in a series of very significant pieces of employment legislation enacted throughout the 1970s and 1980s transposing European directives into Irish law. A comprehensive code of basic rights based on such initiatives was created for Irish workers, which enhanced significantly their employment conditions and working environment. As Irish workers began to experience the real benefits of this legislation through improved working conditions, the ideological pro- and anti-Europe debate began to fade.

Influencing and setting the agenda

When I joined the Irish Congress of Trade Unions in 1977 as EEC information officer (the third since 1972), I found an organisation that was very much at ease with the European dimension of its work. Draft directives and regulations dealing with a wide range of issues were the subject of seminars and workshops and were given detailed consideration by various Congress committees. The approach was to integrate the European dimension, where possible, into mainstream trade union discussion of the particular issue rather than hive it off into a specialist European policy unit. So, discussion on proposals for worker participation (e.g. information and consultation, the European Company Statute and European works councils) took place in the Industrial Democracy Committee, equality-related proposals were dealt with by the Women's Committee, and the extensive range of occupational health and safety initiatives was integrated into trade union health and safety structures. Congress and its affiliated unions actively contributed to these discussions at both national and European level. At national level, the transposition into Irish law of EEC directives that affected workers' rights was normally the subject of detailed consultations with the social partners. At European level, as representatives on various ETUC committees, Irish trade unionists made an input into the consultative process conducted by the European institutions.

These early years of EEC membership were very challenging for the trade union movement. From the position of a failed high-profile campaign of opposition to EEC membership, it quickly came to terms with membership and committed the necessary resources to ensure its effective participation. The substantial minority that had voted in 1972 against the decision to oppose EEC membership (including key unions such as the Workers' Union of Ireland) was instrumental in promoting this pragmatic approach. This was in sharp contrast to the UK trade union movement, which chose to pursue a strategy of ongoing opposition to the EEC throughout the 1970s. Even when UK trade union representatives were nominated to the relevant EEC committees, they pursued an 'abstentionist' line and very rarely attended the meetings. This approach continued right through to the mid-1980s.

But the practical approach of the Irish trade union movement and its enthusiastic participation in European activities belied a growing anti-EEC current of suspicion and hostility just below the surface. This was usually expressed in terms of resentment of the apparent riches which the EEC was bestowing on the farming sector, in sharp contrast to the lack of support for industries that were dealing with closure and job losses in the face of increased competition. The burden of adjustment was felt very much by workers in the traditional industrial sectors, while farmers were enjoying new-found prosperity under the price support regime of the Common Agricultural Policy. Even though the Commission had prepared and adopted its social action programme under the leadership of Dr Paddy Hillery, the first Irish commissioner, the 'social dimension' to the EEC remained underdeveloped. Trade unions were very critical of this and continually pointed to the lack of European policies and instruments to deal with unemployment, social disadvantage, industrial restructuring and social dumping. The period of the late 1970s through to the late 1980s was characterised by a sense of frustration at the apparent inability of the EEC to come to terms with the major challenges of poverty and unemployment. The disproportionate influence during this period of the policies of free trade, unfettered competition and deregulation, pursued in particular by the Conservative British government under Margaret Thatcher, threatened to collapse the EEC into a free-trade zone without any civic, social or political dimension. The general sense of alienation from the European project that this generated among trade unions during this period is best illustrated by the fact that Congress did not participate in the referendum campaign on the Single European Act in 1987.

What kind of Europe?

The adoption in December 1989 of the Community Charter of Fundamental Social Rights of Workers was a milestone in the development of EEC social policy, and engaged the trade union movement across Europe in a real debate for the first time in almost a decade about the kind of Europe that was emerging. The adoption of the Social Charter transformed Community social policy from being a relatively minor policy area (compared for example to the Common Agricultural Policy, competition policy, transport policy) into one of the most critical and controversial areas of Community policy, raising the most fundamental questions about the role of the Community.

Why and how was this fundamental change brought about? First, the increased momentum at the end of the 1980s towards completion of the internal market raised major questions about disparities between member states. These disparities, both economic and social, either directly or indirectly impeded the free movement of labour, which was seen as an essential component of the single market and was the key objective of the Single European Act. The need for a 'level playing field' was obvious if the single market was to be achieved and if the fears about social dumping among the richer member states were to be allayed. Second, there was within the Community, and specifically within the European Commission in the person of Jacques Delors, a recognition of the need for a human face to the

Community that would address the growing alienation felt by European citizens in general and workers in particular. He considered it necessary to make some commitments to improve the position of workers in the hope of gaining their support for and co-operation with the emergence of a single market. The Social Charter was the Community instrument brought forward by the Commission to address these two objectives.

At the European Council summit in December 1988, the conclusions stated that:

> completion of the single market cannot be regarded as an end in itself; it pursues a much wider objective, namely to ensure the maximum well-being of all in line with the tradition of social progress which is part of Europe's history.

At the Madrid summit six months later, the conclusions stated that 'social aspects should be given the same importance as economic aspects and should accordingly be developed in a balanced fashion'. So this growing awareness of and commitment to what now became known as 'the social dimension' to the single market was given expression in the Social Charter, which was adopted by eleven of the twelve member states at the following summit meeting in Strasbourg in December 1989.

The final text of the charter was watered down in an effort to secure the agreement of the UK government. In particular, provisions relating to minimum wage and information and consultation rights were weakened. There was also concern, particularly on the trade union side, about the use of a charter as the mechanism for developing the social dimension. The charter had no legislative base in the Treaty of Rome, and therefore could not have any legally binding effect on member states. It was the first time that such an instrument had been used by the Community (even though it had of course been used by other international organisations such as the UN and the Council of Europe). Nobody was quite sure of its standing at the time. Now – a decade later – it is clear that the charter provided no more than a framework for principles and a statement of political intent on the part of the signatory member states. While trade unions were critical of the watering down of some of the provisions of the charter and were concerned about the nature of the instrument itself, they nevertheless recognised that its adoption was a major development for workers. It was particularly significant that the charter was adopted at a time when deregulation and opposition to government intervention in labour markets dominated political and economic debate in some of the major economies of Europe and the world.

The charter itself did not contain any implementing mechanism. This was provided through the social action programme, which was brought forward by the Commission. It contained 47 specific measures designed to give effect to the principles set down in the charter, and all of these measures were to be implemented by the end of 1992 as part of the single market process. But progress on the implementation of these measures was painfully slow. During 1990 and 1991, the Commission prepared all the proposals required for implementing the social action programme and submitted them to the Council. However, the Commission's commitment to the social dimension was continually undermined by the failure of the Council of Ministers to adopt the proposals brought forward by the Commission within a reasonable time-scale. Because of the existing voting arrangements at Council level, proposals affecting workers' rights, other than health and safety measures, could only be adopted by unanimity. Progress therefore was confined mainly to the area of health and safety. Directives dealing with basic issues such as protection of part-time workers and maximum working hours were being blocked or watered down to such an extent that their provisions were meaningless. On the other hand, substantial progress continued to be made in removing technical barriers to competition and to the free movement of capital and establishing new mechanisms and institutions to achieve economic and monetary union. Therefore a serious imbalance was emerging between the economic and social aspects of the Community, contrary to the stated commitment to progress both in tandem.

The Maastricht Treaty attempted to address this difficulty and to renew the Community's commitment to the social dimension, which is reflected in the social chapter (i.e. social protocol and agreement) which eleven of the twelve member states signed – the UK opting out once again. One of the most important aspects of the Maastricht Treaty was that it provided for qualified majority voting on workers' rights, thereby removing the dead hand of the veto from a number of key areas. This would ensure much speedier adoption of these measures. In addition, Article 118 of the Treaty was substantially revamped at Maastricht to provide for a detailed consultative procedure between the Commission and employers and trade unions on social policy proposals, and opened up the possibility for agreements to be concluded at European level between employers and trade unions. The consultation procedure set down in Article 118a ensured that the views of both sides of industry would be fully considered by the Commission when drafting proposals on social policy.

Article 118b provided for the possibility of European agreements between employers and trade unions. This provision was incorporated on the basis of a joint proposal from ETUC and UNICE/CEEP (the European employers' organisations). Since its adoption, a number of important agreements on parental leave, part-time workers and fixed-term contracts have been successfully negotiated through this process.

These changes contained in the Maastricht Treaty strongly influenced the approach taken by Irish and European trade unions to it. It was clear that the Social Charter had run out of steam and that new thinking and new possibilities for further initiatives in the social policy field would be dependent on the adoption of the Maastricht Treaty. Based on this analysis, Congress and the broader European trade union movement campaigned for a 'yes' vote in the Maastricht Treaty referendum in 1992.

In the lead-up to the Amsterdam Treaty, the trade union movement across Europe formulated a clear policy and strategy to ensure that the Treaty would not just concern itself with institutional and technical issues but that the opportunity would be taken to renew and revitalise the spirit of European solidarity. From the start of the Intergovernmental Conference (IGC) in March 1996 to the signing of the Amsterdam Treaty in June 1997, the trade union movement at European and at national level pressed for the inclusion of the two key issues of employment and social rights in the Treaty. This was part of a European-wide trade union campaign to get the IGC to address some real issues in the Treaty and to propose some real solutions to the problems of unemployment, social protection and citizens' rights in the European Union.

The inclusion in the Amsterdam Treaty of a new Title on Employment marked the culmination of a series of important policy decisions and initiatives taken since the adoption of the Maastricht Treaty which were primarily the result of the pressures for action on employment put on the European institutions and the member states by ETUC and national trade union centres. At the beginning of the IGC process, most member states were opposed to the inclusion of the question of employment on the agenda. Therefore the inclusion of a new Title on Employment in the Treaty linked to specific policies and initiatives was a very important breakthrough for trade unions.

The Luxembourg Summit on Employment, held in November 1997, brought forward the implementation of the Employment Title ahead of ratification of the Treaty. At home, the social partners were consulted on the Irish government's national action plan submitted to the Commission in April 1997, specifying its actions designed to fulfil the different criteria set down in the guidelines adopted at the Luxembourg Summit.

On the question of social rights, the Amsterdam Treaty included in the Recitals a reference to the Charter on Fundamental Social Rights for Workers; it incorporated the social agreement; it strengthened Article 119 of the Treaty dealing with equal pay and broadened the reference to equal treatment in the workplace; it introduced a new article on non-discrimination which empowered the EU to take action to combat discrimination based on sex, race, religion, disability, age and sexual orientation; and it provided for co-operation between the member states to fight social exclusion.

While trade unions understood that the Amsterdam Treaty was not going to change radically the direction in which Europe was going, they recognised that it contained important new commitments in the areas of employment and social rights which had the potential to impact significantly on the lives of workers and the citizens of Europe generally. Trade unions believed that if these provisions could be activated and developed in a meaningful way, then the Amsterdam Treaty could be an important milestone on the way to building a 'citizens' Europe'. Having regard to the significant provisions of the Treaty in the areas of employment and social rights, Congress supported ratification of the Amsterdam Treaty and urged trade union members to vote 'yes' in the referendum held in May 1998.

Looking forward

As the European project continues to evolve, there are many new challenges facing trade unions. The move to a single currency is probably the most significant, and creates new opportunities as well as threats. The impact of the single currency on collective bargaining patterns across the European Union is difficult to foresee at this stage, but clearly there will be growing pressure on trade unions to have regard to the competitive pressures created by the single currency and the need for greater wage flexibility. But industrial relations and collective bargaining systems are still firmly rooted within national boundaries and have so far proved themselves impervious to change.

There is still the challenge of securing the European social model in the face of economic globalisation, which seeks to build competitive edge on low wages and low standards. Enlargement is part of this debate, and trade unions in the European Union will have a critical role to play in ensuring that workers in the new member states will benefit from the code of minimum social standards which has been painstakingly built up over the past 25 years. It is also important that the provisions of the Amsterdam Treaty on fundamental human rights, which include trade union rights, are fully adhered to by these new member states.

Based on experience over the past 25 years, trade unions in Ireland and throughout the European Union are well equipped to face these challenges. They will continue to be a critical voice and an energetic driving force for building a citizens' Europe, while also being capable of acknowledging change and progress towards achieving this goal. This balanced approach has moved the trade union movement beyond the simplistic and sterile pro- or anti-Europe debate of the 1970s to a position where it now plays a constructive and participative role in determining the kind of Europe that will evolve in the future.

1984 – the end of Eurosclerosis

KATHERINE MEENAN

Background

Although the complex of issues currently facing the European Union will provide a very severe test of its capacity for decisive action, it is salutary to look back to the early 1980s and see what things were like then. It seemed that the concept of European integration had been one of those nice ideas – good at the time, but without the strength or capacity to sustain itself. This is the period for which the term 'Eurosclerosis' was invented. There was no momentum in the process, and the European Community was irrelevant to most of the member governments.

There may be considerable differences of opinion at the moment about what kind of European Union is the appropriate one to deal with the challenges of the next century, but there is no doubt of the need to take decisions and that the European Union is at least the forum within which these decisions need to be taken. The queue of applicants at the door of the EU demonstrates this more clearly than any rhetoric.

The 1980s began badly with an awareness that the economies of the European Community, jointly and separately, were falling further and further behind in the economic game. The Luxembourg Compromise of the 1960s, which had given every member state an absolute right of veto, had led to institutional paralysis and an incapacity to deal with the challenges facing the Community.

After the oil crisis, which unhappily had coincided with enlargement from the original six, with the accession of Ireland, the United Kingdom and Denmark, the Community had, as Edward Heath said, lost its momentum. It also lost its fundamental philosophy: that it existed to find common solutions to common problems. There was a failure to provide employment for its citizens, its share in world trade was diminishing, and it was losing out particularly badly in the newer industries.

In the late 1970s the rate of growth in the European Community had exceeded that of both the US and Japan. However, it recovered far more slowly after the 1979 oil crisis and growth rates lagged behind the those of the US and Japan. There was a complete failure to meet the challenge of the south-east Asian tiger economies, with a relative decline in all manufacturing sectors. In particular, all growth in the high-tech sectors seemed to be taking place in Japan and the US. There was also an awareness that while European companies were spending amounts on research and development nearly equivalent to their industrial competitors in Japan and the US, the rate of growth of importation of high-tech goods was increasing. (In 1986, for example, the Community imported $83 billion worth of high-tech goods, but exported only $69 billion worth.) Unemployment was growing rapidly. By 1983 it had reached 11 per cent, and job creation was falling far behind Japan and the US.

Early attempts at reform

By 1982 the extent to which the Community and its members were being left behind was clearly recognised. At the Copenhagen summit of that year, the conclusions stated that the European economy compared poorly with that of the United States and Japan. A declaration was made that the internal market would be completed in ten years, but no measures were put in place to ensure that this would happen.

Governments were seeking to re-invent protectionism after the success of the period of 'negative integration' of the 1960s. Increasing levels of protectionism vis-à-vis third countries and also between member states were prevalent, with a sharp increase in the number of cases of this type being taken to the European Court of Justice. National industrial policies of 'champions', such as the French computer industry, succeeded only in making markets smaller. The accepted benefits of a larger common trading area were being undermined by national policies.

At the same time as the recognition of the problem was becoming more acute, the proposals for a solution were changing. The Keynesian approach of the 1950s and 1960s – which had been the backdrop to great growth and a rapid post-war recovery – was no longer believed to be capable of delivering the required solutions. Comparisons with the success of the US economy in providing for its citizens meant that the lessons of neo-liberalism and deregulation began to be taken on board by governments. However, there was no recognition that the Community was the fulcrum on which these levers should be placed, and no awareness that this type of deregulation does not require 'less government', it actually requires strong institutions to enforce it.

Although the economic picture was fairly uniformly gloomy, and the original concept of the value of a single market had been lost, it was not the case that there had been no progress on the political or institutional front. The establishment of the exchange rate mechanism had been a major step forward, economically and institutionally, and at the time was proving a success.

The election of the European Parliament by universal suffrage in 1979 was already a major constitutional change in the Community, which for the first time had moved from a construct made for and by technocrats to one which involved choices on the part of the citizen.

European political co-operation had been established and, although at that stage it meant only minimal co-ordination of member states' individual foreign policy, it was none the less a first step on the road to integrated policies, with at least the sharing of information, and the very beginning of common analyses of problems.

In November 1981 France and the Federal Republic of Germany presented the Genscher–Colombo Plan, a draft 'European Act' to improve the institutional mechanisms. This initiative of Hans-Dietrich Genscher, the long-serving German foreign minister, and Emilio Colombo, his Italian counterpart, had been to try to bounce the member governments into moving forward together. The process had moved on to the German Presidency and the result was the Stuttgart declaration, agreed at the European Council in Stuttgart in 1983, which summed up the objectives of the time as follows:

- to strengthen and continue the development of the Communities
- to strengthen and develop European political co-operation
- to promote close co-operation in cultural matters
- to promote the 'approximation' of certain areas of the legislation of the member states.

However, none of these incremental changes came across to the citizens as being of particular importance. As far as headline-writers were concerned, and to those involved in the day-to-day running of the process, the Community had been completely absorbed in the acrimonious and sterile British budget question. Although the UK argument was well founded, and there was no doubt that the peculiar vagaries of the Community budget meant that it paid a contribution way above what might have been considered equitable, the way in which the debate was conducted poisoned the atmosphere. It is possible that only the fact that the German Chancellor actually left the table at the European Council in Brussels in early 1984, rather than continue pointless negotiations, made it clear to the UK government that it might not be able to pursue its argument to the very end.

The procedure of preparing for the Iberian enlargement had been difficult and time-consuming, as well as extremely bad-tempered, particularly over issues such as free movement of workers and fisheries. This also meant that there was little time or energy to devote to the bigger picture.

Although it was not recognised at the time, by 1984 changes were appearing both within institutions and between them. The election of the European Parliament by universal suffrage in 1979 created a certain change in the dynamism of public opinion. Direct elections had been promoted by political parties and their leaders as a solution to the problem of legitimacy in the Community, but now the directly elected parliament was recognised as having no say in Community decisions, blocked by the European Council, in which those same party leaders sat. The Parliament could barely propose and could not dispose. However, its very presence as a directly elected chamber was sensitising the electorate, and the political parties nationally, to some of the more pressing problems of the Community.

Because of the frustration of the newly elected Parliament at the lack of change that would enable it to exercise real influence, and because of the impact of a large number of big European names being brought together, Parliament began casting around for an adventure which would allow it to play the kind of role that the members felt it ought to. So in 1984, the Parliament proposed the Treaty on European Union. The inspiration for this had come from one of the grand old men of European federalism, Altiero Spinelli, a leader of the Italian wartime resistance, a founder of the federalist movement at the end of the Second World War and a former member of the Commission. It had been the work of many months within the Parliament to draft and then agree a text. However, that activity energised the Parliament and its members, and gave them a focus for the kind of work that the members believed they should be engaged in.

When the Treaty was put to the plenary session of the Parliament in February 1984, it was accepted by 237 votes to 31. The Parliament then began an offensive to gain acceptance for this proposal among governments, political parties, national parliaments and other interest groups. Certain member governments responded favourably, but the Parliament considered that it had achieved a real breakthrough when, in May, President Mitterand of France, then President of the Council, in a speech to the Parliament expressed his support for the draft Treaty.

The Dooge Committee

At the Fontainebleau European Council, which followed in June of that year, agreement was finally reached on a structure for a fairly substantial UK budget rebate, although the wrangling was not completely over. In handing over the baton, Mitterand identified the issues facing the incoming Irish Presidency as the conclusion of the Lomé Convention, the final steps in agreeing the terms of Spanish and Portuguese accession, the nomination of the next President of the Commission and the 'initiation of a process of strengthening the Community by the establishment of two committees'. According to the memoirs of the incoming President of the Council, Dr Garret FitzGerald, this proposal was supported wholeheartedly by the German Chancellor, Helmut Kohl, who wanted a 'top-notch' group of imaginative and inspirational personalities to be appointed.

At the conclusion of its meeting, the European Council announced that it had decided to set up an *ad hoc* committee consisting of personal representatives of the heads of state and government 'on the lines of the Spaak Committee'. The Ad Hoc Committee's only brief from the European Council was that it should 'make suggestions for the improvement of the operation of European co-operation in both the Community field and that of political or any other co-operation'.

The only other guidance given to the Committee was a letter from Garret FitzGerald, incoming President in Office. He suggested the following 'further guidance for the work of the Committee':

- the functioning and decision-making arrangements of the institutions and inter-relationships between them
- the effectiveness of the Community's action in the socio-economic sphere (including the European Monetary System) and in that of technology
- the possibility and modalities of common action in, for example, the fields of education, culture, health, justice and the fight against terrorism
- progress towards European Union.

It is interesting to compare the brief of the Committee with the vast range of issues that were placed on the table of the Reflection Group, designed on the Dooge Committee model, which prepared the Amsterdam Treaty negotiations. This was not because the President in Office sought to limit the functioning of the Dooge Committee, but it was an indication of the limit of the possible within the political landscape of the time.

The Committee decided early that it would act on the political level. Its report states explicitly that:

> The Committee has placed itself firmly on the political level, and without proposing to draft a new treaty in legal form, proposes to set out the objectives, policies and institutional reforms which are necessary to restore to Europe the vigour and ambition of its inception.

While the make-up of the Committee and the range of backgrounds made for a valuable meeting of minds, the very difference of approach and expectation meant that it would never be an easy grouping to pull together. No guidance was given to the Irish Presidency as to who should chair the

Committee, and Dr FitzGerald immediately proposed the name of Professor James Dooge, former Minister for Foreign Affairs, Senate leader and eminent academic. His chairing skills in the Senate and at university level were legendary, in addition to his capacity to see both trees and forest with equal clarity.

Although no opposition had been voiced either to the Irish Presidency's right to name the chair or to Professor Dooge's nomination, after the Committee had begun its preparations the German government let it be known that it had intended to nominate former Federal President Carstens. If Carstens had been a member of the Committee it was certain that he would have been the chair, given his eminence. The Germans subsequently accepted that they had left their announcement too late and that Professor Dooge was acceptable to them. However, this left the Committee with an uneasy beginning, which might have been avoided.

It was not the intention of the Committee that it should get involved in complicated drafting of texts on which exact agreement would be sought. In fact, the secretariat drafted virtually no documents; its function was to facilitate meetings, deal with documentation, etc. All the documents on which the Committee worked were supplied by individual members, on their own responsibility. Members volunteered to prepare documents on issues that needed discussion. In certain cases, documents were prepared containing views with which the author did not necessarily agree, just to provide a basis for debate. This is an interesting indication of the level of trust and openness with which the Committee operated, which was achieved to a very large extent because of the trust that was laid in the Chairman, Professor Dooge. He had demonstrated very early that he was aware of the possible pitfalls of an exercise such as this, and had managed to persuade the members to maintain the essential cohesiveness of the group. His grasp of the issues and the evident integrity with which he approached the job meant that members knew that a real exploration of the problems facing the next step in the integration process would not be used against them, either then or in any subsequent negotiation.

The meetings of the Committee were planned with great efficiency. Timetables were drawn up and adhered to – another ground-breaking achievement in Community history. The Chairman also succeeded in dividing the issues into ones of real sensitivity and ones of a more general interest for each member. The main themes were slugged out at the meetings of the Committee themselves, with assistants and note-takers present, when it seemed likely that there could be a resolution. But when there was a problem that seemed likely to lead to breakdown, the real progress was made at the informal lunches. It was clear that the members of the Committee did not want breakdown, notwithstanding their very different concerns. For that reason even the format in which the report would be presented took on a significance. The skill and resourcefulness – not to say courage – of the Chairman were key to the process.

The standing of the Chairman was underlined when, after the interim report was published and submitted to the Dublin Council of 1984, his position was unchallenged in spite of the change of Presidency and, in logic, the possible rotation of the chair. To my knowledge this was never even contemplated.

A number of meetings of the assistants to members were held to deal with the less contentious issues, but there was no question of 'drafting groups' or moving things down the line in order to build in the maximum number of different approaches, and arrive at a consensus by watering-down.

The reason why this kind of *modus operandi* was possible, and what gave this Committee its unique flavour, was the extent to which each member was indeed the *personal* representative of the head of state or government that had appointed him. Every member was in very regular contact with the leader that appointed him. In some cases there was a very close personal relationship, and it was obvious that issues were being dealt with on a one-to-one basis; in other cases the relationship was more formal, but the interest from above was no less keen. Certainly from my own point of view as head of secretariat it was interesting to see the hand-written notes of heads of government on documents. The down-side was waiting until 2 a.m. to start drafting documents for a 9 a.m. meeting, because the relevant key political personality, whose OK was essential, had gone to the opera and decided to stay for a drink – thereby copper-fastening my admiration for the extraordinary physical stamina of senior government leaders.

There was a good mix of political figures in the Committee, combined with those who had considerable experience of the administration. Those differences probably contributed in large measure to the dynamics of the Committee, a valuable mixture of the highly political with the very pragmatic. Each member had sufficient standing to take considerable risks on his own account, knowing that he might subsequently be disowned.

It became clear that there was a difference in understanding of the objective of the Committee between a few members and the majority. There was a view that the role of the Committee was to draw up a manifesto on progress towards European Union, and a much stronger view that the most useful thing the Committee could do was to explore the extent to which there was a genuine willingness to bring about change. The Committee made it clear early that it was not in the negotiating business. The members recognised that unanimity was to be desired, but it was not to be achieved at any cost.

The Committee operated by exploring in considerable detail, and at the highest intellectual level, based on the considerable range of experiences of the members, what different attitudes meant and how far they could be made capable of change. A highlight was a four-hour discussion on how exactly a vital national interest could be defined, and whether it would be possible to lay down the conditions under which it could be invoked. It was certainly interesting, as a spectator at the debate, to see the extent to which groups had become prisoners of their current rhetoric. In fact, very often when the layers were peeled back, it turned out that positions were not so different from one another; it was equally clear that some actors were able to disguise their opposition on a particular point by hiding behind a more vociferous partner. It was also interesting how minorities changed from topic to topic. No member of the Committee was in a minority on everything. It consisted of a series of coalitions on different issues, with constantly changing membership.

The most fundamental decision for the Committee to take, towards which it was moving from the early stages, and the one on which the final report could not give a unanimous answer, was whether to call for the holding of an Intergovernmental Conference. This was the concept promoted by the Parliament's Treaty on European Union, but there was a recognition that it would open a Pandora's box of Treaty revision. Whether an IGC was the most useful way of proceeding was an issue for discussion even among the greatest proponents of progress.

Although the work of the Committee was a matter of considerable interest to the rest of the political establishment at the time, its activities were, in theory at least, confidential. Meetings were held with the President of the European Parliament, Pierre Pflimlin, and Altiero Spinelli as chair of the Institutional Affairs Committee (if charm could have won the battle, the appearance of these two ancient warriors in the cause of integration would have overcome every obstacle instantly), representatives of the Spanish and Portuguese governments, which were just concluding the negotiations for membership, and the President of the Economic and Social Committee.

It is a measure of most observers' pessimism that the European project could be driven forward that the activities of the Committee became the focus of so much interest among those involved in political activity in Brussels. Certainly information was leaked from the Committee, and several different spins were put on the leaks, in an effort to be able to claim credit for whatever eventual progress might be made, or to get in some pre-emptive strikes against the likely slow-coaches. However, it should also be said that this did not really damage the frankness of debate within the Committee.

Completing the Single Market

While the Dooge Committee and the parallel committee on a People's Europe, chaired by Adonnino, were operating, the new Commission was taking up office in January 1985. The incoming President of the Commission, the French socialist Jacques Delors, had already understood the need for the 'big idea' to motivate and inspire both the élites involved in the operation of the Community and the member state governments themselves. Given the background of real concern about Europe's position in the global economy, the task was clearly identifiable as restoring competitiveness by establishing and developing the internal market of the Community, which was about to have a membership of twelve states. In Delors' view:

> In the world race against the clock, which the countries of Europe have to win to survive, what was needed was a common objective to enable us to look beyond the everyday difficulties and pool our strengths and energies.

This common objective was identified as the Single Market programme. As it was subsequently defined in the Single European Act, it was be the continuation of the work begun by the Treaty of Rome: 'an area without internal frontiers in which the free movement of goods, persons, services and capital is ensured'. It was packaged politically by Delors as the 1992 project, cleverly giving a name and a comprehensible target date to a highly technical project.

Political imagination was improbably inflamed by the white paper, published under the authorship of Lord Cockfield – another new member of the incoming Commission – which identified 279 measures that needed to be removed in order to create a genuine Single Market. There was a clear recognition that the existing institutional structure had been adequate for 'negative integration', i.e. the removal of tariffs and quotas etc., but attempts to harmonise standards to allow true freedom of circulation of goods had proved that the need for consensus on every issue meant that decision-making was excruciatingly slow.

The Milan European Council

Therefore these two dynamics, the increasing need for institutional change as outlined in the Dooge Committee report and the clearly defined objective of the Single Market programme, which would founder without institutional change, found their way onto the table of the European Council at Milan in June 1985, and it was clear that there was a need to deal with them. The dynamics of the few weeks before the Council and of the Council itself are described in Garret FitzGerald's memoirs. A first discussion had been held on the Dooge Committee report at the European Council in Dublin in December 1984, and the Committee had been asked to continue its work. This it did, but without achieving any greater degree of consensus. In the period immediately preceding the Milan Council, the proposal to hold an

Intergovernmental Conference became the subject of intense activity. However, all the indications at the time were that no clear-cut decision would be made on this crucial question. In fact, it seemed more than likely that a series of agreements on a range of individual issues could be arrived at, but that there would be no question of revising the Treaty.

However, on the second day of the Council it was proposed by Chancellor Kohl and President Mitterand that a vote would be taken as to whether to hold an IGC. Craxi, the Italian Prime Minister who was President of the Council, had in the days leading up to the Council given no indication whether he would push for an Intergovernmental Conference, but he decided to put it to the vote – the first time a vote had ever been taken at a European Council. To the intense surprise of several members of the Council, in particular Mrs Thatcher, the UK Prime Minister, a vote was taken and passed by seven votes to three. (Subsequent studies have shown that the UK Foreign Office was unaware that a vote was likely to take place, while most other countries had at least toyed with the implications of the concept.)

Crucially, Ireland voted with the six founder members of the Community, thereby giving the lie to the idea that enlargement has inevitably weakened commitment to the Community enterprise.

In his memoirs, FitzGerald said that he 'left the meeting exhilarated'. Tensions during the Council were probably exacerbated by the surroundings in which it was held, the Castello Sforza, an important national Italian museum. The delegations were hemmed in by walls many feet thick, with the press in tented corrals in the various courtyards. The galleries of the museum were the delegation rooms, and it may have helped the success of the Council that no member of a delegation could make an expansive gesture, no matter how important the issue, without the fear of breaking priceless porcelain or antique musical instruments, and possibly causing lasting damage to Europe's joint cultural heritage.

Now that Intergovernmental Conferences are constantly on the agenda and each conference has already designated its successor and the time-scale, it is more difficult to understand the impact of the decision. The only changes to the original Treaties had been technical ones, which allowed the executives of the Coal and Steel Community, EURATOM and the Common Market to be merged. The Luxembourg Compromise had locked the institutions of the Community into a completely negative circle where every activity was reduced to the lowest: in Kohl's words, applied to a later state of affairs, 'the convoy was sailing at the speed of the slowest ship'. Now the governments were to sit down and review the changes that were necessary. And if one change was necessary, why not change everything?

No observer could pretend that the immediate outcome of this process, the Single European Act, was perfect. It allowed for real progress to be made towards achieving the Single Market and it institutionalised the Community's foreign policy in a way that improved both efficacy and the transparency of each process. It also allowed the particular concerns of member states to be promoted or protected as required.

It was clear that the Community needed to achieve greater scale in all its activities, and that this could not be done if every single vested interest was to be regarded. It seemed certain that the concept of a vital national interest – as coined for the text of the Luxembourg Compromise – would still exist and that member governments would not ride roughshod over each other. On the other hand, a move towards majority voting was essential if free movement of goods and services was to be achieved.

This capacity to allow for the real concerns of individual member states – however horrendous the constitutional hotchpotch that results – is possibly the basis of the real success of the European adventure. Considerable time was devoted then and since, in the Dooge Committee and in many other fora, to what constituted a vital national interest. The way in which this concept had been promoted in the 1960s and 1970s led many to believe that it could not longer be allowed to be used as a weapon in the institutional debate. But, as in many other cases, it was probably the abuse rather than the use of this weapon that had done so much damage to the Community and its dynamism. The Community could hardly continue if the truly vital interests of its members could not be protected.

The period since the early 1980s has seen numerous developments – too much for some, too little for others – many of which are outside the control of the Community and its members. However, the real value of the changes in the period since the disease of Eurosclerosis was diagnosed, and largely cured, has been the recognition by many that a truly vital interest of a member is better served by the existence and progress of a successful, dynamic and outward-looking European Union than by ongoing warfare in the trenches of individual policy issues.

═══ 6 ═══

Academic studies in Ireland

BRIGID LAFFAN

Introduction

Prior to Ireland's membership of the European Union in 1973 there was extensive teaching about Europe in Irish universities. Students of history, antiquity, geography, modern continental languages, and the social sciences took courses on the character of European development and Ireland's relationship with continental Europe. Membership of the EU did, however, have an important impact in that it marked a commitment by the Irish state to a continuing and active involvement in building a political system that went beyond the state. The Irish electorate opted to embed the Irish state in the wider European system. Ireland in 1973 rejoined or rediscovered Europe in many respects. The international focus of Irish foreign policy at the UN and the societal focus on the United States and other English-speaking societies was augmented by a regional, European, focus. EU membership greatly increased the salience of Europe for the Irish economy, polity and society. Knowledge of the EU became an asset in many fields, and the Union's educational and research policies altered the life of individual academics and the university environment. This essay seeks to capture the impact of EU membership on academia. But first, a personal reflection.

A personal journey

Ireland's membership of the EU instilled in me an interest in the dynamic of European integration, an interest which has been central to my scholarly concerns. I have a very sharp and clear memory of viewing Jack Lynch, on television, signing Ireland's Treaty of Accession in 1972. A sense of a new phase of Irish development led to my decision to apply to what was then the National Institute of Higher Education (NIHE) in Limerick, to do a degree course in European studies. A few weeks earlier, information packs about the new course in Limerick had been distributed at my secondary school, St John Bosco's Secondary School, Cahirciveen, Co. Kerry. The course seemed to offer a fresh approach to the study of the humanities and social sciences. Furthermore, it responded to Ireland's changing orientation. The NIHE opened in autumn 1972 with just over 100 students, 20 of whom did European studies. This was the first undergraduate degree course in Ireland with a European studies core. I was attracted by the interdisciplinary mix and the opportunity to take a continental European language without having to do a language degree. It was challenging and at times very difficult to be pioneers in Limerick. Those first students and staff opted to join a new institution, which had yet to find its place in Ireland's university landscape. It was a college characterised by innovation, and had all the strengths and weaknesses of a young, hungry institution. Freed from inherited legacies and the dead weight of the past, it could and did experiment with course structure, content and delivery. This was both exciting and exhausting for students and staff alike. Not all of the experiments worked, and at times we would have exchanged the unpredictability of Limerick for the calmer waters of an established university. However, the difficulties created by the newness of the institution were more than compensated for by the dedication of the academic staff, whose enthusiasm for their subjects was infectious. We had the privilege of small classes, extensive tutorials and thorough feedback.

Leaving Limerick in 1976 without a degree, because of a row about accreditation, did little to dim my conviction that taking the European studies course was the right decision for me. We were finally awarded our degrees in 1977, one year later, not just well versed in our subjects but with invaluable lobbying skills garnered in a hard-fought campaign for our rights. Four years in Limerick, followed by two at the College of Europe in Brugge (Bruges), sealed my fate. Limerick's system of co-operative education gave me an invaluable opportunity to work in the Department of Foreign Affairs in 1975 during Ireland's first Presidency of the EU. I experienced at first hand the manner in which EU membership was having an impact on Ireland's governmental and administrative system. While there, I had the opportunity to interview Dr FitzGerald, the Foreign Minister, for my undergraduate dissertation entitled 'The impact of membership of the EEC on Irish foreign policy'. I still have the notes I made at that meeting. From that time on, the central focus of my academic work was the politics of European integration and Ireland's relationship with the European Union.

Beyond the personal, membership of the EU had a significant impact on the Irish university system over time. Until the mid-1980s, teaching and research on European integration was restricted to a small group of 'EU specialists' and Brussels-watchers. The primary focus of their work was on the impact of EU membership on the Irish economy and political system. The resurgence of the EU in the mid-1980s with the Single European Act and the 1992 single market programme led to a remarkable increase in the number of academics working in this field. There were a number of reasons for this. First, the 1992 programme made the EU much more visible and the study of integration had become fashionable again after a fallow period in the early 1980s. Second, the growing salience of the EU led to sustained interest by the government in this area. A series of referenda brought EU issues centre-stage. Third, the universities responded to the renewed interest by launching taught master's programmes in this area. Fourth, Commission policies such as the Jean Monnet scheme, Erasmus and later Socrates, and the research programmes (framework programmes) acted as a major incentive for engagement with the Brussels system. The Europeanisation of public policies in the EU had a direct impact on the university environment. Responding to Europe was not just a catch-cry in company boardrooms, but was also apparent in all the universities.

Teaching

The European studies course in Limerick was, for many years, the only undergraduate course in this field. It combined languages with the study of European history, economics, politics and society. The course had a strong social science orientation. An important part of it was the system of co-operative education whereby students were sent on placements in Ireland or abroad. Trinity College followed with a second undergraduate degree in European studies. This course differed somewhat from the course in Limerick in that it combined languages with a humanities focus on the development of European civilisation and the history of European thought. Both Trinity and Limerick have dedicated departments of European studies with staff drawn from a variety of disciplines. The development of teaching on the EU was not limited to designated European studies courses. Over the past 25 years, the study of the Union, once a marginal or non-existent interest in many disciplines, became central to the university curriculum in economics, politics, law, history and, increasingly, sociology. Departments in these disciplines felt the need to recruit specialists in European integration. Courses on the EU became very popular with students in all the traditional social sciences. In fact all disciplines developed a 'European dimension', and knowing something about the EU was seen as relevant to employment prospects.

It was not until the late 1980s that Irish universities began to offer master's-level programmes on European integration and European studies. This was a direct response to the political resurgence of the European Union and its growing visibility. The increased salience of EU courses at undergraduate level was augmented by the growth of graduate courses at MA level. Master's courses with a European focus became a growth industry. These programmes contributed to the training of growing numbers of graduate students in this field. The University of Limerick, Queen's University and University College Dublin developed specialised master's courses on the European Union and European studies. The National University of Ireland at Maynooth developed an MA programme on European social policy. All other universities have MA students working on European themes. Many Irish students have also opted to do courses on Europe in other EU states, and the Irish-based courses attract non-Irish students to Ireland. The students began to come to Ireland from North America, the Far East and continental Europe to take courses in this field. The College of Europe in Brugge and the European University Institute in Florence always have a cohort of Irish students.

The educational policies of the EU reach right into the university lecture hall. What was once known as the Erasmus programme, now Socrates, encouraged the establishment of exchange programmes among European universities in all faculties and disciplines. Establishing European networks became one of the hallmarks of a good department in all our universities. The programme further internationalised university life and gave Irish universities a European perspective to complement existing links with North America. Student and staff exchanges have not only been enormously beneficial to the individuals concerned; they have changed the environment within each university. One finds oneself lecturing to five or six nationalities at undergraduate level. Ireland has proved very popular as a destination for Socrates students for reasons of language and the pastoral care that characterises our system. Irish university campuses are now internationalised in a manner that would have been inconceivable 20 years ago. The Union's educational programmes are contributing in a very direct manner to the strengthening of the social fabric of European integration. A people's Europe is being fashioned over time.

The Jean Monnet programme is another example of the impact of EU policies on the Irish university system. In 1989, Jacques Delors, then Commission President, proposed the establishment of European chairs to promote the study of European integration in the member states and beyond. Universities throughout the EU, associated states and others responded enthusiastically to the proposals, with the result that there are now chairs in politics, economics, history, law and some related disciplines. All Irish universities have their complement of Monnet chairs. There is a highly competitive process of selection at EU level as the universities bid for the available financial resources. In 1998, the Commission launched the concept of 'centres of excellence' in this field. Queen's University Belfast and University College Dublin were among the successful institutions in the first round when 25 awards were made in the Union as a whole.

Research

Membership of the Union led many researchers to focus on Ireland's relationship with the system and the consequences of the EU for the Irish economy, polity and society. A recurring theme in many Irish studies is the question of small states and European integration. This reflects Ireland's position as a small west European state and the growing debate about the balance between small and large states in the Union. Irish scholars are also conducting research on the broad themes of European integration, and not just on Ireland.

The Institute for European Affairs (IEA), established in 1991, has had a major impact on European integration research in Ireland. The institute is a permanent forum for the identification and development of Irish strategic policy responses to the continuing process of European integration and to the wider international issues that impact on Europe. The institute's methodology is based on research into identified subjects of key importance to Ireland and to Europe, organised principally on the basis of expert study groups working with a rapporteur. The output of the groups is in the form of publications, notably reports, occasional papers, books and periodicals. The IEA strengthened the links between academic specialists and the policy community more broadly defined.

Irish research on the EU and Ireland's relationship with Brussels has focused on the following major themes:

- the legal impact of the EU
- institutional and constitutional change in the EU
- the common foreign and security policy
- economic and social cohesion/economic and monetary union/EU sectoral policies
- public opinion and the democratic deficit.

The constitutional implications of accession to the EU, in addition to the impact of the system on the Irish legal system and the operation of the courts, led to extensive legal research on the impact of the EU on Irish law. The federal nature of the EC's legal system with its principle of direct effect and supremacy of EC law over conflicting national law has had substantive and special effects on Irish sovereignty. Ireland now operates within a dual constitutional framework: the national constitution and EC treaties.

The governance structures of the Union are a major focus of research. Institutional and constitutional change in the EU is a central research topic for the IEA, which has produced four volumes on this theme since 1994. The first analysed the context and process of treaty change at the 1996

Intergovernmental Conference (IGC). This was followed by an analysis of relations between the United Kingdom and the EU. The difficult relations between the UK and the EU are a major constraint on Ireland's European policy. After the conclusion of the 1996 IGC, the Institute published an analysis of the Treaty of Amsterdam and an insider's account of the Treaty negotiations.

Ireland's non-membership of NATO and its traditional policy of neutrality led to sustained interest in the development of the common foreign and security policy (CFSP). There is extensive graduate work on European political co-operation and small states, the security politics of small states, the attitude of political parties to neutrality, and the elaboration of alternative security scenarios for Europe. The IEA published a major study on the security policies of small states in the context of the evolving CFSP. The objective of the study was to identify variations in the exposure of individual countries to security risks, and to assess the extent of commitment to collective measures.

Economists have dominated work on EMU, the internal market and economic and social cohesion. Ireland's traditional position as a less developed member state and its geographical peripherality have led to extensive research on economic and social cohesion. This may change, as Ireland has experienced sustained convergence since the early 1990s. The University of Limerick's proximity to Shannon Development (regional development organisation) has stimulated research into centre–periphery relations and the structural funds. In UCD, research has been conducted on the impact of European integration on central–local relations and on the structural funds and regional mobilisation. The impact of EU regional policy on cross-border co-operation in Ireland is a major focus of research at University College Galway (UCG).

The Maastricht ratification crisis led to renewed interest in the role of public opinion in political integration and the problem of democracy in the Union. The Centre for European Economic and Public Affairs (CEEPA) in University College Dublin was centrally involved in a European Science Foundation project on beliefs in government. This project involved an assessment of the relationship between public opinion and internationalised governance. CEEPA was also engaged in a European Parliament/European Union Commission-funded project on turn-outs in the European elections with the European University Institute in Florence. Research on the 'democratic deficit', EU citizenship and the broader implications of a 'social Europe' forms part of an ongoing research project at Limerick.

Research networks/infrastructure

The fabric of teaching and research on European integration continues to strengthen. Because of the small size of the academic community in Ireland and the weakness of funding for social science research, cross-national networks are crucial to Irish scholars. Irish academics have participated in studies of the Trans-European Policy Studies Association (TEPSA), the European Consortium of Political Research (ECPR), the European University Institute (EUI) in Florence, the European Institute in Bonn, the European Community Studies Association (ECSA), and networks grant-aided by the Commission's framework programmes. Collaboration with colleagues in other countries is central to the activity of Irish researchers in this field. There are a number of centres in the universities – CEEPA in UCD and the Centre for European Studies in Limerick. The Jean Monnet project has provided a focus for interdisciplinary work in many of the universities.

Reflections

In this short piece, I have attempted to reflect on the impact of Europe on the Irish university system and the development of European studies as an area of study. My decision in 1972 to do a course in European studies in Limerick was, as it turned out, a decision about my life's work. My interest in the dynamic of European integration which was sparked by my lecturers in Limerick has remained with me throughout my academic career. While many scholars engaged in the study of political systems find the EU uninteresting because it does not conform to the patterns and processes of 'normal', i.e. domestic, politics, this was the attraction for me. I remain fascinated by the EU as a form of political order, precisely because it lies between the national and the international, between what is domestic and what is foreign. The EU has slowly, in an incremental and evolutionary manner, changed the nature of statehood in Europe.

Given Europe's revolutionary tradition, it is fascinating to analyse radical change brought about by the politics of pragmatism rather than war and revolution. EU membership embedded Irish society, economy and political system in the wider European system and hence altered the interaction between Ireland and the outside world. Intrinsic to the contemporary Irish state is its involvement in the wider processes of European integration. Inevitably the effects of such a major repositioning of the Irish state were substantial and felt throughout Irish institutions.

The university system responded to the changes in Ireland's external orientation by developing programmes of teaching and research to ensure that young Irish graduates were knowledgeable about the EU and Europe generally. Teaching on the EU is now part of the curriculum in all social science subjects, and the humanities continue to teach on European civilisation. Two universities run specialist European studies courses at undergraduate level. EU policies, notably Socrates, have internationalised the Irish campuses and added a very attractive multicultural layer.

Research in Ireland on European integration is no longer devoted entirely to the impact of integration on Ireland. There is a growing interest in the dynamics of integration and in relations between the EU and the wider world. Although the scholarly community remains small, a growing number of graduate students are engaged in EU-related research. Cross-national networks are extremely important to Irish academics working in this field, and the Institute of European Affairs provides a national focus for research on European integration.

Part II
Institutions

7

The Council of Ministers

DAVID M. NELIGAN

Introduction

Although learned studies of the Council of the European Union abound, a certain mystery about its nature and activities persists. Well-informed members of the general public often have to ask, when their attention is attracted to the institution by some newspaper headline (usually negative), what really goes on in the Council. How does it function?

The Council's public image is rather unclear, despite recent efforts to improve its press and information services. The image possibly suffers because of the higher attention paid to the European Parliament, whose expanding role has been accompanied by an effective media effort. Besides, everybody knows what a parliament is, and over the years people have come to learn quite a lot about the Commission, which is also not shy about publicising its activities. But the Council – if anybody has even heard of it – is seen as a rather indeterminate body which holds its meetings in private and takes many decisions 'without debate', in the brief intervals between indulgence in Lucullan banquets paid for by the citizenry.

Officials of the Council, even the most senior and best known, and even in Brussels where knowledge of the EU institutions is more widespread, are frequently introduced in social situations as 'working for the Commission'. The temptation in such circumstances is to resort, as Beckett did when an interviewer described him as an English writer, to the formula: '*Au contraire!*'.

The successive presidencies certainly get their fair share of publicity, but although the function should correctly be called the Presidency of the Council, the term 'Presidency of the EU' has become so generally accepted in recent years that to argue for the more accurate usage now appears pedantic. Once more, the Council as a result avoids being identified or defined in the public mind.

Decision-making role

Yet for those more closely concerned in EU affairs, the Council enjoys a degree of recognition and even prestige. It is the institution where the sovereign member states are directly represented. Here sit ministers of the governments which initially concluded the founding treaties or which, by accession, in due turn, accepted the *acquis communautaire*. Here sit the ministers who from time to time, convening as an Intergovernmental Conference, have the power to modify those treaties. It is the Council that prepares and follows up the European Council sessions, where the heads of state and of government take the most important decisions and lay down strategic guidelines for EU policy.

The Council is involved in all legislative decisions of the Union. It is at the Council table that applicant countries above all wish to be able to sit. Even the elaborate arrangements made under the 1992 European Economic Area (EEA) agreement in favour of the residual EFTA countries were not sufficient for Austria, Finland and Sweden. Their desire to be able to take a full part in Council decision-making was the main reason for their applying, within a few years, for membership of the EU. Similarly, one may conclude that it is not the prospect of sending a handful of deputies to the European Parliament, or of ensuring some as yet undefined but certainly modest degree of presence in the European Commission for one of its nationals, that motivates Estonia (shall we say) to press for membership in an enlarged Union. Old-fashioned national governmental diplomacy has not so fallen out of fashion that the member states involved, and to be involved, do not attach predominant importance to the forum where they directly defend their interests, deploy their skills and contribute to decision-making: that is, in the Council of the EU.

It would not be a complete definition to say that the Council is such a forum – a permanent diplomatic conference, as earlier commentators have suggested. That aspect certainly has to be reckoned with. National diplomats of the highest standing and ability occupy the posts of permanent representative of their countries in Brussels. The full resources of a member state's diplomacy can on occasion be mobilised to try to sway a Council decision. It is not possible to forget that, in certain cases, the protagonists have a centuries-old imperial tradition behind them. The nation state, naked and unashamed, can occasionally be glimpsed stalking the corridors. The spectacle does not have the same charm for all observers.

However, side by side with this aspect, the Council is also, and very effectively, an organ of the EU. It is an institution fully capable of playing its part in the inter-institutional politics of Brussels, coherent and tenacious in the defence of its common positions, which are the fruit of successful negotiation within the Council. As a result, EU legislation bears the clear imprint of the

Council view, due recognition being given of course to the significant amendments brought in by the Parliament in very many cases. It may well be asked what enables the 15 governments, in negotiating mode, to function so often and so effectively as a unit. What makes the EU Council different from other world diplomatic fora in this regard? Given the major economic and political interests involved, is there some magic ingredient in the Council that facilitates agreement even on very difficult matters? I believe that four factors in particular (none of them in any way magical) can be identified.

The first is socialisation, as commentators have called it, meaning the close personal rapport that comes about between ministers, and above all between the permanent representatives in Brussels, in the course of years of work together. The men and women in the Coreper – the committee of permanent representatives – regularly spend two days a week together in long meetings at which all the files relating to future legislation, and many other institutional, procedural and administrative matters, are painstakingly examined. In addition, each permanent representative is the immediate adviser of his or her Minister at the Council session which deliberates and decides on those files – this duty can in busy periods involve the remaining days of the week. It is not surprising if the permanent representatives end up knowing and understanding one another as well as (if not better than) the senior officials in their own national capitals who give them their instructions.

The second factor is the degree of influence on national policy-making that the permanent representatives or, as the case may be, ministers deeply involved in Council negotiations can exert. In the judgement of those involved in the intensive work of negotiation, it is sometimes appropriate to report home that the national objectives (in terms of the drafting of new legislation) cannot be attained, and that the emerging compromise solution, being the best that can be achieved, ought now to be accepted as the basis for further negotiation. Often in that situation a permanent representative's colleagues in Coreper rely on his or her ability to get a favourable response from his or her capital. Their confidence is in most cases fully justified, and this contributes greatly to the smooth advancement of Council business.

Thirdly, the function of the presidency is a highly significant factor. Volumes have been written about the development of the presidency's role. In this part of the argument, I would limit myself to saying that the proper exercise of the presidency's prerogative in organising and co-ordinating the Council's work, in establishing priorities and fixing agendas, is a powerful component of the Council's effectiveness. A hard-working and well-organised presidency attracts the loyalty of the other delegations. A real desire to help as much as possible to achieve such a presidency's aims can develop, particularly if the presidency shows its willingness to concede on points of its own national policy in order to facilitate overall agreement.

As a fourth factor, the secretariat of the Council should be mentioned. As in any institution, efficient operations depend on the groundwork provided. In the case of the Council, this involves a great deal of practical preparation. Thirteen meetings a day can be held, requiring the provision of interpretation services and of great volumes of documentation – remember that there are eleven working languages in the EU. Technical and security services have also to be provided. However, the secretariat's most important contribution is certainly in the sphere of policy advice and presentation. Presidencies come and go, and so eventually do permanent representatives and ministers, but the secretariat is perpetual. It combines a full knowledge of precedents and procedural niceties with a detailed awareness of where delegations stand on the issues under examination at any time. Its legal service provides copper-bottomed professional advice which all ignore at their peril (it is the legal service that defends the Council in litigation before the European Court of Justice).

The secretariat's talents are put at the disposal of the Council, and of the presidency in particular. Documents on evolving draft legislation are presented in such a way as to prioritise problems and to facilitate the search for solutions. In addition, confidential tactical notes are prepared for the presidency alone, to help the President of the Council (and of Coreper) to get the best out of his or her colleagues and to make the best use of any elements of compromise on the table. The secretariat helps the President to propose and present compromises and, eventually, successive fall-back solutions. The secretary general or a director general always sits directly beside the President (on his or her left) in order to give immediate oral advice as business proceeds. The Council legal adviser (or his or her most senior representative) is also at hand and sometimes intervenes, at the chairman's request, to clarify a legal aspect.

Of course the whole context of the European Union, constituted by the member states' acceptance of the Treaty framework and of the *acquis communautaire*, their regional affinities, their shared characteristics as open, democratic societies, contributes to the effectiveness of the Council as an institution. But the four operational factors outlined above cannot be ignored in any attempt to portray how it functions, and why in general it functions rather well.

How the Council works

I have only begun to answer the initial question – what goes on in the Council? Let us look in more detail at its structure and procedures. Whether one speaks of the first, second or third 'pillars', and no matter what the subject to be dealt with may be, the basic shape of Council procedure is the same. The file to be examined first goes to a working party for technical analysis and a delimitation of the problem areas (often political rather than technical). Each working party (and more than 200 are recognised, though not all equally active) is composed of 15 delegations, representing the 15 member states, with a president, who is an official coming from the member state holding the presidency of the Council, and a representative of the Commission. The Council secretariat is also present and plays its usual role, as described above in respect of the higher instances of Coreper and Council itself.

Each member state delegation includes the 'attaché', i.e. the leading official in that country's permanent representation competent for the subject matter under advisement. For instance, in the environment working party, the 'environment attachés' lead the delegations around the table. These will be fairly senior officials coming from the member states' environment ministries, residing in Brussels to cover all the work in the area of environmental protection. Each attaché may be accompanied by advisers as necessary, who will usually be people from the ministry, i.e. not resident in Brussels, having special technical knowledge of whatever particular file has come up for examination at a given meeting.

The Commission representative has the task of explaining and defending his institution's proposals to Council, and therefore needs to be a relatively senior official (often a director) capable of speaking authoritatively and also of evaluating the member states' difficulties in his reports back to his own institution.

As a matter of rule, business in the working party is conducted in the eleven working languages of the EU. In practice, interpretation into one or another may not be available because of the demands made on the interpretation services. Delegations can be insistent on having interpretation, not only on principle but also for the practical reason that a national expert on a technical subject cannot be assumed to be (and often isn't) capable of presenting his case in a language other than his own – or of following a discussion which is not interpreted into his own. However, the attachés are assumed, from their being posted in Brussels, to have a mastery of French and English sufficient to enable some urgent work or consultations, in particular circumstances, to be carried on in informal meetings without interpretation and without the presence of experts. (In the area of the common foreign and security policy, where the working parties are composed of diplomats from the foreign ministries, business is conducted as a matter of practice in French and English only.)

At working party level, it often becomes evident that substantial revision of the Commission proposal will be necessary if the draft legislative act is to get the necessary support (typically today qualified majority vote) from among the delegations. Here already the negotiations begin. Revised texts are put forward by the presidency at successive meetings. These will often be accepted by the Commission, if it considers that the main objectives of its proposal can still be attained. The aim of the working party president and the secretariat is to advance the work of analysis and revision as far as possible before reporting (usually within a pre-fixed timetable) to Coreper, the next highest instance.

Some detailed explanation of the structures at this stage is necessary.

Coreper

First of all, the Coreper is in two parts, Coreper I and Coreper II. Coreper II is the higher forum, where the ambassadors and permanent representatives sit, while Coreper I is composed of their deputies. However, the distinction between the two does not arise because Coreper I has to report to Coreper II – although this may originally have been the intention and may explain the designations I and II – but on the basis of an agreed division of work between them. The ambassadors (Coreper II) deal with institutional matters, external relations (both economic and political), certain economic and monetary matters, justice and home affairs and the budget. Coreper I deals with all other matters and in consequence prepares a large number of Council meetings in the so-called pillar I. ('Pillar I' comprises the multitudinous economic and social areas covered in the European Community Treaty (ECT) texts, basically Titles I to IV and VIII to XVII of the Treaty. The informal names 'pillar II' and 'pillar III' are given respectively to the common foreign and security policy (CFSP) and to co-operation in justice and home affairs. These are Titles V and VI of the Maastricht 'Treaty on European Union' (TEU).)

Both Corepers by convention conduct their business in only three languages: French, German and English.

Both Corepers are very busy organs, but the burden on Coreper I – the deputy permanent representatives – can be exceptionally heavy given its role also in the conduct of the co-decision procedure with the European Parliament.

However, in dwelling upon the Coreper and its function as the highest instance before the Council itself, one has to recognise the presence of several other high-level bodies which carry out much of the work of preparation for certain Councils, and to which working parties report in the same way as they do to Coreper. These higher bodies are:

- the special agriculture committee
- the 'Article 36' committee, set up under that Article of the Amsterdam Treaty to co-ordinate and contribute to the work of the justice and home affairs Council (but with reduced competence compared to its predecessor, the 'K4' Committee)

- the political committee, which prepares discussion by foreign ministers of CFSP matters
- the economic and financial committee, which prepares much of the ECOFIN Council's work (and which also has the institutional peculiarity of electing a chairman for two years from among its members, and is thus an exception to the six-monthly presidency rotation rule).

While the existence and operation of these bodies has sometimes been described in terms of their 'rivalling' Coreper in the Council, and while there is undoubtedly a tendency on the part of top-level officials in various ministries in the member state capitals to think that they should prepare the Councils and that they would do it better, the value of Coreper is that it is not too deeply mired in sectoral or technical considerations and that it can co-ordinate all Council work and see all of the field at the same time. This attribute of Coreper has again been emphasised in recent and current deliberations on improving the Council's working methods.

Many accounts of the operation of the Coreper suggest that, having received a report from a working party which clears up all the 'technical' points in a file, Coreper has only to occupy itself with the outstanding 'political' points. Its job is sometimes said to be to solve as many of these 'political' points as possible and to send up the remainder to the Ministers in the Council. Such distinctions are meaningless in practice. The onerous work in Coreper is routinely concerned with technical matters. To do their job, the members of Coreper must be capable of grasping the significance of abstruse technical details and of doing it very rapidly, given the high throughput of very varied files. Of course the difficulty in agreeing on technical aspects is almost always in fact political – can the line ever be drawn clearly? – But Coreper is imaginative and persistent and solves many problems that stymied its 'expert' working parties.

It is certainly true that Coreper recognises at all times the inadvisability of asking Ministers to hold debates on technical questions. It is recognised that Ministers assemble in Council, with limited time at their disposal, for the purpose of taking decisions, rather than engaging in possibly confrontational exchanges about finicky and difficult problems, nearly always of legal drafting. On the other hand, there is a sort of question, such as the determination of figures in the distribution of quotas or the fixing of charges, where ministers have to have the last say and in fact will usually get a good result, without fuss or loss of time.

Coreper has a justifiable sense of pride in its responsibilities and in its discharge of them. A former chairman of the committee recently raised with me certain difficulties he had in understanding the Good Friday Peace Agreement for Northern Ireland. His final comment was: 'It could never have got through Coreper Part I'. No indeed, but the context of its negotiation could hardly have been more different. I have however heard the view expressed that Coreper collectively, for its work in preserving European stability over the years, would fully deserve to be considered for the Nobel peace prize.

Having described briefly the preparatory procedures, let us now look at the Council in the proper sense, i.e. the Ministers' forum at the crown of the edifice.

Legally and institutionally, the Council is a single body. However, from the early years of the Economic Community, it has met in different configurations and has divided its agenda accordingly. Thus agriculture is dealt with in the agriculture Council, social questions in the social affairs Council, and so on. There are about 20 such formations in all. Each of these sectoral Councils is composed of the 15 ministers competent in the respective member state governments for the matters under examination. The chairman is the competent minister of the government holding the presidency. The Commission is represented by the commissioner or commissioners responsible for the policy area concerned.

The Council's agenda is proposed by the chair several weeks in advance and refined during the preparatory process in Coreper described above. The agenda indicates where a decision by vote is to be expected, and in other cases what the nature of the discussion is to be – e.g. a policy debate or the adoption of conclusions (i.e. not a legal act).

Council meetings

Each minister comes to the Council accompanied by a delegation of officials, foremost among whom will be his national permanent representative and a senior official (often the secretary general) from his own ministry. Often a junior minister will also accompany the head of delegation and take over if the latter has to leave early. Officials in the delegation are sometimes too numerous to be accommodated in the Council meeting room, but they can follow the proceedings in a neighbouring 'listening room'.

The Council meeting room is, necessarily, very large. Sixty to seventy people sit around the table. Microphones and earphones are used, not solely to follow the interpreters, but very generally so as to be able to hear what is said in one's own language. The setting and the atmosphere are strictly workmanlike. Ministers meet in the same rooms as those used on other days by Coreper and by the larger working parties. Neither flowers nor flags embellish the scene and the meeting is not an occasion, obviously, for resonant political speeches. Coffee is served discreetly at the table so as not to interrupt in any way the progress of business. If there is an interruption, it is called by the President for a stated period – usually a few minutes – in order to let Ministers study a new text or to allow the President to hold consultations for some clearly defined purpose. The items on the agenda are taken in a predetermined order (which may, by agreement, be different from that set forth in the draft agenda document). Each item in turn is pressed, in so far as possible, to a conclusion. However, in the case of complex and difficult files, the possibility of breaking off the discussion to allow for contacts (e.g. with capitals) or to convoke a special meeting of a working party to try to thrash out some sort of compromise drafting on specific limited points may well be resorted to. In that case, the item will be returned to at a later stage, and the intervening hours will be spent dealing with other items on the agenda.

The work is intense and often prolonged. While great efforts and care are devoted by the secretariat to completing each delegation's file of documents (in the appropriate language) in advance, new pieces of paper are often produced by the delegations, in successive drafts, and can proliferate like snuff at a wake. The President at times needs a strong sense of discipline and clarity to keep things on the rails.

His efforts to wind up the negotiations on complex subjects will typically result in his putting forward a compromise package proposal, designed to do something to meet each difficulty encountered, i.e. to give something to each delegation unable to support the text initially on the table, even after a full discussion. In this context, the package is presented as a whole. All must be agreed, and if one part of the package seems to get general agreement, this is only provisional until the whole deal is done.

In all this work, the Commission's role is of key importance. A good entente between the presidency and the Commission is vital and is established beforehand in a detailed preparatory meeting conducted by the chairman and the commissioner personally. In particular, the Commission will set limits to what it can accept, and it is important to note that if the Council wishes to go beyond these limits and to reject any part of the Commission's final formula, it must under the Treaty do so by unanimity. The Commission also should do the job of explaining the technical consequences of each and any amendment that may be proposed in the debate, and should put forward its own proposals whenever they might be helpful.

Qualified majority voting is now, under the Amsterdam Treaty, very much the predominant method of taking Council decisions. However, it is interesting to observe that the taking of a vote, as laid down in the Treaty and the rules of procedure, is often not followed. The President will simply state, when the position is clear to him or her, that a qualified majority exists, and will propose that, on that basis, the decision be adopted. This statement will be assented to, often silently. It is then up to any delegation outside the majority to state whether it wishes its vote against to be formally recorded in the minutes – such a statement being sometimes accompanied by an explanatory commentary.

What about the Lucullan banquets? This is, I fear, another Euro-myth. The ministers' luncheon is not merely a working one but is the time and place where the most sensitive and important political matters are discussed. The President brings in his permanent representative, but otherwise all the ministers and the commissioner are alone at the table in a private room. The working setting is emphasised by the presence of microphones, earphones and interpreters' booths. The secretary general or a director general of the secretariat takes notes. A light three-course meal is served expeditiously, with one wine and a great deal of water. The conversation, as one would expect, is frank and to the point. The themes for the lunch are set by the presidency in advance. These may include a topic on the day's agenda, not to replace proper discussion of it in the Council, but to permit a preliminary political exchange of views about it in a confidential ambience. The lunchtime discussions are informal, and any conclusions reached over the coffee must be formalised subsequently in the Council itself if they are to be valid.

Council having resumed after lunch and having completed its business, typically after a full afternoon and evening session but quite often after a second day of work, the chairman and the commissioner will give press conferences, very often a joint affair. Individual ministers can use the facilities of the Council press centre to hold their own briefings with journalists. In the Council agenda, a considerable number of files will be listed as 'A' items and, in the press communiqué released at this final stage of the proceedings, will be described as having been 'adopted without debate'. From the latter document, it will be seen that these are often files of the greatest importance. Why and how are they adopted without debate?

Presidents of the Council themselves are sometimes puzzled about this. Lord Carrington's irascible eye once fell upon an 'A' item list when he was about to chair a Council meeting. He was heard to exclaim in outrage: 'Who the hell has put pig-iron on my agenda?' Some overdue decision relating to the Coal and Steel Community was thereby put in peril. Soothing explanations by the bag-eyed brehons and his Lordship's own ambassador were needed to save the situation.

The explanation is that those files on the 'A' item list have, some weeks or months before, been the subject of full Council debate and negotiation, and indeed of political agreement on their content. In the conditions normally obtaining at such moments in the Council, while everybody is clear about what they are agreeing upon, a complete legal text in all the official languages is never available. Under the control of Coreper, the work of verifying the final text is subsequently undertaken by legal and linguistic experts and the texts in all the language versions are scrupulously examined for accuracy in capitals and in the Coreper itself. Only then, some weeks later, is the file sent to the Council for formal adoption, i.e. without debate, as an item on the 'A' list. Following this formal passage through the Council, the text is published in the Official Journal of the Community, and Council's procedure is completed.

Reference to this common misunderstanding about adoption 'without debate' leads to a consideration of the question of openness or transparency in the Council. As far as the Council's documentation is concerned, the great bulk of the papers is accessible to the public and a strict definition and justification is required if any are withheld. The demand sometimes made that Council's proceedings should be public is most unlikely to be granted. Negotiation on matters involving substantial interests, to be successful, requires a confidential setting. The participants proceed typically by using the informal *sondage* and the *ballon d'essai* and by linking matters that are not organically connected. If it were required that this be done *coram populo*, the result would be to drive the real bargaining off the stage and into the smoke-filled committee rooms. This is not what the Council's critics want, but it is what can already be observed in the European Parliament. When the Council does hold 'open debates' (seven per presidency), they consist as a rule of 15 disconnected speeches essentially addressed to the folks at home, and a stirring admonition from the Commission. These proceedings are televised for the benefit of the media.

General Affairs Council

The preceding paragraphs relate more especially to the sectoral Councils and to 'pillar I'. The second 'pillar', and 'horizontal' subjects (meaning institutional and budgetary matters etc.), fall to the charge of the General Affairs Council, that is, the configuration of the Council where the ministers of foreign affairs sit. This Council meets each month, or more frequently as necessary. From the beginning of the Community it has been the leading organ. As the work of the Council covers ever more extensive policy areas and the number of member states increases, this leading and co-ordinating role of the General Affairs Council seems set to be strengthened and developed.

The multifaceted external relations of the EU, trade, economic and political, are handled here, including the still evolving common foreign and security policy (CFSP). There are also very numerous formal obligations such as the regular meetings of Association Councils with various European associated countries, and of ministerial meetings with the African, Caribbean and Pacific countries, and with Asian, Latin-American and Mediterranean countries. The General Affairs Council conducts the 'enlargement' negotiations with applicants for EU membership.

The process by which this Council's files are prepared is basically as described above, but the pace of events is faster. In fact, where the CFSP work is concerned, there is often insufficient time to follow the structural process of preparatory meetings. Where an EU reaction is urgently called for, passage of draft position papers through the political committee or the Coreper (let alone both), to say nothing of the Council itself, is not possible. Co-ordination and consultation are done via the COREU confidential communications network linking the presidency and secretariat with the capitals and the Commission directly. In this way an appropriate and timely declaration by the presidency on behalf of the European Union can be drawn up and issued. This area of work already benefits from the establishment of the CFSP unit within the secretariat, and is shortly to be transformed through the assumption of office by the high representative ('Mr CFSP' – Mr Solana) and the start of the activities of the specialised planning and early warning unit.

It is not only in the CFSP context and in the many formal meetings mentioned above that the presidency acts as spokesman for the Council. This is also the rule in many international organisations of which the Community is a member and where the policy area concerned is not a matter of 'exclusive Community competence'. (Where it is, e.g. trade policy, the Commission speaks and acts for the Community with an appropriate mandate from the Council.) Furthermore, the Council's chairman is its spokesman and negotiator in all inter-institutional business in Brussels, above all the conciliation with the Parliament. In all these cases, in all replies to Parliamentary questions, and in the case of all letters or other communications or declarations which the presidency issues in the course of its duties, the agreement of the 15 delegations is required as to what is said or written in their name.

Adapting to the future

A final word should be added about adaptation to the future. The Council has adapted itself very considerably to the changes wrought by the successive new treaties, but it faces very great challenges on account of the many new member states clamouring at the gates and the institutional transformations that their accession will bring. What is certain is that, to function in a European Union of 21, 26 or more members, the Council will have to concentrate massively on co-ordination and programming (including with the Parliament and Commission) and on streamlining its working methods. The Council is the EU institution most directly affected by enlargement, and it is girding its loins to tackle imaginatively the new tasks that lie ahead.

8

The Parliament

JOE FAHY

Introduction

In the 1960s, the Irish political establishment concentrated, to the exclusion of almost everything else, on preparations for entry to the Common Market. Year after year, reports emanated from the committees on industrial organisation outlining the prospects for the various important sectors of Ireland's economy, and indicating the likely impact of Common Market membership on these facets of Irish life. For some areas, changes were recommended; for others, little hope was held out; and the disappearance of some long-established industries was forecast.

Uncertainty about our application for membership in company with the United Kingdom, Denmark and Norway remained, while preparations for the inevitable changes in the economic and agricultural sectors continued. General de Gaulle's reluctance to accept Britain was well known, giving rise to fears of a dilemma for Ireland – if Britain was excluded, should Ireland go in regardless? Should some other arrangement, such as a form of association on a temporary basis with the EEC, be considered? These were just some of the fundamental issues to be decided by the government of the day.

Small wonder, then, that in all the pre-entry debates, discussions and arguments, very little, if any, attention was given to the more mundane aspects of the changes that were about to occur once we joined. A quarter of a century later, one is not immediately struck by memories of detailed discussions, for example, about Ireland's participation in the institutions of the EEC, and particularly in the nuts and bolts areas of Council, Commission and Parliament. As far as the general public was concerned, once we joined it would fall to the Taoiseach, government ministers and Ireland's sole member of the Commission to see that Ireland's interests were looked after. Not much thought was given, outside the realms of the public service and, perhaps, the academic field, to Ireland's direct participation at other levels of the Common Market institutions. And yet, membership was about to involve Irish parliamentarians in an entirely new level of political activity on an international plane. It is fair to say that, in 1972, the full implications and potential of these impending changes received scant attention.

Here, I should say that the average Irish journalist in those days was as much in the dark about the workings of the Common Market institutions as the public at large. Attention was concentrated on the progress of the negotiations for entry, and outside of the small corps of journalists following these on a day-to-day basis, not much thought was given, I suspect, to the detailed operations of European bodies. Besides, in the late 1960s and early 1970s there was plenty on the home political front to distract us.

Thus, it was with mixed feelings that, on the morning of the count in the general election of March 1973, I cut out of the *Irish Independent* an advertisement for an information officer for something called the European Parliament, and tucked it away in my wallet. A new adventure was about to begin!

The European Parliament in 1973

From 1 January 1973, the European Parliament consisted of 198 members, all of whom had to be members of their national parliament; they were, therefore, delegates of the national parliaments of the Nine. Ten members of the Oireachtas were nominated by the Dáil and Seanad to represent Ireland. The delegation reflected the political balance in the Dáil. A similar procedure had obtained for a number of years in relation to our membership of the Parliamentary Assembly of the Council of Europe; many members of the Oireachtas, therefore, had had considerable experience of working in that body.

There was a major distinction, however, and one which was instantly apparent, between the Council of Europe Assembly and the European Parliament. Members of the former body sat in national delegations, behind the name-plate of their country; the European Parliament had organised itself along party political lines, and so the delegates aligned themselves in groups according to their political philosophy. This was the first hurdle (if that be the correct word) facing the Irish members. Fine Gael had already established close links with the Christian Democrat movement in Europe, and joining the appropriate group in the European Parliament presented it with no difficulty; similarly, the delegates of the Irish Labour Party associated with the Socialist group. For Fianna Fáil, there was a dilemma: many observers at the time felt that its natural allies would be the Christian Democrat formation, but since Fine Gael was already established there, the presence of two parties vehemently opposed to each other in their national parliament in the same group in Europe would seem incongruous, to say the least. The problem was solved by the inimitable Brian Lenihan who, with Michael O'Kennedy, brought into being an entirely new political group, in alliance principally with the French Gaullists. Herein was an early, and graphic, illustration of the potential for a broadening of the political spectrum offered by membership of the European Parliament. Ireland now had not one voice, as was the case in the Council of Europe assembly, but representation in three of the principal groups in the developing European Parliament.

For the first six years of our membership of the EEC, Ireland continued to be represented by delegates of the Oireachtas. Personnel changed quite frequently; as vacancies occurred, they were filled on the nomination of the party in which the vacancy had occurred, making no change in the overall balance. From a practical point of view, the dual mandate caused serious difficulty for the delegates. As the European Parliament evolved, seeking more and more influence on the development of EEC policy, and pressing for the introduction of direct elections, as envisaged by the Treaty of Rome, the demands on members' time increased. The Parliament operated a highly developed committee system, which was another important difference from Oireachtas organisation. It soon became clear that the dual mandate was unworkable: if the European Parliament was to become a body with real influence in the interplay between Community institutions, then its members would have to devote their full time and efforts to it.

In those early years, while the Community as an entity was getting to grips with the introduction of new policies in agriculture, regional development and social affairs, there were growing pressures for greater integration in the economic and monetary spheres. In the political field, there was an unstoppable move towards early direct elections. There were practical problems too: the location of Parliament's work in three different cities, and the physical limitations of the buildings concerned.

The division of the work-places was a problem that was outside the competence of Parliament to solve. It was also a cause of much press criticism. These practical difficulties arose from the failure of the original six member states of the European Coal and Steel Community to agree on a single seat for the institutions about to be created. In a compromise, which in subsequent years was repeated in many other fields of European policy, the governments decided that the secretariat of the Parliament should be located in Luxembourg, plenary sessions would be held in both Luxembourg and Strasbourg, and the committees would meet in Brussels. In the days of the Community of six, not much consideration was given to resolving what was clearly an inefficient and costly procedure; with the growth of the European Union to its present size, the logistics of moving the Parliament about continued to consume enormous amounts of time and money. Under current arrangements, the secretariat continues to be centralised in Luxembourg, and sessions are held in both Strasbourg and Brussels, with most committee meetings also taking place in the Belgian capital. With such huge investments by the governments concerned in buildings and infrastructure in these centres, the ideal of locating all the institutions in one place is unlikely to be achieved in the foreseeable future.

For those like myself, whose first direct contact with the EEC occurred following Ireland's accession in 1973, one of the great attractions of the Parliament, in particular, was its informality. In Strasbourg, the part-sessions (as they were described) were held in Maison de l'Europe, constructed by the French to house the Council of Europe from 1950. It was intended to be used for five years, by which time a more imposing Palais de l'Europe would be erected on the adjoining site. In Luxembourg, a meeting place was included in the Schuman Building. Neither centre was adequate for accommodating the public in any significant numbers, and the media facilities also left a lot to be desired. Despite these drawbacks, however, there was an atmosphere of much greater intimacy, bringing together MEPs, journalists, officials and visitors, than one tends to find nowadays. Of course, far smaller numbers were involved, so that it was possible to become acquainted with representatives from the various member states in a relatively short time. Members of the Commission, for example, mixed freely in the precincts of the hemicycle with journalists, officials and visitors. Gradually, this informality helped to improve Parliament's image; it was seen as a place where those at the very centre of European policy-making could exchange ideas or engage in discussion in pleasant and relaxed surroundings. For all the early cynicism about Parliament – and there was a lot of it around – those who had real contact with it in those early days were often taken aback by its openness and informality, and the accessibility of high-ranking European personalities. The membership of Parliament was an impressive roll-call of many who had played leading roles in the post-war development of the continent; before Irish accession, members had included such figures as Schuman, Scheel, de Gasperi, Scelba, Mitterand and Spaak.

A feature of Parliament's composition was the wealth of political experience it encompassed. Many of those who served there from 1952, and into the era of the Nine, had extensive ministerial experience in their own countries; some critics used this to suggest that the Parliament was a kind of retirement home for politicians who had served their time in national affairs, rather than a place to which young, ambitious politicians should aspire. In the long run, I believe, the combined experience of its membership was what enabled Parliament to grow in influence and largely achieve its aims.

The position of the Irish political parties at the time of nomination of the first members of the delegation to the European Parliament is of some interest. Fianna Fáil was in government and would nominate five of the ten prospective members. Because of the dual mandate, it was clear that the Taoiseach, Jack Lynch, would not be able to put forward those members of the party with a high profile: ministers in national governments were ineligible to sit in the European Parliament. He chose three Dáil deputies (Michael Herbert, Michael Hilliard and Tom Nolan) and two Senators

(Michael Yeats and Farrell McElgunn). Fine Gael leader Liam Cosgrave appointed Sir Anthony Esmonde TD, Richie Ryan TD and Senator Charles McDonald, while the Labour Party was represented by Deputies Justin Keating and Conor Cruise O'Brien. Within a matter of months, the operation of the dual mandate, combined with the results of the March 1973 election which I mentioned above, brought about almost an 'all change' situation. Mr Lynch's government fell, and in the new coalition led by Mr Cosgrave and Brendan Corish, Deputies Ryan, Keating and Cruise O'Brien became ministers.

In subsequent changes, Fianna Fáil was able to nominate former ministers, which gave it added influence within its political group and in committees. It is noteworthy also that in those early years Irish members held a vice-presidency of Parliament: Sir Anthony Esmonde was the first to do so, and subsequently Senators Yeats and McDonald. Mr Yeats also became a Quaestor, which gave him a position of considerable influence in dealing with members' practical issues, such as office accommodation, and building development projects. The changes necessitated by the change of government at home brought people like Brian Lenihan, Jim Gibbons, Liam Kavanagh and David Thornley to Europe.

I am sure that all those who served in Parliament at that time experienced many differences in their day-to-day activities: my own experience certainly was different from my former existence in broadcasting journalism with RTE and previously in Independent Newspapers and the *Connacht Tribune*. At the outset, I referred to the advertisement that I had taken from the *Irish Independent* on the day of the election count. In the frenzy of covering the election, and the subsequent political developments, I had forgotten all about the European Parliament. Indeed, some time passed before I discovered the advertisement in my wallet and, having read it again, decided to apply. With a number of other strong candidates, I faced an extensive interview before a jury of senior Parliament officials with an independent chairman, and in the early summer was offered the job as head of information in Ireland. A lovely-sounding title, but what to do? My first question (to myself initially, and subsequently to others) was why should a Parliament, if it was really functioning properly, need an information office? Should not a Parliament be able to generate sufficient interest in its proceedings to have media people, if not the public, clamouring to be present for its debates? Well, if not clamouring, at least interested! Seeking direction or guidelines as to what was expected of me brought little enlightenment. In hindsight, it is easy to understand that the continentals – my European colleagues, especially my French Director-General – were as unsure of what methods I should adopt in promoting Parliament and its work before the Irish public as I was of what they expected from me. And in the end, that was not a bad starting point. I had the support of, and an excellent rapport with, Jack McGowan-Smith, former clerk of the Seanad, who had taken up a post as director of information and public relations in the European Parliament from January 1973. The message, simply put, was: 'Get on with it (and keep us out of trouble!)'.

There were aspects of the bureaucracy surrounding the Parliament that surprised me: in some respects, perhaps, I was a little naïve. I soon discovered that, in contrast to the Irish public service, the administration of Parliament was heavily politically oriented, and that this was widely accepted and taken for granted. In one of my earliest encounters with colleagues in Luxembourg, I spent some time trying to convince them that I was not politically aligned with any of the Irish parties, and was not a nominee of either Mr Cosgrave or Mr Lynch. This was regarded by some of them as quite bizarre! The administrative structures of the European institutions I found quite complex and at times, frustrating. Eventually, with time and patience, most problems were overcome.

At the outset, there was the question of where the Parliament's office in Dublin should be located. Relations between Commission and Parliament were cool; there was a distinct view in the Commission that Parliament should be kept at arm's length, and it took some time for closer working relationships between the two bodies to be established on a Community-wide basis. In this connection, it is worth noting that the co-operation between the two offices in Ireland was subsequently cited as an example to other member states.

The major problem facing the European Parliament (and those, like myself, charged with trying to promote it) was the perception that it was irrelevant, powerless, and nothing more than a talking-shop, and a costly one at that. How was this impression to be overcome, and whose was the primary responsibility in the effort to do so? From the earliest days, there was an element of conflict here between officials and members of the institution. The information service could use its best endeavours to publicise as widely as possible what the Parliament was doing, but if, realistically, the Parliament could make no impact on Community decisions, then little notice was likely to be taken of it. To the credit of all concerned, determined efforts were made, firstly at the political level by Parliament to make its presence felt, and secondly at the administrative level to generate awareness on as wide a scale as possible of what the Parliament was striving to achieve.

What could be done was subject, of course, to budgetary constraints. It is often overlooked that the total EEC budget in those early years did not match the defence expenditure, for example, of any of the larger member states. Within the overall Community budget, all the activities of the Commission, Council of Ministers, European Parliament and other bodies had to be provided for, and then, within each institution, there had to be a share-out of funds for the various directorates. Contrary to popular belief, the pit was far from bottomless.

Against this background, and within these limitations, efforts were made to interest opinion-leaders in as many sectors as possible in the activities of Parliament. Visits by journalists and representative groups drawn from the economic, industrial, trade union and academic fields were subsidised financially; over the years, these schemes were expanded as far as financial provisions would allow. The practical operation of the visits scheme provided numerous headaches, but also some interesting reactions from the public. I recall an article written by the late Fergus Pyle in the *Irish Times*, outlining our proposed group visits scheme; days later I received a note written on a shop letter-heading from a remote village in a Border area: 'Please send on two tickets to Strasbourg and oblige'! Individuals called to the office demanding, as of right, free travel to sessions of Parliament. In another case, an irate county secretary berated me for having dared to invite the county librarian to a special seminar in Luxembourg without having first invited the chairman of the council, and, of course, himself. Over the years, many thousands of Irish people have participated in these subsidised group visits to see the Parliament in session. In Strasbourg, Luxembourg and (in more recent years) Brussels, they were given an opportunity to follow part of the debates in plenary session, usually followed by a question-and-answer session with MEPs from the various parties, and very often also the Irish member of the Commission. At the same time, through the Dublin office, an extensive programme of lectures and information visits within Ireland was undertaken. In my own case, I visited every county in Ireland to talk to different groups, from schools to third-level institutions, political party groups, vocational organisations in different fields, and to participants in adult education schemes conducted through the universities. In all this work, I was fortunate to have the support of excellent colleagues in Dermot Scott, Nancy Mullins, Mary Killoran, Cecily Ryan and others.

Attitudes to the European Parliament

Attitudes to the Parliament remained very mixed: people in general were sceptical, if not hostile, in their assessment of its usefulness. The role of the Parliament was clearly defined, and its limitations clearly expressed, in the Treaty of Rome. It was not surprising that the majority of people would not have been aware of how circumscribed the Parliament was. In speaking to groups, I regularly made the point that the average person tended not to be concerned on a day-to-day basis with whatever happened to be going on in Europe. Brussels, which was equated by many people with the EEC, was often described as remote. The huge majority in the 1972 referendum on entry to the EEC brought us into the Community with an outstanding pro-Europe reputation compared with Britain and Denmark. Yet there was a noticeable suspicion about the possible future impact that Community membership would have on Irish life. The Parliament, in which we had only ten representatives at the time, became a particular target for those who felt that sovereignty and all kinds of constitutional protections had been put at risk.

I stress this merely to emphasise the contrasting view which emerged among those who came in direct contact with the Parliament, and who took the time to learn more about how it really worked, and its role in the EEC. The fact that individual parliamentarians could influence both Commission and Council in the development of economic, regional and social policies began to come across during the 1970s. Local issues could also be raised, when commissioners took part in question time in the Parliament. For those involved in particular sectors of the economy, lobbying in the European Parliament became an important aspect of their dealings with the EEC, even before the Parliament took on a completely new dimension with the introduction of direct elections in 1979. The spread of Irish representation across the political groups also was an important factor in ensuring that Ireland's needs were broadly recognised. For our politicians, as Brian Lenihan always made a point of underlining in his talks with visitors, a new form of politics was under way – compromise rather than confrontation. In the European Parliament there was no government, and no opposition. Consensus politics became the order of the day; it took a little time for that to sink in too.

Direct elections

In 1973 there were high hopes for rapid development of the common market. Numerous ambitious projects were initiated and, all going well, 1980 would see monetary union in place. Regional and social policies began to take shape. As a result of intense lobbying within the Parliament, and by the Parliament among the member states, 1978 was set to be the year of the first direct elections. The oil crises of 1973 and 1975 shattered those aspirations temporarily.

The move towards direct election of the Parliament accelerated quite rapidly through the 1970s. For Parliament, a Dutch Socialist member, Schelto Patijn, drew up a comprehensive report setting out various options, taking account of the different electoral systems operating in the nine member states at the time. Mr Patijn consulted political leaders, both government and opposition, and legal authorities right across the Community. Some of the difficulties in electing a Parliament on a uniform system were immediately apparent, and it was a considerable achievement on Mr Patijn's part that he managed to create a broad consensus which enabled the Council of Ministers, on 20 September 1976, to adopt the Act providing for the holding of the first direct elections on a single date within the period May/June 1978. The date was later put back by one year, and the first Community-wide elections took place in June 1979.

One of the issues that arose in Ireland was the question of filling casual vacancies which could occur for many different reasons. The legislation provided for the election of 15 members in four constituencies, broadly based on the provincial boundaries, with Dublin city and county as a separate entity, electing four MEPs. Because of the huge size of the constituencies, in terms of both population and territorial spread, the government decided that holding by-elections would be impractical and costly. A compromise proposal was accepted, namely that casual vacancies would be filled by nomination of Dáil Éireann: if a member vacating a European Parliament seat belonged to a political party, then that party would have the right to nominate the successor. This seemed fine on paper, but in practice it turned out to be unacceptable. There were objections to people whose names had never appeared on the ballot paper taking seats in a European Parliament deemed to have been elected on a uniform system. Simply through a combination of circumstances outside their control, and in perfect accordance with the law in operation at the time, no fewer than 13 members of the Labour Party occupied the four seats won in the 1979 election in the following five years. Further negotiations took place to cure this problem; the result was that in all future European Parliament elections each selected candidate or independent would have to have a list of substitutes, whose names would appear on the ballot paper.

Apart from these questions in Ireland, there were wider-ranging issues at Community level. In contemplating a Parliament whose members would be able to maintain some reasonable contact with those they were supposed to represent, the governments had to engage in some complex mathematical calculations. The larger member states – Britain, Germany, France and Italy – were to have 81 seats each, the Netherlands 25, Belgium 24, Denmark 16 (including one representative from Greenland) and Ireland 15. What to do about Luxembourg, if real uniformity and equality were to be maintained? Of course, mathematical equality could not be achieved in such a case because, on any method of calculation, Luxembourg would be entitled to half a member! And so Luxembourg was allocated six seats. Ireland also gained as a result of this situation. The then Minister for Foreign Affairs, Dr Garret FitzGerald, was able to push for stronger Irish representation, and did well to achieve a figure of 15, which gives us a higher membership than the country was entitled to on the population figures. The Irish government also succeeded in ensuring that within the UK total there would be three seats allocated to Northern Ireland, to be elected by proportional representation, in contrast to the standard 'first past the post' system obtaining throughout the rest of the UK. Thus, the minority nationalist population in the North was virtually assured of an elected voice in Europe.

17 July 1979 was, by any standard, a historic day in European history. In Strasbourg, the 410 members elected by 61 per cent of the eligible voters among the millions of Europeans in nine countries came together for the first time, and elected Simone Veil, a former Minister for Health in France, and a survivor of the notorious Auschwitz death camp in Poland, as President. She was the first in a panoply of influential political figures to fill the role. Pierre Pflimlin, who as prime minister of France in the 1950s was responsible for bringing General de Gaulle back to political power, and who was for many years mayor of Strasbourg, was a later occupant of the post.

With the installation of the elected Parliament, all the powers and functions held by the former Parliament, and earlier the Assembly of the Coal and Steel Community, ceased to exist. What, then, were to be the real functions of this fledgling elected body? Much of the preceding system continued. Although larger in numbers (with the accession of Greece in 1981, Parliament had 434 members; 518 when Spain and Portugal followed in 1986; and currently, with Finland, Sweden and Austria bringing the number of member states to 15, the Parliament has 626 members), Parliament continued and developed its organisational structure of political groups and committees.

Increased powers

For many years, Parliament had been pressing for a number of things: a greater say in the development of Community legislation, increased budgetary powers and, perhaps more importantly, far greater impetus towards political development and co-operation among the member states. As far back as 1975, Parliament had adopted a report by former Belgian Premier Leo Tindemans on European Union, and it followed this in 1981 with the establishment of a Committee on Institutional Affairs, which became a driving force in proposing initiatives for the creation of the European Union which exists today. In the endeavour, one of the Parliament's most colourful and enthusiastic members, Altiero Spinelli, came to the fore. He criss-crossed the Community, meeting with parliamentarians, academics and others, encouraging them to put pressure on their governments to take the courageous decisions necessary to bring the Union into being. Through the 1980s and 1990s, Parliament has increased its role bit by bit. Today, no major decision can be taken without Parliament's agreement, a position which effectively provides a democratic aspect to EU policy. Parliament is still the only European institution that debates the issues in public, and to which the public has regular access.

In the beginning, the powers of the European Parliament were limited. It was, however, unrealistic to expect members of a body such as this to sit tamely and watch the world go by, without at least attempting to bring their influence to bear on events. Over the years, Parliament managed to raise hackles by appearing to interfere in areas where it had no legal standing. Member states, through the Council of Ministers, were placed in uncomfortable positions from time to time when the Parliament, perhaps judging public opinion more accurately, adopted significant policies in such matters as women's rights, racial intolerance, human rights violations, transport, and political co-operation. Nowhere in the Treaties were these or many other issues placed directly within the ambit of Parliament. Nowadays, Parliament's interest is pretty much taken for granted across the spectrum of European Union affairs. One might say that this kind of intervention, outside the scope of the Treaties, has brought Parliament into much greater focus with the public, and has not gone unnoticed by the communications media.

In Ireland, there was a growing perception that the European Parliament, somehow, was a body that should not be ignored. Interest in it was undoubtedly heightened by numerous articles, and radio and television features. One of the country's leading political commentators, the late John Healy, became rather enchanted with it, and his series of articles in the *Irish Times* certainly contributed to a much wider understanding of just what could be achieved by effective lobbying. John Healy was keenly aware of the shift in the balance of political power that was taking place before his eyes, and he would often remark that the real action would be found in future in Brussels and Strasbourg.

In many respects, the Parliament is the very public face of the European Union. From its earliest days, it has developed contacts with other countries, especially those in the Third World. Inter-parliamentary delegations meet regularly, bringing together representatives of the United States, Canada, South American countries, Australasia and Africa. Heads of state and government regularly address their concerns on world affairs through speeches in the plenary sessions of the European Parliament.

The fifth elected Parliament begins its five-year term exercising a range of specific powers and a degree of influence on EU matters that were virtually unimaginable when the first elected body met 20 years ago. Future enlargement of the Union will undoubtedly bring further obstacles to be surmounted, but with the level of experience accumulated over the past three decades, there is no reason to fear that these cannot be tackled effectively by a confident Parliament, whose place in the European Union is assured.

9

The Court of Justice

TOM O'HIGGINS

The Court of Justice of the European Communities was established in 1958 in succession to the Court of the European Coal and Steel Community. I became a member of the Court on 15 January 1985 and served as such until October 1991. My two distinguished predecessors were first of all Cearbhall Ó Dálaigh, former Chief Justice of Ireland, who became a member following Ireland's accession to the Community, and Andreas O'Keeffe, former president of the High Court, who joined the Court on Cearbhall Ó Dálaigh's election as President of Ireland. My successor and the present Irish member of the Court is the former attorney-general, John Murray SC.

In this essay I shall endeavour to examine how the Court has developed since its establishment and how that development, already in progress when Ireland acceded to the Community, has affected Ireland and its laws.

The Court of Justice and the Community legal order

I think I can commence by describing the task of the Court as laid down in the founding Treaty of Rome. This task, in accordance with Article 164 (now renumbered 220), is:

> to ensure that in the interpretation and application of this Treaty the law is observed.

It will be noted that this mandate is not limited to the mere interpretation of the Treaty in accordance with the cold wording of its text, but requires that in such interpretation and application 'the law is observed'. The term 'law' is not qualified in any way, and as such indicates a concept which is wide in its scope, comprising not only written precepts and regulations but also those unwritten principles whose observance is essential to the achievement of a just social and legal order. Viewing the term in that sense, the Court held at any early stage that its duty under Art 164 included the observance of certain principles which, although not mentioned in the Treaty or in secondary legislation where such was in question, were common to the legal systems of member states. Considerations of justice and equity, of the necessity for legal certainty, of equality and proportionality, of fair procedures and respect for human rights were thus gradually adopted by the Court as part of the law it was required to administer.

Having thus described the Court's mandate and duty under Art 164, I now refer to certain developments which are key to understanding the legal order that has grown up in the Community under the aegis of the Court.

Firstly, and as early as 1963, the Court held that a Treaty Article could under certain conditions have direct effect within a Member State and be there enforceable (Van Gend en Loos[1]). This meant that it could be invoked before a national court and thus give rise to enforceable rights and duties. This ruling was later extended to Community Directives. It was already the case with regard to Community Regulations, as provided by the explicit wording of Article 189 (now Art 249). In this way, under the conditions specified, legal certainty was sought.

Secondly, the Court held in 1964 that Community law took priority over national law in relation to those activities that were within the ambit of the Treaty (Costa v. Enel[2]). The corollary was that in the event of a conflict between a national law, even a constitutional provision, and a Community rule the national judge had to disregard or fail to apply the national law in favour of the Community rule (Simmenthal[3]).

Thirdly, the Court relied upon and applied the doctrine of pre-emption. This was a technique familiar in federal legal systems according to which member states retained the power to legislate in a given area but lost that power once the Community, being empowered to act under the Treaty, had legislated for that particular matter (Walt Wilhelm[4]).

A final principle which strikes me as being of truly great significance is the doctrine of member states' liability for breaches of Community law. This arose in the Francovich case.[5] The doctrine is founded on the duty of loyalty to the Community owed by each member state under Art 5 (now 10) of the Treaty, which duty, if breached, calls for redress where particular loss has been suffered by an individual or individuals within that state. The obvious redress is a claim for damages in the national Courts.

Most of these developments resulted from judgments of the Court in the 1960s. Thus, by the time Ireland joined the Community in 1973, Irish lawyers and judges were aware of the legal implications of such action for the Irish legal system. Even the Francovich doctrine which emerged in 1991 was not entirely surprising, given its basis in Art 5 of the Treaty. It could therefore be said that by the time Ireland joined, a well-rounded intelligible system of Community law was beginning to emerge which promised, within the scope of the Treaty, fairness and equal treatment for member states and their citizens. This perception of Community law with its distinctive character is the great achievement of the Court. It has been instrumental in developing a legal system which, while reposing on the founding Treaty, has been amplified by doctrines that it has expounded to make that Treaty work. This form of judicial activity has been necessary because the Court has been dealing with, interpreting and applying a Treaty that is remarkably laconic or even silent on issues, such as individual rights and the relationship of Community law with natural law, that needed to be dealt with if the Community was to operate.

It may be useful at this stage to point to the practical consequences for the domestic law of member states of the foregoing developments. The principle of the primacy of Community law requires national Courts to acknowledge the supremacy of a directly effective Community Regulation or Directive (and *a fortiori* of a Treaty Article) over any conflicting provision of domestic law. Thus national judges may be required to act not only as judges determining their own law in respect of its purported effect and ambit, but also as Community judges, applying Community law. When a conflict arises the national judge must decide whether the issue before the court is covered by a relevant Community measure as interpreted, if necessary, by the Court. If it is, then the judge is obliged to enforce it and to declare the national measure inapplicable (without, however, declaring it invalid). In member states, such as Ireland, with written constitutions this may mean the setting aside as inapplicable of even a constitutional article.

A celebrated example of this came in a case relating to the phenomenon of the re-registration of Spanish fishing vessels under the Irish and British flags in order to qualify for Irish and British fishing quotas. British legislation was enacted to prevent the 'Spanish fishermen' qualifying for quotas. When the British legislation was tested before the Court of Justice, following a reference by the House of Lords, the Court held that a British Court had to disapply or set aside the British legal rule according to which no Court in Britain could grant an injunction to suspend application of an Act of parliament. When this case came back before the House of Lords, that Court had no difficulty in recognising its duty to set aside this British rule.[6] The important point to note here is that in order to protect rights of individuals under Community law, the national court is empowered, as a matter of Community law, to take measures that it could not take under national law – in this case the grant of an injunction against an Act of parliament. Community law thus grants national Courts powers that they do not have under national law.

Another example of the duties of national Courts comes when there is a conflict between Community law and national law, but the Community provision, usually a Directive, does not have direct effect, and thus may not be relied upon directly before the national Court. The Court of Justice has held in the Marleasing case,[7] for which I was Judge Rapporteur, that in such circumstances the national Court is under an obligation to apply national law so far as possible in the light of the wording and the purpose of the Community rule, in order to achieve the result pursued by Community law. It is particularly noteworthy that the Court held that this obligation applies to national law adopted both before and after the Community rule. The obligation to interpret national law in this way, especially as regards legislation adopted before the Community rule, places a particularly heavy burden on the Irish Courts, but one that is necessary in order to ensure the *effet utile*, or useful effect, of Community law.

The Court as an institution

The Court is currently composed of 15 judges, one for each member state, and nine Advocates General. It is an institution that has a remarkably strong supranational character and has inculcated an institutional loyalty in its members. It is quite remarkable that it has built a coherent case-law, composed as it has been of judges of first six, then nine, and at the moment of 15 nationalities, all coming from different legal systems (16 including the Scottish one, from which two of the British judges have come) and speaking different languages.

Viewed from the outside, the Court is a multilingual institution as cases are heard in twelve procedural languages – the eleven official working languages of the Community and Irish. However, internally, the court has chosen French as its working language, with the result that all Court documents and judicial discussions are in that language. This is perhaps inevitable given the early formation of the Court (with both the UK and Ireland absent), but it is nowadays less obvious that there should be only one working language. Given the linguistic preferences of judges of several states that have acceded to the Community since 1973, including most recently Finland, Sweden and Austria, and given the probable linguistic preferences of judges from the countries that will accede in the forthcoming waves of accession from Central and Eastern Europe, this is a decision that should be reviewed.

The common argument to defend the status quo is that Community law has such a specialised vocabulary that the Court's judgments should always be written in a single language in the interests of consistency. While this may have been true in the beginning, I am not persuaded that this is still a valid argument as the terminology of Community law has now stabilised, both in French and in English. It would be quite a remarkable facilitation for members of the Court to be able to express themselves in a working language with which they are more familiar. It should be recalled that the International Court of Justice in The Hague, whose statute was the model for the European Court of Justice, has always used the two working languages, English and French, without obvious ill-effects.

In 1988, the European Court of First Instance was established to assume some of the jurisdiction of the Court of Justice, first in four areas (cases brought by officials of the European Communities, cases concerning the European Coal and Steel Treaty, competition cases and damages actions in all these areas) and later, with added jurisdiction, in all cases brought by natural or legal persons. This now includes the important sector of trade law where dumping by non-Community enterprises or industries has been found or alleged. The purpose of setting up the Court of First Instance was both to relieve the Court of Justice of some of its ever growing case-load and to establish a forum where complex issues of fact could be examined in greater detail than was possible before the Court of Justice, given its workload. Mr Justice Donal Barrington, then a judge of the High Court and now judge of the Supreme Court, was appointed as the first Irish judge of the European Court of First Instance. He has been succeeded by Mr John Cooke SC.

Nowadays, any case brought directly by an Irish firm or individual before the European Court will be heard by the Court of First Instance and appeals from that Court will be heard by the Court of Justice. On the other hand, cases referred by Irish Courts continue to be heard directly by the Court of Justice under the procedure set up by Article 177 (now Article 234) of the EC Treaty according to which national courts may refer cases to the Court of Justice for an authoritative ruling on points of Community law.

Doubtless in the future the whole question of what has come to be known as the judicial architecture of the Community will have to be reviewed. At the very least, the composition and working methods of the Court of Justice and Court of First Instance will have to be examined, given the probable accession of the Central and Eastern European states and of Cyprus. The institutional challenge posed by a Community composed of between 20 and 27 member states is easily appreciated. If the practice continued that every member state should have the right to nominate a judge to both the Court of Justice and the Court of First Instance, these Courts would lose their present character. The working methods would probably have to change, with more cases being heard by chambers, and possibly a 'full panel' of the Court consisting of less than all the judges. In such circumstances one issue that might arise is the question of a divergence of case-law between chambers or even panels of the full Court. If this were so, one might have to envisage a system of reconciling the case-law, perhaps by a hearing before a plenary court of all judges. Some continental systems, such as in Germany, already have this system.

Finally, it should be borne in mind that the scope of Community law is expanding, as both the Maastricht and Amsterdam Treaties show. The Court's jurisdiction will increase particularly as a result of the Amsterdam

Treaty, according to which the Court will have jurisdiction in cases concerning immigration, asylum and visa issues under the proposed European immigration policy as well as in cases concerning police and judicial co-operation under Title VI of the Treaty on European Union. Recent Conventions such as the Trademark Convention also give a jurisdiction to the Court. There will also be the accessions of Central and Eastern European countries. As a result, the Court will find its workload increasing, and the problems coming before it will be more varied. The consequent impetus for change in the Court's working method and composition may be substantial.

In the 25 years of Irish membership, there has been, having regard to Ireland's size, a substantial number of Irish cases before the Court. Irish cases usually come before the Court in three ways:

1   they may be brought as a direct action by the state, or under certain circumstances by undertakings or individuals to challenge a Community act or failure to act
2   the Commission may sue Ireland by virtue of its enforcement powers under the Treaty
3   cases may be referred by Irish Courts for a ruling on Community law under Article 177 of the EC Treaty.

The last category is by far the most numerous.

I propose to examine two cases decided by the Court during my mandate, to illustrate the impact of the Court's case-law for the Irish legal order: the Groener and the Grogan cases.

The Groener case

The Groener case[8] concerned the requirement that teachers in Ireland should be proficient in Irish. Ms Anita Groener was a national of the Netherlands. She was engaged in 1982 on a temporary basis as a part-time art teacher in the College of Marketing and Design, Dublin. In 1984, she applied for a permanent full-time post as a lecturer in art at that college. Pursuant to a measure adopted by the minister for education acting under statutory powers, a person could not be appointed to a permanent full-time post in certain areas of teaching, including art, unless that person held the Ceard-Teastas Gaeilge or had an equivalent qualification recognised by the minister. The minister reserved the right to exempt candidates from countries other than Ireland from the obligation to know Irish, provided that there were no other fully qualified candidates for the post. Candidates who did not hold the Ceard-Teastas Gaeilge or an equivalent qualification could be required to pass a special oral test in Irish.

Ms Groener, who did not hold the Ceard-Teastas Gaeilge, first asked for an exemption but was refused on the ground that there were other fully qualified candidates for the post. She subsequently studied Irish, but (apparently uniquely) did not pass the relevant oral test. She then instituted proceedings for judicial review before the High Court in Dublin maintaining that her rights as a migrant worker were violated by the measures adopted by the minister. The High Court referred to the Court of Justice questions concerning the compatibility of the Irish rules with Article 48(3) of the EC Treaty and Article 3 of Council Regulation 1612/68 on freedom of movement for workers within the Community.

The case thus concerned the right of a Community migrant worker to work in Ireland, a right conferred by Article 48 of the EC Treaty and forming part of the fundamental freedoms of Community law. On the other hand, it also concerned what Advocate General Marco Darmon, in a brilliant Opinion, called 'one of the most sensitive aspects of cultural identity'. He went on: 'The importance of the Court's reply and its consequences for the member states and for the diversity of the Community as a whole are so evident that I should not dwell on them, for at issue here is the power of a state to protect and foster the use of a national language.'

In its judgment, the Court reviewed the provisions of Community law granting the right of free movement to workers. It noted that Article 3 of Regulation 1612/68 provides that national provisions or administrative measures are not to apply where their exclusive aim is to keep nationals of other member states away from the employment offered. It also provided that this principle did not to apply to conditions relating to linguistic knowledge required by reason of the nature of the post to be filled.

From the point of view of Community law, the question was whether the Irish measures in question constituted a discrimination against Ms Groener, or whether they could be justified by reason of the post to be filled. It should be noted immediately that the Irish measures were not overtly discriminatory: they applied to Irish and other Community nationals without distinction. However, the question here was whether they were covertly discriminatory, that is whether in fact they had the effect of reserving full-time teachers' posts to Irish nationals to the exclusion of other Community nationals. The Court took a slightly different tack. Although noting that the teaching of art in the college in question was in English, and thus a knowledge of Irish was not necessary for the performance of the post, the Court found that this was not sufficient to decide the issue.

Instead, the Court examined the position of Irish in some detail. It referred to Article 8 of Bunreacht na hÉireann, according to which:

(1) The Irish language as the national language is the first official language.

(2) The English language is recognised as a second official language.

It noted the policy of Irish governments to promote the use of Irish as a means of expressing national identity and culture, including its use in schools. The obligation for lecturers to have a knowledge of Irish was put in this context.

The Court held that the Treaty does not prohibit the adoption of a policy for the protection and promotion of a language of a member state, which is both the national language and the first official language, but such a policy must not encroach on the free movement of workers. Accordingly, it must not be disproportionate in relation to the aim pursued, and the manner in which it is applied must not bring about discrimination against nationals of other member states.

Following this preamble, the Court found that the language requirement was not disproportionate as it was not unreasonable to require teachers to have some knowledge of the first official language, provided the level of knowledge required was not itself disproportionate. The Court also laid down guidelines for the non-discriminatory application of the Irish measures.

The result of the case was that Ireland was able to maintain its policy of promoting Irish provided that it did so in a way that was both proportionate and non-discriminatory. Moreover, it established a wider Community principle of respect for national culture and national identity. The importance of this issue has been subsequently stressed by both the Maastricht and Amsterdam Treaties on European Union. Article 6(3) of the Amsterdam Treaty provides that 'The Union shall respect the national identities of its member states'. Moreover, both Treaties contain provisions requiring respect for national and regional cultural diversity.

The Court's judgement in the Groener case is an excellent example of a concern for the diversity of national cultures within the Community, of which language is a vital part. It is particularly important in countries that have what Community jargon calls 'lesser-known languages'. It is also of course important in countries with several linguistic regimes, or linguistic minorities. It is of paramount significance where the language is synonymous with the culture, as in the case of France. It is thus not surprising that France made both written and oral observations in the hearing before the Court. Finally, one should reflect that, had the case been decided differently, respect for cultural diversity in the community could have been threatened.

The Grogan case

The Grogan case[9] concerned proceedings brought against Mr Grogan and Others, officers of students' associations, in connection with the distribution in Ireland of specific information relating to the identity and location of clinics in another member state where medical termination of pregnancy was carried out. In September 1989, the Society for the Protection of Unborn Children (SPUC) brought proceedings in the High Court in Dublin for a declaration that the distribution of such information was unlawful and for an injunction restraining its distribution. The High Court referred questions to the Court of Justice for a preliminary ruling concerning the application of Community law, in particular Article 60 concerning the free provision of services within the Community.

Article 40, section 3, subsection 3 of Bunreacht na hÉireann was inserted following a referendum in 1983 and provided as follows: 'The state acknowledges the right to life of the unborn and, with due regard to the equal right to life of the mother, guarantees in its laws to respect, and, as far as practicable, by its laws to defend and vindicate that right'.

Let me preface my account of this case by stating that this was a truly unexpected development. I doubt if the Treaty-makers in 1957 had envisaged abortion as being a subject of what was then a Treaty dealing almost exclusively with economic issues. Moreover, although the Court of Justice had developed a case-law concerning respect for human rights, this was developed without an explicit basis in the Treaty, apart from the Court's general task, as set out in Article 164, to which I have referred above. This lacuna was remedied by the Maastricht Treaty. Article 6 of the Treaty on European Union provides that 'The Union shall respect fundamental rights, as guaranteed by the European Convention for the protection of Human Rights and Fundamental Freedoms signed in Rome on 4 November 1950 and as they result from constitutional traditions common to the member states, as general principles of Community law'. This phrasing is taken almost word-for-word from the Court's human rights case-law, of which it represents an accurate summary.

However, it seems to me that in the pre-Maastricht era in which the Grogan case was decided, the Court of Justice had a fundamental difficulty in deciding issues such as abortion. It did not have an explicit Treaty-based mandate to decide human right issues. Although national constitutional courts recognised the Court's authority to make judgments in this area (and indeed the German Constitutional Court made it a specific condition for recognising the supremacy of Community law that the Court of Justice should protect human rights), I cannot help but feel that the Court of Justice, at least at that time, was not the best forum to discuss fundamental human rights of a non-economic nature, as they normally arose only incidentally in a case concerning the application of the economic law of the Community.

An issue such as abortion is a prime example of a national constitutional issue with which national constitutional judges and the European Court of Human Rights are familiar.

In order to bring the issue of abortion before the European Court of Justice, it had to be shown that it concerned Community law in some way. Since the Treaty did not mention fundamental rights at all, still less abortion, the issue was discussed before the Court of Justice in the context of the free provision of services in the Community. However, the provisions concerning services are essentially economic provisions and concern the rights of individuals and undertakings to carry out an economic activity in another member state for a limited period or to provide a service in another member state from one's own state. Since the abortion issue was sought to be brought into the framework of Community law by means of arguments relating to the free movement of services under EC law, it is not surprising that the pleadings and the Court's judgments concern this issue, and do not reflect the sort of discussion that would take place before a national constitutional court or the European Court of Human Rights. Thus, the European Court of Justice's decision on this issue was essentially concerned with abortion as the provision of services, rather than with abortion as a human right. This gives a slightly unreal flavour to the judgment but, on the other hand, given its jurisdiction, the Court of Justice could only deal with this case in this way.

In its judgment, the Court first held that the termination of pregnancy as lawfully practised in several member states was a medical activity, which was normally provided for remuneration and might be carried out as part of a professional activity. It thus constituted a service within the meaning of the Treaty. The Court dismissed the argument of SPUC that the provision of abortion could not be regarded as being a service on the grounds that it was grossly immoral. The Court stated: 'Whatever the merits of those arguments on the moral plane… it is not for the Court to substitute its assessment for that of the legislature in those member states where the activities in question are practised legally.' The point here was that the Court was considering the question of the provision of legal services in countries other than Ireland. It did not address the interesting question of whether a service that was legal in some member states but illegal in others should be considered to be a service within the meaning of Community law.

The Court then examined the question of whether it was contrary to Community law for a member state in which medical termination of pregnancy is forbidden to prohibit student associations from distributing information about the identity and location of clinics in another member state where medical termination of pregnancy is lawfully carried out and the means of communicating with those clinics, where the clinics in question have no involvement in the distribution of the same information.

First and decisively, the Court held that the link between the activity of the students' associations and medical terminations carried out in clinics in another member state was too tenuous for a prohibition on the distribution of information to be capable of being regarded as a restriction within the meaning of Article 59 of the Treaty, as the information being given by the students' associations was not distributed on behalf of an economic operator in another member state.

The Court then addressed the human rights issue in the following way. Although the Court noted that where national law falls within the scope of application of Community law, the Court would have jurisdiction to give a ruling concerning fundamental rights, and in particular the European Convention of Human Rights, the Court held that it had not such jurisdiction as regards national legislation falling outside the scope of Community law. That was the case here, as the Court had already held that the national prohibition in question did not constitute a restriction on services within the meaning of Community law, and therefore the national legislation fell outside the scope of Community law. The Court therefore held that it was not contrary to Community law to prohibit the distribution of information which was at issue in the case.

Subsequently, the Maastricht Treaty on European Union provided in Protocol 17 that 'Nothing in the Treaty on European Union, or in the Treaties establishing the European Communities, or in the Treaties or Acts modifying or supplementing those Treaties, shall affect the application in Ireland of Article 40.3.3 of the constitution of Ireland'.

It should be pointed out that at no stage before the Court did the Grogan case concern the legality or morality of providing abortions as such. That was not the issue under EC law.

It is interesting to compare the Court's judgment with the approach taken by Advocate General Van Gerven, who inquired whether the national rule prohibiting the distribution of information on abortion pursued an objective which was justified under Community law, that is whether it was justified by imperative requirements of public policy known as the general good. The Advocate General was of the opinion that the issue related to a policy choice of a moral and philosophical nature, the assessment of which was a matter for the member states, and in respect of which they are entitled to invoke the public policy exception under Articles 56 and 66 of the Treaty. The public policy exception is subject to the principle of proportionality in areas covered by Community law: the Advocate General found that this was satisfied in this case. According to this reasoning, Ireland would have been able to justify its rules on the grounds of national public policy.

The Advocate General conducted an extremely detailed examination of the human rights issue but concluded that the individual state must be allowed a fairly considerable margin of discretion. Although the result is the same, the way of reaching the conclusion was quite different: for the Advocate General, the issue of abortion raised a question of a legitimate policy choice taken by the member state which could be justified under the public policy exception of the Treaty with regard to services, and which did not violate existing European human rights law. For the Court, on the other hand, the link with services was too tenuous in the first place (a finding of fact which is unusual in the context of Article 177 proceedings). The Court was thus not required to consider issues such as public policy or to address the human rights issues.

There have of course been other Irish cases before the Court of great importance in the past 25 years. The Campus Oil case concerning oil refining in Ireland and the Buy Irish Campaign case come to mind as two important cases concerning the free movement of goods, but space does not permit their discussion. In general, most Irish cases have tended to concern more technical issues, such as agricultural and fisheries issues, the free movement of capital, and so on. However, the two cases on which I have chosen to concentrate show the effect of Community law, and of the Court's judgments, on areas that go to the root of national concerns, in Ireland and in any other country, concerning culture and morality. They also show the limits of Community law. In their own way, they can be considered to be harbingers of the principle of subsidiarity.

Conclusions

Irish courts have shown commendable familiarity with the new legal system, and have not hesitated to use the system of referring cases to the Court of Justice for a preliminary ruling concerning points of Community law. This system is essential for the uniform application of Community law. Irish lawyers who have appeared before the Court have distinguished themselves: I recall the very high appreciation of the standard of oral pleading by Irish lawyers who appeared before the Court expressed by members of the Court of all nationalities and legal traditions.

For the Community legal order to be firmly rooted in the Irish legal system, it is essential that judges and lawyers should have an adequate familiarity with Community law. The universities and the professional law schools have a major role to play here, as do the professional bodies in ensuring that there is adequate post-qualification professional training to keep practitioners up to date with the most recent developments. The Irish situation is unique in the Community legal order as it is the only country of the common law tradition with a written constitution, and there is no doubt that Irish judges and lawyers can make a contribution to the development of the Community legal system. I particularly appreciate in this context the work of the Irish Centre for European Law at Trinity College Dublin (of which, with the then Professor Mary Robinson, I was co-founder and later chairman for a number of years), and welcome initiatives such as the Irish European Law Forum in University College Dublin. It is vital to maintain an ongoing dialogue among ourselves and with judges and lawyers from other jurisdictions concerning the relationship between Community law and Irish law.

Finally, it should be recalled that the legal dimension, which I have described, is not technical but the essential framework for European integration. The Court's role in the integration process has been vital and will continue to be so as the authentic interpreter of Community and Union law.

NOTES

1   *Van Gend en Loos* [1963] ECR 1.
2   Case 6/64 *Costa v. Enel* [1964] ECR 585.
3   Case 106/77 *Simmenthal* [1978] ECR 629.
4   14/68 *Wilhelm v. Bundeskartellamt* [1969] ECR 1.
5   Joined Cases C-6/90 and C-9/90 *Francovich and Others* [1991] ECR I-5357.
6   Case C-213/89 *The Queen v. Secretary of State for Transport*, ex parte: *Factortame Ltd* [1990] ECR I-2433.
7   106/89 *Marleasing* [1990] ECR I-4135.
8   *Anita Groener v. Minister for Education & Or.* [1984] ECR 1.
9   127/80 *Grogan v. Commission* [1982] ECR 869.

10

The European Court of Auditors

BARRY DESMOND

Introduction

Although the European Economic Community (EEC) came into existence with the Treaty of Rome in 1957, it was not until 20 years later that the European Court of Auditors was established as the independent, external auditor of the Communities (the EEC, the European Coal and Steel Community and EURATOM). As a result of pressure from the European Parliament and, in particular, from the German president of the committee on budgetary control, Dr Heinrich Aigner, provision for the setting-up of the Court was made in the Treaty of Brussels in 1975. It took a further 15 months for the Treaty to be ratified by all the member states and for the necessary preparations to be made. The inaugural meeting of the Court of Auditors took place in October 1977. The creation of the Court coincided with two particularly important events – the extension of the European Parliament's powers in the field of budgetary control and the use of own resources to finance the whole of the European Union budget.

Mr Hans Kutscher, President of the Court of Justice, presided over the swearing-in of the first members and among those being sworn in was the first Irish member of the Court, Mr Michael Murphy. Nine members were appointed, corresponding to one member from each member state, in accordance with the Treaty provisions. The Court now comprises 15 members. The creation of the Court confirmed the Community's need for a 'financial conscience', as Mr Kutscher defined it at the swearing-in of the first members. It was not until the Treaty on European Union (Maastricht, 1992), however, that the Court was formally recognised as one of the Community institutions alongside the European Parliament, the Council, the Commission and the Court of Justice.

The role of the Court

The Court is the external auditor of the European Union and bodies set up by it. The Treaty stipulates that the Court is to assist the European Parliament and the Council of the European Union in exercising their control over the implementation of the budget and, more generally, that it may, at any time, submit observations on specific questions and deliver opinions at the request of one of the European institutions. The Court carries out its control and consultative functions independently and autonomously. It is responsible for the audit of all EU expenditure and revenue in much the same way as the comptroller and auditor general audits government departments and certain state bodies in Ireland. (See Tables 10.1 and 10.2 for payments to and from Ireland.)

Table 10.1. Payments from Ireland to EU budget

Year	M ECU	% of total
1994	638.9	1.0
1995	664.8	1.0
1996	681.5	1.0
1997	687.0	0.9
1998	984.9	1.2

Table 10.2. Payments to Ireland from EU budget

Year	M ECU	% of total
1994	2406.8	4.0
1995	2578.3	3.9
1996	2997.7	3.9
1997	3363.7	4.2
1998	3119.7	4.1

In 1998, the EU general budget will amount to some £65 billion. However, the Court not only audits the general budget but also Community loans and borrowings, the revenue and expenditure entered in the European Coal and Steel Community (ECSC) budget and various other EU bodies as well as the revenue and expenditure of the European Development Funds (EDF). The assets and liabilities of the Community amounted to £38.6 billion at the end of 1998. The EDF represents an overall allocation of almost £9 billion for the period 1996–2000 (eighth EDF) and the budget of the ECSC and other EU bodies will amount to some £400 million in 1999.

The Court has considerable powers under the Treaties to audit and report on the reliability of the Union's accounts and the legality and regularity of the underlying transactions. It also checks, on a systematic basis, that the financial management of these resources is sound. The Court's principal interlocutor is the Commission, which is responsible for implementing the EU budget each year. The Court reports the results of its audits to the European Parliament and to the Council of Ministers, which jointly form the budget authority. The Court conducts its audits not only at the Commission but also in the member states where some 80 per cent of EU expenditure, notably under the Common Agricultural Policy and the structural funds, is, in practice, administered by government departments, regional authorities and other agencies.

The organisation of the Court

Despite its title, the European Court of Auditors has no judicial powers or functions. The Court is organised in accordance with the principle of collective responsibility similar to that of the Irish government. Suitably qualified members are nominated by the government of each member state and appointed for six years (renewable) by the Council of the European Union after it has consulted the European Parliament. Each member takes an oath of office to act in a completely independent manner. In the performance of their duties, members may neither seek nor take instructions from any government or other body, and they may not engage in any other occupation. The members of the Court can only be removed from office by a decision of the European Court of Justice. The annual remuneration of members is fixed by the Council at a level 8 per cent higher than that of a director general. The President of the Court is elected by the members for a term of three years and may be re-elected. The current President is the Swedish member, Jan Karlsson.

I was the third Irish appointee since the Court was set up. I have now served ten years in two of the institutions of the Union, commencing in the European Parliament from 1989 to 1994. A fellow Corkman, Michael Murphy, former Secretary of the Department of Finance, served at the Court from its setting-up in 1977 until 1986, and was President of the Court from 1977 to 1981. Mr Murphy's successor from 1986 to 1994 was Richie Ryan, the former national coalition Minister for Finance and the Public Service and a former Fine Gael TD and MEP. Each member of the Court is appointed to a specific audit sector within an audit group. From 1994 to 1996 I was responsible for the agricultural guidance expenditure, and then in 1996 I was appointed chairperson of the audit group responsible for the agricultural guarantee expenditure (EAGGF). At present there are 16 Irish persons working at the Court, on either a permanent or a temporary basis, of a total staff of 550, including 90 translation staff. The staff are generally recruited in open and internal EU competitions. The Irish in the Court worked initially in the offices of the Irish Comptroller and Auditor General, the Revenue Commissioners, the Department of Finance and the private sector.

The outcome of the Court's audits

The results of the Court's audit of the relevant accounts and its analysis of the quality and reliability of the systems of management and internal control, as published in the Court's annual and special reports, are forwarded to the Council and the Parliament so that they can draw the necessary conclusions from a legislative point of view, determine the areas of management in which improvements are necessary, and make the necessary recommendations. The reports of the Court are taken into account by the European Parliament in considering the budget discharge each year. In 1998 the Court published 25 special reports on BSE, water pollution, fisheries, MEP allowances, etc. The annual report of the Court is available on the Internet (http://www.eca.eu.int), as are all its published special reports. The Court also provides opinions when requested by one of the other EU institutions, one of the latest being an opinion following a request from the Council concerning the Commission's Agenda 2000 proposals. The Court may also prepare opinions on its own initiative.

The Commission's financial controller

Of special relevance to the work of the Court is the role of the financial control directorate general of the Commission. Its task is to guarantee internally to the Commission that its budget is implemented in accordance with the Treaty principles of legality, regularity and sound financial management. The Commission's financial controller has independent status. His central function is that of prior approval of financial transactions. He must satisfy himself that any proposed expenditure is properly authorised and that there are budgetary and legislative provisions for it. In addition, he must check that the necessary funds are available, that the supporting documentation is in order and that the expenditure is justified. If the financial controller refuses approval, the Commission may overrule that decision but must table a reasoned decision for doing so. That decision is open to examination by the budgetary control committee of the European Parliament and the Court of Auditors. The financial controller increasingly makes use of risk analysis in order to strengthen his effectiveness.

How the Court's audits are performed

The audits carried out by the Court may, if necessary, be performed on the spot in the other European institutions and in the member states. Documents and information which the Court needs to carry out its task are forwarded to it, at its request, by the other European institutions, by the national audit institutions (NAIs) and the competent national departments. We have access to data held on the computer systems of the Commission and the member states in connection with their operations under the Union budget. The Court's audit arrangements are co-ordinated through a nominated liaison officer from each NAI. In Ireland this work is currently done by Michael Buckley, a deputy director in the office of the comptroller and auditor general. Meetings are held regularly with the liaison officers to exchange views and information on audit matters. All on-the-spot audit missions undertaken by the Court are notified six weeks in advance to the NAIs.

Throughout the Community there are 90 national and regional paying agencies, with, for example, 23 in Germany and 17 in Spain, where they have considerable autonomy. In the Commission's budget alone there are some 400,000 commitment and payment transactions each year; there are millions in member states. In Ireland alone in 1996 there were half a million claims in the Department of Agriculture and Food for animal premiums! It is clearly impossible to check every transaction. The Court has, therefore, adopted a systems-based audit approach. Financial and sound financial management audits are often carried out simultaneously in a comprehensive audit of a given subject.

The Court's annual statement of assurance

The Maastricht Treaty added a new and vital element to the Court's tasks. It requires the Court to provide the Council of the Union and the European Parliament with an annual statement of assurance as to the reliability of the accounts and the legality and regularity of the underlying transactions. As in previous years, in 1997 the incidence of errors affecting the transactions underlying the Commission's payments was so high that the Court was unable to give an assurance in their regard. Many of the errors found in the payments provided direct evidence of failure to implement the control mechanisms foreseen in the regulations or to apply requisite checks before payments were made.

In 1997 (budget £65 billion) the rate of substantive errors affecting the amounts of the transactions underlying payments (i.e. errors having a direct quantifiable effect on the amount of the underlying operation financed from the Community budget) was in the same range as in previous years. Substantive errors include payments to beneficiaries who do not meet the conditions for receiving aid, or the payment of incorrect amounts. Audit evidence indicated that the most likely rate of error was 5.1 per cent (£3.5 billion) for the budget as a whole, with rates of 3.3 per cent for agriculture, 8.2 per cent for structural funds and 4.5 per cent for expenditure managed directly by the Commission.

For 1997 the Court has found that the error rate for agricultural guarantee expenditure (approximately 3.3 per cent) remains material. The majority of the substantive errors concerned misrepresentation by the beneficiaries, which often resulted in relatively small overpayments in percentage terms. Examples of substantive errors in the EAGGF-guarantee section in 1997 were as follows.

- Overdeclaration of arable area for a given crop, either of the size of the field concerned, or by erroneously including land not being put to productive use such as areas occupied by woods or buildings. Also, overdeclaration of area set-aside, due to inclusion of cultivated areas, or of land which had never been used for agricultural production.
- Supplementary milk levies not being paid by the producers who exceeded their quotas, but being borne by the member state administrations concerned and, for example, incorrect classification of the olive oil producer as a 'small' producer through an underdeclaration of olive trees, leading to overpayment of aid.

In 1997 the substantive error rate in the structural funds (approximately 30 per cent of the budget) remained high. Some errors involved public authorities in member states putting forward projects for co-financing by the Commission that were ineligible under the regulations. Other examples were:

- declaration of expenditure by member states which included significant investments outside the eligible zone, or outside the eligible period; charging costs that were not directly related to a training project including an arbitrary and unjustified overhead rate of 12 per cent
- for a gas pipeline co-financed by a local authority and private company, the expenditure incurred by the private company was put forward for community co-financing; and a member state declared as expenditure the amount it had agreed with the promoter, instead of the actual expenditure, which was 27 per cent lower.

Two-thirds of all payments from the Community budget are made on the basis of information provided by the recipients themselves. Thus farmers may often find it tempting to give themselves the benefit of the doubt when measuring their fields, or counting their flocks. This leads to a large number of overpayments, often of relatively small amounts, but with a significant impact on overall spending. Similarly, local and regional authorities putting forward projects for Community support too often fail to follow the rules on eligibility. This sometimes means that one element of the cost is not eligible for funding – such as the rental cost of a building owned by the authority itself. It sometimes means that the entire project is ineligible – such as a project outside the region covered by the relevant structural fund.

Agenda 2000 and CAP reform

Contrary to some popular mythology in Ireland, I am acutely aware that the £850 million of EU direct payments to Irish farmers in 1998 constitutes a huge proportion of their income and is of vital importance to farm families and the entire rural economy (Table 10.3). However, readers will appreciate that many agricultural products are extremely difficult to monitor in terms of production, marketing and the payment of subsidies. The subsidisation of oranges, lemons, tomatoes, apples, peaches, citrus processing, cereals, olive oil, skim milk powder and tobacco, for example, poses acute audit difficulties. The major problems relating to payments for cattle and sheep are also well documented. In the agriculture guarantee section alone the Commission's DG VI audit staff is confronted with checking expenditure in excess of £32.5 billion annually in 15 member states paid through over 90 paying agencies to several million individuals and other agencies.

Table 10.3. EAGGF guarantee expenditure: payments to Ireland in 1998

Category	*M ECU*	*% Share per category of EU expenditure*
Arable crops*	131	.7
Sugar	14	.8
Milk and milk products	192	7.4
Beef/veal*	870	16.08
Sheep and goatmeat	109	7.1
Fisheries	2	7.5
Non-Annex 11 products	46	8.3
Clearance of accounts	5	–
Accompanying measures:		
early retirement	63	30.1
environment	122	9.5
forestry	31	9.4
Other measures	48	8.0
Total[†]	1633	

* Overall, cereals accounted for 46.2% of EAGGF guarantee expenditure in 1998 and beef and veal accounted for 13.3%.

[†] Total EAGGF guarantee expenditure in all member states: 38,810 m ECU. Ireland's share of this expenditure: 4.2%.

In 1998 the Court was asked, by the Council of Ministers, to comment on the Commission Agenda 2000 programme, which sets out the framework of the EU's main expenditure programmes on agriculture and the structural funds for the period 2000 to 2006, taking account of the prospective enlargement of the Union. The Court's main points in relation to agriculture were as follows.

- The key Commission proposal was a reduction in guaranteed price for agricultural products, coupled with a further increase in direct aid payments. The Court said that the Commission proposals for a price cut did not go far enough. The impact of commitments already made in the context of the World Trade Organisation agreement means that Community prices will need to move towards prices prevailing on the world market. Failure to take account of the Asian crisis and problems in Russia may mean an overspend lasting from 2002 to 2005.
- The Court drew attention to the fact that the bulk of the benefit from the CAP accrues to the largest farmers. Direct aid for arable crops already accounts for well over 40 per cent of CAP expenditure, by far the largest element in this total. 40 per cent of current payments for arable crops of about £12.5 billion a year accrue to 4 per cent of farmers, and 70 per cent to 10 per cent of farmers. Less than a third of the money goes to 90 per cent of farmers. It is doubtful whether the Commission's proposals responded adequately to this situation. In the Court's opinion, more far-reaching measures needed to be considered to reduce the share of the aid received by the largest farmers.

The Rural Environment Protection Scheme

One particular scheme which has been of major benefit to Irish farmers is the Rural Environment Protection Scheme (REPS). The scheme is administered by the Irish Department of Agriculture and Food, operates throughout the state and is audited by the department's internal audit unit, the Comptroller and Auditor General, the Court's auditors and Arthur Andersen auditors. Since 1995 37,500 participants have joined the scheme, which is voluntary; expenditure has amounted to over £500 million (75 per cent European Union and 25 per cent national exchequer) in direct payments to farmers since 1995, and the lands farmed under REPS amount to 1.27 million hectares throughout the country. Production methods and farming practices in the scheme reflect the need for environmental conservation and the protection of wildlife habitats and endangered species of flora and fauna and ensuring that quality food is produced. This scheme is of major benefit to the farming community, to rural life and to the economy as a whole, provided effective financial and administrative controls are fully maintained. Teagasc estimates that in four or five years some 80,000 farmers will have availed of the scheme.

Agenda 2000 and the structural funds

The Court supports efforts to simplify the administration of the structural funds and to make them more effective. This can only be achieved if objectives are more clearly defined and better information is available about projects. The accounting arrangements need to be improved in regard to advances to member states. The Court supports the proposal to cancel commitments for expenditure which have not been used at the end of a given period. At present these are allowed to accumulate, with the result that spending plans are continually extended, but do not lapse. Similarly the Court supports the tighter arrangements proposed for the control and audit of Community funds within the member states. At present the situation applying to the structural funds compares unfavourably with that applying to agriculture. Member states that fail to comply with rules on agricultural spending can be penalised by the Commission. Such action has hitherto been effectively ruled out for structural funds spending.

EU external aid programmes

I am strongly of the view that the financial accountability of the Commission's external aid programmes is in need of standardisation and transparency. External aid in the Union comes from no fewer than 75 budget lines, 87 legal bases and nine different committees. There are some 10,000 contracts each year and about 3,000 public tenders. The Commission has in this area 47 different procedures. One can only imagine the difficulties which arise in the financial management of the programmes. I am hopeful that the proposed new external relations common service will improve the situation. Better value for every EU euro spent must be the overriding criterion. Major resources are involved. For example, the reconstruction and modernisation of Soviet-type nuclear plants will cost at least 50 billion euros. So far some 700 to 800 million euros have been spent. The Court has been very critical of some of this expenditure in a recent special report.

Fraud and irregularity

One of the outcomes of the Court's ongoing work is that it makes reports and recommendations to improve the financial controls against fraud. Part of the explanation for the alienation of citizens from Union affairs relates to the embezzlement of Union funds and cases of incompetent management of these funds. The Court is obliged to bring these issues to the notice of the European public. Unfortunately, these frauds set off an avalanche of media and Eurosceptic reaction, and can destroy citizens' faith in Community legislation and in the staff of the institutions. Public acceptance of the single currency, the future work of the European Central Bank and adherence to economic policy guidelines by every member state demand that the resources of the Union be fully transparent and accounted for. All suspected frauds and irregularities uncovered during Court audits are promptly reported to the Community institution in question and to the national audit institutions to enable the necessary corrective measures to be undertaken. Very close liaison is also maintained with OLAF, the control and anti-fraud unit of the Commission. Frauds are frequently of a complex transnational nature. For example, in recent years criminal charges were brought against 119 people for a conspiracy of fraud against the Community budget, involving smuggling, tax evasion, forgery and corruption concerning a 'meat carousel'. This concerned imports of live cattle from Eastern Europe to Italy, which were re-exported as low-quality cuts and offal to Malta, re-exported from Malta to Italy, and further re-exported to non-member countries, mostly Gabon, with refunds. ECU 18.5 million in evaded levies and ECU 24 million in wrongly paid export refunds were involved; 42 persons were convicted. The investigative difficulties in this work are, of course, immense because some 18 million transit documents are issued annually in the Union.

Some fundamental reforms

There are some 30,000 European civil servants working in the institutions of the Union. There are over 8,000 retired staff. They work in an extremely complex and demanding multilingual and multinational environment. For the most part they serve the institutions very well. However, the staff regulations within which they work are, in my experience, in need of considerable reform, having first been framed some 30 years ago. No fewer than 76 staff regulations have now been consolidated into a complex text of 229 pages in eleven languages. These range from the special conditions of employment for officials serving in third countries to the weighting of the purchasing power of Community staff allowances in member states. Staff are recruited in outmoded public service categories of A, B, C and D. Category A, for example, ranges over eight steps from director general to administrative assistant. A fundamental reform I would advocate is that the posts of director general and director in all the institutions be made by an absolutely independent appointments board. These appointments are currently made by the members of the institutions (the Bureau in the case of the European Parliament), although they are subject to some constraints and appeal to the European Court of Justice. Effectively, the European institutions have a top-level appointments system which we in Ireland abolished in the mid-1980s in favour of an independent system. This basic reform in the European civil service is long overdue.

Having served as a member of the European Court of Auditors for the past six years, I am convinced that there is a very urgent need for the fundamental reform of the financial regulations of the institutions. These are initiated by the Commission and decided by the Council of Ministers, acting unanimously, following consultation with the European Parliament and having received the opinion of the Court of Auditors. In my opinion the regulations urgently need reform to ensure that there is full transparency of all transactions at institution and member state level. I have long held the view that these regulations are drafted with undue flexibility and ambiguity to enable member states and their paying agencies to appeal at three or four levels, to the Commission, the conciliation committee and the European Court of Justice, in the event of corrections or penalties being imposed by the Commission. If irregularities and fraud are to be rooted out, this basic change must be implemented. Secondly, the role of financial controller in the Commission must be strengthened. In recent years only about 10 per cent of the 400,000 transactions each year have been examined by financial control staffs of the Commission prior to payment. In my personal opinion the Commission needs the equivalent, as we have in Ireland, of a 'ministry of finance'. Far too many powerful centres of influence over financial commitments exist at commissioner, cabinet and DG levels. The serious problems arising from the horizontal structure of the Commission's administration have been well documented. Thirdly, the regulations relating to the tendering procedures and controls over outside contractors engaged by the Commission and its agencies are also in clear need of urgent reform. There are many large-scale technical assistance programmes where financial control, value for money audits, and reporting systems are entirely unsatisfactory. The Court of Auditors has pinpointed many of these defects. Does real political will exist at Council, Commission and member state level to tackle this serious problem?

In June 1999 a new European Fraud Office, OLAF (Office pour la Lutte Antifraude), was created to replace and improve on its immediate predecessor, UCLAF. It is essential that the head of this office be an independent director general with very substantial authority in the discharge of clear functions. Everybody in the Commission, from the President to the most temporary of temporary agents, must be fully aware that such a DG would have total authority of immediate intervention in the event of any irregularity being suspected. Moreover, it is imperative that the level of direct co-operation between such a DG and the authorities in all the member states be enhanced.

Above all else, I am convinced that the basic structure of the European Union's budget is in dire need of fundamental reform. The differentiated system of multiannual programming of commitments and payments is fatally conducive to maladministration. For example, have you ever tried examining a cancelled expenditure commitment which is carried over, revived in the following year, partly paid in that year, with the balance being refused in year three? This is an audit nightmare. The lack of annuality in the budget is a constant source of criticism, a recipe for malmanagement, an incentive for misappropriations and conducive to ever-mounting layers in the financial regulations and a budget structure of deliberate complexity suited to many member states, particularly those that are net beneficiaries. One must stress again and again that 80 per cent of the EU budget is spent at the level of the member states. And those that are net contributors are so beholden politically to their agricultural lobbies they are most reluctant to propose a root-and-branch reform of the Common Agricultural Policy and its regulations. Meanwhile, the agri-food conglomerates and the major farmers cream off the taxes of Europe's industrial labour force. It would also be an enormous sea change if the EU budget were to be transformed into a real cash-based annual budget. We urgently need compulsory year-end closures with absolutely transparent carry-overs and mandatory reversions to the general budget.

The future

As we approach the millennium, the European Union is still maintaining its momentum. A new Treaty was agreed at Amsterdam; the historic goal of democratic economic and monetary union is within reach; common strategies towards the fullest possible employment of all our citizens continue to preoccupy the body politic; there is consolidation and completion of the single market; the largest enlargement in the Union's history is being planned; and slowly but surely elements of a common foreign and security policy are being forged. It is our duty to ensure that 'no longer will old men make war and young men die'. In relation to CAP reform there is a real imperative to create a healthy, highly efficient and competitive farming industry; guaranteeing the future of high-quality food production; rewarding food producers fairly; controlling the agri monopolies; maintaining the rural environment; meeting consumer entitlements to high quality and safe food at a reasonable cost; enabling the agriculture of the new Eastern European states to enter the markets on a fair, competitive, non-excessively subsidised basis; and ensuring that in this framework Europe will negotiate on a solid footing in the next round of WTO negotiations. Great political vision, far greater than that which existed during the recent reforms, will be required. By the year 2010 the European Union may well comprise some 20 member states with a population of over 440 million and an annual budget in excess of £110 billion. By then, the Union will have expanded from the initial common market to include comprehensive economic, monetary, social, environmental and security objectives. With the prospect of considerable changes in the Union's budget, the Court of Auditors faces formidable challenges in the years ahead to ensure full public accountability and transparency in the effective utilisation of the resources of the Union.

11

The European Council

GARRET FITZGERALD

Introduction

The idea of a European Union, undefined, but going beyond the concept of the European Economic Community established by the Rome Treaty, was implicit in the very first clause of the preamble to that Treaty, which spoke of a determination 'to lay the foundations of an ever closer union among the peoples of Europe'. At the 1972 summit that immediately preceded the accession of Ireland, the United Kingdom and Denmark – a summit attended by the three acceding countries – the establishment of such a European Union by the year 1980 was decided upon, but the nature of this Union was left vague.

When, in the aftermath of the Copenhagen summit of December 1973, the EEC foreign ministers met informally at Gymnich near Bonn in April 1974, a first attempt was made to establish just what such a Union might entail. The new British Labour foreign secretary, James Callaghan, opened the discussion with the comment that presumably it did not mean a Union like that between Britain and Ireland, which had not been exactly a success, nor like that between England and Scotland. Taking a more positive line, I asked whether it might perhaps mean modification of the need for unanimity in Council decision-making, increased democratic control by the European Parliament, and closer working of the economic and political sides of our work.

In the discussion that followed, the French, German, Italian, Dutch and Luxembourg ministers all said that they did not know what the European Union decided on in 1972 meant. I was not too surprised at this, for at the Copenhagen summit some months earlier the foreign ministers had been unable to work out what the heads of government had agreed during their morning 'fireside chat'. The foreign ministers had spent the subsequent afternoon trying to invent what we thought they might have decided!

However, the French foreign minister, Michel Jobert, then suggested that the further development of the concept of European Union be delegated to representatives of the governments, meeting without the Commission. This attempt to marginalise the Commission was, however, blocked by a number of us representing smaller countries.

With President Pompidou's death shortly afterwards, and the election of Giscard d'Estaing, a further effort was made to bypass the Commission by establishing an intergovernmental system centred on the three large member states – France, Germany and Britain. Giscard invited the heads of government to dine with him in the Elysée on 14 September – pointedly excluding the French President of the Commission, Francois Ortoli, from this occasion. When the foreign ministers met two days later, the new French foreign minister, Jean Sauvagnargues, attempted to suggest that at that dinner agreement had been reached among the heads of government on new proposals for the Community. A number of foreign ministers contested this, explaining that our heads of government had not reported any such dinner decisions to us.

As to the proposals themselves: having described as 'idiotic' the 1972 summit European Union project – to which President Pompidou had subscribed on behalf of France! – Sauvagnargues put forward several generally acceptable ideas, such as the identification of areas not involving vital national interests in respect of which qualified majority voting might be permitted, and direct elections to the European Parliament, which was to be given some legislative functions. These functions were to include a right of legislative initiative.

Genesis of the European Council

However, he also proposed intergovernmental discussions to be held on subjects such as energy, transport and aviation, the environment and youth. As all of these, except perhaps youth, were in fact Community competences, this proposal would have undermined the Community's role over wide areas. His proposals also involved the sensible merging of Council and Political Co-operation meetings – a merging which the French had previously resisted (a year earlier they had in fact required the foreign ministers to fly from Copenhagen to Brussels for two such meetings on the same day). These proposed joint meetings (to be described as 'meetings of the European Community') were in future to be attended by heads of government. They were also to be private; were not to be followed by any communiqué; were to be prepared by a 'light secretariat'; and were not to discuss foreign policy relating to issues outside Europe. The proposals were the genesis of the European Council.

While the German Foreign Minister, Hans Dietrich Genscher, was 'happy' with these proposals, and James Callaghan was suspiciously enthusiastic (clearly they had both been tipped off in advance about the French initiative), all the other foreign ministers made it clear that they saw the proposals as a most serious threat to the balance of the Community, and in particular to the balance between larger and smaller states.

Why was this? First of all, there was widespread reticence about the concept of frequent meetings of heads of government. Regardless of how they are organised, such meetings tend to favour the interests of larger states: because the prime ministers of such states have major external interests outside as well as inside Europe, they are usually better equipped to deal with external matters than are the leaders of some smaller countries, many of whom tend to concentrate rather on domestic affairs, leaving external matters largely to their foreign ministers.

At least in those Councils which meet monthly and sometimes more often, e.g. foreign affairs, finance, agriculture, a certain collegiality develops between the ministers, who tend to try to help each other when possible. In this format this is true of ministers from larger as well as smaller countries. But at heads of government level this is less likely to happen, partly because they meet much less frequently – only two or three times a year – but also because heads of government from larger states sometimes tend to be impatient with the narrower range of interests of some of their colleagues from smaller countries.

Next, when it comes to concerting positions in advance of meetings, France and Germany have the advantage of being able to do this bilaterally, whereas effective co-ordination of policy by the smaller states, whether to initiate action or to counter a Franco-German initiative, would require multilateral consultation by the larger number of small states. Also, multilateral consultation is open to being stigmatised as 'conspiring' or 'plotting', and is thus vulnerable to negative reactions from one or more larger states. Thus, in 1973 when I arranged pre-Council lunches with the Benelux foreign ministers, these did not long survive what appeared to be private hints of disapproval from some larger member states.

So, the foreign ministers of smaller states have concrete reasons for being unenthusiastic about regular heads of government meetings – to which has to be added their own private vested interest in holding on to as much control as possible over foreign affairs and minimising the prime ministerial involvement in their policy area!

But the French proposal of September had other features that worried the smaller states. The Commission – whose role is crucial for smaller states – was to be marginalised in more than one way. Members of the Commission other than its President were to be excluded from these 'meetings of the European Community' even when their particular competences were under discussion. Moreover, the Commission's exclusive right of legislative initiative, which offers great protection to the interests of smaller countries, was to be shared with Parliament.

Furthermore, the role of the secretariat of the Council was also to be marginalised by transferring to a new secretariat the task of preparing for and following up the Political Co-operation parts of these meetings. And finally, the proposal to limit the role of Political Co-operation to Europe seemed designed to free France, Germany and Britain – and perhaps Italy – from the obligation to formulate foreign policy in consultation with their EEC partners.

When at this meeting the French foreign minister seemed to challenge my assertion that decisions on matters involving Community competences could be taken only on the basis of Commission proposals, he was forced to back off after the French President of the Commission, Francois Ortoli, supported my position. My hand thus strengthened, I went on to add that if it was proposed to increase the role of the heads of government, Parliament's legislative role would need also to enhanced in order to maintain the institutional balance of the Community.

At the next meeting of the General, or Foreign Affairs, Council, the French Minister began to pull back on some aspects of his proposal for the establishment of what he now described as 'the European Council'. This body was not to replace the Council of Ministers, or to act as court of appeal from the Council, but was merely to 'mark the globality of combined Council and Political Co-operation meetings'. And he implied acceptance of the need for decisions taken by heads of government acting as a Council of Ministers to be taken in accordance with Community rules.

By this time it was being proposed that decisions on these matters be taken by heads of government at a summit in Paris in December. When Jim Callaghan rejected as 'impossible' an assertion of mine that a Paris summit would also have to deal with concrete economic problems such as regional and energy policy, I responded robustly that if that was impossible, it would be better not to have any summit at all.

A number of objectionable features of the French proposals were eliminated at this meeting, namely the proposal for intergovernmental discussion of matters involving Community competences; the suggested limitation of Political Co-operation to European issues; and the preparation of European Councils by a new secretariat. Moreover, the political directors were to agree a record of the conclusions of this meeting as a basis for the work of a joint meeting of political directors and permanent representatives – which would be important from our point of view, for at joint meetings we might be able to trade some institutional concessions for a decision on the establishment of the regional fund which at that point seemed to be in some doubt.

For some reason this record of our meeting was not in fact prepared, and instead of the joint group meeting, it was decided that its two components would meet separately. When I learnt of this official level reversal of the ministers' decision I was furious. Phone calls to the President of the Commission and the Dutch foreign minister disclosed that they were not aware of this 'coup', and within hours effect had been given belatedly to our ministerial decision. From then on the run-in to the Paris summit went smoothly.

At the summit, the regional fund was established, and we secured an increase in our share to over 6 per cent. Originally we had been offered 3.9 per cent, but as, due to the oil crisis, the fund itself had been reduced by over two-fifths from the amount initially proposed by the Commission, we ended up with a figure that was no more than the amount we had originally been offered. But then everyone else ended up with far less than they had intended! As for the heads of government meetings, it was agreed that the role of the Council of Ministers secretariat would be safeguarded by limiting the role of the European Council administrative secretariat – moreover, the role and powers of the Commission were explicitly preserved. The battle to preserve the balance of the Community had been won.

However, perhaps because the heads of government of some larger countries did not wish to subject themselves to the Community procedures, European Councils did not in the event act as a Council of Ministers, taking formal decisions. Instead the European Council gave general orientations, and if General Council was unable to reach agreement on some Commission proposal, with the result that it was referred to the heads of government, whatever solution was agreed by the European Council would be referred back to the General Council for it to take the formal legal decision on this matter. As to the frequency of European Council meetings, the eventual compromise took the form of agreement to meet three times a year, 'and when necessary'.

So much for the genesis of the European Council.

The European Council in operation

It was ironic that, after all this, it fell to Ireland to host the first meeting of this new Community body, for our first presidency began in January 1975, a couple of weeks after the Paris summit. By a happy chance, this first Irish Presidency was an eventful one. During the first two months of the Presidency we had completed the delayed negotiation of the first Lomé Agreement, and signed it in that city, and we also implemented in the General Council the Paris summit decision to introduce qualified majority voting on matters not involving vital national interests – a practice which, however, immediately lapsed after the end of our Presidency. And we also launched a new process of EEC foreign policy co-ordination with the United States. Much more was to follow during the later months of that half-year, but by the time the first

European Council took place in March, we had already acquitted ourselves well enough to create a favourable atmosphere for that meeting.

We took a lot of trouble with the arrangements for the Council which was held in the 18th century St Patrick's Hall in Dublin Castle – a chamber decorated with the banners of the Knights of the extinct Order of St Patrick. In contrast to earlier summit meetings, when journalists were housed several miles away from the site of the meetings, we located them in a space immediately *below* the conference hall, and we installed telecommunications equipment giving them direct access to the outside world – something that was far from common at that time, as I knew from visiting Paris and Rome and, indeed, the diplomatic quarter of Washington, where at that time all international phone calls had to be routed via an operator in Pittsburgh!

While the agenda for this first European Council was quite long, it included only one issue of real substance. This was the resolution of the outstanding issues involved in the first British 'renegotiation', namely the budgetary corrective mechanism and the arrangement for New Zealand butter. Harold Wilson told us that if these problems were settled, Britain would no longer be a reluctant partner in the Community, would play its part in Community development and would have a vested interest in its cohesion. He added that Britain did not retract its commitment to the EMU as expressed in the communiqué from the Paris summit, and he pointed out that no one else had gone any further than that! But more than a dozen years were to elapse before EMU became a real issue in the Community.

After a well-choreographed ritual dance of negotiation between the principal heads of government, solutions were found to these two outstanding problems and the Council was judged to have been a success. It was subsequently contrasted with immediately following European Councils, which, as it happened, did not have any significant issues into which they could get their teeth.

It was almost to become a standard practice on these occasions that the heads of government and foreign ministers dined separately, but met together afterwards for coffee. On this occasion the coffee discussion was about the negotiations in the Conference for Security and Co-operation in Europe. As on many subsequent occasions I was struck by the fact that this discussion seemed to be informed by relatively few hard facts and appeared, indeed, somewhat amateurish. When, some years later, I became Taoiseach and joined the heads of government at their dinner table discussions, I found that these varied considerably in quality. On some occasions quite serious issues were discussed, including the Cold War strategic issues. But at other dinners the discussion was frankly somewhat frivolous. I recall one which was taken up with a historical account by Helmut Kohl of four plots against Hitler's life – though I don't think he even actually reached the fourth one.

But to return to the meetings of the Council itself. The format of these meetings involved the presence of the heads of government and foreign ministers only. No civil servants were in attendance, which thus left to the foreign ministers the task of recording for the benefit of their governments the main features of the discussions and any conclusions that might be reached. The Council's secretariat was, of course, in attendance and made a record of the proceedings which could, if necessary, be referred to, but which was not circulated after meetings. Contact with the outside world was maintained through an arrangement under which each government nominated an official who could be summoned, if necessary, to pass a message outside. All this was in marked contrast to the Council of Ministers meetings, which involve attendance by several hundred officials or, in restricted session, by several civil servants as well as the ministers.

The task of foreign ministers on these occasions was quite onerous. In addition to recording the main points of the discussion and any conclusion that was reached, they also simultaneously had to advise their heads of government on points on which they might have to intervene and, on occasions, with the permission of their heads of government, they actually intervened themselves. Moreover, some of us sent out notes from time to time to our civil servants to keep them informed of the trend of the debate, and, when appropriate, to communicate some of this information to the press – including, on suitable occasions, a note of statements made by the head of government. Carrying out these three functions simultaneously could be quite a strain, although for my part I enjoyed the challenge. A good deal of time was often wasted by virtue of the convention under which each head of government made statements on issues before the Council. Not all of these were equally interesting or relevant.

As was the practice at meetings of the Council of Ministers, breaks were called in the proceedings of the European Council at moments when a combination of problems had to be resolved, thus enabling ministers to talk informally with each other in order to work out possible compromises before resuming the general discussion. As regards the time-scale for the meetings, they normally started at lunchtime, breaking for dinner around 7 p.m. to 8 p.m. – and on certain occasions when the discussion was fraught, even later. The discussions resumed on the following morning, often preceded by bilateral breakfast tête-à-têtes between heads of government. The meeting might end anytime from lunchtime on the second day up to 6 p.m. or 7 p.m., depending on the amount of business to be discussed. At the later stages of such meetings, or when people were anxious to get away but were unable to reach an agreed conclusion, a certain amount of tension would arise.

The foreign ministers normally arrived with a number of draft statements on international issues, prepared for them by their political directors through the process of Political Co-operation. These were then discussed and refined or modified by the foreign ministers at their separate dinner in the course of the first evening. They then came before the heads of government on the second day. However, it would frequently happen that due to the pressure of work on the second day there was little or no time for these statements to be considered, and it was not unknown for the head of government of one of the larger states to dismiss these last statements airily as unimportant, leaving them to moulder in the files of the political directors.

Much of the time of the heads of government was taken up with drafting and redrafting parts of the communiqué, which had often been prepared before the meeting started. Although this seems an extraordinary misuse of the time of heads of government, it was often an inevitable consequence of the need to paper over cracks. Much often depended on the precise choice of words, which could obscure rather than clarify issues. On occasions these drafting sessions enabled me to suggest improvements in English drafts prepared by or in the process of being modified by a British Prime Minister. It gave me particular pleasure to improve on the English of the English!

Although initially the European Council meetings took place in the capitals of member states, it became increasingly the practice to hold them in provincial centres, where they certainly aroused more interest than was the case in capital cities. Particularly I recall the European Council held in Stuttgart, when the heads of government and the foreign ministers appeared on the balcony to receive the applause of a substantial crowd of citizens in the square below. This would never happen in a capital city!

The impact of the European Council

There was always a likelihood that these meetings would be used as some kind of court of appeal from the General Council, and would thus diminish the authority of that Council. It did not take long before this began to happen. Indeed, the existence of these regular European Council meetings seems to have limited the decision-making capacity of the General Council to the point where it almost seemed bad form for that Council to settle an issue and thus exclude the European Council from playing a role in the matter! That may be a somewhat exaggerated view, but I am certain that in the absence of regular European Council meetings, many issues that were allowed to drift up to European Council level would have been settled at General Council level.

There are both advantages and disadvantages to this. Because of the greater expertise of ministers on many of the issues under debate, and because of the 'legality' factor referred to earlier, a General Council is technically better equipped to settle many of these issues than the heads of government.

On the other hand, there *are* occasions when the greater weight of authority
of the heads of government may help to resolve a problem with significant
political implications for some or all member states. I doubt, however,
whether the decision as to the precise colour of the European passport really
fits in to this latter category. I could not help but be struck by the absurdity
of heads of government debating the relative merits of shades of burgundy
and claret for this purpose!

One important issue that was resolved at the European Council level –
but only after it had been discussed there on no fewer than three occasions –
was the introduction of direct elections to the European Parliament. From
the time the Assembly of the European Coal and Steel Community had been
established a quarter of a century earlier, members of it and of the subsequent
Assembly of the European Economic Community had been chosen indirectly
– nominally elected by their national parliaments but in practice selected by
the parties in these parliaments, more or less in proportion to their strengths,
but with the pointed exclusion of Communists during most of that period. A
proposal in 1974 for direct elections had envisaged the first direct elections
taking place in 1980. However, I saw an advantage in having these elections
in 1979, when they would coincide with our local elections, thus ensuring a
better turn-out than if they were held on their own. On our proposal the Paris
summit had decided that the elections should be held in 1978 but, as I had
foreseen, they subsequently slipped to 1979 – so the coincidence of Irish local
elections and European elections was secured in that year.

The debate on European elections within the European Council proved
protracted because it raised the issue of how far the introduction of direct
elections should be permitted to dilute the over-representation of smaller
countries in the earlier indirectly elected assembly. Naturally enough, some
larger countries took the line that we should go much or even all the way
towards proportional representation of the electors of member states on a
population basis. Inevitably, those of us from smaller countries sought to
retain the over-representation which had been such a striking feature of the
earlier system of indirect elections. In our case, this over-representation had
given us 5 per cent of the seats in the European Parliament, despite the fact
that our population was then only 1 per cent of that of the Community.

There was, however, a further consideration from an Irish point of view.
As it seemed likely that we would be permitted to retain our multi-seat
electoral system for the purpose of a European election, it would be important
that the actual number of seats, as distinct from our proportion, would be
sufficient to enable us without undue problems to divide the country into
Euro constituencies that could be represented more or less proportionally to
their population. I judged that for this purpose we would need 15 seats.

In the protracted debate that followed at the European Council meetings of December 1975 and April and July 1976, we fought this case pugnaciously. Eventually, we secured our 15 seats rather than the 13 that had been proposed; however, other countries' representation was also increased by two-thirteenths, so that our share remained at the level initially proposed. But a further 24 seats were then added so as to increase the representation of the dissatisfied larger member states. And even with this increased representation the British were still unwilling to allocate more than two seats to Northern Ireland. Our insistence that Northern Ireland should have three seats eventually led to each of the three large member states being allocated a further three seats. Thus our double intervention in this debate on behalf of our own state and subsequently on behalf of Northern Ireland had the effect of increasing the total size of the European Parliament by almost one-fifth!

Evolution of the European Council

When I returned to the European Council as Taoiseach in 1981, and again in 1983 for a longer stint, I found that little had changed – apart from the personnel of its membership. Margaret Thatcher had replaced Jim Callaghan; Helmut Kohl had replaced Helmut Schmidt; and Francois Mitterand had replaced Giscard d'Estaing.

Because of the number and complexity of issues that the Community has to deal with, the practice had grown up over the decades of seeking solutions to the multiple problems by way of 'package deals' at ministerial Council meetings. It might appear that by accumulating issues in this way problems would become more difficult to resolve, but in practice there are situations in which a solution to a bunch of issues may be easier to achieve because everyone can gain something in relation to one or other of the combination of issues under negotiation.

Such a package deal emerged in 1984 after a period in which the European Councils of June 1983, December 1983 and March 1984 had struggled to resolve three complex problems:

- an increase in the Community's own resources (which up to that time had been limited to a maximum 1 per cent of member state VAT)
- the 'British budgetary imbalances' problem
- a reform of the Common Agricultural Policy in relation to milk.

In the event, the milk problem was resolved before the other two. By leaving the Brussels European Council Meeting of March 1984 and remaining in my room throughout the latter part of the meeting, I dramatised the Irish problem in relation to milk and thus created a climate in which the French Presidency was able to find a compromise solution in the days that followed

– one that gave us an additional quota, thus making us the only country to be allowed to increase its milk output at that point.

The issue of the British rebate was settled at the subsequent Fontainebleau European Council of June 1984. Although that issue was linked to the resolution of the dispute over the increase in the Community budget, a dispute subsequently arose about the supplementary budget for 1984 which we then had to resolve during our presidency in the second half of that year.

In fact the Fontainebleau European Council of June 1984 marked a turning point in the history of the Community. It was at that meeting that France, through President Mitterand, indicated its willingness to abandon the Luxembourg Compromise agreed in 1965, which had effectively undermined the qualified majority voting system through which alone the Community could overcome the many obstacles that stood in the way of the creation of the single market.

President Mitterand identified three of the principal tasks that Ireland had to tackle in its presidency: the conclusion of the third Lomé Convention; the achievement of an agreement on enlargement of the Communities by the inclusion of Spain and Portugal; and the securing of a consensus on the nomination of the next President of the Commission. But he also proposed to re-ignite the process of strengthening the Community by establishing two committees of representatives of heads of government to look at the changes needed in the structure of the Community's institutions and to make the Community more meaningful to ordinary people.

In the event, we successfully negotiated the Lomé Convention, and I secured – not without difficulty in the case of Margaret Thatcher – the agreement of member governments to the appointment of Jacques Delors as the next President of the Commission. But the achievement of an agreement on enlargement of the Community by inclusion of Spain and Portugal proved more difficult.

Throughout the second half of 1984, attempts had been made to resolve French and Italian difficulties about the impact that Spanish wine would have on their wine industries. But neither the agricultural ministers nor the foreign ministers had succeeded in resolving this wine deadlock. Indeed, it seemed to me that they had even failed to identify precisely where the problem lay as between the French and Italians. However, on visits to Paris and Rome shortly before the European Council meeting, I was able to identify precisely what was bothering the two governments, and to propose a solution at the European Council meeting in Dublin that could satisfy them both. Having got informal agreement of the two governments during the course of the weekend before the Council meeting, I suggested that at the Council itself they should respond in a grudging manner to my suggestion as to how it could be resolved, thus creating a time-frame within which it might be possible to resolve another wine problem created by Germany's and Luxembourg's insistence on retaining the right to sugar some of their wine.

In the event the French and Italian wine problem was resolved, but we and our partners were forced to agree to allowing Germany and Luxembourg to continue to sugar their wines so as to secure EU subsidies for their surplus wine. However, we secured an agreement designed to limit to some degree the cost of that arrangement. This agreement on wine cleared the way for Spain and Portugal's accession, which was agreed on the eve of the next European Council meeting in March 1985.

In the meantime, I had succeeded in establishing the two committees proposed by President Mitterand, arranging that the institutional committee be chaired by our former Foreign Minister, Jim Dooge, whom I knew had the capacity to bring its work to a successful conclusion. This he succeeded in doing before the March 1985 European Council, thus paving the way for a breakthrough to a reformed Community institutional structure, upon which agreement was reached at the Milan European Council in June 1985.

This latter European Council meeting was quite dramatic, because Margaret Thatcher had been led to believe that the issue of establishing an Intergovernmental Conference with a view to agreeing the necessary reforms to the Treaty was not going to be pressed at this meeting. But overnight discussions between the Italians, Germans and French had led to a decision on their part to go ahead with the proposal to summon such an Intergovernmental Council. When this proposal was unexpectedly put formally to the Council during the morning session of the second day, Margaret Thatcher reacted with fury. Together with the Greek and Danish prime ministers she voted against the proposal. I had no hesitation in voting with the original Six in favour of the calling of this Conference, thus marking in the clearest way possible the difference between Ireland's position as a new member state and that of the other three countries that had joined the Community between 1973 and 1981.

In the event, and on mature reflection, Margaret Thatcher reversed her position, not merely supporting the reform of the institutional structure of the Community at a Luxembourg European Council in December of that year, but herself claiming credit for the Single European Act which was the product of that Intergovernmental Council.

At that Luxembourg European Council, Ireland played a particularly active role, pressing for the introduction of the concept of 'cohesion' into the Rome Treaty. We were more successful in this respect that we had expected, and these new provisions subsequently proved extremely effective in expanding several times over the scale of structural funds made available to the peripheral members of the Community during the early 1990s.

During 1986 the business of the European Council was quite light, but informal contacts during these meetings made it possible to prevent a breakdown of a project for a programme of university student exchanges (Erasmus). Before I went to one of these meetings the recently-appointed President of University College Dublin, Paddy Masterson, had contacted me to tell me that this programme was at risk because of reluctance by the education ministers of the larger EEC countries to approve spending on the scheme at the level recommended by the European Commission. Accordingly, in a break at the European Council in London in December 1986, I took the opportunity of raising this matter informally with the French Prime Minister, Jacques Chirac.

Like myself he had known nothing of this problem, but responded enthusiastically, and we jointly approached the German Foreign Minister, Hans Dietrich Genscher, and secured immediate support to overrule the ministers of education who, it appeared, had been among those opposing the project; the result of this informal chat was that the Erasmus programme got off the ground quite soon thereafter.

Looking back now at the work of the European Council since its establishment in 1975, I recognise the value of engaging the interest of heads of government in the work of the European Community through the operation of this body. Most of the dangers that the establishment of the European Council initially seemed to pose for the balance of the Community have been avoided – largely, I feel, because of the tough reaction of the smaller member countries to the proposals put forward by the French in the autumn of 1974. On the other hand, the European Council has certainly contributed to the weakening of the authority of the General Council, from which it has too often acted as a court of appeal.

12

Changing balance between European institutions

FRANK A. WALL

Introduction

Over the past 25 years, the relations between the various European institutions have evolved significantly. As the member states transferred more and more responsibilities to the European framework, the respective roles of the institutions took on a new shape. For some the changes were dramatic, for others very little changed.

In this essay, concentration is focused on the main players in the political and policy areas – the European Council, the Council of Ministers, the European Parliament and the Commission – and on how European evolution has influenced the interaction between them. Other institutions have not made an obvious impact, to the extent that their relations with the principal institutions have not changed much. Thus the Court of Justice, in common with court systems generally, remains aloof from the other institutions. The Economic and Social Committee has never achieved its full potential, probably due to its lack of political ambition. To be fair, it has not been helped by the budgetary restrictions imposed on it by the Council of Ministers, but it has suffered from a lack of imagination in establishing a role for itself. To illustrate this, the example of the European Parliament's success in building up the role of public hearings on aspects of draft legislation, many of them technical, can be put forward. This would have been an ideal road for the Economic and Social Committee to follow, as it already has direct or indirect access, through its members, to the experts that can contribute to the work of such public hearings.

The committee of the regions is a relative newcomer, having been established in 1994 by the Maastricht Treaty. Although it is a political body, it has yet to make a serious impact on the institutional scene. Its role is limited, and it shares the 'regional' platform with some other Europe-wide bodies.

European Council

The European Council started as occasional meetings of heads of state or government, convened to discuss major political issues and to address the more difficult problems that remained unresolved at the level of the Council of Ministers. The frequency of meetings increased from one to two per presidency as the heads of state and government, together with the President of the Commission, took a more active role in key political decision-making. Their evolving involvement in these key decisions led to their role being institutionalised by the Maastricht Treaty 1992. Certain major responsibilities have become their exclusive preserve. Thus the European Council is now the particular body that decides who can be proposed as President of the Commission and who can be appointed president of the European Central Bank. The former power is exercised on behalf of the governments of the member states, while the latter is explicitly endowed on the European Council by the Maastricht Treaty. As the political buck stops with the European Council, it is also called on to find solutions to major problems such as agreeing on compromises on such dossiers as the Maastricht and Amsterdam Treaties and Agenda 2000. The Maastricht Treaty charges it with charting the future of the European Union by providing it 'with the necessary impetus for its development' and defining 'the general political guidelines thereof'.

The increased and more active role of the European Council has cut across the traditional role of the Council of Ministers, and in particular the General Affairs Council, which is made up of ministers for foreign affairs. The latter group traditionally enjoyed a catch-all role of running the European Communities, but the expansion of policy areas coming within the ambit of the treaties led to a steady development of the role of other ministers in specialised Council meetings. Thus, in recent years, the ministers responsible for economic and monetary issues and justice and home affairs have become highly prolific in terms of discussion and output. This led to the need for the General Affairs Council to take a hard look at its current and future role.

The European Parliament has been casting an envious eye in the direction of the European Council for some time. It has questioned the right of the Commission President to be a member while it has no corresponding role. So far, its efforts to join this élite club have never got beyond an invitation to the European Parliament President to present the views of that institution at the beginning of European Council meetings.

In the early years, the President of the European Parliament would make a statement before the European Council meeting formally got under way, with no discussion on his or her comments whatsoever. In recent years a little progress has been achieved in that the President of the European Parliament now speaks at the beginning of the European Council meeting and a short discussion normally follows.

Council of Ministers

The Council of Ministers enjoyed the role of dominant institution for many years with its power of legislative decision. The Ministers are, after all, the representatives of the member states, and it is those member states that decide what goes into and what does not go into the Treaties. Thus the Council could always display a certain amount of diffidence, if not arrogance, towards the other institutions. That was to change utterly when adoption of legislation by codecision was introduced by the Maastricht Treaty. Since then the Council has to take full consideration of the views of another institution – the European Parliament – when considering its own position, and to negotiate a compromise when differences persist. This was a culture shock for some but, interestingly, a changeover was successfully made without too many hiccups. On the other hand, the Council has many new areas of responsibility arising from the Maastricht and Amsterdam Treaties, which it exercises without too much influence from the other institutions, in such areas as the common foreign and security policy and justice and home affairs.

The common foreign and security policy has remained the major area of activity for the General Affairs Council since the Amsterdam Treaty came into force. However, this Treaty also brings in a new challenge to the ministers in the shape of Mr/Ms CFSP – the newly enhanced Secretary-General of the Council and High Representative for the CFSP. While the new CFSP post will assist the presidency of the Council, to be successful he or she will have to adopt a high profile and implement an ambitious programme of activities. This could possibly bring him or her into competition with some individual ministers who have been used to an unrestricted international role heretofore.

This potential for internal tension brings to mind a clash between the then President of the Commission, Jacques Delors, and the then President of the Council of Ministers, Hans Van den Broek (who was Dutch Minister for Foreign Affairs) on the occasion of the escalation of violence in Yugoslavia in 1991. The incident took place in August, when traditionally European institutions and national governments are on holidays. President Delors was, however, in touch with the situation and quickly issued a statement on the affair. Council President Van den Broek was also up to date with the crisis, but before issuing a statement he had to consult with the member states. He was not amused at President Delors' rapid and personal interjection and, conscious that the Commission had no competence in foreign policy matters, told Delors as much. Some days later the foreign affairs committee of the European Parliament held an extraordinary meeting to discuss the crisis and invited both personalities to address the meeting. In accordance with tradition, the Council President spoke first. When invited to take the floor, Commission President Delors hesitated, turned towards Van den Broek and pointedly asked if it was in order for the Commission to speak. Van den Broek (who went on later to serve as a Commissioner under Delors) had no problems on this occasion, as he had already re-established the supremacy of his own institution over the Commission.

European Parliament

Over any period of history there are always winners and losers. The clear winner of the European institutions' power stakes in the past quarter-century has been the European Parliament. Alternatively described as 'a rabble without responsibility' by the late Brian Lenihan, a Minister for Foreign Affairs who had been a MEP from 1973 to 1977, and as 'the institution of the future whose real influence in decision-making already goes far beyond its theoretical powers' by Jacques Delors, President of the European Commission, the European Parliament has graduated from being a gentleman's club in the period before direct elections in 1979 to being a dynamic force for change and reform within the existing structures and thereby shifting the balance of power between the institutions. Not only did the European Parliament gain the legitimacy of a directly elected mandate in 1979, but it was now made up of ambitious politicians, some of them already established personalities and others out to make a name for themselves, and it made full use of its substantial budgetary powers and resources to create a high-powered and well-staffed secretariat to support the achievement of its ambitions.

How the Parliament pursued its strategy to effect changes in its favour can be illustrated by two stories from different periods of its history.

The first example relates to the creation of the title of the European Parliament. When the Treaty establishing the Coal and Steel Community was adopted in 1952, it provided for the establishment of a Common Assembly. This in all probability reflected France's preference of title – its own democratically elected body is called the 'Assemblée Nationale', as De Gaulle is supposed to have disliked the word 'parliament' – but over the years the members of this new European Assembly felt that the title 'Parliament' was more appropriate. Thus in 1958 they decided to call themselves the European Parliament in the German and Dutch languages, and this was extended to all other languages in 1962. The Parliament promoted the new title extensively over several years so that it became the description of the institution that was commonly and publicly used. In formal legislative procedures it would adopt its opinions in the name of the European Parliament while the Council, in adopting the final legislative Act, would refer to the opinion of the Assembly. Success finally came in 1976 when the member states accepted the title change on the occasion of the adoption of the Act concerning the election of the representatives of the European Parliament by direct universal suffrage.

The Parliament had won the argument through its persistence. In the end it would have looked strange for member state governments to call on their citizens to vote in new Europe-wide parliamentary elections to an institution formally known as an assembly while popularly spoken of as a parliament.

The second example concerns the origins of the term 'codecision'. I have placed the term in inverted commas to highlight the fact that it is nowhere to be found in the Treaties. (It is mentioned in a Declaration annexed to the Amsterdam Treaty.) Nevertheless, those who are in any way familiar with European procedures will know what you are referring to when codecision is spoken of, but far fewer will be familiar with the term 'procedure in accordance with Article 189 b of the EC Treaty'. The latter term is technically correct but is now the preserve of the legalistically pure.

Once again, the Parliament is responsible for this situation. The Parliament had campaigned over several years for changes to the Treaty that would give it a right of codeciding with the Council in legislative areas. The Single Act of 1987 had given the Parliament an enhanced role in the legislative process in a limited number of areas, but Parliament was not happy and sustained a constant campaign before and during the Intergovernmental Conference negotiations leading up to the adoption of the Maastricht Treaty. Parliament wanted equal rights with the Council to codecide on European legislation, and nothing less would do. The member states were sympathetic but were not yet prepared to go the whole way, and what emerged was a complicated procedure giving the Parliament two opportunities to put forward amendments to draft legislative proposals and a right to obligatory conciliation with the Council where amendments were not accepted. However, the Council could still overrule the Parliament by unanimous decision at the end of the procedure if agreement had not been found during conciliation (a right that has never been exercised and which disappears with the entry into force of the Amsterdam Treaty).

You could hardly call this codecision in the strict sense, but the Parliament was intent on making the most of it and proceeded to use the term in its official texts and in its press and public statements. The rest is history.

Parliament continues to challenge the powers reserved for the Council and continually seeks to enhance its influence over the exercise of those powers. Through its own budgetary powers the Parliament is able to interfere indirectly in, for example, the CFSP area which remains very much an area of intergovernmental competence. We can confidently expect the Parliament to persist in its efforts to increase its influence over the Council's activities, as it has never accepted that the Treaties do not make the Council answerable to the Parliament, a situation which is contrary to the normal relationship between a national government and a national parliament.

European Commission

While the Parliament has been the obvious winner in enhancing its role, the main loser has been the Commission. The Commission is a unique institution in historical terms. Never before in history had sovereign states endowed an independent body with such powers of a legislative and executive nature. The right to propose legislation, the responsibility for executing European Community policies, the right to control competition policy and the disbursement of a massive budget are substantial powers indeed, and an ambitious Parliament would naturally look in this direction for a bigger slice of the action.

Using its budgetary powers, the Parliament regularly seeks to influence what the Commission does. While any executive welcomes more funds to pursue particular policies, less funds can effectively cripple such policies. The Parliament has become very adept at negotiating trade-offs with the Commission in order to change the emphasis in certain policy areas.

However, it has not been a total success for the Parliament against the Commission, as exemplified by the attempt in the early 1990s by the Parliament to control the Commission's right to propose legislation. Parliament initially requested the Commission to present each autumn an annual legislative programme – a list of legislative proposals that would be presented during the following calendar year. This was not an unreasonable request, as it would allow the Commission to make a political impact by publishing its programme and would also allow the other institutions to plan their work in dealing with the proposals announced in the programme. However, the Parliament had other ideas and was not happy just to debate the Commission's programme and give an opinion on it, but also wanted to negotiate changes to the programme. The Parliament invited the Council to join in these discussions with a view to agreeing a joint legislative programme. The Council refused to be drawn into the exercise, and the Commission resisted the Parliament's pressure. The final outcome was that the Commission presents an annual work programme (which includes its list of legislative proposals as well as its plans in many other areas of activity – green papers, international relations, etc.) on which Parliament votes an opinion. The Council, in a spirit of compromise, agreed to make a general statement in relation to the exercise. This statement consists of a list of priority policy areas and legislative issues to be addressed in the following year by the Council.

The Parliament's backing-off in this case may reflect an acceptance that it could not win this particular battle. Everything it had acquired had been fought for over a protracted period. So perhaps the Parliament may have seen better opportunities arising through its new powers under the Maastricht Treaty, which was about to enter into force.

Appointment of the Commission

One of the new powers endowed on the Parliament by the Maastricht Treaty was the right to approve the appointment of the President and members of the Commission. The new Treaty had dovetailed the appointment of the Commission to commence at the beginning of January following the June 1994 elections to the European Parliament. This would allow sufficient time for the various stages foreseen in the Treaty to be respected – designation of the future Commission President by the heads of state or government, consultation of the Parliament, nomination of the other members of the Commission by the member states, a vote of approval of the future college of commissioners as a whole by the Parliament, and finally their formal appointment by the representatives of the governments of the member states.

Not for the first time, or indeed the last, the Parliament was not altogether happy with this straightforward procedure. The Parliament had never enjoyed a formal role, or an informal one of any consequence, in negotiations concerning changes to the Treaties. As a result of not being party to the negotiations, it did not accept the Treaties with the high degree of respect automatically granted by the other institutions. For the Parliament the real bible is its own rules of procedure. Thus, when the Treaties have been amended such as by the Maastricht Treaty and, more recently, the Amsterdam Treaty, the Parliament has established its own elaborate version and interpretation of the new Treaty provisions by creating new, or amending its existing, detailed rules of procedure. By this means the Parliament has sought to impose obligations on other institutions, often taking advantage of vagueness in the Treaty texts. If something is not expressly forbidden in the Treaties, the Parliament sees no reason why it cannot be inventive and, of course, this will always be to the advantage of the Parliament against the other institutions.

Thus the Parliament proceeded to lay down detailed rules for fulfilling its role in the nomination procedure of the President and members of the Commission. The individual candidates, their future portfolios already identified, would have to appear at public hearings of the relevant

Parliamentary Committees and answer any questions put to them by members of the European Parliament. The Parliament saw an opportunity to establish procedures similar to those in the US Congress when appointments of ambassadors or judges to the Supreme Court are being made.

The Maastricht Treaty did not foresee this kind of procedure, and it was a direct challenge to the new incoming Commission. However, Jacques Santer, Prime Minister of Luxembourg, was the President designate of the new Commission and he accepted the new procedures being imposed by the Parliament. The other candidates for the Commission had little choice but to follow suit. The Parliament generated substantial publicity for the public hearings, and the media expectations were high. In reality the hearings turned out to be boring and repetitive. All of the nominees were highly qualified for the job, having already served as commissioners, as government ministers or as senior public officials.

Towards the end of the hearings some MEPs realised that the exercise was not working out as expected, and the media reaction would not be to Parliament's advantage. To rescue the operation the nomination of one or more of the candidates had to be called into question so as to create a bit of controversy and to send a message to the incoming commissioners that they would have to respect, if not obey, the wishes of Parliament.

Pádraig Flynn was Ireland's nominee for the Commission. He was already a member of the Commission primarily responsible for employment and social affairs. He was designated to retain this portfolio in the new Commission. He had already completed his hearing, which had passed off satisfactorily. During the hearing, he had been questioned about his controversial remarks concerning Mary Robinson during the 1990 Presidential election campaign, but this passed off without incident. In the private meeting of the Parliamentary committee members after the hearing, it was agreed to recommend Pádraig Flynn for nomination as a member of the Commission with the responsibilities as foreseen in his designated portfolio.

Within 24 hours Pádraig Flynn had been pinpointed as the candidate whose nomination was to be questioned, and in particular his competence as the Commissioner responsible for women's affairs in the light of his remarks during the 1990 presidential election campaign. The political reality of his being singled out had probably a lot more to do with the fact that he did not have the protection of the Socialists or the Christian Democrats, the two largest political groups in the European Parliament.

The pressure was now on Jacques Santer, and he eventually secured agreement to a compromise whereby Pádraig Flynn's responsibility for women's affairs would be shared with another Commissioner.

In this whole exercise the Parliament had established two new powers over the Commission which were not envisaged by the Treaties. Firstly, it had established a procedure of hearings of candidates for nomination to the Commission with their prospective portfolios already identified and, secondly, it had forced a change, although minor, in the allocation of portfolios. Once a precedent is established in the eyes of the European Parliament, it is cast in stone and becomes a foundation on which to build.

One may ask what role the Council played during this episode. The answer is simply 'none'. The Council, as an institution, does not have any role to play. The candidates for the Commission are put forward by the member states and they are formally appointed by the representatives of the member states. The question of how the candidates for nomination are to conduct their relations with the Parliament is a matter for themselves alone. Should the member states become unhappy with any procedures unilaterally imposed by the Parliament, they can always amend the Treaties. Such a happening is unlikely in the near future merely to address this issue.

Management of the budget

Recent developments in the relations between the Parliament and the Commission, arising from allegations of fraud, mismanagement and nepotism against the Commission, have further weakened the Commission against the Parliament. Over several months the members of one institution – the Commission – have had to endure sustained criticism and attack from the members of another institution – the European Parliament. In an effort to curtail the criticism and respond to the allegations, the Commission accepted a substantial number of demands from the Parliament. Nevertheless, the Parliament refused to grant a discharge to the Commission in relation to its management of the 1996 budget, it debated motions of censure in the Commission which did not have adequate support for adoption by qualified majority, and it established a committee of independent experts to investigate the allegations against the Commission. The publication of this Committee's first report on 15 March 1999 led to the resignation of the Commission as a whole within a matter of hours. This episode presents a good opportunity to examine the structural faults inherent in the European Parliament and which present regular problems for its relations with other institutions.

While the European Parliament can be compared with national parliaments in many ways, there are some fundamental differences. A government normally enjoys the clear support of the majority in a national parliament, as it is elected by the parliament and ministers will invariably be drawn from the elected representatives of the political parties in that majority. This brings about an automatic discipline in the running of parliament, with the government majority effectively in charge of the agenda. In the European

Parliament a government is not elected and its role in the appointment of the Commission is limited. Consequently, neither the Council nor the Commission is in charge of the agenda or conduct of Parliament, nor do they enjoy the regular support of the majority of its members to carry through their wishes.

In practice, the national political parties making up the governments of the member states cannot command a majority of the members of the European Parliament. It is often the case that in elections to the European Parliament there is a mid-term reaction against the government parties, thus returning a majority of opposition candidates. This scenario is illustrated by the fact that in March 1999 12 out of 15 prime ministers were socialist, but the Socialist Group, with one-third of MEPs, was a long way from having a majority in the European Parliament.

In reality there is no disciplined majority in the European Parliament, and it is often difficult to know who is in charge. Parliament's President holds a titular office with limited powers. The conference of presidents, made up of the leaders of the political groups, is probably the most influential body within Parliament, but its members are regularly frustrated by the divisions within their own political groups, not to mind the divisions between the groups.

Against this background of no majority in charge, it is easy for a loud minority to grasp the initiative. In the case of the allegations against the Commission mentioned above, motions of censure on the Commission were proposed and debated in January 1999. It was always clear that the necessary qualified majority of MEPs (absolute majority of MEPs plus two-thirds of those voting) would never be achieved to fire the Commission, so certain members shifted the debate to seeking the resignation of two individual named commissioners. The Treaties only provide a procedure whereby the Parliament can fire the Commission as a whole, and no right is granted in respect of firing an individual commissioner. It was argued that the absence in the Treaties of such a right meant that a motion calling for the resignation of an individual Commissioner was inadmissible. This argument was rejected because Parliament will never limit its possibilities where the Treaties are vague.

When the debate was over and the votes were counted, the clear result was that the Commission of Jacques Santer had been seriously damaged politically. Several prominent MEPs were quick to claim that Parliament had established its ability to fire individual commissioners. Yet the statistics of the various votes would indicate a somewhat different story. When votes were taken on motions to seek individually the resignations of two commissioners, the figures in favour were 165 and 155 respectively. However, when the motion to censure the Commission as a whole was put, 232 voted in favour out of 552 votes cast. Listening to the loudest MEPs would give one the impression that substantially more members were in favour of firing those individual commissioners identified in the allegations than in sacking the Commission as a whole. The votes speak otherwise, and indicate that MEPs were still a long way from seeking to fire an individual commissioner as opposed to sacking the lot. The resignation of the Commission following the publication of the report from the committee of independent experts and its subsequent treatment by Parliament will cast additional light on this subject.

Reflecting on these recent events brings to mind the procedure for the appointment of the next Commission, which got under way at the Berlin European Council Meeting. Parliament had already dictated how it wanted the procedure to apply when adopting a resolution in January 1999 – the European Council should not select its nominee for President until after the European Parliament elections are over, the political background of the President designate should correspond to the majority within Parliament, members of the Commission should be drawn from the ranks of MEPs, etc. Needless to say, none of these demands were inspired by the Treaties, and the European Council proceeded to propose Romano Prodi as the President of the next Commission.

This situation does, however, raise the scenario of what could be done should an institutional stand-off develop between Parliament and the member states over the nomination of the next President of the Commission or, indeed, some other fundamental issue, such as continuous disagreements on legislation under codecision. Should efforts to reach a compromise fail, there is no provision in the Treaties to dissolve the European Parliament and call new elections. It is unthinkable that the 15 member state governments would dissolve the national parliaments so as to seek a resolution to the impasse. As has often been the case in the evolution of the European Union, it has taken a crisis to force those in power to address a problem and find a solution. The next Intergovernmental Conference due to be convened in the coming year presents an opportunity to consider this scenario. Hopefully it will not be an item for discussion arising from a crisis.

Part III
Policies

Defence, peace-keeping and arms control

TONY BROWN

Introduction

In this essay I shall look at the history of the security/defence debate in the European Union as it has affected the discussion of European integration in this country. I shall also look at the related question of Ireland's role in peace-keeping and at the vexed question of the arms industry and arms control, with particular reference to the Irish stance on nuclear weapons.

My involvement in these areas has principally arisen from almost 20 years in the position of international secretary of the Labour Party. I held that honorary position throughout Dick Spring's leadership of the party, and had the privilege of working closely with him on the formulation of policy in these areas.

More recently, as an active member both of the European Movement (EM, formerly ICEM) and of the Institute of European Affairs, I have sought to contribute to rational debate in Ireland on the security/defence issue. There have been times when that has appeared to be a 'mission impossible'.

My approach to these questions has always been driven by the concept of a coherent Irish foreign policy grounded on clear principles, seen not as immutable 'tablets of stone' but as guidelines for dealing with ever-changing circumstances. I have also held a view of the European Union as first and foremost a zone of peace. In the words of Monnet's biographer, Francois Duchene, it 'will only make the most of its opportunities if it remains true to its inner characteristics. These are primarily civilian ends and means, which in turn express, however imperfectly, social values of equality, justice and tolerance.'[1]

That profound insight means, I submit, that the European Union, as such, does not have a vocation in the sphere of military power. Of course, the recent tragic phase of history in the Balkans has very clearly demonstrated that a Union without the political means to contribute positively and decisively to the solution of such crises is not meeting the wishes and aspirations of its citizens. Diplomacy, peace-keeping, humanitarian missions and, in the last resort, peace-making will all have a place and there must be adequate resources and institutions to deliver these, within the frameworks and guidelines provided by the United Nations and the Organisation for Security and Co-operation in Europe (OSCE).

Yet, as Dick Spring stated as Minister for Foreign Affairs in 1994, when discussing the possibility of air strikes against the Serb positions around Gorazde:

> these are not easy choices for the international community; nor easy things for an Irish Foreign Minister to contemplate. Every fibre of my being tells me that an international order cannot be built on the use of force. And this must remain the cornerstone of Irish policy. But the events in Gorazde have shown once again that where an aggressive power uses military force to achieve political and ethnic ambitions the world, acting with the full authority of the UN Security Council, must at some point be prepared to say stop and mean it.[2]

The Irish approach

Ireland has debated the question of European foreign and security policy over the past 30 years without ever achieving a really objective, thoughtful and balanced approach. Rather it has been tackled ideologically and emotionally. Roger MacGinty of Queen's University was very close to the truth when he gave a paper on Irish security policy the title 'Almost like Talking Dirty'.[3]

A particular aspect of the Irish approach has been the unhappy tendency to permit the most short-term party political interests to cloud and divert serious debate. This is most clearly seen in the Partnership for Peace (PfP) 'debate', much of which has shown an almost total disregard for facts or for the long-term national interest. This entirely voluntary arrangement, tailored to the needs of individual participating states, was initially welcomed by the Fianna Fáil/Labour government as an initiative which bridged the Cold War divide in Europe. It was recognised as having real interest for the defence forces in developing their capacity as a peace-keeping resource for both UN and OSCE. However, with the arrival in office of the Rainbow Coalition it was suddenly denounced in the new opposition circles as an exercise in military adventurism. A referendum, it was asserted, would be required before Ireland could sign up – to an arrangement which is not treaty-based and which could be entered or left at will, as demonstrated by Malta! The Rainbow itself fell victim to internal disputes on the issue, delaying the 1996 white paper on foreign policy for months.

Now the present Taoiseach has discovered that:

there is no fundamental reason of principle why we should not be prepared to participate in PfP arrangements with NATO on our own terms as all other European neutrals and even Russia have done[4]

and the Minister for Foreign Affairs has made it clear that no question of a referendum arises. Almost five years have been wasted on this.

These unhappy elements of the party political system have spilled over into the area of academic analysis and discourse. For example, in 1981 the Royal Irish Academy (RIA) organised a seminar on neutrality which was addressed by, among others, the Finnish statesman Kalevi Sorsa, who eloquently demonstrated the relevance of neutrality for his country in the Cold War situation then prevailing. The seminar arose from an original proposal from myself to the RIA national committee on international affairs. It was ritually condemned by the unique voice of Sean MacBride as a clear case of US/Trilateral Commission infiltration of the Irish body politic, and resulted in deep heart-searching in the academy's highest circles.

Shortly afterwards, organised vandalism led to the total abandonment of an EM seminar on the same subject. Ever vigilant, Sean MacBride admonished the EM for its collaboration with the CIA! It should be recalled that the same Sean MacBride, as Minister for External Affairs, actively worked for a bilateral defence pact with the USA when his republican principles got in the way of his desire to join NATO!

In the 1990s, the Institute of European Affairs (IEA) organised important seminars and studies on aspects of Ireland's place in the evolution of European security systems and institutions, under the expert direction of Professor Patrick Keatinge of Trinity College Dublin. The IEA rapidly found itself under attack from politicians and periodicals, armed with the usual arsenal of leaked documents and leaky logic, as the centre of yet another conspiracy.

At times it is very difficult to put up with the nonsense that is the stock-in-trade of some people who like to be heard on international affairs, who have remarkable access to the media and who expect the Irish people to believe that European capitals are devoted to sinister plots against this country. The absurd distortions about Jacques Delors and so-called 'resources wars' caused real concern to some Irish parents who were told that conscription to a European army would immediately follow the Single European Act in 1987 – and the Maastricht Treaty in 1993 – and, of course, the Amsterdam Treaty in 1998! Bertie Ahern has rightly expressed his impatience with those 'whose main role in life seems to be to whip up irrational fear'.[5]

Happily, current evidence is that organisations such as the RIA, the EM and the IEA, and others, have chosen to ignore the conspiracy theorists and are setting out to establish a sound basis of scholarship and analysis in this area, which must, in time, have a positive influence on both political and media discourse. The effort made to involve the greatest possible number of interested individuals and groups in the preparatory phase of the drafting of the 1996 white paper on foreign policy marked a genuine advance in this connection.

The Labour Party and the EC security debate

I became involved, over a number of years, in drafting a series of policy papers for the Labour Party on security-related matters. While these did not result in the desired in-depth debate, they did establish a basis for analysis of the changing international scene. The first of these papers was published in 1980 and it set out a number of principles of international policy, which, it was argued, should inform all of Ireland's foreign policy positions. A stance of military neutrality – and, in Cold War circumstances, of effective non-alignment – was seen at that time to be the correct interpretation of those principles. The document concluded with the assertion that 'it is only through a neutral and non-aligned position that a small country such as Ireland can play a worthwhile and positive role within the world community… Labour's commitment to neutrality is inspired by its concept of a world no longer divided into potentially warring camps but united by a shared objective of human and social development.'[6]

That 1980 paper was written in a period when the rhetoric of the Cold War had reached the point where Ronald Reagan was talking of the Soviet Union as the 'evil empire', while surrogate 'hot' wars were being fought in Central America and Africa. The US was embroiled in the Iran–Contra scandal, while the Soviet invasion of Afghanistan, with its overtones of Hungary and Czechoslovakia in the 1950s and 1960s, led to heated debate on the rights and wrongs of participation in the Moscow Olympics.

Ten years later, however, the Berlin wall had fallen and everything had changed utterly when President Mitterrand and Federal Chancellor Kohl wrote to Taoiseach Charles Haughey, as President of the European Council, in April 1990 to propose an Intergovernmental Conference (IGC) on political union, arguing that:

> in particular, the objective is to strengthen the democratic legitimation of the Union; render its institutions more efficient; ensure unity and coherence of the Union's economic, monetary *and political action; define and implement a common foreign and security policy.*[7]

The special European Council in Dublin later in the same month agreed to establish the parallel IGC which, in time, produced the three pillars of the Maastricht Treaty with its implications for security policy in Europe.[8]

As these developments unfolded, the need to revisit the principles underpinning Labour Party policy and to apply them to a new situation became obvious. Policy documents through most of the 1980s – such as the 1984 European election manifesto[9] – tended to arrive at the same conclusions as the earlier paper. However, the scale of the changes arising from the collapse of the communist system and the effective end of the divisions of the Cold War opened up new possibilities and raised new questions.

The debate within Labour on the Single European Act (SEA) saw the emergence of a growing commitment to long-term integration, replacing to a considerable degree the scepticism that had been at the heart of the 'no' campaign in 1972 and had been reflected in the 1979 European election campaign.[10] The arguments surrounding Title III of the SEA with its introduction of foreign policy and security issues into the Treaty framework led to a split which saw the Labour Party pragmatically adopting a neutral stance on the referendum while its leader openly called for a 'yes' vote on the grounds of overall commitment to the Community and its complex political and economic goals.

The Maastricht period saw significant movement in Labour Party thinking on European security. A 1994 paper, looking to the Intergovernmental Conference foreshadowed in the Treaty text, concluded that:

> in the period up to 1996 Ireland must argue and work – in close co-operation with like-minded member states and notably with new arrivals such as Sweden, Austria and Finland – for acceptable and progressive common policies capable of providing the whole of Europe with genuine security, disarmament and development and a defence policy at the minimum levels necessary to ensure peace and justice.[11]

The Maastricht Treaty itself led to particular problems, mainly in the area of interpretation. Its convoluted propositions about the special positions of member states within and outside military alliances made clarification in the heat of the referendum debate rather difficult.

And so the evolution of thinking has continued. The report of a special Labour Party committee on the IGC which led to the Amsterdam Treaty, with its minimal provisions on foreign policy and security, argued that:

> Ireland should play a positive role in the debate on a common defence policy. That debate should be based on a definition of European

security which recognises new geo-political realities and which is designed to end past divisions and produce pan-European policies and structures.[12]

Stressing the long-held Irish view on the unacceptability of nuclear force, the report supported the emerging role of the OSCE and clearly indicated that the Partnership for Peace arrangement 'on a tightly defined peace-keeping agenda is entirely compatible with Irish neutrality and would contribute constructively to the desirable concept of pan-European security, taking account of Russian sensibilities'.[13] Russia, of course, was an early participant in PfP.

The evolution of the European debate

The long history of the evolution of debate and decision on foreign and security policy within the European integration process goes back to the years immediately prior to the launching of the European Economic Community. The failed attempt in 1954 to establish a European Defence Community led to a concentration of thought and effort on new fields of co-operation. Thus, Monnet and his collaborators were quickly able to convince the leaders of the six countries which had responded to the Schuman Declaration of May 1950 by setting up the Coal and Steel Community that the path of economic partnership might actually lead them towards deeper political integration.

However, when Ireland applied for membership, the Taoiseach, Sean Lemass, in formally presenting that application to the EEC Council in Brussels in January 1962, placed a clear emphasis on the political objectives of the project.

> Political considerations, we know, played a considerable part in the motivation and the successful outcome of the negotiations for the Treaty and the aims of the European Economic Community go much beyond purely economic matters.... I desire to emphasise that the political aims of the Community are aims to which the Irish government and people are ready to subscribe and in the realisation of which they wish to play an active part.[14]

Significantly, Mr Lemass went further. Pointing out that Ireland had played an active role in the establishment of the OEEC and the Council of Europe, he stated that:

> while Ireland did not accede to the North Atlantic Treaty, we have always agreed with the general aim of that Treaty. The fact that we did

not accede to it was due to special circumstances and does not qualify in any way our acceptance of the ideal of European unity and of the conception... of the duties, obligations and responsibilities which European unity would impose.[15]

That effort foundered on the rock of French opposition to the inclusion of the UK in the Community. However, with recognition of the benefits arising from freer trade in an expanding market, the applications of the UK, Ireland, Denmark and Norway were reactivated in 1967. The emphasis at this time was very much on economic matters. When the then Taoiseach, Jack Lynch, addressed the Dáil in July 1967 most of his lengthy speech was devoted to the economic implications of entry, and he frankly admitted that he did not think that 'there is anyone in this House who is prepared to say that we should not seek participation in an enlarged European Community which includes Britain'.[16]

He did, however, echo Sean Lemass's views on the political finality of the integration project, arguing that 'the ultimate goal of the Treaty is essentially to bring about a united Europe through the fusion of national economies',[17] and went on to speak pointedly about the concept of shared sovereignty.

The second application also met with the de Gaulle *non*, and it was only with the departure of that remarkable figure from the Elysée in 1968 that the prospect of entry for this country and the other applicants became real. While entry negotiations were getting under way and Irish attention turned to sugar quotas and intervention regimes, the question of progress towards the political ideals of the Community surfaced within the Six.

In a move that was formally outside the Treaty framework, the leaders of the Six began to consider ways in which they might strengthen political co-operation. In 1970 they agreed to a proposal for twice-yearly meetings of foreign ministers 'in political co-operation', for the creation of a political committee of senior national civil servants, and the involvement of the then non-elected European Parliament. All such co-operation was to be based on consensus, with decisions taken unanimously.

None the less, the security/defence question became an issue in the 1972 referendum campaign in Ireland which culminated in an overwhelming – 83 per cent – vote in favour of accession. The main elements of the debate were economic, concentrating on the opportunities presented by the Common Agricultural Policy and on the continuing dependence of Irish business on the UK market, while the security issue arose mainly in connection with discussion of the limitations on sovereignty entailed in Community membership.

The Labour Party, which campaigned for an association agreement rather than full membership, argued that the government has gratuitously offered to abandon Ireland's policy of neutrality as an indication of its earnestness in seeking EEC membership. The Treaties of Rome and Paris require no such undertaking and any future political development of the Communities which involved defence would require a completely new Treaty. Nonetheless, the government has given public, but unsolicited, assurances of its willingness to enter into common defence arrangements with the other members of the European Communities. To do so would be to forfeit one of the few advantages which Ireland possesses in international politics, limited though it is.[18]

In October 1972, President Georges Pompidou convened a summit in Paris of the leaders of the Six and of the three applicant countries which had completed negotiations and ratified the formal arrangements for entry contained in the Accession Treaty. This meeting approved a remarkable communiqué which, *inter alia*, set 1980 as the date for EMU! This document, while largely devoted to economic and social concerns – it laid the basis for the Social Action Programme of 1974 drawn up by Dr Patrick Hillery as Vice-President of the Commission – took the political initiatives of 1970 a step further.[19]

The 1970 provisions for political co-operation were intensified, with more frequent meetings of ministers, and specific mention was made of security issues. The leaders pledged 'a concerted and constructive contribution' by member states to the Helsinki Process, which led eventually to the establishment of the Organisation for Security and Co-operation in Europe (OSCE). Thus, Ireland entered a Community that was about to extend its range of activities into clearly political fields.

1975 saw the publication of a document that significantly expanded the agenda. The 1974 Paris summit had requested the Belgian prime minister, Leo Tindemans, to define the term 'European Union'. He attempted to do so in a lengthy report which, at the time, was discussed mainly in terms of its proposals on institutional development. The report also contained the seminal statement that:

'European Union' implies that we present a unified front to the outside world. We must tend to act in common in all the main fields of our external relations, whether in foreign policy, security, economic relations or development aid. Our action is aimed at defending our interests but also at using our collective strength in support of law and justice in world discussions.[20]

Leo Tindemans went on to discuss a common foreign policy, relations between Europe and the United States, a new world economic order and security. On the last of these points he concluded that:

> during the gradual development of the European Union, the member states will therefore have to solve the problems of maintaining their external security. *European Union will not be complete until it has drawn up a common defence policy*.[21] (my italics)

The circumstances that led, during the second half of the 1970s, to the second round of Community enlargement negotiations brought the security/defence issue more clearly on to the agenda. The London Report of 1981 first mentioned security as a matter for discussion and co-operation between member states, and laid the basis for changes in the system of political co-operation including the establishment of a small, permanent secretariat in Brussels, the 'troika' approach to international representation of the EC, closer involvement of the Commission in international political matters, and the introduction of a crisis response procedure.

As the 1980s moved on, the security issue became of increasing relevance. The Genscher–Colombo plan of 1981, the consequent 1983 Stuttgart declaration on European Union and the European Parliament's 1984 draft Treaty Establishing the European Union created a momentum which transformed political debate and led to the extraordinary period between 1986 and 1997 in which three major reforms of the Community's Treaty base took place, which between them brought security and even defence to the centre of debate and, in Ireland, controversy.

The new phase began with the establishment, in 1984, of the *ad hoc* committee on institutional affairs under the chairmanship of Senator Jim Dooge, the former Irish Foreign Minister, which was asked to bring forward ideas on the changes needed in Community structures to meet the growing challenges of the 1980s. The Committee reported in 1985, and proposed the establishment of an Intergovernmental Conference to prepare Treaty amendments.

Speaking in the Seanad on the report of the Dooge committee, the then Taoiseach, Dr Garret FitzGerald, drew attention to a section of the report which dealt with security and defence matters. He pointed out that the Committee report contained proposals that went beyond the existing provisions for political co-operation and that were seen by the government – and by Senator Dooge himself, who dissociated himself from them – as 'more appropriate to military alliance frameworks'.[22] The report contained a section devoted specifically to security and defence, which envisaged 'developing and strengthening consultation on security problems as part of political co-operation' to include evaluation of external threats.[23]

A major driving force at that time was the commitment to move towards a single market. The so-called 1992 project dominated Community life and legislation from 1985, and necessitated the formulation of the Single European Act. This was based to a considerable degree on the Dooge Committee recommendations. It was chiefly designed to ensure the passage of the nearly 300 pieces of legislation needed to facilitate the single market project, and thus extended qualified majority voting in Council. But it also contained a new Title on European political co-operation, thus bringing this subject within the formal Treaty framework for the first time. Title III provided that member states should be ready to co-ordinate their positions more closely on the political and economic aspects of security.

The Single European Act was adopted by the Luxembourg meeting of the European Council in December 1985 and the text was finalised early in 1986. For a variety of reasons, the Irish government, which was advised that the Single Act could be ratified simply by the Oireachtas as an amendment of the Rome Treaty, delayed the start of the ratification procedure so that formalities were completed at a moment very close to the deadline. It was then that Raymond Crotty launched his initiative to have the Single Act declared unconstitutional on the grounds that Title III affected Irish sovereignty in international relations to such a degree that it could only stand if approved by the people in a referendum. Although the High Court ruled in favour of the government, Raymond Crotty took his case to the Supreme Court, where he won the victory that delayed final ratification of the SEA by six months and ensured that all subsequent Treaty amendments would automatically be put to the people.

The judgment of the Supreme Court in the Crotty case is a significant milestone in the consideration of Ireland's position in relation to European foreign and security policy. The concluding passage of the judgment of Mr Justice Brian Walsh contains the distillation of the majority opinion of the court:

> The freedom to formulate foreign policy is just as much a mark of sovereignty as the freedom to form economic policy and the freedom to legislate. The latter two have now been curtailed by the consent of the people to the amendment of the Constitution which is contained in Article 29.4.3 of the Constitution. If it is now desired to qualify, curtail or inhibit the existing sovereign power to formulate and to pursue such foreign policies as from time to time to the government may seem proper, it is not within the power of the government to do so.... To acquire the power to do so would, in my opinion, require a recourse to the people.... In my view, the assent of the people is a necessary prerequisite to the ratification of so much of the Single

European Act as consists of Title III thereof. On these grounds I would allow this appeal.[24] (Article 29.4.3 is the 1972 amendment on EEC accession.)

The referendum campaign saw the security issue moving to the centre of debate, with much intense argument about the meaning of 'the political and economic aspects of security'. This was still within the Cold War era, but the implications of European Community enlargement to the South and the increasingly volatile situation in central Europe raised demanding questions about the future political role of the Community, which clearly required a response. However, the debate brought out much talk of threats to neutrality and a disturbing tendency to categorise many of our European partners as aggressive. In the final analysis, the campaign on the ground came to concentrate on the importance of the single market and on the significant advantages to Ireland of the regional and structural policies – linked under the new concept of cohesion – that would accompany the 1992 project. A relatively small turn-out – 44.1 per cent – saw the SEA endorsed by a margin of 69.1 per cent to 30.9 per cent.

The impetus created by the single market project, the moves towards an enlargement involving three traditionally neutral states and the historic events of 1989–1991 combined to push the Community towards further integration. The decision to convene an Intergovernmental Conference on the long-studied and much-discussed issue of monetary union was paralleled, and complicated, by the addition of an IGC on political union. At Maastricht, in December 1991, these two processes converged in the almost incomprehensible text of the Treaty on European Union. The concept of a three-pillar Union emerged as the policy areas of justice and home affairs, and common foreign and security policy, were distinguished institutionally from the economic, social and monetary dimensions, which were to lead to the single currency and the social chapter.

On the security and defence front, Maastricht introduced measures for the strengthening of foreign policy co-operation, including the new concept of 'joint actions' to be taken by the Union in a co-ordinated manner. In the controversial Article J4, it stated that the common foreign and security policy 'shall include all questions related to the security of the Union, including the eventual framing of a common defence policy, which might, in time, lead to a common defence'.[25] The Western European Union was referred to as 'an integral part of the development of the Union' and the text was equipped with declarations and protocols spelling out various options for the practical implementation of agreed policies.[26] The Treaty included clauses providing for the circumstances of a country such as Ireland remaining outside alliance structures.

The Maastricht referendum campaign once again saw a largely superficial debate on security questions, but with the usual mixture of evasion and exaggeration. Those promoting a 'yes' vote chose to defer discussion of some of the more complex questions by referring to the provision in the Treaty for a further Intergovernmental Conference in 1996 charged with looking at institutional and security matters in the context of the likely further expansion of the Union to the East. As the Union was on the brink of the 1995 enlargement to Finland, Austria and Sweden, the challenge of expansion had weighed heavily on the Maastricht deliberations. But the decisive issue in the 1992 referendum was the promise of substantial funding for development projects under the terms of the so-called Delors II package of structural and cohesion aids. On 18 June 1992, a turn-out of 57.3 per cent saw the Treaty ratified by 69.1 per cent to 30.9 per cent.

The final chapter of the story to date was written at Amsterdam in June 1997, when yet another Treaty amendment was agreed by the European Council. This was intended to provide a sound basis in both policies and institutional provisions for the huge project of enlargement to the countries of Central and Eastern Europe. It turned out to be modest in its outcome, with many key decisions deferred to a later date because of the major internal differences on such questions as the size of the European Commission and the extent of qualified majority voting.

On security, little of real substance changed, although important steps were taken to enhance the foreign policy capacity of the Union by establishing a policy and planning unit and creating the position of high representative of the Union in foreign policy matters. Speaking on the new Treaty in Dáil Éireann, the minister for Foreign Affairs, Ray Burke, said that:

> the outcome on security and defence is satisfactory from Ireland's standpoint. Although many of our EU partners wished to see substantial movement towards common defence arrangements, this has not happened.[27]

The Treaty did make provision for greater EU capability in peace-keeping and related tasks through the incorporation of the so-called Petersberg tasks, which the minister saw as fully in line with Ireland's traditional role under the UN's aegis.

There had been some discussion, in the preparatory stages, of possible moves towards a stronger concept of common defence policy and, even, common defence arrangements. These did not materialise because of the serious divisions among the various alliance members and the concerns of the now much stronger 'neutral' grouping within the Union. Defence policy emerged as very much a peace-keeping/peace-making role in line with the Petersberg Tasks while, as the Taoiseach, Bertie Ahern, insisted:

> the Treaty of Amsterdam in effect makes the question of any future EU common defence subject to a number of locks… if anything, the Treaty of Amsterdam has made an EU common defence less, not more, likely.[28]

The referendum debate, seriously affected by the impact of the McKenna judgement on campaign funding and the related broadcasting restrictions, was notable for its lack of transparent information on either side and of a serious 'yes' campaign on the part of politicians whose real attention was on the concurrent campaign on the Good Friday Agreement. The content of the security debate was of an even lower level than usual, with assertions that acceptance of the Treaty would result in 'body bags' bringing home Irish conscripts. However, the failure to provide clarity on many aspects of the text provided an opening for a telling slogan – 'If you don't know – vote no' – and the poll on 22 May 1998 saw a surprisingly low turn-out of 54 per cent return a 62–38 acceptance of the Treaty of Amsterdam, the worst result in any European poll in Ireland to date.

Peace-keeping

Ireland has established a role and reputation in the field of peace-keeping of which the nation can be proud, and which must be seen as the basis of the key themes and values in Irish foreign policy. Since 1958, 42,000 Irish troops and Gardaí have participated in United Nations peace-keeping missions, of whom 76 have died in the service of world peace. At the time of writing, Irish personnel are active in eleven UN missions, including the SFOR peace-enforcement project, under NATO leadership, in Bosnia-Herzegovina.

Irish participation in peace-keeping has been carried out under the relevant Articles of the UN Charter and subject to specific Irish legislation. In 1993, the Defence Act was amended to provide for participation in the UNOSOM II operation in Somalia, which was designed to enforce a settlement. Dáil Éireann gave specific approval in 1997 for the deployment of personnel in SFOR, and in 1999 for participation in KFOR.

Recent initiatives on nuclear testing and non-proliferation by the present Foreign Minister, David Andrews TD, follow directly in this tradition. Thus, it is very clear that Ireland rejects nuclear weapons, which are widely perceived as beyond any reasonable bounds of civilised acceptability. It is therefore clear that Ireland cannot accept membership of a security arrangement which maintains a nuclear capacity. For many – including the present writer – this concern, above all others, lies at the heart of the debate on Ireland and NATO.

The 1996 white paper on foreign policy points out that:

> the classic peace-keeping operation of the Cold War era was primarily concerned with policing a ceasefire and containing tension. In response to the changing international situation, the nature and scale of peace-keeping operations have altered significantly.[29]

Operations now extend to organising and monitoring elections, participating in civil administration, monitoring human rights situations and assisting with refugee crises. They further extend to preventive deployment and, of course, there is an increasing call for the ultimate commitment to peace enforcement, with its attendant complexities and dangers.

Enforcement is clearly envisaged in the UN Charter. In the past, enforcement operations did take place through the mandating of groups of UN member states, as in Korea in the 1950s and in the Gulf War with Iraq. More recently, the issue of enforcement has arisen in the former Yugoslavia, notably in Bosnia-Herzegovina. The main question here is the evident incapacity of the UN itself to carry out such missions, given its lack of command structures and capability to move personnel and military hardware. This has led to the effective subcontracting of the SFOR operation to NATO. Questions thus arise for Ireland. The white paper sets down two issues for consideration – the basic attitude to such operations, and the approach to be taken to mandates for non-UN forces.

Irish policy has been clearly set down in the white paper. Central to this policy are the principle that 'the objectives are clear and unambiguous and of sufficient urgency and importance to justify the use of force' and the insistence that 'diplomatic efforts to resolve the underlying disputes should be resumed at the earliest possible moment'.[30]

The Somalia experience was that basic requirements for success were not present, with the result that the operation was badly flawed. Irish troops were withdrawn from that mission, but the lessons learned have been applied subsequently in preparations for the SFOR operation. Ireland is prepared to see the development of the OSCE as a suitable regional peace-keeping organisation, in collaboration with the UN. The breadth of the OSCE membership gives it a particular legitimacy.

Ireland is contributing to the training of peace-keeping personnel by the establishment of the specialist UN training school at the Curragh. The question of appropriate training and preparation for peace-keeping arises in connection with the debate on Irish participation in the Partnership for Peace. The PfP can provide a framework within which to undertake 'joint planning, training and exercises to strengthen states' abilities to undertake peace-keeping, search and rescue and humanitarian missions'. PfP is a truly pan-European organisation and I personally have seen, in the past year, much evidence in airports across Central and Eastern Europe of the movement of troops from countries as diverse as Denmark, Croatia, Ukraine and Latvia to and from PfP exercises. PfP has rapidly established itself as a key player in the evolution of joint security and confidence-building efforts in the wider Europe.

Disarmament and arms control

In very much the same way as peace-keeping, disarmament and arms control are characteristic elements of the most positive part of Irish involvement in world security. They merited a lengthy chapter in the 1996 white paper, which states that:

> Ireland's approach to issues of disarmament and arms control is closely linked to other aspects of our foreign policy. For example, there are close links with our policy on human rights abuse – the prohibition of inhumane weapons, the elimination of weapons of mass destruction and control on arms exports are all issues with a strong human rights dimension.[31]

There is also a perceived link with Third World development policy, since it is an unhappy fact that scarce resources are too often diverted to arms purchases by regimes in the poorest countries, to the benefit only of the arms industry and its greedy dealers.

Irish policy has always been to maintain only the minimum level of weapons needed for the relatively small national defence forces. The country – despite some concern about the controversial issue of 'dual use' products of the electronic and engineering sectors – does not have an indigenous arms industry and is not dependent on armaments exports. This situation has, however, led to some criticism of Ireland's assertion of neutrality. I vividly recall the astonishment of an Irish minister who was quizzed at length, by a Swiss socialist politician attending a seminar on neutrality which I organised during the 1980s, on the level of Irish industrial preparedness to support our army in the event of an invasion. The visitor could not understand our lack of military provision, declaring that a neutral country must be ready at all times to defend its chosen status.

Ireland has always supported moves, within both the UN and the EU, to control the arms industry and arms exports. This is a difficult matter, since arms manufacture is a major employer in many of our European partners, and a top export earner. One of the positive elements of the Amsterdam Treaty was the conclusion that there must be a concerted world-wide effort to regulate arms exports and an acceptance that any EU co-operation on armaments production must be paralleled with effective controls on exports in line with agreed principles.

Perhaps the most important and consistent element of Irish foreign policy has been the effort to achieve nuclear disarmament and to halt nuclear proliferation. Resolution 1665, which was adopted unanimously by the general assembly on 4 December 1961, is still referred to as the 'Irish resolution': '...[it] contained the essence of the Non-proliferation Treaty which over the past 25 years has developed into a strong, global norm of nuclear non-proliferation'.[32] With this seminal initiative the name of External Affairs Minister Frank Aiken will always be honourably linked. He strongly demonstrated how a small country can play a positive role on the world stage.

Ireland supports all international moves to ban chemical and biological weapons, and is fully committed to the campaign against landmines. Dick Spring's remarks, quoted above, about the use of force and the need to seek a world order in which military options are truly the last resort reflect the basis of Irish policy under all governments – a policy which reflects a clear national consensus. All forms of militarism are rejected, and there is an understanding, in a country which has a genuine empathy for the developing countries in their search for a more just world order, that Willy Brandt was right when he memorably commented that 'weapons do not make mankind safer, only poorer'.

Conclusion

Addressing a European Movement conference in 1996, Patrick Keatinge spoke of European security as a subject which, compared to economic and monetary Union, 'is a less clearly defined aspect of the current debate on European integration'.

He went on to suggest that:

> the relative unfamiliarity of security policy derives from Ireland's experience of Europe's security problems... [which] has been a good deal less traumatic than that of most European states during this century. We are more relaxed about it, and perhaps just a little complacent.[33]

He argued that there is a need 'to create for all of Europe that same balance between political stability and peaceful change which was achieved for western Europe between 1945 and 1989'. Then, there is the objective of coping 'in the short term with the consequences of the breakdown of political authority, including the sort of internal war we have seen in the former Yugoslavia....'. And there is the troublesome issue for this country of 'collective self-defence, based on the promise, in the legal form of a mutual assistance guarantee, to offer military assistance to another member state which has been attacked'. Many European states desire such guarantees, as the recent expansion of NATO to Hungary, Poland and the Czech Republic clearly indicates. This is an understandable position for those states, but one that must, from an Irish viewpoint, be seen in the light of the case for nuclear and conventional disarmament. We must face up to the fact that this debate will continue for the foreseeable future, and that it will pose key questions for Irish politics. While Amsterdam has weakened the impetus in the EU itself, these issues are not likely to go away, as recent initiatives by both the British and German governments demonstrate.[34]

My concluding point is that we must be prepared to enter into that debate positively and with full understanding. This is not an issue that can be dealt with by the incantation of slogans from another era. Nor can it be constantly deferred in the search for a quiet life. It is certainly not a matter to be approached with that 'holier than thou' attitude which too often displays a particularly repugnant arrogance. Above all, it is a subject that requires sober and well-resourced analysis and open discussion.

The long-standing tendency to avoid the debate is being successfully countered by the work of a number of organisations and individuals. The existence of relevant Oireachtas committees is a most positive development. But it remains a fact that even this advance has yet to be matched by the provision of proper back-up. What is needed now is the will to provide the funding and human resources necessary to ensure that all sides of the debate can be developed on a sound basis of research and study. This presupposes the political courage to withstand inevitable distortions and calumnies from those with an agenda that is transparently isolationist, reactionary and anti-European. There must be a willingness to copy the model of other, more enlightened, European countries, where parliamentary committees, institutes and think-tanks are well staffed and well financed and, in return, expected to give value to the tax-payer in terms of informed public debate on issues of prime national significance.

Disclaimer

This chapter is an expression of personal opinion, which does not reflect the policies or views of the EBRD.

NOTES

1   Duchene, Francois, quoted in Laursen, F. (1991) 'Towards a Common EC Foreign and Security Policy', 2nd International Conference of the European Community Studies Association, George Mason University, Fairfax, Virginia.
2   Spring, Dick (1994) Speech by the Tánaiste and Minister for Foreign Affairs to the Association of European Journalists, Dublin, April.
3   MacGinty, R. (1994) 'Almost like Talking Dirty: Irish Security Policy in Post-Cold War Europe' Annual Conference of the Political Studies Association of Ireland, Belfast, October.
4   Ahern, Bertie (1999) Address by the Taoiseach to the UCD Cumann of Fianna Fáil.
5   Ahern, Bertie (1999), op. cit.
6   Labour Party (1980) 'Ireland: A Neutral Nation', Policy Paper No. 1.
7   Communication from President Francois Mitterrand and Chancellor Helmut Kohl to the Taoiseach, Charles J. Haughey, President of the European Council, April 1990.
8   Presidency Conclusions of the Special European Council, Dublin, 28 April 1990.
9   Labour Party (1984) 'The European Community', Policy Paper No.5.
10 Labour Party (1979) 'Ireland and the European Community', Policy statement for the European Parliament elections.
11 Labour Party (1994) Policy statement: 'Security and Neutrality: Principle in Foreign Policy'.
12 Labour Party (1996) Report of Special Committee on the Intergovernmental Conference. Adopted by the General Council, September.
13 Labour Party (1996), op. cit.
14 Lemass, Sean (1962) Statement by the Taoiseach to the Council of Ministers on Ireland's application for membership of the European Economic Community, Brussels, 18 January.
15 Lemass, Sean (1962) op. cit.
16 Lynch, Jack (1967) Statement to Dáil Éireann by the Taoiseach on the reactivation of Ireland's application for membership of the EEC, 25 July.
17 Lynch, Jack (1967) op. cit.
18 Labour Party (1971) Statement on Irish entry into the EEC.
19 Conference of the Heads of State or Government of the European Community (1972) Communiqué issued on 20 October.
20 Tindemans, Leo (1975) 'European Union', Report to the European Council, December.
21 Tindemans, Leo (1975) op. cit.

22 FitzGerald, Garret (1985) Statement by the Taoiseach to Seanad Éireann on the Report of the Dooge Committee, 26 June.

23 Ad Hoc Committee on Institutional Affairs (Dooge Committee) (1985) Report to the European Council at Milan, June.

24 Walsh, Mr Justice (1987) Judgment delivered in the Supreme Court on 9 April 1987, in the case of Raymond Crotty and an Taoiseach and others.

25 Treaty on European Union (1993).

26 Treaty on European Union (1993).

27 Burke, Ray (1997) Statement of the Minister for Foreign Affairs to Dáil Éireann on the Treaty of Amsterdam.

28 Ahern, Bertie (1998) 'The Amsterdam Treaty', Address by the Taoiseach to the Institute of European Affairs, Dublin, 3 March.

29 Government of Ireland (1996) 'Challenges and Opportunities Abroad', white paper on foreign policy, Dublin, Department of Foreign Affairs.

30 Government of Ireland (1996) op. cit.

31 Government of Ireland (1996) op. cit.

32 Government of Ireland (1996) op. cit.

33 Keatinge, P. (1996) 'Security Policy as a Core Issue', Paper presented to the European Movement Conference, Dublin, 22 March.

34 German government proposals on ESDI, March 1999.

14

Regional policy and Ireland

WILLIAM G. CARROLL
AND THOMAS BYRNE

Introduction

Since the 1930s, almost all developed countries have implemented regional policies in order to achieve defined physical, social, economic and political goals. The objectives of such policies usually include the stimulation of development in backward and disadvantaged areas of the territory, the promotion of balanced development and an equitable distribution of economic activity, income, and access to opportunity. Concerns about equity and social justice, a desire to share the fruits of national economic growth and prosperity, and the elimination of inter-regional disparities have been among the principal factors influencing governments to promote regional policies. The European Union as a transnational entity has also been concerned about regional convergence on a Union-wide basis. This essay sets out to identify the policy objectives and instruments employed by the European Union in regional development and their impact in an Irish context.

Background to development of regional policy in Ireland

A central component of regional development policies is the definition of the 'region'. While initially this may seem a relatively easy task, it becomes clear that a certain ambiguity is attached to the term, not least when the entire country may for certain purposes be termed a region, as in the case of Ireland for EU assistance up to 1999.

Geographical regions can be classified as *homogeneous* regions, which are effectively constant in some principal characteristics such as physical features, land form and common cultural traditions, and *nodal* regions, which are noted for their people and economic and social interests focusing upon nodal centres for trade, administration and services. Regions are very often defined by *political circumstances* and to suit planning, administrative, functional or other particular purposes. There is a general absence of consistency in the designation of regions in different countries, and this tends to fluctuate over time as physical, economic, political and other factors change.

In Ireland it is almost impossible to define the 'region' as the term is in common currency, it being used in many different contexts. There are no historic or cultural regions apart from four vestigial 'provinces'. Yet there is a proliferation of 'regions' in use in Ireland for different purposes, as many national bodies with local responsibilities organise and operate on a regional basis, albeit for the most part in a differently constituted set of regions and, to a great extent, independently of each other. This, together with a traditional strong loyalty to the county, contrives to make a definition and understanding of the 'region' in Ireland somewhat problematic.

Provision for regional structures in Ireland initially emerged in the Town and Regional Planning Act 1934, but the Act's provisions had little impact. It was not until the 1950s that public policy-makers focused on the need to promote and assist economic development and to attract foreign investment, particularly to the poorer areas of the state. The enactment of the Undeveloped Areas Act 1952, which contained intervention measures to be implemented on a spatially selective and positive discrimination basis in favour of designated poor areas of the country, marked the beginning of Irish regional policy. The Act introduced a scheme of grants and subsidies as inducements to industry to locate in designated western counties to create long-term employment in areas where manufacturing firms would not normally locate without the availability of financial incentives. Although the large body of legislation that emerged in the following years – which contained grants and subsidies schemes to assist industrial development – was geared towards achieving the objective of increasing national economic performance, its effect was also to impact positively on regional development.

The economic growth experienced in the late 1950s and early 1960s highlighted the need for spatial planning. This saw the introduction of a comprehensive local physical planning framework through the enactment of the Local Government (Planning and Development) Act 1963, which empowered local authorities to facilitate industrial and commercial development, to influence its location through zoning policy and to secure renewal and redevelopment of run-down urban areas.

In its 1969 statement on regional policy, the government announced the establishment of a Regional Development Organisation (RDO) in each of the nine physical planning regions that had been designated in 1964. The RDOs, composed of representatives of planning authorities at both elected member and official level and of other public authorities and government departments, were to be given a remit to co-ordinate the programmes for regional development in each region. The bodies had an advisory and co-ordinating role in relation to regional planning, investment and development and they provided advice to government on implementation of regional policy. They also prepared regional development strategies for their regions in the shape of regional plans based on assessment of overall development needs, objectives and priorities. Although they were non-statutory and not possessing executive functions or any significant resources, the creation of the RDOs was an important formal recognition of the regional dimension of economic and development policy and of the value of co-ordination and a local input into the development process.

The RDOs were abolished as part of a government package of budgetary cost-cutting measures in 1987. Their demise left a void at the regional level which, a mere two years later, it was necessary to fill. Mindful of the European Commission's desire to promote the partnership principle, the government established a regional structure to advise and assist in the preparation of the national development plan for the 1989–93 round of the enlarged structural funds. This structure was based on seven regions (not on the nine planning regions that were in existence since 1964) and comprised: (a) working groups representative of government departments, state agencies and local authority managers, and (b) advisory groups composed of local authority chairmen and representatives of the social partners and interest groups. There was much local and regional criticism of these arrangements, particularly as the shape and content of the national plan that was submitted to the Commission bore little resemblance to the regional submissions. It was generally felt that the arrangements represented something of a 'cosmetic' exercise to satisfy the desire of the Commission for regional consultation and involvement in the process. As a result, the two groups were merged to form sub-regional review committees.

The Barrington committee, set up by the government to advise on local government reform, concluded that there was a clear case for a regional level of government and recommended the establishment of regional authorities based on eight regions consisting of groups of entire counties. The government response to the Barrington committee's recommendations on the regional tier represented a typically minimalist approach and the traditional reluctance to embrace regionalism in any real sense.

The eight regional authorities were created on 1 January 1994, with different geographical areas from those recommended (the proposed East region was subdivided into the Dublin region and the Mid-east region, while the proposed North-east and North-west regions were amalgamated into the inhomogeneous border region). In addition, the powers and functions of the authorities were considerably changed. Instead of overseeing co-operation between authorities, the regional authorities were to promote co-ordination. They were given no responsibility for the direct provision of any services or any role in proposing specific projects, determination of priorities or resource allocation. That the regional authorities were designed to be weak is clear from the nature of the powers and functions assigned to them, from the meagre resources given to them and, most graphically, from the limitations to their competencies spelled out by the minister for the environment shortly after their establishment. Despite these constraints, the authorities have played a positive and useful role in providing co-ordination, in monitoring, reviewing and advising on the spending of EU funding and in the articulation of the needs and priorities of their regions.

Regional planning has had an intermittent existence. It had a meaningful presence during the time of the RDOs in the 1970s and up to 1987 and it has some relevance again since 1994 through the regional authorities. However, as stated above, there are considerable limitations on the authorities in achieving effective regional planning and co-ordination within their regions. The focus of national planning has been on achieving national economic and social development and progress, and a spatial dimension has generally been absent.

Overview of EU policy on regions

The EU's aims to promote harmonious development by reducing the economic differences between the various regions and the backwardness of the less favoured regions provided the impetus for its strong emphasis on regional policies to promote integration, social and economic convergence and cohesion across the member states and regions of the Union.

The European Union has employed a number of instruments, including regional policy and social policy, to promote and assist regional development.

In the early days of community regional and social policy there was only limited direct Community involvement in the implementation of the individual national policies – projects were supported without any overall purpose. Indeed, very often these projects were in isolation, with little or no consideration for their inter-sectional impact.

The accession of Spain and Portugal in 1986 added new impetus by bringing a widening of regional inequalities and doubling the population of the Community living in regions with average income per head of less than half the Community average. The Single European Act, adopted the following year, committed member states not only to establishing a single market but also to strengthening the Community's economic and social cohesion by reducing regional disparities.

In Objective 1 areas, defined as the less favoured regions in terms of income per head (measured by GDP), the aim was to promote economic development and structural adjustment. In Objective 2 areas, those with severe labour market imbalances linked to the decline in their industrial base, the aim was to strengthen and assist the readjustment of the local economy. In Objective 5b areas, those either agricultural or rural in character, the aim was similar to that in Objective 1 areas, of assisting adjustment and promoting development.

Three additional objectives without an explicit regional dimension were specified – combating long-term unemployment and helping young people to find work (Objectives 3 and 4) and promoting structural improvement in the agricultural sector (Objective 5a). In practice, significant shares of the funds aimed at Objectives 3 and 4 have also been allocated to Objective 1 regions in line with overall objectives.

In December 1992, at the Edinburgh summit, member states agreed to further increases of regional aid between 1993 and 1999, in the form of an expansion of the existing structural funds (from 21.3 billion ECU in 1993 to 30 billion ECU in 1999). They also agreed the creation of a new financial instrument, the cohesion fund (amounting to 1.5 billion ECU in 1993, rising to 2.6 billion ECU by 1999). This extension of support reflected the reiteration of the importance of economic and social cohesion in the Maastricht Treaty 1992, as well as concern about possible adverse effects on problem regions of the move towards monetary unification – a concern heightened by the likely consequences of the budgetary consolidation called for as a condition of membership of the monetary union. Eligibility for cohesion fund assistance is aimed at member states (rather than regions) having GNP per head less than 90 per cent of the Community average. Assistance is therefore restricted to Greece, Portugal, Ireland and Spain, and is conditional on the country concerned taking measures to bring public debt and government deficits to the benchmark levels specified in the Maastricht Treaty.

While there have been moves towards convergence, a number of impediments can be identified. These include the following.

- The imbalance in Community policy in favour of agricultural price policy.

- Agricultural price policy has not helped convergence, either in terms of actual measures it contained or in the way in which they were implemented.

- Structural measures were insufficient, were very often inappropriate, and only took on a real regional focus in the early to mid-1980s.

- Community expenditure on correcting regional structural imbalances was insignificant compared with the corresponding national expenditure, thus leading to some intra-national convergence but to international divergence.

The EU and Irish regional development

The decade prior to Ireland joining the EEC witnessed the issues of regionalism and regional development coming to the fore. Questions of how to promote, regulate and spread economic development elicited policy responses in the shape of three major regional planning studies, the creation of a large number of regional organisations and the publication of major regional policy statements by government. EEC membership in 1973, with the prospect of accessing significant grants and subsidies, and, to a lesser extent, the economic recessions that rapidly followed gradually shifted the focus away from regional development to concerns about national development and welfare. As a peripheral, poorly developed, agriculturally-dependent economy with a GDP per head of less than half the Community average, it was perhaps understandable that an ubiquitous attitude of squeezing money from Europe should have prevailed in the early years of membership. However, its continuance must be questioned, particularly as it has been pursued at the expense of a regional policy designed to address inter-regional disparities within Ireland.

Exposure to the ethos, values and policies of the EU and the availability of large amounts of funds have obliged Ireland to embrace a more analytical and methodical approach to regional development strategies. This involves planning, multi-annual programming and budgeting, *ex ante* and *ex post* evaluation by external experts, monitoring, adjustment and review of programmes. In addition, development strategies such as the national development plans have had to be agreed with the Commission, thus ensuring their co-ordination with the relevant policies of the EU and those of other member states. However, the designation of the entire country as a single region has been criticised as a paradox of Community regional policy that has effectively scotched domestic concern for formulating a balanced development of all regions in the country. The differences in regional economic performance and welfare as measured by gross value added (GVA) in the regional accounts published by the Central Statistics Office for 1991, 1993, 1995 and 1996 and the government decision in November 1998 to divide the country into two 'regions' at NUTS II (Nomenclature Statistical Territorial Units) level for the next round of structural and cohesion funds for the period 2000–2006 would bear out this view.

The EU principles of partnership, sustainability, respect for the environment and the bottom-up approach have found their way into Irish regional development strategy, even if the other key principle of subsidiarity has yet to gain a firm foothold. However, the desire of the EU for devolution of responsibilities and for a greater involvement of regions, and its constant exhortations in this regard, have resulted in the establishment of statutory regional authorities in Ireland in 1994 and more empowered structures in the new NUTS II 'regions' in 1999.

EU membership has facilitated and encouraged interaction and co-operation with other regions both within and outside the Union. Many of the community initiatives, innovative actions and pilot projects involve inter-regional and transnational co-operation, as in the case of the INTERREG programmes. Such interaction brings Irish regions into contact with different systems of government, policy and administration and generates mutual benefits from co-operation and the exchange of experience. Office-holders at both political and executive level had to become familiar with and expert in Community affairs and to devote a greater proportion of their time and attention to EU matters. Practically all ministers and their departments now interact on a regular basis with the EU, as do many subsidiary state agencies and authorities. However, due to our excessive degree of centralisation and the tight control exercised by government departments, especially by the department of finance, over policy implementation and funding, local government, regrettably, has had little or no direct involvement with the EU. This reflects the Irish antipathy to devolution and our proclivity to pursue a sectoral and fragmented approach to governance and policy implementation.

Impact of EU regional policies

From the time the country joined the EEC, Ireland has benefited from Community policies such as the CAP and the social policy. In addition, a significant flow of funds from the EAGGF, both the guarantee and guidance sections, from the ESF and from European Investment Bank (EIB) loans has been ever-present since 1973. The emergence of a regional policy, underpinned by the ERDF since 1975, considerably added to those benefits and financial flows for this country. Because of the evolution and development of more focused regional policies and the reform and expansion of the funds, their impact on Ireland has been greatest over the past decade.

Ireland in the early 1970s had a GDP per head of less than half the Community average. The country was heavily dependent on the agricultural sector, with about a quarter of the total workforce of Ireland engaged in farm work. In the case of industrial development, the state was not long after emerging from decades of protectionist policies and had just started to reap the fruits of the new outward-oriented approach. At entry to the Community the expectations for economic advancement were high, particularly for agriculture, which was a key sector in the national and regional economies. Those early years after accession witnessed a substantial inflow of funds under the CAP, which raised farm incomes and the performance of the agricultural sector in terms of output and exports. For example, between 1970 and 1978 prices for Irish agricultural products increased by a factor of 4.5, while aggregate farm income increased by 72 per cent, after allowing for inflation. Grants and subsidies received from the Community under all headings amounted to more than four billion pounds for the period from 1973 to 1983. At the same time the Irish contribution to the EC was less than 700 million pounds, with the largest proportion of net receipts coming from the guarantee section of the EAGGF. In the first 15 years of membership the financial transfers from the price support mechanism of the CAP were much more significant than receipts from the structural funds, such as the regional fund, the social fund and the agricultural guidance fund. By 1988, having considerably benefited from the impact of EC policies and funding, Ireland's GDP per capita had increased to 64 per cent of the Community average. It is since 1988 that the country has experienced the greatest impact of EU regional policy and the increased level of structural and cohesion funds.

Despite the progress made since 1973, Ireland's economic position in 1988 was still very poor *vis-à-vis* the average for the then twelve member states of the Community. GDP per head was 64.1 per cent, unemployment was the second highest, and the levels of the national debt, the exchequer borrowing requirement and the current budget deficit were very high. Other factors also affected Irish economic performance, such as the low level of private sector investment, major infrastructure weaknesses and educational underperformance of significant sections of the population. Thus, the 1988 reform of the structural funds and the commitment to double the budget by 1992 came at a most opportune time for Ireland. Despite the accession of Spain and Portugal, which brought strong competition for the enlarged funds, Ireland stood poised to claim a substantial share and to benefit accordingly.

The reform of the structural funds, which was agreed in 1988 and implemented from 1989, was an important watershed for regional policies at the Community level. It introduced a genuine Community vision of regional problems, whereas previous policy had essentially taken the form of intervention in support of the regional policies pursued by each member state individually. In the 1989–93 programming period the total financial transfers from the Community to Ireland in structural funds amounted to 4.5 billion ECU, or 253 ECU per capita. When the national exchequer and the private match-funding elements are added, the total scale of investment over this period amounted to 10.3 billion ECU. The EIB provided loans totalling 500 million ECU for Irish projects in the energy, transport and telecommunications sectors as well as for productive environment and vocational training schemes and for other infrastructure projects. This level of investment and financial transfers represented a huge increase in public capital expenditure in the 1989–93 period over previous years. Furthermore, the new programming approach involved a Community Support Framework (CSF) containing twelve operational programmes targeted at four priority areas. These were: (1) agriculture, fisheries, forestry, tourism and rural development, (2) industry and services, (3) human resources and (4) measures to offset the effects of peripherality. The CSF commenced the process of addressing the problems of these sectors, which was to continue in the following programming period.

The impact of the first five-year CSF was indeed tangible. Over the period Ireland achieved the highest growth of GDP of any member state, averaging 5 per cent per annum, compared with a Community average of 1.7 per cent. In addition, prudent fiscal policies contributed to reducing inflation and to improving the balance of payments and the budget deficit/GDP ratio to better than the Community average, although the level of unemployment remained high. The Economic and Social Research Institute (ESRI) has estimated that the effect of the structural funds interventions in this period was to raise the level of GDP by 2.6 per cent in 1992, with the peak impact on unemployment being around 31,000. It further asserts that:

> the advent of the first CSF in 1989 was particularly apposite given the prevailing pessimism about the future and the drive to cut all forms of public expenditure. The CSF encouraged a return to investment in public infrastructure at a crucial time. Without such investment the economy today would be encountering more problems of bottlenecks.

The EU also was well satisfied with the performance and impact of the policy measures and funding in the period, and proclaimed that 'the implementation of the Irish CSF (1989–93) achieved its goal at the end of 1993'.

EU regional policy for the 1994–99 programming period was formulated against the background of the completion of the Single Market, the objective of achieving EMU by the end of the century and moves towards greater integration. Recognising the need for increased solidarity and cohesion within the Community as a basis for economic and social progress, EU regional policy, with the enthusiastic backing of Commission President, Jacques Delors, called for and secured agreement for a massive increase in structural expenditure to promote economic and social cohesion. The Maastricht Treaty 1992, which had made economic and social cohesion one of its key pillars, upgraded the importance of EU regional policy and, as a result, the structural fund budget was increased from approximately 43.8 billion ECU over the 1989–93 period to over 141 billion ECU for 1994–99 (at 1992 prices). With 74 per cent of the total budget being allocated to Objective 1 regions, Ireland's share of the structural funds increased to 5.6 billion ECU, or 262 ECU per person per year. In addition, the indicative allocation to Ireland from the new cohesion fund for the 1994–99 period is 1.3 billion ECU, while EIB lending of 1.8 billion ECU is projected. EU funds together with public and private matched funding will represent a total investment of almost 12 billion ECU over the period.

The current CSF is being delivered through nine operational programmes targeting four priority areas – the productive sector, economic infrastructure, human resources, and local urban and rural development. Ireland has made enormous progress over recent years in achieving economic recovery and sustained high levels of growth and development. The impact of EU regional policy and the huge financial transfers have contributed in large measure to this process. In its mid-term review the ESRI concluded that the Irish CSF 'represents a notable success story' where 'capacity and capability has been increased in the productive sectors; there has been a quantum-leap in the provision of public infrastructure; education and training attainment forges ahead; and experimental institutional arrangements have galvanised local initiatives'. It further asserts that, without the support of the structural funds, congestion in public infrastructure and constraints in third-level education would have limited the economic recovery that has been achieved since 1989. The present CSF programming period has seen Ireland enjoy a sustained high annual level of economic growth, a significant increase in employment and a fall in the level of unemployment to single figures, a transformation of the public finances to a current budget surplus and one of the best debt/GDP ratios in the EU, and convergence to the EU average in terms of GDP per capita. The impact of the spending under all operational programmes has been positive, with the most visible impact being seen in the road improvement programme.

Regional impact

While the impact of the CSF on national economic development and performance has been very impressive, the impact at regional level has been more difficult to assess accurately due to the lack of defined regions for all purposes and the absence of reliable regional data, such as GDP/GNP figures, over any meaningful time-frame. Furthermore, it has long been recognised that there has been a tendency in Ireland to focus on the national and sectoral aspects of programmes – accompanied by a desire to maximise the receipt of EU funding – rather than on the regional impact of policies and programmes. The EU has charged that 'there has been little national debate over regional disparity, perhaps understandably given that Ireland as a whole forms a single NUTS II level region of the EC' and also alleges 'that "regional policy" has been more concerned with promoting industrial employment in the less developed regions to compensate for agricultural decline'.

Table 14.1. Ranking of regional performance under selected indicators

Region	Employ-ment growth 1993–96	Fall in unemploy-ment 1993–96	Growth in new private car registrations 1993–95	Change in long-term unemploy-ment 1993–96	Growth in R&D expenditure 1993–95	Growth in tourism revenue 1993–95
Dublin	3	5	7	6	6	4
South-east	6	4	3	5	3	1
South-west	5	7	6	7	5	5
Mid-west	4	2=	1	2	4	7
West	7	6	5	8	7	8
Border	8	8	8	4	1	6
Midland	2	1	4	1	2	3
Mid-east	1	2=	2	3	8	2

Source: *Mid-Term Evaluation: Regional Impact of the Community Support Framework for Ireland 1994–97* (Fitzpatrick Associates, 1997)

Nevertheless, the mid-term evaluations of the CSF concluded that the impact on all Irish regions has been positive. Fitzpatrick states that the CSF target of having 1,220,000 in employment by 1999 had actually been achieved by 1995, that the economy is well ahead of target in relation to the CSF's macroeconomic performance indicators, a position that provides a very healthy background for the performance of the eight regions within Ireland. Using a range of indicators, the mid-term evaluation of the regional impact states that, with respect to the central objective of the CSF to ensure the best long-term return for the economy by increasing output, economic potential and long-term jobs and reintegrating the long-term unemployed and those at risk of becoming so into the mainstream, all regions appear to be sharing in the development of the Irish economy, even though the reintegration of the long-term unemployed has not been balanced across all regions.

Table 14.1 gives a comparison of regional performance over a range of selected indicators. It shows the uneven impact of EU-assisted policies and programmes and clearly points to the need for a more focused approach to the achievement of a better spatial distribution of enterprise and economic growth and the realisation of the stated national and CSF objective of ensuring the promotion of balanced regional development. The ESRI analysis of comparative regional performance, which 'suggests neither a convergence of performance nor a systematic tendency for the more prosperous regions to pull further ahead', would also lead to this conclusion and brings to mind other negative aspects of the Irish approach to regional development.

The impact of EU regional policies, of the large-scale financial transfers from the structural and cohesion funds and of the income and price supports under the CAP on Ireland's socio-economic development has clearly been very considerable, particularly over recent years. However, the impact has been predominantly economic and has impinged more on national than on regional development, while the impact at the political, institutional and administrative levels has been far less positive. The persistence in designating the entire state as a single region for the purpose of EU assistance and the over-preoccupation with maximising the draw-down of funding from Brussels have been clearly at the expense of effectively tackling and remedying the problem of disparities between the regions within Ireland. This approach has also been responsible for a marked absence of strategic and spatial planning and policy-making and for the pursuance of centrally driven, sectoral and fragmented development strategies with generally poor co-ordination at both the regional and local levels. The EU and its regional policies have not engendered any willingness on the part of Irish policy-makers to embrace and implement radical reform of government and public administration involving a deconcentration and devolution of power and responsibilities in accordance with the principle of subsidiarity.

The widespread unfamiliarity with EU affairs and the lack of contact and involvement with the EU on the part of local government is symptomatic of this centralised nature of Irish governance. This is in sharp contrast with the approach of other member states.

Future prospects for regional development in Ireland

Today, regionalisation has edged onto the political agenda in the context of the ending of Ireland's designation as a single region and the splitting of the country into at least two regions for the purpose of EU structural funds assistance in the period 2000–06. In the run-up to decisions on the next round we have seen robust debate on regional issues. The calls for continued Objective 1 designation for the Border, Midland and West regions and the proposals for greater regional and spatial emphasis mean that regional policy is now more than ever back on the political agenda. The European Commission's acceptance of the government's proposal for a two-region strategy for of the next round from 2000 to 2006 means that in addition to having different regimes for EU funding in different parts of the country, institutional structures, decision-making and implementation arrangements will require devolved structures. The European summit meeting of 26 March 1999 agreed a funding package that totalled IR£3.4 billion (4.25 billion euro). As we move towards a major decrease in the level of EU funding, critical analysis of our current needs is now necessary. These needs, substantially different from those of 1993, will in large measure focus on infrastructural bottlenecks in the economy. In determining priorities for these regions, the respective regional authorities have proposed regional development strategies to government which were expressed in the national development plan published in July 1999. The national development plan will form the basis for detailed negotiation with the European Commission regarding decisions on the nature and shape of the next round of funding after 1999.

Ireland's emergence as an economy that has moved from the lower to the higher stream has been aided in no small way by the influence of the European Union and its policies. Financial aid has been important, but there have also been intangible benefits, such as increasing openness in Ireland to European influences. Support for domestic policies, such as strong emphasis on education, attractive tax regime, and proactive inward investment has also been vital over a long period. If there is one lesson from the Irish experience for the less developed regions of the EU and the new applicant countries, it is that EU regional development funding is important, but without flanking domestic social and economic policies success will be restricted.

Conclusion

The EU has had, and continues to have, a major impact on its member states and their regions at political, administrative and economic levels, which has resulted in peace in Western Europe, progress towards integration and economic and social cohesion, and the fostering of co-operation between the states and regions of the Union. The EU has added a new dimension to the national political systems, and in its promotion of the diffusion of power and the interdependence of states it has eroded the power of national governments and their capacity to control their own destiny. As progress towards greater socio-economic and political integration continues, the EU's influence and impact on its member states is set to increase in the years ahead.

Ireland has been an enthusiastic member state since joining the Community in 1973, and the country has benefited to a great extent from its many policies, especially its regional policy. The receipt of large tranches of structural and cohesion funds as well as vast amounts of funding under the CAP has made a major contribution to the transformation of the Irish economy from one of the poorest at entry to a position where it is now converging with the Community average. Apart from the economic impact, the EU has influenced Irish policies and policy-making to the extent that its objectives, principles and regulations must be taken into account and complied with. This obligation has greatly improved the planning, implementation, monitoring and evaluation of public sector investment. An unfortunate failure in the Irish approach has been the obsession with accessing EU funds to the neglect of developing and implementing regional policies to address the reduction of inter-regional disparities within Ireland and the promotion of balanced regional development in the country. That this approach still persists is exemplified by the decision to regionalise the country for the purpose of maximising the amount of EU assistance for the state under the next round of structural and cohesion funds rather than because of any new conversion to the merits of regionalism. Moreover, Ireland has failed to embrace the principle of subsidiarity and to implement reform of government and people empowerment, preferring to maintain a highly centralised system, in contrast to the approach adopted in many EU member states.

15

Adjusting to industrial policy

LIAM CONNELLAN

Background

There have been many changes in European industrial policy since this country joined the then EEC in 1973. In the early days of membership, industry in Ireland had to adapt to the enormous corpus of European legislation which had been developed ever since the establishment of the EEC in 1957. As time progressed, Ireland sought to influence new measures being proposed, and to take initiatives which would stimulate more rapid development in this and other regions of the EEC.

The present writer was fortunate to have been involved as an Irish member of the executive committee of UNICE (the Confederation of European Industry) for the first 20 years of Ireland's membership, and also as an Irish member of the Economic and Social Committee of the European Communities, an advisory assembly to the European Commission, for a five-year period until 1994. For the purposes of this chapter, industrial policy is defined as all the main actions, whether economic, social or political, which have a direct impact on industrial development. The reflections that follow are personal. Before discussing the impact of the evolution of European industrial policy on Irish industry, it may be helpful to reflect on how Irish industry had developed prior to 1973.

When Ireland achieved independence in 1922, its industry was very underdeveloped and based mainly on agricultural raw materials. The first major policy change was the imposition of tariff barriers in 1932, partly in response to the Great Depression following the Wall Street crash, but also as a means to build up its infant manufacturing base. The imposition of tariff barriers was quite common in small European countries at this time. The protectionist policy was moderately successful, and Irish industry achieved a rate of expansion of about 3 per cent per annum until the early 1950s. It became attractive economically to set up a wide variety of food processing and packaging, final assembly, textile, clothing and furniture industries which were protected against competition by customs duties ranging from 40 to 60 per cent. Jobs were created in manufacturing, but costs were high due to the small scale of production for a home market of only 3 million. Exports were modest, as few of the firms outside industries such as brewing, distilling, and crystal glass could compete abroad. Even some of those, such as distilling, were encouraged to supply home market needs first before becoming involved in exporting. To ensure that industry remained in Irish control, the Control of Manufactures Act prohibited the setting-up of new manufacturing firms with majority foreign ownership. One of the main concerns of Irish industrialists during this period was to ensure that the tariff regime operated effectively and that no methods of circumventing it would be found by enterprising foreign competitors. While the overall effect of the extended period of protection and the active discouragement of inward investment had a suffocating impact, it is worth noting that two of the top five industrial firms quoted on the Irish stock exchange today were established during that era.

In the mid-1950s, industrial output was stagnant. Irish industry did not participate in the strong growth being experienced elsewhere in Europe during the post-war expansion. The country's trade balance deteriorated, and cash deposits equivalent to six months' imports had to be lodged in advance by importers in addition to the customs duty so as to slow down the flow of imports. Some commentators even began to question the economic viability of the state.

It was a happy coincidence that at this very time the original six member states were deciding to set up the European Economic Communities, or Common Market, by signing the Treaty of Rome in 1957. The EEC would create a mutual dependence between recent enemies to prevent a recurrence of war in Europe, and would create a customs union to achieve economies of scale in industry resulting in more competitive European firms on world markets.

In Ireland there were also signs of a new beginning. The phoenix of Irish enterprise was to rise from the ashes of the despair of the mid-1950s. The publication of the first programme for economic expansion in 1958 set a modest target of 2 per cent growth in the national economy over the following five years. While this may seem extraordinarily low today, it was a response to years of stagnation and had the desired effect of restoring confidence. By now the Control of Manufactures Act was repealed, foreign investment was encouraged and, most importantly, exports were stimulated by the introduction of a zero tax rate on any profits generated from export sales. The first foundations of modern Irish industry were thus put in place.

The next step was to start the process of removing protection. When Britain's initial negotiations to join what was then the EEC in 1963 were unsuccessful, it was clear that Ireland, which at that time was dependent almost exclusively on trade with Britain, could not contemplate joining alone. Nevertheless, the process of dismantling tariff barriers had to commence, and the Anglo-Irish Free Trade Area Agreement was negotiated whereby Ireland would retain Commonwealth preference for its exports to Britain, and the 40 per cent Irish customs duties on competing British imports would be eliminated in equal steps over a ten-year period. The agreement became operational in 1964. The first steps in preparing for wider European free trade were thus taken. Industry accepted the challenge with relish, the trickle of inward investment gathered momentum, and throughout the 1960s the output of industry in Ireland increased by 6 per cent per annum, the highest rate achieved since independence.

When Ireland's negotiations to join the EEC commenced, industry threw its full weight behind the campaign for membership. It was recognised that many firms, and even industries, viable behind what were still very high protective barriers, would have to adapt or die. Nevertheless, an optimistic view was taken that the overall impact would be beneficial. The magnitude of the impending change can be gauged from the fact that at the time of entry in 1973 tariffs of 16 per cent were applied on competing British imports, and 60 per cent on those from the other seven member states.

The perceived advantages to industry included the opportunity to participate in the more rapidly growing EEC economy; diversification of trade away from over-dependence on one market; the increased attractiveness of Ireland as a location for inward investment; the substantial benefits to agriculture, which employed 25 per cent of the Irish workforce; and the fact that Britain, our largest trading partner, intended to join.

In the May 1972 referendum, 83 per cent of the votes cast were in favour of membership. There was a feeling of hope, confidence and excitement at the prospect of participating in the wider European economic arena as a sovereign nation for the first time. Unfortunately, this optimism was to suffer a severe setback on 18 June 1972, when twelve leading Irish business representatives died in an air disaster at Staines, shortly after take-off from Heathrow Airport on their way to Brussels to set up the Irish Business Bureau to represent the interests of Irish business there. Their wisdom and experience were sadly missed at a crucial time. The Irish Business Bureau was formally opened towards the end of the year.

The transition phase, 1973–77

As part of the entry negotiations, all customs duties on competing products from other member states were to be eliminated by the end of 1977, and goods from the rest of the world were to be subject to the Common External Tariff, which averaged about 8 per cent. The Irish economy would gain from the Common Agricultural Policy, and it was hoped that industry would gain from free access to continental markets and also from additional new inward investment.

The first year of membership was a boom year for the economy. Disaster struck late in the year with the restrictions on oil output by the oil-producing states led by Saudi Arabia, and a substantial increase in oil prices causing an economic slowdown which would last for three years. At the time Ireland had a substantial trade deficit due to the underdeveloped state of its industrial base. Inflation gathered momentum, spurred on by the rise in international commodity prices and further exacerbated by the devaluation of sterling and consequently of the Irish pound, which still maintained a one-for-one parity with sterling as it had done for over 150 years.

During the first years of membership, the promise of new industrial investment from abroad was fulfilled. Reflecting this new investment, the output of the modern new-technology sectors increased by 15 per cent per annum; the food-processing and drink sector grew by 3 per cent per annum. In contrast, the output of the traditional sectors, which included textiles, clothing and footwear, fell by some 3 per cent per annum.

The negotiation of the Multi-fibre Agreement between the EEC and developing countries would soon cause difficulties for the textile and clothing industries. Irish industry supported and obtained a system of individual national quotas for imports from the main low-cost producers in Asia. Without these quotas, it was feared that imports into the larger member states could quickly be diverted to small states such as Ireland and could eliminate their textile and clothing industries overnight. Nevertheless, the labour-intensive clothing and footwear sectors, dependent in large measure on protection, began to feel the pain.

The decline of these sectors was hastened by the introduction of an employment subsidy in Britain to help manufacturing firms hold on to staff who were in danger of being made redundant. Since the measure had its primary effect in these labour-intensive sectors, it resulted in a distortion of competition in trade between Ireland and Britain. The assistance of the European Commission was sought by Irish industry, and the measure was eventually withdrawn. In the interim period a more generally applicable temporary employment subsidy for labour-intensive industries was introduced by the Irish government, which went some way to offsetting the damage caused by the British initiative. This was one of the first experiences for Ireland of Commission action to counter and ultimately prevent the distortion of competition within the European Communities.

Sectoral policies were also being developed in the EEC. It was considered that there was over-capacity in the textile sector and that no state aids should be given to encourage new firms to start up. This was difficult for Ireland, which was less industrialised than most other member states. There was thus a conflict between industrial and regional policy. In the end a compromise was reached which enabled Ireland to attract a small number of new textile investments from abroad with limited grant assistance. However, the IDA was shifting its promotional emphasis increasingly towards the fast-growing new-technology sectors.

Another example of the emerging Commission philosophy regarding state aids came in relation to the wish of the Irish government to inject additional funds into Ireland's only steel-producing company. At the time there was a sectoral policy in the Commission to encourage the closure of inefficient steel mills due to over-capacity. Eventually the Industry Commissioner agreed to allow an injection of funds, on a one-off basis, to restructure the company provided that no operating subsidy would be paid.

The attitude of the Commission and of some member states to inward investment from outside the European Community at this time was somewhat ambivalent. Some states wanted to place a minimum threshold for manufactured added value in Europe at 60 per cent or more before products would be regarded as of European origin and could thus enjoy the advantage of free circulation within the Communities. Initially large US multinationals with extensive manufacturing capacity in Europe had difficulty in being allowed to participate in Commission-funded research programmes. Had these attitudes persisted they would have had serious implications for industrial development in Ireland. Fortunately, they did not.

The overall result of the first five years of EEC membership was an average annual increase in manufacturing output of 5 per cent. Gains achieved by the emerging new-technology sectors more than offset the losses incurred in the traditional sectors. Encouragement could be taken even at this early stage of our membership from the fact that the performance of industry in Ireland was significantly better than that of British industry, which had shown almost no increase in output in those initial years of membership of the EEC.

During this phase there was a very rapid change in the destination of Irish exports. Exports to Britain, which had accounted for 55 per cent of total exports in 1971, had dropped to a 38 per cent share of a much larger total by 1976. This shift in the pattern of trade was due to the opening-up of the original EEC markets to Irish food products, and the exports of new foreign companies set up in Ireland to supply the European market. In addition, Irish firms gained in competitiveness as a result of the devaluation of sterling and therefore of the Irish pound.

The national prices commission, set up in 1971 to control price increases allowed to firms subject primarily to home market competition during a time of substantial protection against competing imports, was particularly active during this time of high inflation in Ireland and Britain. Industry had also to learn to cope with the vagaries of green pound devaluations and their differing impacts on various sectors of meat- and food-processing which, while neutral in intent, were not always so in practice. At times industry and agriculture in Ireland adopted different approaches. Agriculture usually wanted a rapid devaluation of the green pound; industry was more concerned to keep inflation under control.

By the end of 1977 Ireland was in a customs-free zone with the other eight member states. Since many barriers remained in the form of different national standards, trading and fiscal regulations, there was still some distance to go in creating a Single European Market. Nevertheless, the first major hurdle had been overcome with the elimination of customs duties.

The consolidation phase, 1978–86

The first two years of this phase were dominated by the decision of the Irish government to join the European Monetary System although Britain decided not to do so. The great majority of industries in Ireland favoured this approach, provided some help could be assured in the event of a significant devaluation of sterling against the Irish pound. As part of the arrangement, the government negotiated with the European Commission a substantial loan at a subsidised interest rate for the purpose of modernising the Irish telecommunications infrastructure. And so the one-for-one parity with sterling, which had existed for over 150 years, came to an end. A key influence on the decision was the high inflation in Britain at the time, and a perception that Ireland's best interests lay in participation with what appeared to be more stable and dynamic continental economies. In practice there was a change of government in Britain and, following substantial oil discoveries in the North Sea, sterling became a petrocurrency. It was indeed fortunate that Ireland had taken the decision to break the link, and in this way could avoid the consequences of having the strength of its currency determined by an oil discovery that yielded no advantage to the Irish economy.

However, it was some years before national fiscal and monetary disciplines reflected fully the requirement to manage an independent currency. Maintenance of the central rate parity of the Irish pound within the European Monetary System was an option that could be exercised only if fiscal, incomes and monetary disciplines in Ireland were similar to those adopted in the other member states of the system. Since this was not the case during the initial years of membership, the government had to request and obtain currency devaluations on three occasions to accommodate the reality of international competitive pressures.

Meanwhile, the Commission expressed its unease about the distortion of competition arising from the different treatment given by the Irish government to profits earned from the export of manufactured products and those sold on the home market. After protracted negotiations, the government agreed that all manufactured profits would be taxed at 10 per cent.

During this consolidation phase, the impact of operating in a customs-free zone of 280 million people took some time to take effect. The trend which had been established during the transition phase continued. New industries from abroad were attracted to Ireland in increasing numbers. The new-technology industries such as computers, microelectronics and pharmaceutical industries sustained a 15 per cent rate of expansion, and by 1986 accounted for over 40 per cent of total manufacturing output.

The food industry continued a modest 3 per cent rate of growth, which was broadly in line with the increase in agricultural output. Unfortunately, the output of other traditional industries continued to decline sharply. This was due to four main factors:

1   delayed reaction to the elimination of tariff protection – many firms tried to continue in production but eventually had to recognise their inability to compete
2   the high cost-inflation in the late 1970s and early 1980s resulting from excessive Exchequer borrowing at the start of the period and an inability to reduce government spending in the latter half of the period
3   depressed consumption in the latter half of the period due to the impact of measures taken to redress the balance of payments and budget deficits
4   the impact of the second oil crisis in depressing international demand.

The combined impact of these factors was that the traditional sectors of Irish industry continued to suffer a decline in output of about 3 per cent per annum over the period. By 1986 the great majority of firms that were incapable of surviving in a free and open international market had disappeared. If the surviving firms could be given the opportunity to operate in a well-managed economy, there was a prospect that output of the traditional sectors would again begin to expand. Despite these difficulties, the overall growth of manufacturing industry during the consolidation phase was sustained at 5 per cent per annum. Once again, the expansion of new foreign industries more than compensated for the decline of traditional sectors.

Irish industry continued to diversify its export markets; the United Kingdom's share of Irish exports fell to 35 per cent while the share of continental member states rose to 35 per cent. Then in 1986 Spain and Portugal joined the Community amid concern that labour-intensive industry might be attracted to those countries rather than Ireland. These fears subsequently proved to be unfounded. Instead, these countries provided further markets for Irish manufactured products, and Ireland has maintained a very positive trade balance with both countries to this day.

Two events in 1986 had a significant influence in preparing the ground for the next phase of industrial development. The first was the National Economic and Social Council (NESC) report signed by all the social partners, which stated that the first priority of the Irish government must be to reduce the national debt by reducing expenditure. This recommendation was accepted by all the main government and opposition parties.

The second event was a 10 per cent devaluation of the Irish pound within the EMS. Industry had avoided calling for devaluation because it recognised that the problem lay in the domestic management of the economy. Nevertheless, it recognised that if the NESC recommendations were implemented there was a prospect that the devaluation could be an effective long-term solution.

Meanwhile, a white paper published by the Commission in 1985 showed that some 300 non-tariff barriers remained within the European Community even though a customs union had been in operation for over 20 years. These prevented open competition between many industries in the different member states. Border controls were still necessary between member states so that the variety of national regulations could be policed. Industry in Ireland was a strong advocate of the elimination of all barriers.

The expansion phase, 1987–92

This period commenced with the passage of the Single European Act which would create a genuine Single Internal Market by adopting a programme to implement the recommendations of the 1985 white paper. Apart from an acceptance of the logic of the Single Market, there was an enlightened self-interest in Irish industry's advocacy of the proposed Act.

By that time industry in Ireland was exporting over 70 per cent of its output, mainly to other member states. It was therefore far more interested in having free access to this large market than in protecting a very limited home market.

The Irish government vigorously set about the task of reducing the accumulated public sector debt which had been a millstone around the neck of the economy and had been a major factor in the outflow of funds despite the high level of domestic interest rates. Investor confidence had been at a low ebb. Public spending was reduced, interest rates began to fall and, paradoxically, money began to flow back from abroad. A new programme for national development was agreed between the government and the social partners which incorporated modest pay increases over the following three years. These changes, in combination with favourable international developments, ensured that inflation fell sharply and that there was a marked improvement in competitiveness; industrial output started to rise sharply.

The currency crisis of 1992 showed up some major inadequacies of the narrow band European Monetary System. Britain, which had left the system, devalued sterling by 20 per cent; Spain and Italy also devalued their currencies. The Irish pound came under pressure because it was incorrectly perceived as a clone of sterling. The other central banks with the EMS proved unable or unwilling to provide sufficient support for the Irish pound, and interest rates escalated. Irish industry had to cope simultaneously with a sharp devaluation in the currency of its largest trading partner and a sharp rise in the cost of money. The Irish Central Bank, correctly in my view, held out for five months before eventually seeking a 10 per cent devaluation. The decision to resist immediate devaluation demonstrated that Ireland was a serious member of the EMS club and wished to pursue an independent strategy. Regrettably, some commentators missed the point when calling for a realignment of currency policy to maintain a fixed relationship with sterling. They appeared to ignore the diversification of Ireland's trading and economic interests that had occurred across the wider European market. After this unhappy experience the fluctuation bands in the EMS were widened.

Despite the disruption to international trade caused by the Gulf War in 1991 and the currency crisis, the rate of growth in the output of Irish manufacturing industry accelerated to an average of 8 per cent per annum during this period. The flow of new industries from abroad continued unabated; the output of computers and pharmaceuticals maintained a growth rate of some 15 per cent per annum; the food-processing sector showed a sustained steady expansion of about 3 per cent per annum; and, for the first time, the traditional sectors of industry showed a marked increase of some 5 per cent per annum. This performance provided the clearest indication yet that almost all of Irish industry was now competitive and capable of growing in a large single market of almost 300 million people. The structure of the industrial base was now healthy, and a continuation of the same broad policies seemed the best way forward. In addition, the innovative establishment of the International Financial Services Centre in the Dublin Docklands, with a favourable corporate tax regime agreed with the European Commission, was making a significant impact towards the end of this phase.

The completion of the Single European Market in 1992 had an important side-effect on the island of Ireland. All customs posts would be removed between member states, including at the border between the Republic and Northern Ireland. A major conference in Belfast in 1990 identified the barriers to increased trade between the two parts of the island. These were fiscal, security, physical and psychological. Subsequently the present writer estimated that a fully integrated island market, where industrialists in either part of the island would sell a similar amount per capita in both parts of the island, could add £3 billion to annual sales on the island and create up to 75,000 jobs.

In 1991, industrialists on the island had formed a joint council to promote cross-border trade; considerable progress has been made despite the absence of a peace agreement until 1998. In 1992 the European Commission agreed to co-sponsor a report on the feasibility of developing an economic corridor of European significance linking the cities of Dublin and Belfast, similar to existing corridors between other regions of the Community such as that between Montpelier and Barcelona. The study indicated that there was considerable scope for cross-trading between industries along the corridor if the logistics of transport could be improved and if there was a greater awareness of the potential benefits.

At the end of 1992, border controls on merchandise being traded across the European Community were removed on schedule, and an estimated 75 per cent of the programme for the elimination of non-tariff barriers had been completed.

The Single European Act 1987 had also placed a new emphasis on the need to achieve economic and social cohesion between the member states. EU structural funds contributed to improving the competitiveness of the economy. In 1992 proposals were published by the Commission to establish a cohesion fund which would assist the member states lagging behind to accelerate progress towards bridging the development gap with the rest of the Community. The present writer was chairman of the UNICE regional policy group which recommended that the fund should be applied to substantial infrastructure projects in eligible members, preferably those forming part of trans-European transport networks or environmental projects which would enhance the competitiveness of industry.

The emergence of the Celtic Tiger, 1993–98

The Maastricht Treaty in 1992 set the wheels in motion for economic and monetary union throughout what was now called the European Union. Prospective participating member states were required to manage their economies so that inflation rates, exchequer borrowing, public debt, and interest rates would converge towards specific targets. A common currency, the euro, would be introduced and exchange rate parities with the euro would be set irrevocably at the end of 1998. Industry in Ireland was enthusiastically in favour. Currency fluctuations create uncertainty for business, and there was evidence that the volume of trade between member states varied substantially because of relative currency fluctuations over which firms had no control. These fluctuations militated against the establishment of stable trading relationships governed by predictability of prices and reliability of supply. Wide variations in the volume of Irish trade with Germany in 1995, 1996 and 1997 illustrated this point. It was of little surprise, therefore, that a survey conducted in 1996 of members of the German–Irish chamber of industry and commerce indicated 85 per cent in favour of the euro.

The implementation of the internal market programme to eliminate non-tariff barriers was still not complete. The present writer was rapporteur for a hearing conducted by the Economic and Social Committee of the European Communities in June 1994, during which 64 remaining barriers to the free movement of capital, goods, services and people were identified. These included:

1   insufficient application of the principle of mutual recognition of standards in many areas
2   practical difficulties in winning public procurement contracts unless the company had a local establishment
3   the fact that the application of VAT at destination rather than at source caused distortion of trade due to different rules for local products.

By the end of 1998 it was estimated that 95 per cent of the internal market legislation had been transposed into Irish law.

Irish industry has consistently welcomed the expansion of the European Union. Ireland's role, like that of any other region of the Union, is to be a specialist supplier of those goods and services for which it enjoys a comparative advantage. For example, more than 50 per cent of Irish merchandise exports comprises five product groups: computers, pharmaceuticals, meat, electrical machinery and dairy products. In the services area, information technology, financial services and tourism dominate. Other regions of the European Union have a quite different mix of key sectors, and it is appropriate that they should have.

The modern new-technology industries of computers and pharmaceuticals have shown a remarkable average rate of annual expansion of some 20 per cent, and now account for almost 60 per cent of the total value of manufacturing output; the food- and drink-processing and the traditional industrial sectors have grown moderately. The total output of manufacturing industry has increased by about 15 per cent per annum over the past six years – almost twice the average annual growth rate achieved during the previous five-year period. This phenomenal growth has led to the appellation 'the Celtic Tiger'.

The diversification of Ireland's trade has continued unabated. The continental member states of the Union now account for about 40 per cent, Britain for about 16 per cent and Northern Ireland for 3 per cent. It is likely that the proportion of goods purchased by mainland European customers, who account for 85 per cent of the Union market, will increase further. The enlargement of the Union by three new member states – Sweden, Finland

and Austria – in 1995 brought the total population to 340 million. Trade is likely to develop most rapidly with the 'Euroland' member states.

Towards the end of this period the European Commission returned to the issue of the distorting effect of Ireland's much lower rate of corporate profits taxation for manufacturing and internationally traded services than for other businesses. Finally in August 1998 the Commission agreed to the gradual phasing-in of a 12.5 per cent tax rate in 2003 for all businesses. The Commission has accepted that differences in corporate taxation rates between member states do not fall within the definition of state aids.

Conclusion

The evolution of European industrial policy continues. It has moved a long way from the protectionist and somewhat xenophobic attitudes of the 1970s and early 1980s. The Union was an active and positive participant in the conclusion of the Uruguay Round of global trade negotiations in the early 1990s. It is willing to accept the consequences of further enlargement to the East. It accepts the need to deregulate, while seeking to preserve the desirable attributes of the European social model.

This brief overview of the development of Irish industry since Ireland joined the EEC demonstrates the exceptional importance of evolving European industrial policy. A positive framework for development has been provided by the interaction of European and Irish policies. This has made possible the emergence of the so-called Celtic Tiger. On the domestic front some have suggested that its origins can be summarised in two words – talent and tax. While this is a gross oversimplification, the two factors are very important.

'Talent' comprises all the attributes that make up the high-quality Irish workforce today. These include youth, education, the speaking of English, openness to new ideas, confidence, dynamism, willingness to change and international orientation. The strong family links with the US are of considerable help in positioning Ireland as a gateway to the new Europe.

'Tax' points to the foresight shown by successive Irish governments since 1958 in promoting inward investment and subsequently Irish investment, by offering a low rate of corporate tax on the profits of manufacturing and internationally traded service companies. Only firms likely to have significant profits were attracted. Little if any money was wasted on feather-bedding inefficiency.

Membership of the European Union has enabled industry in Ireland to expand at an unprecedented rate. It has ensured the application of the four freedoms for the movement of capital, goods, services and people throughout the Union, irrespective of whether the member state is large or small. It has also provided Ireland with considerable cohesion fund and structural fund assistance to develop its industrial infrastructure in areas such as transport, water, sewerage, telecommunications and training.

Ireland can look back on its first 25 years of membership of the European Union as a most exciting and productive period. Irish living standards are now converging rapidly with the European average, having been only 55 per cent in 1973. The Irish experience is a model which demonstrates clearly that the principles of economic and social cohesion across the European Union can be made to work in practice. There is a solid foundation on which to build the future in Euroland.

════════ 16 ════════

EU industrial research programmes

BRENDAN FINUCANE

Introduction

Prior to Ireland's accession to the EEC, various government departments had undertaken intensive studies on the impact of membership in such areas as agriculture, forestry, fishing, industry and commerce, employment and tourism. All the main lobby groups and economic commentators had also done their own analysis of the main issues, and these were extensively reported in the press and debated at great length on radio and television. By the time Ireland joined in January 1973, politicians, public servants and lobbyists already had reasonable expectations of how the new arrangements would work and how they would impact (almost all seen as favourable) on the Irish economic system.

But initially the Irish scientific and technical community was not so well prepared. There were many reasons for this. In the 1950s and 1960s many European countries invested heavily in new national science and technology facilities, to begin to close the perceived technological gap with the US. Nuclear physics was chosen as a priority research area, reflecting the spirit of the times, and it was seen as a symbol of power, prestige and progress. For physicists atomic research was a new frontier, whose study required finance beyond the means of any single country. Politicians saw in nuclear research an area of vital national interest which had energy, economic and military aspects. The coincidence of political and scientific interests led in turn to a series of European initiatives which resulted, after years of debate, in the establishment of European Nuclear Research Organisation (CERN) in 1953 and to the European Atomic Energy Community (EURATOM) in 1957. The Irish scientific community was not part of the movements that formed these new institutions.

In space science it was recognised that the European institutions were too small to mount programmes in 'big' science and that collaboration would provide the size and scale to match the efforts of the US and the USSR. In 1962 two new European organisations came into being, the European Southern Observatory (ESO) and the European Space Research Organisation (ESRO). Ireland belonged to neither of these organisations.

The Irish government in the late 1950s and early 1960s set up research institutes in agriculture, industry and standards, and physical planning and construction research. During this period there was a considerable expansion in the universities, and in their capacity to undertake research. A high proportion of the Irish research community had undertaken postgraduate training in either the UK or the US. Research links and research networks revolved largely around these. For historical and linguistic reasons research contacts with counterpart European laboratories were seriously underdeveloped.

The nuclear energy debate

Quite quickly after joining the EEC we found ourselves confronted by a series of major Community crises and conflicts on the nuclear energy front. There were serious policy conflicts on the objectives and operations of the nuclear programmes in EURATOM. Deep divisions existed among the member states on the future of the Community's joint research centres, particularly the Ispra facility. Some member states regarded it as a costly and unreliable research centre and proposed its closure. The Italians wanted its position strengthened, and the Commission was proposing a new role for it in the light of changing circumstances.

There were very mixed feelings in the Irish delegation about getting involved in this row. Some argued that this was part of the legacy of the EURATOM dream that went sour and it did not really concern us. In addition, as we had no nuclear facilities it was hard to see what benefit the facility and its research results would bring us. We were reminded by our permanent representation office in Brussels that this dispute concerned the Community, and all members were expected to become involved in finding a solution.

The UK, US and USSR in the 1940s had been studying plasma physics with the intention of creating controlled nuclear fusion which would provide a limitless supply of energy. This work was conducted in strict secrecy. But in the late 1950s the results were largely declassified and researchers began to contemplate large-scale co-operation. The EEC considered that it would have to join in the development of this exciting new technology and push the research to new boundaries by building very large experimental machines. Thus the Joint European Torus (JET) project was born.

Somewhat unexpectedly, the project was quickly approved by the Council. But seven sites were proposed and of these there were four main contenders: UK, France, Germany and Ispra (area in Northern Italy). Justin Keating, who was the Irish minister, found himself caught up in the midst of serious internal wrangling, as members lobbied for their preferred site. He remarked that it would be difficult to explain to his constituents the immediate benefits of this arcane 'fusion' technology and why the resolution of this problem required so much of his time. After six meetings of the Council of Research Ministers, two meetings of the Council of Foreign Ministers and a European Council, the UK was chosen.

The lexicon used by the Commission in describing its programmes was not familiar to us. Aside from all the technical terms used in the nuclear area, we had not come across the commonly used descriptions for the various types of EEC programmes. Soon, terms such as direct action, indirect action, concerted action and joint research centres began to enter the vocabulary of the Irish delegation. At the same time we became accustomed to the lengthy, discursive decision-taking processes used in the EEC. As there was very limited debate in government departments, or the Dáil, on scientific and technical issues, this new process was a revelation.

During our presidencies the Irish administration was seriously stretched. Part of the problem was the sheer logistics of dealing with the myriad reports and recommendations emanating from the Commission and getting them to the right departments in Dublin. Sometimes documents went astray. At other times non-English versions arrived. In the research area, many of the research topics, particularly in the early years of accession, were of little or no interest to us. And yet our system coped well with pressure. A good example of the frantic pace of developments arose when Jim Tunney TD had to step in at a day's notice to chair a Council meeting on Super SARA – a simulation of a nuclear meltdown accident. This was proposed by the Commission as Europe's response to the understanding of such phenomena following the Three Mile Island incident in the US.

Discussions in EEC expert groups had made no headway on Super SARA. By the time Jim Tunney was called in, the other ministers were deeply divided. He was briefed by his officials in Dublin, and went to Brussels that evening where the Commission and the permanent representation again outlined the issues. Having listened carefully to the advice he remarked that 'what you really want me to do is to be fair but firm like a school headmaster and keep a tight discipline on the meeting. As a former headmaster I am quite accustomed to that.' He played a remarkable role in moving the issue forward, especially since he was probably the only member of the Council who was neither a scientist/technologist nor in charge of science affairs in his own country.

Impact of the oil crisis on research priorities

The oil crisis which followed the Arab–Israeli war prompted the Community to evaluate the current model of economic growth, which was based on limitless expansion and the continuous consumption of non-renewable resources. It raised questions about the wisdom of investing in 'big research' as against research that was more responsive to the immediate needs of society. At the request of the Council, the Commission prepared an evaluation of the work it had undertaken with a series of proposals for future action. These centred around three general objectives, which could be summarised as:

- long-term supply and conservation of resources
- promotion of economic development through industrial competitiveness
- improvement of living and working conditions and protection of the environment.

These were enormously ambitious tasks, particularly when account was taken of the Community's research budget (1–2 per cent per cent of the public research budget of member states) and industrial rivalry between the major member states and between them and the Commission. CREST, an advisory body to both the Commission and the Council, had the task of moving the business forward, to ensure that action was taken.

Michael Manahan, the Irish Scientific and Technical Research Committee (CREST) delegate, reminded the Commission that the research budget was unbalanced, with an undue emphasis on energy research, which accounted at the time for some 70 per cent of the budget: of that a very high proportion was devoted to nuclear energy. This was going to be an ongoing criticism by the Irish side which would be echoed at various Council meetings over the next few years.

Framework programmes

In the early 1980s, research in the Community was organised on a highly disaggregated basis, with almost no attempts at bringing the various strands together. Commissioner Davignon, with Professor Paolo Fasella, the newly appointed DG for research, together with CREST began to reorganise the various Community research programmes into a coherent framework programme covering several years. There was much opposition to this from some of the member states and from parts of the Commission. The first framework programme covered the period 1984–87. The Irish delegations had continued to make the case for a rebalancing of the budget away from its preoccupation with energy, particularly nuclear energy. It was noted with satisfaction by us that energy research had declined from 66 to 50 per cent of the total budget. This was a trend we would strenuously continue to support.

The framework programme essentially provided us with the first real opportunity to contribute meaningfully to the emerging science debate in Europe and to draw on the scientific community in Ireland. The Irish

National Science Council co-ordinated much of the scientific input up to 1987, when it was replaced by the National Board for Science and Technology (NBST). The NBST appointed national delegates (with the concurrence of the department of industry and commerce) to all the main research activities (with the exceptions of agriculture and nuclear energy). The delegates' tasks were to input into the research programmes that were emerging and to actively encourage Irish participation.

The relatively small, closely knit Irish scientific community was accessible and eager to give its views on research priorities. This meant that the Irish representative at Community committees such as CREST could provide a quick response to a Commission research proposal. In contrast, large member states such as Germany, France and the UK had to co-ordinate views across many different government departments and research institutes (often with competing or conflicting views), and this was always a time-consuming process.

One of the first examples of this occurred when the Commission presented a list of proposed topics in the field of raw materials, which to us seemed heavily biased towards prospecting. Within two weeks the head of the industrial materials department in IIRS (the Institute for Industrial Research and Standards), Killian Halpin, had the Commission's proposal evaluated and was proposing an amended set of research themes. Subsequently most of these were accepted by the Commission, thereby giving the Irish research community a better chance to compete.

There were many sceptics on the industrial policy side, as well as academics, who were of the opinion that it would be very difficult for Irish researchers to become involved in Community research. One of the early promotion tasks of the NBST was to produce a simple guide to EEC programmes, explaining all the arcane terms, the programme priorities, budgets, addresses and deadlines. It was enormously popular with the researchers, and over the years it was revised and updated to take account of each framework programme as it emerged. Finally the Commission produced its own framework programme guide, based very much on the format of our early designs.

Irish involvement in EEC research started slowly because of a misalignment between Community R&D and Irish R&D priorities. But even in the nuclear research area, research groups in University College Cork (UCC) and Kevin Street, under the leadership of Professor Michael Sexton and Dr Carmel Mothersill respectively, found a niche for themselves. In the early phase of the Community research, Irish researchers did not have networks of European contacts who knew their capabilities and who would invite them in as joint partners. This problem was tackled very directly by the NBST initiating a travel grant scheme which subsidised researchers to travel to Europe to seek out partners.

In many of the early programmes, Irish researchers either found themselves as subcontractors or were given small elements of the research work. Over a period the active researchers deepened their involvement and gradually became significant players, sometimes taking a project leadership role. In terms of numbers, the second framework programme involved 84 Irish researchers; this increased to almost 390 some twelve years later in the fourth framework programme.

While on a visit to UCC a few years ago, I called unannounced to see Professor Charles Daly, who was involved in a successful EU-sponsored research network. That day I was sixth in the queue behind three Europeans, one American and one Australian researcher who had all come to visit him to hear about the latest research results in cheese starter cultures. Through his EU research he had become a recognised research authority in his chosen field. A few years prior to this, he remarked, he would be doing the 'visitations'.

Promoting mobility of European research

Many commentators had noted that by comparison with the US there were serious barriers to scientific mobility in Europe. It was recommended that the Commission should play a leading role in stimulating such mobility. The Commission had always run limited programmes in scientific mobility, but these were confined to postgraduate and post-doctoral fellowships with the Joint Research Centre at ISPRA. The European physics community spotted an opportunity to open up access to large-scale European facilities, such as synchrotrons, electron lasers and neutron sources. It was proposed that a limited number of facilities would receive substantial Community funding in order to allow researchers from all over Europe to use these unique facilities.

The Irish delegation had mixed feelings about this proposal. On the one hand it would open up new facilities to our researchers: facilities that we could never afford to build ourselves. As against that, it was obvious that Community funding would encourage every 'large-scale' institution to seek support, that it would be difficult to control, and would end up being very costly with only limited Irish interest. There was intense competition for funding amongst the institutions, and in the end a satisfactory solution was arrived at which included the National Microelectronics Research Centre (NMRC) in UCC being selected as a large-scale facility – the only one in Ireland.

The second leg of the mobility initiative was the extension of the mobility scheme beyond the JRC. The scheme, which commenced in the early 1990s, has proved very popular in Ireland. Ireland now has the highest success rate in postgraduate fellowships in Europe. Of equal interest is the number of European scientists coming to Irish research institutes/universities. There had been concerns that the traffic would be largely one way, but there is now a steady stream of European researchers coming here. Most of the incoming researchers tend to come to either University College Dublin or Trinity College Dublin. It is expected over the next five years that increasing numbers of incoming researchers will take up places in colleges outside Dublin, driven to some extent by contacts forged through stays in Ireland under the Erasmus programme.

Regaining competitiveness through research

Europe was a net exporter of electronic goods in the 1960s. A decade later Europe's share of its home market in IT products, aerospace, biotechnology and new materials had deteriorated in the face of intense Japanese, US and South-East Asian competition. The tendency of European companies to form partnerships with US companies, rather than other European companies, hindered the process of co-operation and consolidation of high-tech European enterprise.

When Commissioner Davignon initiated the first 'Round Table' discussions in 1979 with twelve of Europe's leading IT firms, the portents were not encouraging. Attempts by some of the larger member states to revitalise their 1T industries by means of generous research subsidies and encouraging mergers did not succeed. National rivalries undermined two European industrial IT consortia, Eurodata and Unidata. But this time the large IT companies could see that their market share, even on the home market, was likely to continue to decline, and unless this was arrested soon the indigenous IT industry would disappear. Recognition of this problem did not necessarily mean that it would be easy to find a prescription that would mollify everyone.

National governments considered that this problem should be solved by intergovernmental agreements because of the strategic interests involved. There were doubts that the Commission would have the flexibility and capacity to manage a fast-moving industrial programme. This strongly pro-European IT programme contrasted sharply with Irish industry policy under which overseas, mainly US, IT companies were encouraged to establish and put down roots in Ireland.

There were clear warning signals that the overseas IT companies located in Ireland would not be welcome to apply. It also seemed, at least at the outset, that it would be very difficult for the small indigenous IT companies to become meaningfully involved. And furthermore, this would be an expensive programme, which would drain resources away from other parts of the framework programme. In the end the Irish delegation felt it had no option but to support the European Strategic Programme for R&D in Information Technology, dubbed the ESPRIT programme, and to work very hard at maximising Irish involvement in it at all levels.

One of the programme's greatest success stories started in Trinity College Dublin. Three of the college's computer science lecturers, Chris Horn, Sean Baker and Annrai O'Toole, spent six years working on ESPRIT projects directed at coupling together modules of software from different sources. Using the knowledge and expertise that they acquired through this work, they established Iona Technologies in 1991, which today is hailed as one of Europe's leading entrepreneurial companies. It exports its flagship product, Orbix, throughout the world. In the past five years it has increased its revenue by 22,900 per cent, and its workforce has expanded by 8,300 per cent. Iona continues to participate in ESPRIT.

In Cork, the National Microelectronics Research Centre, led by Professor Gerry Wrixon (who is now President of UCC), has been a major player in ESPRIT. It has worked on projects with all the major European electronics companies including Philips, Siemens, Bell and SGS Thomson in the development of state-of-the-art microelectronic devices. In Monaghan, a small software company, Datacare Computers, has been carving out a niche for itself with software to assist companies in filing returns with company offices throughout Europe. Managing Director John Kelly values the contribution of ESPRIT to his company in helping to develop its business links throughout Europe.

The first framework programme became a bridge for transferring industrial proposals that had been conceived in an industrial policy context (to which a number of member states had fundamental objections) into a redefined science and technology milieu. There was much debate about the nature and form of such research. In the end there was broad consensus that it should be precompetitive, i.e. not close to the market, and that it would be carried out by transnational consortia of business, universities and technology institutes.

The Basic Research in Industrial Technologies (BRITE) programme, which started in 1985, marked a watershed in the evolution of Community R&D policy. In contrast with the ESPRIT programme which was focused on the IT sector, the BRITE programme aimed to develop generic technologies relating to both products and processes. Nine broadly-based research areas were identified. In parallel with BRITE, the Community also set up the European Research in Advanced Materials (EURAM) programme to research new materials, using a multidisciplinary approach. Not surprisingly, the two programmes were later merged to form BRITE/EURAM. Interestingly, an aeronautics initiative that had been rejected some years previously by the member states became an element in the amalgamated BRITE/EURAM format.

BRITE/EURAM provided one of the best opportunities for scientists and engineers in the Irish Science and Technology Agency (EOLAS) (and its successor organisations) to work on large industrial technology projects. The projects are always multipartner and transnational and enabled the technologists to 'benchmark' themselves against the best in Europe. Tom Kelly, then director of the Joint Ceramics Research Centre, EOLAS, summarised his research team's involvement as follows:

> Usually EOLAS was the only Irish partner in projects. This enabled us to gain a considerable level of specialisation and expertise which in turn could be diffused into Irish companies. We have had some notable success including working with Harris Ireland on developing multifunctional electronic ceramic components and Cameron Limited on using diamond films to enhance the erosive wear resistance of tungsten carbide components used in oil extraction. We are currently working with Wavin (Irl) in Balbriggan on coatings for internal surfaces for certain engineering components. Daimler Benz, Teer Coatings (UK) and a small German grinding wheel manufacturer, Diamant Werkseuge in Hameln are the other partners. Our involvement in BRITE/EURAM has also led to considerable north–south co-operation on this island. We have for many years availed of the excellent surface analysis facilities in the University of Ulster at Coleraine under the direction of Professor Norman Brown and we have worked in partnership with Dr Bill Graham in the Physics Department in Queens University, Belfast. We also enjoy a very close relationship with Seagoe Ceramics, in Portadown. They formed a critical part of a consortium to develop machining technology for advanced ceramics and we continue to rely on each other for various forms of technical support. BRITE/EURAM has helped us develop new technologies and it has also helped us to cut our teeth in large-scale R&D project planning and management. Most valuable of all is the extensive network of contracts that we have built up across Europe. Technical institutes, university departments and manufacturing companies all form part of the repository of expertise accessible to Enterprise Ireland and our clients.

Co-ordinating national research

One of the most effective methods of co-ordinating national research in Europe was put in place in November 1971 through the formation of Scientific and Technical Co-operation (COST), with 23 countries joining. This was an intergovernmental agreement with the Commission providing the secretariat. Under this arrangement, which functioned like a club, members were encouraged, but not obliged, to collaborate and exchange information on selected research topics. Each research project would take two to five years, and the Commission provided the scientific and administrative secretariat. Many critics considered it a minimalist approach, with the bureaucracy involved in preparing research proposals greatly outweighing the actual research. The Commission was not enamoured at being relegated, as it saw it, to a reactive administrative role. In addition, the agreement began to absorb Commission staff time increasingly. COST selected seven broad areas of scientific interest, but within these no priorities were established – this was regarded by some member states as too open-ended and likely to dissipate the energy of the COST system.

Despite these difficulties European collaboration began quickly in a number of areas, and particularly in the IT and telecoms areas. In fact, the co-operation and results were in one respect so effective that the Commission appropriated a number of projects and they were transferred to the framework programme as part of ESPRIT, RACE or BRITE/EURAM, as appropriate.

Accession to COST projects also gave rise to tedious internal difficulties in most member states. This arose because COST agreements were considered to be intergovernmental and hence had to be ratified by the Dáil. One of the first COST actions Ireland joined was in the environment area, involving research on the analysis of micropollutants in water. This was a narrowly defined piece of research involving eleven countries. When the accession to this project was being ratified by the Dáil, it sparked a lively and topical debate on the state of pollution of various Irish rivers: a parliamentary interest quite disproportionate to the importance of this project.

For the first 15 years Irish participation in COST was among the lowest in Europe. The principal reason for this was that researchers had to undertake all their research and their travel from their own resources. Travel costs were not a particular burden for continental Europeans, but were a big disincentive to most Irish research groups. At the COST senior officials' meetings the Irish delegation was for many years a lone voice in seeking a travel compensation fund from the Commission.

Finally the budgetary system was reorganised and the Commission was given a travel budget so that researchers could attend project meetings. This had a dramatic effect on the level and spread of Irish participation, which grew from involvement in an average of five COST actions to about 50 per annum. Of the seven 'standing committees', Irish delegates were elected to the chairmanship of three: Brendan McWilliams (Met Office) to Meteorology, Joe O'Dwyer (Telecom Éireann) to Telecommunications, and Sean Dunleavy (Forbairt) to Construction. Dr Ronan Gormley and Dr Finbarr O'Riordan of Teagasc played important roles in leading or co-ordinating various research actions. At an earlier stage Dr Stan Nielsen, then the secretary general of the Irish National Science Council, was elected Chairman of the COST Senior Officials' Committee and guided it through a difficult growth phase.

Following the oil shocks of the 1970s the Commission considered that one of the most effective means of promoting new energy-saving technology was through a demonstration programme. In the period 1981 to 1988 Ireland secured some £14m for energy-related demonstration projects representing a capital investment of some £40m. Many of these focused on milk evaporation technologies/cheese-making and associated enterprises, which are relatively very energy-intensive. Dairy co-ops in the remotest areas now employ the best technologies. At Listowel, the fluidised-bed boiler can burn anything organic. At Kantoher co-op there is a reverse osmosis process for milk dewatering. Overseas suppliers of combined heat and power systems and mechanical vapour recompression systems were attracted by this EC programme to demonstrate, at the time, the latest technologies and designs at remote Irish dairies and breweries. This proved to be a win-win formula both for the large equipment suppliers in Britain and Germany and for many agri-food companies based in a peripheral region of the EU. One could say that Irish co-ops such as Kerry and Avonmore were more open to innovation than their EU counterparts and are now world leaders in energy efficiency in the food sector. When Dick Spring, as Minister for Energy, came to open the new EU-funded plant at Listowel, it was raining heavily. His host exclaimed, 'It is terrible weather for the time of year, Tánaiste'. The minister replied, 'Yerra, 'tis not that time of year at all man'.

Finally, it is important to ask what impact membership of the Community had on the development of scientific and technical policy in Ireland. Probably the first effect was to expose Irish policy-makers to a much broader context, and one where their European partners placed science and technology in a more central role in the process of industrial development. It heralded the end of our isolation from Europe as Ireland joined the European Science Foundation (ESF), the European Molecular Biology Laboratory (EMBL), the European Space Agency (ESA) and the European Research Co-ordination Agency (EUREKA). Co-operation agreements were signed with scientific bodies in France and the UK, and for some years there was a highly productive co-operation arrangement with German institutions.

When preparing the Irish input to the structural funds programme on industrial development, the Irish policy-makers were able to draw on some European experiences from the various framework programmes as well as best practice in some member states. In particular, the evolution of the programmes in advanced technology (PATs) in which national research efforts were focused around the best university and institute departments found much of its inspiration in the 'European laboratory with walls' concept.

The impact on the researchers was profound. For many it provided the opportunity to become partners in leading-edge research in major European consortia. The researchers had to find their own niches, and their continued survival in the EU system depended on doing high-quality research on time and on budget. This was not as easy at it sounds, because in many cases the Irish research groups would have been considerably less well resourced than their counterparts. Community-wide research provided a unique opportunity for Irish research groups to benchmark themselves against best practice elsewhere in Europe. The initial fears that the Irish research community would not have the capacity to win its *juste retour* in terms of contracts from Commission programmes turned out to be completely unfounded.

Though we are among the least developed member states scientifically, the question arises: did we have any influence in the pace, structure and mix and content of the framework programme? We had no direct interest in, nor could we foresee immediate benefits from, the various nuclear research programmes. But despite this, I think we contributed to the debate by taking an interest in the issues, at both political and technical (via the then Nuclear Energy Board and its successor, the Radiological Protection Institute of Ireland) levels; we attempted to calm some fraught situations and adopted a *communautaire* approach. During the last Irish Presidency, Michael Smith, the Irish minister for science and technology, acting on behalf of the Council of Ministers, played a seminal role during the conciliation meetings with the Parliament. His vigorous defence of the Council's position contributed to the adoption of the research programme.

For the first ten years of membership there was a consistent Irish position, closely argued by our delegates, that the framework programme needed to have increased resources to tackle pan-European science and technology problems and that areas such as marine, environment and natural resources should be strengthened. It is with some satisfaction that we have watched the evolution of the various framework programmes with their increasing emphasis on these areas.

More recently, Irish representatives have drawn attention to a new imbalance – the skewing of the framework programme towards large companies. Michael Fahy, formerly head of the Office of Science and Technology, pressed the Commission to take account of the importance of promoting SMEs, particularly in view of their importance in job creation in Europe. The fifth framework programme has given special recognition to the European small and medium-sized businesses (SMEs), and it is hoped that they will now become more involved in Community research.

The whole Irish policy and research system is, relative to almost all our partners, very small. But this has proved to be an advantage in dealing with the myriad science and technology programmes emanating from Brussels.

With a small team dedicated to 'Euro-watching', we have been able to ensure consistency of approach. The chain of command from the minister to the policy co-ordinators and the experts is short, and has often operated at an informal level in parallel to the official procedures. Most Irish ministers for science and technology have not only been very well briefed and taken a keen interest in European science and technology issues, but have also been in touch with many of the main Irish researchers and their interests.

Another key part of the national system has been the appointment of delegates to the programmes. All have been nominated based on their technical expertise and links to the research and industrial sectors. Most have been in place for more than four years, and they have built up invaluable networks of contacts in various Commission departments with delegates from other member states and also with the home base. This familiarity and experience assists them in influencing Commission decisions, maintaining informal contacts with other delegates, and passing information and advice back home. They have been able to offer counselling, information and advice to potential applicants and to disseminate research results very rapidly to their clients. The respective roles of policy-makers, national delegates and researchers/contractors have become clearer over the past ten years, and this has aided co-operation and no doubt contributed to the success of Ireland.

In terms of the framework programmes, the major key challenge facing us will be to assist more indigenous companies to become involved in Europe-wide industrial research.

17

Twenty-five years of
European environment policy

TOM GARVEY

Not only does 1998 mark 25 years of Irish membership of the European Community, it is also the 25th anniversary of European environment policy. None of those who were interested in or concerned with our negotiations for membership could have imagined that within a period of 25 years, Ireland would be legally bound to implement and enforce on its territory some 200 European Directives whose aim is the protection of the environment. Moreover, it is safe to say that nobody could have foreseen that in a five-year period (1994–98), Ireland would have been in receipt of a capital inflow of almost £600 million from Brussels, in co-financing of investment in the physical infrastructure necessary for the implementation of some of those Directives. Yet this is precisely what has come to pass – 'Brussels' has provided two-thirds of all capital investments in the public water sector in Ireland since 1994.

These figures bear striking testimony to the extent to which the environment and its protection have become major political preoccupations for the Community, and for Ireland and its citizens. In the early days, most Irish people would, perhaps, have recognised that environmental problems existed – but not in Ireland. Untouched by the industrial revolution and its smokestack industries, Ireland was seen then by its citizens as an exception to the general judgement that Europe was becoming dangerously polluted. I was at that time the chief executive of the Irish Export Board (CT), and it was a unique selling proposition of Irish produce around the world that it came from an environment that was 'clean' and 'green', and it was generally believed that our environment would ever remain so. Yet today you have only to read the daily paper to find accounts of fish kills, deteriorating water quality in our lakes and rivers, and protests about the location of waste disposal plants for our ever-increasing tonnage of waste.

In the late 1960s and 1970s, the writings of Rachel Carson[1] and Barbara Ward,[2] among others, and the pronouncements of the 'Club of Rome' (of which Professor Patrick Lynch, a longstanding member of the European Movement, who made many contributions to European affairs in Ireland, was

212

a member) caught the attention of the media and politicians in the developed world, and especially in mainland Europe.[3] The First Global Conference on the Human Environment was held in Stockholm in 1972, as a consequence of which the UNEP (United Nations Environment Programme) was set up. The European Commission published its first Environmental Action Programme in 1973. It is interesting today to reflect on the fact that the Treaty of Rome, which Ireland signed on entry to the Communities, had no reference whatever to the environment and it would take a further ten years before the European Communities had a coherent policy dealing with the environment. Nevertheless, the political momentum for environmental protection was gathering pace during the 1970s and early 1980s as many of the global environmental conventions and treaties were adopted to which the Communities became a party.[4]

All this was achieved by the Communities and their member states without a specific environmental article in the Treaty. A decision of the European Court of Justice in 1971 stipulated that if the Communities had power directly or indirectly under the Treaty to legislate internally, they therefore, implicitly, had power to act externally as well. In fact, despite the absence of a specific article in the Treaty dealing with the environment, the Community was legislating internally on environmental matters on the basis of Articles 100 and 230 of the Treaty.

My first encounter with the Community's increasing readiness to legislate on matters touching the environment came in 1984 when I joined Directorate General III of the Commission, and became involved in the planning and subsequent construction of the Single Market. This 'construction' was the most important development of the Community since the achievement of 'customs union', coming after a decade or more of 'Eurosclerosis' and stagnation. I was a director in charge of preparing much of the necessary legislative proposals to remove technical barriers to trade and distortions of competition. It was increasingly clear that whereas up to then most trade barriers arose from the different health and safety regulations applied by individual member states, a rapidly growing source of trade barriers comprised the different and differing national environmental rules, regulations and standards which were proliferating in member states. During the 1970s, Community Directives had been adopted, as we have seen, on the basis of Articles 100 and 235, and set down basic requirements for the protection of water quality and the management of waste.

Thus the direction of Community environmental legislation for more than a decade was significantly influenced by the need to eliminate barriers to trade. This was no bad thing, as the areas covered by rigorous national regulations were presumably the areas that, for the national administrations, were priority ones. What the absence of a special Treaty provision on the environment did do, however, was to give priority to Community legislation that was focused on products rather than on the processes of production. It was not until the coming into force of the Single European Act in 1987 that it was possible to develop a coherent Community environment policy.

Eastern Europe

At the end of 1989, I left DG III for what was then DG I, to take responsibility for the launching of the Commission's programme of technical assistance and aid for the slowly emerging democracies in Central and Eastern Europe (PHARE). This was a massive aid programme, which, even in its first years, was valued at almost 1 billion ECU. Interestingly, both Poland and Hungary, the first countries to qualify for the assistance, devoted a high proportion of the funds available from the Commission to environmental protection. I was to learn that this was a reaction to a 50-year period during which the environment simply did not figure in the policy and investment priorities of the previous centrally planned regimes. I was further to learn that this 'ignoring' of the environment owed nothing to the form of economic organisation (central planning) practised in those days – I began to realise that, *per se*, neither the capitalist or the centrally planned model was intrinsically environment-friendly or environment-unfriendly. The difference between 'East' and 'West' lay in the democratic right to protest, which we in the West had – and used, to great effect, in the case of environmental problems. This freedom of expression and protest was denied to Central and Eastern Europeans, so it was natural that the environment would be a major item on the political agenda after 'liberation'. Indeed, the previous regimes' neglect of environmental problems provided one of the rallying points of the protest movement through such organisations as ECO-Glasnost.

For anyone who travelled during the 1980s in Central Europe, the results of environmental neglect were plain to see. The pollution of surface water, the low quality of drinking water and the degree of air pollution were striking. In the area of Upper Bohemia–Lower Silesia–German Democratic Republic known as the 'Black Triangle', so awful were the effects of open-cast mining of lignite to feed adjacent large power generation and industrial plants that the life expectancy of the inhabitants was some five years below the average, and the very countryside had the appearance of a lunar landscape.

I mention this because it was at this point that I personally became convinced that the protection of our natural resources (what the classical economists called 'free goods') must form a part of any rational system of economics. I came to understand in a very direct way the importance of 'sustainable development' – of decoupling economic growth and environmental degradation. It was therefore with a great deal of pleasure that I accepted the offer of Carlo Ripa de Mena (commissioner) and Laurens Jan Brinkhorst (director general) to take up the post of deputy director general in DG XI (environment and nuclear safety) in the middle of 1992.

Policy development

So, in 1992, I came to DG XI at a time when public awareness of environment, the threats to it, and the economic and people-related implications of those threats was increasing exponentially! In short, it was the year of the Earth Summit in Rio. It was also the year in which the Commission issued its Fifth Action Programme on the environment – the first that made a coherent statement of policy priorities and strategies, and gave an outline programme of implementation (its principal author was Philip Ryan, then one of the few Irish in DG XI, and now in the Commission's office in Dublin). There is a further Irish connection in relation to the Fifth Action Programme. It was formally requested by the European heads of state meeting in Dublin in June 1990, which took place under the chairmanship of the then Taoiseach Charles J. Haughey. From this 'Dublin summit' issued the 'Declaration on the Environment', which was subsequently known in environmental circles as the Dublin Declaration. Brendan O'Donoghue, then Secretary in the Department of the Environment, had the major input into the preparation of this seminal document, which set out the European Community position on a number of global problems, and classified the respective roles of the member states and the Community in the conduct of international environmental negotiations. Moreover, the 'Dublin Declaration' also set out the head of states' position on review of implementation, economic and fiscal measures to protect the environment, damage to the ozone layer, climate change and soil erosion. It also endorsed the agreement reached in Dublin earlier in the same month by the first-ever joint meeting of environment ministers of the Community and those of Central and Eastern Europe, on the steps to be taken to improve the environment throughout the whole of Europe.

That meeting was chaired by the then Irish Minister for the Environment, Pádraig Flynn. I was present as part of the Commission delegation led by Commissioner Carlo Ripa de Meana, because of my position as director of the PHARE programme. Both that meeting and the subsequent European Council were major steps on the road to an environmentally cleaner European continent, and it was greatly to the credit of the Irish that they achieved such progress during their 1990 presidency.

The Dublin Declaration on the Environment also called on the Commission to 'expedite proposals for concrete action, and in particular, measures relating to carbon dioxide emissions, with a view to establishing a strong Community position in preparation for the second world climate conference'.

In 1992, the Commission responded with a major proposal for a Community carbon/energy tax to reduce emissions of CO_2, the main 'greenhouse gas' contributing to climate change. This proposal was never adopted by the member states, although at one stage all except two member states could have accepted it in a modified form. It should be said in this connection that British opposition to this proposal, which needed unanimity in Council as it was a fiscal measure, was down to a hard-line and doctrinaire Conservative approach to Community involvement in tax harmonisation – and not necessarily the view of the then British Secretary of State for the Environment, John Gummer, who was a dedicated and persuasive proponent of environmental protection. Ireland's position was close to the official British line.

An enormous amount had been achieved by DG XI since the ratification of the Single European Act, in establishing a Community environment policy and a Community presence in the important international fora. The Commission and the Community had established themselves as global players, and this had been achieved by the manner in which the director general, Laurens Jan Brinkhorst, had forcefully built on a European Court of Justice ruling that:

> Each time the Community, with a view to implementing a common policy envisaged by the Treaty, lays down common rules, whatever form these may take, the member states no longer have the right, acting individually, or even collectively, to contract obligations towards non-member states affecting these rules.

This ruling, as we have seen, provided the definitive decision clearing the Commission and Community's role in international environmental politics. Subsequently, the Single European and then the Maastricht Treaty gave specific competence to the Community to conclude international environmental agreements which bind the institutions of the Community – and the member states – and thus the Commission's role in international negotiations was clarified.

On the domestic front, 1993 saw a number of significant developments on the environment question. In the first place, a new European Commissioner, Iannis Paleokrassas, was appointed – he had previously been the Greek Finance Minister. It was largely through his influence that the topic of fiscal instruments as determinants of environmental behaviour was raised to public discussion. The use of fiscal instruments for the achievement of environmental goals had been already mooted in the fifth action programme, but – as unanimity was required in Council for any proposal dealing with taxation – it had not got very far. What Paleokrassas did was to persuade Jacques Delors that if some of the massive tax burden that fell on employment and the employed could be transferred to polluting products and activities, then pollution could be made more costly and employment less costly – two birds with one stone. In the Commission's white paper 'Growth, Competitiveness and Employment' such a shift was advocated. While it was sympathetically received in some quarters, the conservatism of tax authorities, together with the reluctance on the part of some member states to hand over any competence to the Commission in matters of taxation, ensured that this aspect of the white paper was effectively ignored in political terms. This has remained the position of member states to this day – perhaps with the arrival of a common European currency system we will see more flexibility on this crucial issue of environmental taxation at Community level.

During the early 1990s, the Commission, spurred by a deregulatory crusade on the part of certain member states, reviewed its environmental regulations and, while proposing no withdrawal, launched an exercise in revising some major pieces of regulations with a view to making them more flexible and cost-effective. In this process, we in DG I examined and proposed revisions in a series of Directives dealing with water, waste and air pollution. It was during this period too that DG I and DG III devised and implemented a completely new system for proposing limit values for noxious emissions from motor vehicles – the source of major pollutants such as carbon monoxide, nitrous oxides (NOx) and particulates. The limit values proposed by the Commission were in fact developed in a joint research project with the motor industry and oil industry (the first ever in Europe!), and following a cost-effectiveness study to determine a least-cost set of measures that would achieve the Community air quality standards. This Auto-Oil Programme was designed to respond to all of the strictures contained in Article 130 of the Treaty – solid scientific base, knowledge of costs and benefits, etc. It remains a model for the development of future environment regulations in the Community.

Personalities

During my period in DG XI, the European Environment Council has been dominated by a number of superb Environment Ministers: Klaus Töpfer from Germany, Svend Auken from Denmark and John Gummer from Britain. In my view, it has been largely through the force of these personalities and capabilities that much of the Commission's proposals have been adopted. Dr Töpfer was a decisive force in the early 1990s; he was clearly the 'doyen' at that time, and a man responsible in his own country for one of the clearest applications of the 'polluter pays' principles in the German packaging waste ordinance – the DUALE system.

Svend Auken is a big man, in every sense. He also has a big job, for he is Danish Minister for the Environment and Energy. He is perhaps the most persuasive politician I have ever met, and his contribution to European environment policy through his advocacy at Council and elsewhere is substantial. John Gummer was a committed environment supporter even before he became Secretary of State for the Environment. I first encountered him when he was still Secretary of State for Agriculture, Food and Fisheries at a conference on 'agriculture, trade and the environment' in Scheveningen, Holland; his commitment to environmental protection was quite obvious even at that stage. An immensely skilled debater with a mischievous sense of humour and great charm, he made a major contribution to European and global environmental affairs.

On the Irish side, quite a few of our more prominent politicians have held the environment portfolio. Since my 'conversion' to environmental aims, the Irish ministers have been Pádraig Flynn, Michael Smith and Brendan Howlin. I met Pádraig Flynn initially at the historic first meeting of Environment Ministers from the Communities and from Central and Eastern Europe, over which he presided in Dublin Castle in June 1990. As a Commissioner he has always been supportive of the environment viewpoint. Michael Smith was a well-respected member of the Environment Council – always open, approachable and worth listening to. It was at one informal meeting of Environment Ministers in Dresden that I got to know him on a more informal basis. Brendan Howlin, as Pádraig Flynn before him, was Irish Minister for the Environment during an Irish Presidency in 1995. He is remembered with great affection both by his fellow ministers of the time, and by those European civil servants (including me) who had the occasion to meet and work with him. His participations in Council discussions were always impressive – and he had both linguistic ability and a sense of fun, which endeared him to all. He carried out his duties as President of the European Environment council conscientiously and effectively. Noel Dempsey, the present minister, I first met when he was the shadow Minister for the Environment, on the occasion of a two-day visit he made to Brussels to acquaint himself with the major problems on the European environmental agenda… this, for me, was impressive. He subsequently produced a Fianna Fáil policy document on environmental policy.

In general, Irish positions at European Councils have been constructive. Only on two issues, in my experience, have they been in direct opposition to

Commission proposals or to majority consensus. The first was Irish opposition to the Commission proposal, called for at the Dublin 1990 summit, for a carbon energy tax. The second was Ireland's opposition to the Commission proposal on water charging in the content of the new Water Framework Directive. This latter was a point on which Ireland lost a considerable amount of the standing it had built up in European environmental circles.

There has always been, during my contact with them, an extremely good *esprit de corps* among Community Environment Ministers. I recall one incident in Sofia in October 1995 at the third ministerial conference, 'Environment for Europe'. The Council President at the time was Jose Borel (now leader of the Spanish Socialist opposition), and I was leading the Commission delegation in the absence of Commissioner Ritt Bjerregaard. The particular question at issue was the date and venue of the next 'Environment for Europe' conference. The Danes wanted it for Aarhus before the summer of 1998; all other ministers were unanimous that a two-and-a-half-year gap was too short, and that the next meeting should be in 1999 at the earliest. It was agreed that the matter would be settled at a meeting on the penultimate evening of the conference, on which the Bulgarians had arranged a state reception for participants. All the arguments, persuasive skills and charm of Danish minister Svend Auken were to no avail. Finally, he appealed to political susceptibilities, revealing that an election was likely in Denmark in June 1998, and the holding of this important conference in his own constituency would be 'not unhelpful'. On this basis he managed to melt the opposition of the others, who rallied around their 'political' friend. In the event, it proved to be an excellent decision, as the 'Environment for Europe' process was in need of reorientation in 1998. Furthermore, the time pressure was useful in forcing a number of issues at the UN–ECE negotiations for a convention on access to information, public participation in decision-making, and access to justice in environmental matters – now known as the Aarhus Convention, as it was signed at the conference.

Evolution

During the period since 1994, I have invested a substantial proportion of my time in a campaign to help the countries of central and eastern Europe prepare for accession to the Union. The environmental *acquis* that they will be expected to transpose, implement and enforce as a precondition for accession is extensive, and the implementation costs are enormous. To make good the neglect of 50 years in a short space of time represents a major challenge. Commissioner Ritt Bjerregaard (who took up office in January 1995) always gave top priority to this task. Under her leadership we have, I believe, been able to provide significant support to the countries in providing know-how, guidance, support, technical assistance, and even some capital investment support. Enlargement to the East is important for Ireland, as it is clear that the incoming countries will need considerable 'funds from Brussels' to assist their transition and early life in the European Union. Their arrival, together with world trade pressures, will demand a significant reform of the Common Agricultural Policy.

In 1995 the European Environment Agency (EEA) was set up by the Commission with the main task of developing and disseminating accurate and timely data on the actual physical state of the European environment so as to help legislators to focus on, and subsequently evaluate, the results of the various policy measures, regulations and other actions taken over 25 years to protect the environment. The EEA published a major 'state of the environment' reform in early 1998 (it is fair to say that it contained a great deal of bad news!) and another in 1999. In short, the reports show that in only four out of twelve major sectors of environmental concern have the protections, regulations and measures implemented achieved the desired result, namely an improvement in environmental status, or at least the arrest of environmental degradation. This was a shock to many. Immediately, a great deal of soul-searching was initiated – were the Directives strict enough, had they been implemented and enforced adequately enough? The main reason why many environmental Directives have not achieved the hoped-for results is that other important sectoral policies continued to have inherently polluting effects – the Community and member states had simply failed to heed their own strictures which were written into the Treaty ten years previously:

> Environment concerns and requirements shall be incorporated into the design and implementation of other sectoral policies.

Two examples of this 'ignoring' may be helpful. I was personally involved in the regulation of motor vehicle emissions as far back as 1984. By 1994 the Community regulations had succeeded in decreasing noxious emissions from new vehicles by 80 per cent. Nevertheless, the total tonnage of pollutants released into the atmosphere by the transport sector continued (and still continues) to increase. In this case it was not that the regulations were not strict – they were at the limit of the technological possibilities. It was not that they were not implemented – they were. It was because of a transport policy (or lack of a transport policy) that failed to take account of consequences of growth of motor vehicle fleets and their use, that took no action to stem the flow of freight from rail to road, and that paid scant attention to the alternative public transport systems.

The old Common Agricultural Policy of the Communities (and to a lesser extent the revised one) was inherently intensive and polluting. When

Community policy encourages actions that are fatal for the health of our rivers and lakes, what chance have regulations of turning the tide?

At the end of 1997, the heads of state called on the Commission to provide a blueprint for the integration of environmental concerns and requirements into sectoral Community policies; at the Cardiff summit in June 1998 they adopted a series of regulations requiring the Commission and the sectoral ministerial Councils to take account of the integration imperative in their work and to report to the heads of state regularly on its implementation. This, one hopes, is the new beginning. We shall, of course, have to wait and see how effective this new approach will be. One can say that it will only be as effective as Community-wide policy is effective in any sector. Thus, for instance, it is clear that in relation to sectors where Community policy really bites – agriculture, external trade, regional development – the integration imperative should produce results, but what real effect it will have in transport and energy, for example, remains to be seen.

Thus we are at the start of a third phase in EU environmental policy. Having commenced 25 years ago an intensive, though *ad hoc*, regulatory phase, we passed in the early 1990s into a phase where regulation was reviewed and rationalised, and where new instruments for achieving specific environmental goals were discussed (e.g. voluntary agreements with industry, economic and fiscal instruments). Now at the end of the 1990s we pass into the third phase, whose cornerstone is the 'integration' of environmental requirements into sectoral policies. This integration has in fact been a Treaty obligation since the SEA, but has been largely ignored. The Amsterdam Treaty makes the 'integration' imperative a lot more specific – hence the decision taken at the European Council in Cardiff in June 1998. Progress is also likely to be made, in certain areas of environmental concern, on the development of voluntary or negotiated agreements with the business sector – the agreement between the Commission and the European automobile industry on CO_2 emissions from car motors marks a beginning. Again, the whole question of 'environmental liability' will be treated in a white paper soon to be issued by the Commission. Many commentators have established that our present life-styles based on planned product obsolescence, convenience, our use of resources, and use of independent means of locomotion are inherently polluting, and that changing consumer behaviour is the key to restoring environmental equilibrium. Here the approach would be one of 'prevention' rather than 'cure'. For me, progress along these lines will only be achieved when we in the EU have the means, through taxation, to alter consumer motivation and behaviour on a Community-wide basis. Hopefully, EMU will lead to an acceptance of greater tax harmonisation, thus providing a basis for tax differentiation to encourage the production and use of 'greener' products through 'green' processes.

Judgements

Any judgement on Ireland's performance in relation to Community environment policy must be based on two things: firstly, the Irish record in implementing Community Directives, and secondly, the Irish contribution to the development of Community environment policies. In the matter of implementation, Ireland's record is a good one. In a recent conversation I had with Dr Ludwig Kraemer (probably Europe's most distinguished environmental lawyer and a long-time senior official in DG II), we touched on this question. He takes the view that in the matter of implementing Community Directives, Ireland's performance is good. He points to the fact that there has never been a single European Court of Justice decision against Ireland in the field of the environment. He also points to the considerable achievement during the 1980s in improving air quality in Dublin (25 per cent of the population benefited). Ireland had to finance since 1972 a catching-up process in the development of physical environmental infrastructure, and this has been largely achieved (with structural and cohesion funds intelligently used). Ludwig Kraemer also points out that it was Ireland that demonstrated that it was possible for a country with a 'common law' system to transpose European Directives into binding legal obligations which could be implemented. Ireland has also been to the fore in cleaning up beaches and thus qualifying for a high number of 'blue flags'. Only in the implementation of Directives dealing with water quality and biodiversity protection has our performance been somewhat slow; this is not because of any administrative neglect, but arises from the need to convince the agricultural sector of the necessity of these measures.

In the matter of policy formation and development, it must be said that the Irish representatives in the environment group of Council have always been constructive and at times creative in solving apparent impasses. Although we have not yet produced an acknowledged leader in environmental thinking or writing, the contributions of Professor Yvonne Scannell (TCD – environmental law) and Professor Frank Convery (UCD) have been widely acknowledged.

For Ireland, beset as it is with two significant environmental challenges, namely degradation of surface water (lakes, rivers, streams) and waste disposal, the way ahead is clear enough. The only question is whether the political will remains to implement and enforce EU legislation, and to integrate environmental requirements into other sectoral policies. The present minister and his predecessor have produced strategies for sustainable development for Ireland. They are excellent, and will be an example to other member states when they are fully implemented and enforced, but recent news is far from encouraging.

It is in our own business interests to take whatever actions are necessary to reverse present trends and to restore the quality of our rivers and lakes, and preserve the 'green' image from which we have prospered in the past.

For the European Union as a whole, the path to the achievement of sustainable economic growth has been clearly indicated by the heads of state. The 'integration' of environmental concerns and requirements into sectoral policies, in particular transport and agriculture, is the *sine qua non*. It is also widely acknowledged that we need to streamline the procedures at Union level for enforcing the directives. So far as the ever-increasing waste disposal problems are concerned, I remain firmly of the view that such problems will never be solved until first we solve the problem of waste prevention, and for this we still lack one crucial instrument, namely the capacity to create fiscal incentives and disincentives at Community level. It is, I think, salutary to recall how effective a small variation in tax was in promoting the introduction of, and sales growth in, lead-free petrol.

I think there are many areas where fiscal incentives, carefully used at Community level, can gradually produce changes in consumer behaviour and expenditure that could never be achieved by regulation alone. But for this instrument to be used across the European Union, the Treaty, which requires unanimity for any fiscal measure, will need to be modified by the introduction of qualified majority voting for this issue.

Finally, it is my hope that the European Union will continue to give leadership at a global level in the matter of tackling global environmental problems. It has done this up to now, and it continues to do so in the face of apathy and obstruction on the issue of climate change. We in Ireland need to be conscious of the duty we have to support EU positions on global environment issues in all our contacts with third countries.

NOTES

1   R. Carson, *The Silent Spring*, Houghton Mifflin, Boston, 1962.

2   Barbara Ward and R. Dudos, *One Earth: the Care and Maintenance of a Small World*, Penguin, Harmondsworth, 1972.

3   The Club of Rome Report, *Limit to Growth*, 1972.

4   Paris Convention for the Prevention of Marine Pollution, 1974; Bonn Convention for the Protection of the Rhine, 1976; Bonn Convention on the Conservation of Migratory Species, 1979; Bonn Convention on the Conservation of the European Wildlife and Habitats, 1979; Geneva Convention on the Long Range Transboundary Air Pollution, 1979; Vienna Convention on the Ozone Layer, 1978.

18

Equality and gender balance

JOAN HART

Introduction

Membership of the European Union has helped transform Ireland, not least from a perspective that is less tangible but arguably as potent as the more obvious benefits of membership – the opportunity to see how others do things and, in so doing, to hold a mirror to ourselves. 'The only true voyage of discovery is not to go to new places, but to have other eyes.' (Marcel Proust, *Remembrance of Things Past*). As inhabitants of a small, insular, economically vulnerable island, membership of the EU in 1973 offered the Irish people new access opportunities and new perspectives.[1] Membership ultimately offered us the prospect of working and moving around freely in the EU, trading freely in goods and services and having an open capital market. In essence, the combined political energy of the member states and the European institutions over the past 25 years at European level has been channelled towards making a reality of these simple principles as originally enshrined in the Treaty of Rome.

However, membership of the EU also gave us access to new sets of institutions, new legislative, judicial and policy-making processes and new cultures in the fullest sense of the word, which in effect gave us 'other eyes' and new perspectives. It gave us the opportunity to look at ourselves while retaining our distinct identity. Even in a small environment such as the College of Europe in Bruges[2] (founded by the International European Movement), which I attended, the real learning took place not so much from the formal learning opportunities but from watching how others do things, and using that learning for exploring our own distinctive approaches. The college was in many ways a microcosm of the European institutions themselves – it exposed the real difficulties of managing in multicultural environments, balancing the need for sensitivity to differences, and the imperative of not allowing the process of dealing with those differences to interfere with the achievement of policy goals and objectives. The college was formative for a second reason: it moved what was initially an intellectual exercise – studying and understanding the principles, processes and policies of the European Union – onto the emotional level.

Most people nowadays tend to associate Belgium, and Brussels in particular, with the centre of power of the European Union. Its troubled past tends to be overlooked. One of the most formative journeys I took was the annual 'pilgrimage' organised by Professor Marie-Joseph Lory of the college on 11 November each year to the trenches and battlefields of the First World War and to the war cemeteries. Being Irish, we are rarely confronted with the harsh reality and landmarks serving as reminders of what that war really meant. We had many casualties of our own in the war, but the Irish involvement has not really percolated through to our national psyche. That first journey on 11 November 1978 vividly and poignantly underlined for me what the European Union was really about. Living and studying with peers from other member states whose family histories bore testimony to the wars was also instrumental in shifting perspectives. The political rationale and impetus for the European Union very often gets lost in the quagmire of the complex and technical nature of the EU policy agenda.

Our membership of the Union has been important, therefore, not just in policy terms but also because of the opportunity to develop new insights about ourselves as a society, our values and beliefs. When we joined the EU in 1973, Irish society was shaped by a very distinct set of values with significant implications in particular for the role of women in society – not least their participation in the labour market. Ireland was not, however, unique in this respect. From its inception the EU recognised that there were issues to be addressed in terms of the role of women as economic actors and participants in the labour force. The Treaty of Rome's provisions in relation to equal pay (Art 119) and the European Social Fund proved to be important catalysts in placing issues associated with women's participation, in the labour market and in society in general, on the European political agenda. The European Commission would now argue that it has a comprehensive enabling legal framework covering the area of equal opportunity.[3] Both the Amsterdam Treaty (Articles 2, 3 and 141.4) and the 1999 employment guidelines copper-fasten the political commitment to equality and gender balance. In an important development, they extended the scope of the equality agenda to apply to all EU policy areas, and so introduced one of the key changes in the equality agenda over recent years, i.e. mainstreaming.

Any study of Ireland's membership of the EU therefore has to ask whether and how the role of women has changed as a result of EU and national initiatives. It is, however, a very broad question inviting analysis from a number of different perspectives. One could, for example, look at the question from a gender, economic, social, political, organisational, national, cultural or European perspective. The approach in this essay is informed by two perspectives: that of a woman who is committed to the European ideal and who has tried to influence the translation of ideals into reality, mainly but not only through the European Movement; and that of a woman who has worked in both the public and private sectors in Ireland. An inevitable part of this experience has been the constant questions in relation to the role of women in organisations and in society: are there sufficient real opportunities for women to participate fully in a meaningful way in the labour market, in the policy-making institutions within the public and private sectors, in those critical interest groups that shape policy, and in the social economy? What are the factors affecting women's participation? Has the EU made a difference through its legal and financial frameworks? How can we move from aspirational to operational policies on equality? These are difficult questions to answer. It is not easy to attribute change (or the lack of it) to one particular set of factors – more usually a combination of factors and circumstances apply. In this essay, my main interest is to look at these questions in the context of women at work, including their contribution to the social economy, and women in decision-making.

Women and work

Looking back at the position in 1973, the most obvious single structural barrier – the marriage bar – was a very powerful, but not the only, impediment to participation, particularly in the public sector. As a consequence the labour market at the time was characterised by low female participation rates and, of course, low pay. Those who were successful in climbing the career ladder were inevitably single. Up to the late 1980s it was unusual in both the public and private sectors to meet female senior managers who were not single.

Prior to our membership of the EU, the Irish government had taken the first tentative steps to look at the role of women in society and particularly their participation in the labour market. Interestingly, the establishment of the first Commission on the Status of Women was triggered by Ireland's involvement in another international organisation, the United Nations. Importantly, though, there were also parallel developments at national level to mobilise women and to frame an agenda on women's issues, with the trade union movement playing an active role. The legal framework of the EU through its Directives was an important catalyst in bringing about the ground-breaking legislation at national level to remove the most critical areas of discrimination in relation to the employment of women, in particular equal pay for equal work.[4] In the mid-1970s, the Irish economy was in recession and so the government sought a derogation from EU Directives. There was a real concern on the part of the government, fuelled by the business lobby, about the potential cost of implementing EU Directives both for the national finances and for the private sector. As a well-established, influential lobby, business interests had initially been more effective in influencing the government's agenda than the advocates of equal pay. But in the end the government did not get its derogation and had to implement the equality Directives. The Irish commissioner at the time, Patrick Hillery, in response to pressure from women's groups and the trade union movement, investigated the need for the derogation and refused it. This was an important achievement for both women's groups and the trade union movement, and showed how the Commission can be and has been used as a channel by pressure and interest groups to influence national policy-makers. It also put down a marker to the government that the equality agenda was not going to be shaped only by business interest groups. Without the legal imperative of implementing EU legislation, and the success of women's groups and the trade unions in setting the agenda at national level, the ground-breaking legislation could have been delayed longer.

It is one thing to have legislation in place, but another to implement it so that it actually brings about desired changes. The picture in 1998, compared to 1973, is in many ways a healthier one, but there are still areas of concern. While women's pay improved in the initial period after the legislation was enacted, there are still considerable pay differentials between men and women, irrespective of their seniority within an organisation, it would appear. In 1997, the average industrial hourly earnings of women were 73 per cent of those earned by men – surprisingly, the differential also applies to female managing directors, who earn only 75 per cent of their male equivalents' salaries.[5] Undoubtedly there has been an increase in women's participation in the labour force, from 26 per cent[6] in the early 1970s to 39 per cent in 1997, although the participation rate is still lower than the EU rate of 45 per cent in 1997. In 1998, a strong economic imperative was likely to drive participation rates for women upwards. On the supply side, the shortage of labour means that more women will have to be encouraged to enter the labour market to avoid wage inflation, while the demand for work by women is being driven by economic necessity. So women are definitely entering the labour market in larger numbers – but to do what? Once in work, do women see themselves as having real opportunities to progress within organisations?

The services sector is still the single biggest source of employment for women – four out of every five employed women work in this sector. While the services sector is growing, over 67 per cent of employed women work in one of three occupations: clerical workers, professional and technical workers, and service workers. There is a high concentration of women in low-paid semi-skilled occupations. One in every five women employed works part-time, and women account for almost 75 per cent of those employed on a part-time basis. Women are slowly gaining ground in some professions,

notably the legal and accountancy professions, but are still marginal players
in others, particularly engineering, and to a lesser extent the medical
profession. A worrying trend for the future is that women tend to be under-
represented in the higher echelons of the new emerging sectors such as
electronics and information technology. In 1997, only 30 per cent of those
with a scientific or technological qualification were women – this is clearly
an area that needs to be addressed.

There is a widespread perception that opportunities exist for women to
progress within organisations if only they would equip themselves with the
necessary skills to take advantage of them. So, are these real opportunities for
women? The facts would suggest not. While there has been progress in some
sectors, there are still glaring discrepancies in the extent to which women are
represented at senior level in organisations. In the private sector, 3 per cent
of managing directors are female while 15 per cent of heads of function are
female. The proportion of women at middle management level is better,
perhaps giving cause for optimism for the future. However, the number of
women presenting for management training is low, at about 17 per cent, so
there are some mixed signals.[7] Despite the high participation rate of women
in the financial sector, and the explicit commitment to equality, women are
under-represented in the senior and executive ranks. At one of the annual
social functions for the sector where the overall attendance would typically
be over 800, the proportion of women represented up to the mid-1990s was
less than 5 per cent, reflecting their absence from the executive ranks within
the sector and the broader business community. In the public sector there is
evidence of women being promoted to senior management level, but again
they are still substantially under-represented. Less than 6 per cent of
secretaries and assistant secretaries are women; there is still only one female
county manager, only one female senior person in the ranks of the gardaí, and
very low representation of women in senior academic circles. The overall
picture in both the public and private sectors is one where women are still
only slowly making their way up the corporate ladder.

What are the obstacles? In a 1996 survey conducted by Eurobarometer
into attitudes to opportunity in the labour market, the two most important
obstacles cited preventing women from holding positions of responsibility
were that women have less time because of family responsibility, and the
work environment is dominated by men who do not have enough trust in
women.[8] Most women with family responsibilities will identify with the first
reason. The second reason brings us into the realm of perception – it is less
tangible and therefore easy to dismiss. But this perception is revealing in
terms of how people see the problem.

People work for different reasons – some are motivated by career, money,
power, status, achievement; others work simply out of economic necessity.

Increasingly, both men and women are opting for a balanced lifestyle – balancing the needs of work and family. This is a particular reality for women with children at work. Hence there is both a need and a desire for more flexible options in relation to the context and organisation of work. The EU has helped to stimulate debate and has been a catalyst in terms of promoting flexible and innovative approaches to work. Through its legal and financial frameworks, it not only has tried to create a supportive and enabling environment but also has introduced specific initiatives aimed at encouraging women's participation, such as the NOW (New Opportunities for Women) initiative. In essence, NOW is a learning framework for testing and implementing new approaches to the training and employment of women through a cross-section of projects and sectors. Projects were set up so as to facilitate women, breaking away from more traditional practices, and therefore have been instrumental in developing models of best practice in critical areas, e.g. childcare facilities.[9] What is striking is the amount of activity, in the form of projects and initiatives sponsored by the EU, to promote equal opportunity, particularly during the 1990s. Its impact is more difficult to assess. In a more general work context, Ireland is often cited for its innovative approaches to the organisation of work. However, recent research indicates that the picture in Ireland is not as progressive as might at first appear with regard to the nature and scope of innovation taking place in the workplace.[10] The climate and factors contributing to the development of innovative work practices are broadly similar to those required if women are to participate at all levels of organisations in a significant way. Are the numerous projects and initiatives having the desired impact on national and organisational policies? There is a palpable sense of frustration on the part of some women's groups on the lack of progress and the perceived inertia on the part of national government to 'mainstream' gender issues. The European Commission was critical of the national action plans (NAPs) on employment produced by each member state because they did not give sufficient details on how pillar IV, relating to mainstreaming of equality issues, would be applied at national level.[11]

Interestingly, one of the essential principles guiding the Irish government's approach to overseas development issues is gender. All aid projects have to be assessed from a gender perspective. There is a sense of irony that we set principles to be implemented in developing countries that somehow still elude us at home. This is not a criticism of the focus on gender in a development context, but our commitment becomes more convincing when we feel that we have our own house in order first.

There have been many assessments of the barriers preventing women from participating fully in the labour market, the social economy and decision-making at all levels and sectors. The EU has played a central animating role in helping to set the agenda, provide incentives for specific actions and provide 'moral' support for women's groups and projects. But it also recognises that, of necessity, each member state has primary responsibility for making equality a reality. It is a very complex issue and has to be seen from different perspectives. A perspective that is often overlooked is the impact of organisational culture at the level of individual enterprises/institutions. Organisational culture is itself a complex phenomenon – it has an elusive quality often compounded by the fact that the stated culture (to the extent that culture is stated) can be at variance with the 'real' norms and values that actually determine behaviour. So an organisation may be saying the 'right things', using the correct language, while the real norms determining behaviour are quite different to those stated. This would appear to be the case on issues relating to equality. The mismatch between organisational culture and policy certainly confuses and distorts our view of the real impediments to change. Organisations may have policies that indicate commitment, but they are not internalised into behaviours. Organisational change will only happen if there is an enabling, supportive organisational culture. Who and what determines the culture of an organisation? In theory, everybody does; in practice, senior – and therefore predominantly male – managers are the critical shapers. Does the external regulatory environment affect organisational culture? Eventually, yes – but to move from compliance to commitment is a slow process.

Women and the social economy

Traditionally, women have played a central, although voluntary, role in the burgeoning social economy. The voluntary sector receives almost £500m from the government and the EU each year – a figure that considerably understates its importance because of the voluntary nature of many of its services.

The social economy is characterised by a complex, decentralised and largely uncoordinated delivery system consisting of a vast array of voluntary and community groups, all competing with each other for the limited financial resources available.[12] While voluntary groups have been a feature of the social economy for some time, the growth in the number and diversity of community groups is a relatively recent phenomenon which the EU, through its structural funds, helped to stimulate. The challenge for the government is to harness the resources of the sector by giving it recognition and a voice at national level, while ensuring that it retains the diversity that is its core strength. The number and diversity of organisations involved in the social economy have made it difficult to find an appropriate platform at central level for formulating and articulating a common agenda. However, the importance of the sector is now being recognised by its inclusion in the partnership dialogue through the Community Platform.

There are issues for women in this sector. The increased participation of women in the labour market combined with changing demographic patterns may mean that this sector will be deprived of arguably its greatest asset – voluntary carers and workers. A related issue is what support can and should be made available for those working in the social economy. Finally, voluntary and community groups seem to suffer from the structural weaknesses evident in the public and private sectors – women are central to service delivery but appear to be under-represented on the management structures of the delivery organisations, based on the evidence of the area partnerships, county enterprise boards and LEADER boards.[13] The size of the sector makes it difficult to monitor the participation of women in decision-making, but it would appear to lag behind the public sector.

Women in decision-making

As suggested above, exposure to and interaction with European institutions and other member states opens up new possibilities for influencing and being influenced. It is difficult to assess the precise impact of this process of interaction, but the evidence would suggest that it is highly formative. There are many examples of how the 'demonstration effect' applies, but perhaps the most striking, because of its central importance in driving recent economic success and because it is becoming an important forum for setting the equality agenda, is the partnership approach that has evolved since the mid-1980s. This was the result of a process that involved taking a hard look at the institutional architecture for managing our economy and adapting it based on experiences in other national and European institutions. The participation of the social partners in the EU process was important in preparing the ground for the partnership approach. So how has this unique interaction process worked for women?

The first self-evident point is that it only works to the extent that women are involved in decision-making processes and networks at national level. Looking at European decision-making fora, there are potentially two avenues for women to become involved: women can participate in shaping and negotiating Irish interests in Europe either through government channels or the many interest groups seeking to influence policy at national and European level, including those dealing exclusively with equality issues; or they can join one of the European institutions either as an employee or as an elected or nominated representative.

In relation to the first avenue, the very real problem is a structural one – women can only participate to the extent that they are included in decision-making at national level. The Community process therefore reflects structural inequalities in national policy-making processes. Measuring the extent to which women participate in decision-making is difficult because of the lack of indicators and benchmarks. This is an area that the EU is encouraging member states to address, and in fact they are now required to produce reports on progress achieved. A couple of points can be made, however. The figures suggest that women are still considerably under-represented at senior and middle management level in the civil service – critical actors in the negotiation process. Concerns have been expressed about the lack of involvement of women in monitoring arrangements for the structural funds.[14] In relation to interest groups, women have obviously been well represented on those dealing with equality issues. However, women have been under-represented in some of the most influential sectoral groups, notably agriculture and business, both of which are important policy areas in the Union.

The approach of local authorities to the EU provides a specific insight into how they tried to increase their leverage in their relationship with central government by influencing the agenda at EU level. Ironically, the initial drive towards regional development in the EU through the regional development fund coincided with a period of centralisation in Ireland. Although not very well organised initially, local authorities turned their attention in the 1980s to various European networks of local authorities such as the CEMR (Council of European Municipalities and Regions) and IULA (International Union of Local Authorities). Their agenda was clear: to learn from other models of local government and to put pressure on the government, via the Commission, to increase their power nationally. But again, those interacting with these networks at either political or executive level reflected the distortions in terms of women's representation on local structures. Local authorities substantially failed to use the EU as leverage because of the resistance of central government. The Commission tried to use the financial incentive of the structural funds to promote more participative, locally-driven approaches to development in Ireland, but this wasn't sufficient to overcome the resistance of central government. In summary, the extent to which women have been able to benefit from the interaction and socialisation process that is such an integral part of the Community process has been unavoidably intertwined with the realities of their participation in decision-making on the national domestic scene.

One area where there has been considerable progress is the representation of women on state boards. When the National Women's Council of Ireland (NWCI) first started monitoring representation of women on state boards in 1979, only 9.6 per cent of the appointees were women. In 1997 there were 812 women and 2002 men on 211 nationally appointed boards.[15] This significant change is directly attributable to the government's policy adopted in 1991 to introduce a 40 per cent gender policy on state boards. The quota system has been contentious in the past, but it is definitely having an impact in the public sector – the vigilance of organisations such as the NWCI helps. There are still some outstanding areas to address, for example the gender balance on the relatively new local institutions such as the area partnerships (12–45 per cent women), the county enterprise boards (11–43 per cent women) and LEADER boards (0–36 per cent women); the number of female chairmen (39 out of 172); and the interpretation of the quota as a maximum rather than a minimum. The overall picture, though, is promising in the public sector. The contrast with the private sector could not be more stark. In 1993, only two out of 128 (1.6 per cent) of the board members of the top ten companies were women.[16] The achievements in the public sector agencies possibly suggest that their visibility puts more pressure on them to comply with EU and their own guidelines – in the longer term, the increased representation should put gender issues firmly on the political and organisational agenda.

An interesting development is now occurring with the likely inclusion of some of the current round of applicants from central and eastern Europe and the Baltic states. The profile of the Irish civil service in the early 1970s could not be more different to the profile, for example, of the Latvian civil service, currently preparing for their accession negotiations. Between the ministry of foreign affairs and the European Integration Bureau, there are a significant number of young, assertive, confident women with the ability to network and immerse themselves in policy issues. This does not necessarily reflect the situation throughout the sectors – there are difficulties in other areas of the public and private sectors, despite a constitutional commitment to equal opportunity, and the traditional high participation rates of women in socialist economies. In addition, their interest groups and NGO sector are still in their formative stage – it is too early to indicate what their profile and their influence will be like.

Women also participate directly in the European institutions, some in positions of power and influence. The most high-profile of these are the MEPs. Irish women were more successful in getting elected to the European Parliament than the Dáil in the last elections to both institutions. There are currently five female MEPs[17] out of a total of 15, while the number of female TDs stands at 20 out of a total of 166 (12 per cent). Why have women been more successful at European elections? Getting elected at local level is an important starting point on the road to national politics – only 11 per cent of councillors elected in 1991 were women.[18] Election to local government is not as critical a factor for the European elections. The election of two female presidents in succession has forced a re-think on the part of the political parties in terms of their selection procedures – they have finally been confronted with the significance of the women's vote and therefore the need to put forward strong female candidates. Women have been making their voices heard through the ballot box. The fact that two of the female MEPs are members of the Green Party also reflects the growing importance of the 'environmental' agenda – an area consistently emerging in opinion polls that is perceived to be of more importance to women than to men. The calibre of MEPs is critical for two reasons. First, they project an image of Ireland – how they behave and project themselves personally is important. Second, they have an opportunity to influence and shape policy and the direction of the Parliament itself. Because the European Parliament is a fledgling institution in legislative terms, with growing but limited formal powers, an important source of its informal power is the calibre of its individual MEPs. The main channel of influence is through the committee system, where the detailed policy investigation takes place. The European Parliament is therefore an important avenue whereby Irish men and women can contribute to the development of the European Union. Is it possible to make an overall comment/observation on the specific role/contribution of female MEPs as opposed to male MEPs? This is difficult to say – female MEPs have certainly tried to set an agenda in terms of social and environmental policy, and are possibly more vocal than most of their male colleagues. Probably the most important aspect of their success is the very presence of such a high number of female MEPs – evidence that women are capable of breaking important electoral thresholds.

The European Commission, as a central institution in driving the European policy agenda, is also a potential target institution for women seeking to influence the policy agenda. The most influential posts in the Commission are those in the respective cabinets of the commissioners and high-ranking posts in the Commission itself. Women have been represented on the cabinets of Irish commissioners, although not in great numbers. Because the cabinet acts like the eyes, ears and voice of the commissioner, they play a pivotal role in the Commission bureaucracy. The possibility of Irish women aspiring to high-ranking posts in the Commission is constrained both by the traditional barriers and by the 'quota' system on the number of high-ranking positions assigned to different nationals. Given Ireland's size, the number of senior posts open to it is limited. The most senior ranking female Irish Commission officials are at director level, one of whom works on the enlargement desk – playing a central role on a dossier that is arguably one of the most important on the European political agenda. The Commission has recognised the need to introduce equality policies in its own organisation, and is taking steps to do so.

Concluding remarks

Looking at the role of women in Irish society today compared to 1973, there have undoubtedly been important changes. Women are more active in the labour market, they are having some success in climbing the career ladder and they are more involved in decision-making. The EU has played its part in a number of important ways: it has introduced legislation that provides a supportive and progressive legal framework for women participating in the labour market and ensured compliance through its judicial system; its financial supports have facilitated women in training and employment; it has helped to shape the agenda at European and national level on equality issues; it has provided learning opportunities through transnational experiences; it has generated ideas and raised questions about the organisation of work and the development of indicators and benchmarks on equality issues; and it has assertively monitored the evolution and implementation of policy at national level.

In recent years, the EU has put down important markers to the member states on how equality issues should be integrated and incorporated into all aspects of national and EU policy. Mainstreaming the equality policy agenda is now firmly placed at the top of the EU political priorities, as evidenced by the Amsterdam Treaty. But the EU is just one player. Without the co-operation of the member states it can basically only ensure compliance with its equality policy – it cannot secure the commitment needed to internalise and operationalise it within public and private sector organisations.

This is the nub of the problem on equality and gender – how to move from rhetoric on the need for equality to generating the kind of commitment throughout society and more specifically in individual organisations and institutions to make it a reality. Are our values and beliefs reflecting the political importance attached to equality? Do we look at what we do and who we are from an equality perspective? While the statistical and documentary evidence points to progress and most sectors have appropriate policy positions on equality, many sectors are still segregated and women are not highly visible at the upper echelons of organisational life. The structural barriers are at least tangible and slowly being dismantled. The attitudinal barriers are more difficult to shift, but shifting them is a necessary precondition for generating commitment to sustainable change.

NOTES

1   The European Union has undergone several name changes over the years, reflecting its political and institutional growth. In the interests of simplicity, it is referred to as the EU throughout this essay, irrespective of the period to which the reference relates.

2   'The College of Europe, Bruges, Belgium and the sister College of Europe, Natolin, Poland, were founded by the International European Movement, 1949.'

3   Annual report from the Commission, *Equal Opportunities for Women and Men in the European Union, 1998*, COM (1999) 106 final, 05.03.1999, p. 24.

4   For a comprehensive account of the policy-making process in Ireland on employment equality see Y. Galligan, *Women and Politics in Contemporary Ireland – From the Margins to the Mainstream* (Pinter, London, 1998), chapter 4. See also Chapter 4 of this volume.

5   The figures used in this section are taken mainly (unless otherwise specified) from Frances Ruane and Julie Sutherland, *Women in the Labour Force*, Employment Equality Agency, 1999. This publication also refers to a survey conducted by Inbucon in 1998 which found that female managing directors received 75 per cent of the salary of their male equivalents – the salary for females employed in other management ranks was consistently around 86 per cent of men's salaries (p. 69).

6   Y. Galligan, op. cit., p. 32.

7   ESF/Program Evaluation Unit, *Evaluation Report, Women's Training Provision*, April 1994.

8   Eurobarometer 44.3, *Equal Opportunities for Women and Men in Europe*, December 1996, p. 55.

9   Evaluation of the NOW initiative 1991–94, August 1995.

10   J. Geary, *The New Workplace: Change at Work in Ireland* (research paper), December 1998, UCD.

11   Annual report from the Commission, *Equal Opportunities for Women and Men in the European Union, 1998*, COM (1999) 106 final, 05.03.1999, p. 13.

12   For an outline of the development and importance of voluntary and community groups see *Supporting Voluntary Activity – A Green Paper on the Community and Voluntary Sector and its Relationship with the State*, Government Publications, 1997.

13   National Women's Council of Ireland, *Who makes decisions in 1997? A Review of Gender Balance on State Boards in Ireland*.

14   National Women's Council of Ireland, *This Time Round – Gender and the Structural Funds*, October 1998.

15   As per note 12.

16   Y. Galligan, op. cit., p. 41.

17   In the European Parliament elections of 11 June 1999 five women won seats (Nuala Ahern, Mary Banotti, Avril Doyle, Patricia McKenna and Dana Rosemary Scallon).

18   Y. Galligan, op. cit., p. 38.

19

Consumer policy

JIM MURRAY

Consumer policy is not mentioned in the Treaty of Rome. References to 'the improvement of living and working conditions' in the Preamble and to 'an accelerated raising of the standard of living' in Article 2 could be cited as a basis for such a policy, but clearly could not carry the same weight as the more explicit references elsewhere to specific common policies. One of the stated objectives of the Common Agricultural Policy is 'To ensure that supplies reach consumers at reasonable prices'. The question of what constitutes a reasonable price is of course open to interpretation, but even the strongest supporters of the CAP would hesitate to describe it as consumer-driven. Consumer benefits are also mentioned in the competition Articles 85 and 86. Under Article 85, certain restrictions on competition may be justified if, for example, they improve production or distribution, or promote technical or economic progress, 'while allowing consumers a fair share of the resulting benefit'. Under Article 86, an abuse of dominant position may include limiting production, markets or technical development 'to the prejudice of consumers'.

In overall terms, however, these indirect or passing references could not be said to provide a firm basis for a Community consumer policy. None the less, a consumer policy of some kind did emerge slowly, albeit as a complement to, or component of, other policies such as the completion of the common market. Indeed, consumer policy issues inescapably arose within the global policy of creating a common market. What would be the effect of mutual recognition? Would it lead to a reduction in standards towards the lowest common denominator or would the increased competition ensure higher standards? At what level of consumer protection should laws be harmonised? Should the member state with the strictest laws be taken as a model, or should some other standard be applied? These were questions that had to be answered, if only by default, across a wide range of policy sectors.
Even when agreement was reached on a particular level of harmonisation, a second question arose. To what extent, if any, might member states be permitted to introduce or maintain stricter consumer protection laws at national level?

The question of representation of the consumer interest also arose, perhaps partly due to the foundation of a number of consumer organisations at national level during the 1950s. In 1961, Sicco Mansholt, then Commissioner for Agriculture, suggested that consumers should set up their own organisations since 'it has to be observed that the general interests of consumers in the Common Market are not represented to the same extent as are those of producers'. Doubtless encouraged by those words, BEUC, the European Consumers' Organisation, of which I am now the director, was established in 1962 and became a founding member of the contact committee for consumer questions set up by the Commission in that year. The other members included trade unions, family organisations and co-operatives. Some years later, in 1968, the Commission set up a new administrative unit to deal with consumer affairs, within the competition directorate.

From these somewhat scattered beginnings, the first real 'lift-off' for a Community consumer policy came at the 1972 Paris summit, on the eve of the admission of Ireland, Denmark and the UK. In Paris, the six founder members emphasised, perhaps for the first time, the importance to be accorded to the human dimension of the European Community and the need to improve the quality of life for the people within an enlarging community, and called on the Commission to develop programmes of action to this end. The Commission followed up the Paris summit with the establishment of a special consumer policy service, the setting-up of a new consumers' consultative committee (CCC), and the preparation of what became the preliminary programme for a consumer protection and information policy, approved by the Council in April 1975. This programme included a statement of basic consumer rights, based on those first enunciated by President Kennedy. This first programme was followed by a second programme and various new initiatives, action plans and priority programmes, whose details need not detain us here. Within the Commission the consumer policy service became part of DG XI, later a separate stand-alone service and now DG XXIV, with a much expanded brief.

Even with the adoption of the preliminary programme in 1975, the fact remained that the Treaty had little to say about consumers or consumer policy. The Single European Act, which came into force in 1987, brought two significant changes. The more important change was the abolition of the unanimity rule for directives in numerous matters relating to consumer protection. The less important change, also in Article 100A, required the Commission to adopt as a base a high level of consumer protection in proposing single market measures. From the perspective of a consumer advocate, this provision had more of a polemic value than anything else. It applied only to proposals by the Commission and not to final outcomes. It left ample room for argument on the definition of a 'high' level of protection, and it was not clear what redress was available to anyone who felt that a Commission proposal was not based on a high level of protection. It may be, however, that the clause had some impact in internal discussions within the Commission, and as consumer advocates we certainly tried to make the most of this provision in our lobbying. The ending of the unanimity rule was of great importance in the development of consumer protection measures, as in other areas. There was no longer the prospect of an effective veto being wielded by one member state. Much more important, however, was the Maastricht Treaty, which contained for the first time a Treaty article on consumer policy (Article 129A). BEUC was extremely active in pressing for this provision. We started our campaign in November 1990 by writing to the Presidents of the Commission (Jacques Delors) and the Council (Giulio Andreotti), arguing that protection of consumers should be one of the explicit objectives of the Community and that the Community should have the necessary competence to do what needs to be done to ensure a high level of protection for consumers across the entire market. The Danish government had made a somewhat similar proposal in October 1990, and we therefore sought to secure wider support for a proposal that could be said to be already on the table. The major breakthrough came when the Luxembourg Presidency included an article on consumer policy in its draft version of the Treaty (Title XVI in its draft). There seemed to be a fair degree of support for this proposal from most member states, but we were worried that this support was not very deep. We feared that the draft article would not survive determined opposition from one or a few member states, or perhaps that it might 'fall off the table' in the general press of business in the Intergovernmental Conference. We therefore targeted a number of governments that we feared might be hostile, notably the UK.

In the end it was the Dutch Presidency that caused the greatest problem, by preparing a draft text which did not include an article on consumer policy. As is well known, the Dutch text attracted wide criticism for reasons unconnected with consumer policy, but we had an anxious few final months before the Maastricht summit trying to do what we could as consumer advocates to keep the proposal on the table. In this we had a valiant ally in Karel Van Miert, then responsible for consumer policy, but we were not especially hopeful on the eve of Maastricht. In fact a new article 129A was agreed. Subsequently, Jacques Delors and John Major each claimed the credit for the new article. Success has many fathers.

In contrast with the time of the Amsterdam Treaty, my impression was that relatively few NGOs were actively interested in, or consulted about, the Maastricht Treaty. There was very much more consultation and public discourse in the preparations for the Amsterdam Treaty. From the consumer policy perspective, moreover, we found what seemed to be a general acceptance early on that the Amsterdam Treaty should include stronger consumer policy provisions. Discussion was more about wording than about principles.

The major change in the Maastricht Treaty 1992 was of course the increase in powers for the European Parliament. For consumer advocates, this was especially welcome because the Parliament is often more 'consumer-friendly' than the other institutions (although exceptions abound). Previously, there had sometimes been a sense among advocacy groups that the key battles were lost or won when the Commission had decided on its proposal; a feeling perhaps that the other institutions would not amend the proposal to any great degree. Co-decision changed that perspective almost immediately, and in BEUC we intensified to very good effect our work and contacts with the Parliament. Co-decision and the conciliation procedure have also had a positive influence on decisions of the Council, which is always the hardest nut to crack.

I should not like to give the impression that there was little progress in consumer policy before the Maastricht Treaty. In fact a great deal was achieved. Despite the absence of an explicit treaty base for a consumer policy prior to 1992, many directives dealing with consumer protection were passed before that date, usually under Article 100. As mentioned above, harmonisation of laws immediately raises the question of harmonisation at what level of consumer protection. To take one example among many, the Directive on misleading advertising was passed in 1984, not as a consumer protection measure (although it is) but as a harmonising measure. The Directive was agreed during the Irish Presidency. I chaired the Council working group at which final agreement was reached, but was not called upon to display any great diplomatic skills – the main outstanding issues had been resolved informally by the French Presidency which had ended just a few days previously.

On a personal level, my main introduction to the Community decision-making process was in the Council working group on the misleading advertising Directive. It was an enriching experience, perhaps particularly for those coming from the two common-law member states. Added to the inherent interest of seeing how other member states dealt with the same problems, it was also intriguing to grapple with very different legal concepts and systems, and to try to reach solutions that made sense in both.

The impact of Community law on Irish consumer policy can hardly be overestimated. At the time of Ireland's accession, there were very few modern consumer protection laws on the statute books. The Hire Purchase Acts were relatively modern, but consumers' rights in the sale of goods were still governed by the pre-independence (1893!) Act. There were a series of

Merchandise Marks Acts and accompanying orders, but these were more concerned with identifying foreign or imported goods than with information that might be more directly useful to consumers. In fairness, I should not over-emphasise the bad state of affairs in consumer policy in Ireland prior to accession. Modern consumer protection laws were of relatively recent origin in many other countries. We may have been behind, but not that far.

The Consumer Information Act 1978 was one of the first, successful in my view, steps taken to modernise consumer policy in Ireland. The purpose of the Act was first to try to protect consumers from false or misleading information, and to establish the office of Director of Consumer Affairs to enforce the law. Chronologically, the 1978 Act cannot be said to have derived from the Misleading Advertising Directive of 1984, but this is not perhaps the point. The directive was a long time in gestation and the 1978 Act nicely anticipated many of its provisions. This, I believe, was not by chance.

Whatever about the 1978 Act, the impact on Ireland of community consumer protection measures had been enormous. Irish laws on food labelling, food additives, product liability, product safety, textile labelling, consumer credit, unfair contract terms, doorstep selling and footwear labelling, among many others, are substantially implementing measures for Community law. I suppose that many of these Irish measures would have passed anyway if we had not entered the Community, but I think they might have been very different if they had been purely domestic in origin and subject only to domestic political pressures. To put it bluntly, I think they would have been more influenced by specific interest groups. Whatever criticisms we might have about food labelling Directives, for example, the law would not have been so comprehensive as a purely domestic piece of legislation, given the political weight in Ireland of the food industry. The same might be said for the law on product liability. To prove my point, when the Consumer Information Act 1978 was passed, banks were exempted from the scope of the Act. The banks, therefore, were not subject to the normal laws on misleading advertising (*O tempora! O mores!*). That exemption was removed, and had to be removed of course, with the advent of the Misleading Advertising Directive.

Community law has influenced not only the content of domestic law but also its administration. As Director of Consumer Affairs it was my task, *inter alia*, to administer the European Communities (Misleading Advertising Regulations) 1988, implementing the Misleading Advertising Directive. The protection of consumers and traders was stated to be one of the purposes of the Directive, and likewise of the implementing regulations. The significance of this may be seen in the two following examples. In the first case, inspectors acting on my behalf were refused access to the premises and records of a share

promoting company. The company argued, *inter alia*, that they were selling
shares only to people outside Ireland and that the (domestic) laws, under
which the inspectors were acting, were intended for the protection of persons
in Ireland. In my view that argument was not correct in relation to Irish law,
but clearly it could not be raised at all in relation to the Directive. The
inspectors sought access again to the relevant records, but this time acting
under the regulations implementing the Directive. They were again refused
access and prosecution proceedings were instituted. The company and two
executives of the company were convicted on various charges of obstruction,
including one charge under the Misleading Advertising Regulations. In this
particular case, the practices under investigation involved the selling of
shares by telephone. I took the view that this constituted 'advertising' within
the meaning of the Directive, which refers to the making of a 'representation
in any form'. Although the Court did not consider the point, it is generally
accepted that the scope of the Directive is wide enough to cover such cases.

The definition of advertising was also relevant in another case involving
the export from Ireland to the US of a whiskey product. The question of how
the name of the product should be spelled was of some significance to the
issues in dispute, as readers might appreciate. The product was labelled in
Ireland and a dispute arose as to whether or not the labelling was misleading.
Whatever the merits of the case, there were a number of issues of jurisdiction
to be considered. Firstly, did the labelling on the product constitute
advertising within the meaning of the directive? In my opinion the definition
of advertising in the Directive was wide enough to include labelling of this
kind. Secondly, was the directive intended to provide protection to
consumers outside the Community against advertising originating within the
Community? In my opinion the answer here was also yes. In intervening in
the case, however, I also relied on another argument in claiming jurisdiction
for the Directive. If the product in question was misleadingly labelled, as
alleged, there was little doubt that it might affect sales in the US of other
whiskey products exported from Ireland. It seemed to me, therefore, that I
had ample grounds to intervene under the Directive on the basis that we were
dealing with an alleged case of misleading advertising originating from within
the Community which might damage a competitor within the Community.
It was therefore irrelevant that the damage would be done to the competitor's
export market outside the Community. While I was, and remain, confident
on these issues of jurisdiction, they were not argued in court, as there was a
resolution of the problem with the labelling of the product in question.

One passing comment: it was my task as Director of Consumer Affairs to
enforce the Consumer Information Act 1978 and later the Misleading
Advertising Regulations. I found the 1978 Act to be an effective and flexible
means of dealing with misleading advertising and for implementing the

Directive when it arrived. My later experience of the corresponding regimes in other member states has confirmed that view. Lest I might be thought to be biased, I should stress that I had no involvement whatever in the drafting or making of the 1978 Act.

In overall terms, therefore, EU membership has brought to Ireland the benefits of a substantial body of consumer legislation which, in my opinion, would not have been produced by domestic forces alone. On the economic side the benefits to consumers are more mixed. Irish consumers have undoubtedly benefited from free movement and the increase of competition, economies of scale, and consumer choice, but they have also had to contend with derogations from free movement, in relation to cars, for example, and telecommunications for a time. Like other European consumers, Irish consumers have also had to bear the costs of the CAP, whether in terms of increased food prices or as taxpayers. It is not only in Ireland that the ministers of agriculture are praised for their ability to raise food prices in negotiations in Brussels. Ireland has played its part in the development of EU consumer policy, with a commissioner, Richard Burke, and, in Jerry Sheehan and Peter Prendergast, long-serving directors of the consumer policy service. Indeed, for a long time, the director of the consumer policy service and the director of the main European consumer organisation were both Irish. This fact was often noted, at least in consumer policy circles, and may have given a somewhat rosy picture of the strength in depth of consumer policy in Ireland.

The recent appointment of David Byrne as Commissioner for Health and Consumer Protection marks the coming of age of EU consumer policy. It is a sign of the new importance of the dossier that he is the first Commissioner to be responsible only for consumer policy and health. He will have a key role to play, not only on substantive issues of consumer policy, but also in terms of how the EU is perceived by European citizens/customers. It is clear also that consumer concerns and expectations must be addressed if there is to be further progress in Europe on such issues as trade, genetically modified food and food ingredients, and on food policy more generally. These are just some of the formidable challenges facing the new Commissioner.

========= 20 =========

Agricultural policy

SEAMUS J. SHEEHY

Introduction

Accession to the European Community in 1973 was enthusiastically welcomed by the people of Ireland, largely because of the prospective benefits to agriculture that it promised. At that time Irish agricultural exports were almost entirely dependent on the British market, and that market became progressively more restrictive as Britain became increasingly self-sufficient. At the same time Western European markets were being fenced off by the new Common Agricultural Policy (CAP) which was being implemented. Because of these market problems, Irish governments throughout the 1960s were reluctantly forced to provide an increasing amount of income support for agriculture. Before EU accession in the early 1970s this support had reached about 3.4 per cent of Irish GDP, which may be contrasted with the cost of the CAP today to EU taxpayers at just 0.6 per cent of EU GDP.

Against this background EU membership offered the prospect of substantial price increases, a doubling of real incomes, and market access to nearly 300 million people. These were of enormous consequence, not just for farmers but for the economy generally, in which agriculture then represented about 50 per cent of total net exports.

The 1970s: price and structural policy

The comprehensive CAP support system also promised price and income stability. But in fact the 1970s turned out to be a period of unprecedented turbulence. Inflation rates grew, interest rates rose and exchange rates fluctuated. A new vocabulary had to be learned in relation to agricultural trade, as Agriculture Ministers refused to adjust the exchange rates relating to agricultural trade fully in line with general exchange rates. Subsequent adjustment of the agricultural or *green* exchange rates were a source of price increases for devaluing currencies such as the Irish pound, and price decreases for revaluing currencies such as the Deutschmark. The manipulation of these green exchange rates became a troublesome but important part of CAP management.

As this monetary chaos was unfolding in 1974, a crisis was developing in the beef sector. At world and EU level, beef markets swung from scarcity to oversupply. In Ireland cattle numbers had been increased rapidly in anticipation of EU markets, but winter feed supplies had not been increased proportionally. Then, as misfortune would have it, appalling weather struck in the summer of 1974, leading to an acute feed shortage that winter. Farmers desperately tried to sell off their cattle, but all market outlets were choked, including factories slaughtering for sale to intervention. As a result cattle prices and incomes tumbled, as may be seen in Table 20.1.

Happily the 1974 cattle crisis was a transient event, and prices recovered strongly in the following years. Indeed, the agriculture sector as a whole entered a boom period, and despite all the monetary volatility, average real income per worker had in fact doubled by 1978, as had been forecast before joining the EU (see Table 20.1). Of course around this average there was a very wide range of individual farmer outcomes.

While most of this essay relates to price and trade policies, some reference to structural policy is appropriate here. In the 1960s there was an upsurge of interest in structural policies internationally, led by the OECD. This was an era of full employment in most developed countries, so the concept of encouraging labour to leave farming, thereby enabling more rapid enlargement of surviving farms, made a lot of economic sense. It was against this background that the Mansholt plan was launched in 1968. It had the ambitious aim of restructuring EU farming by 1980 into a mixture of commercial farmers and part-time farmers, having weeded out large numbers of non-viable farmers. This was to be achieved by a combination of selective

Table 20.1. Real FFI per family worker (1970 = 100)

1970	100.0	1980	108.1	1990	198.6
1971	106.1	1981	112.7	1991	188.8
1972	136.1	1982	124.6	1992	228.1
1973	167.6	1983	142.0	1993	245.2
1974	130.2	1984	171.7	1994	260.9
1975	167.0	1985	160.9	1995	274.1
1976	161.5	1986	145.1	1996	280.1
1977	202.5	1987	182.3	1997	254.2
1978	209.6	1988	217.3	1998	247.9
1979	152.1	1989	218.8		

investment aids to potentially viable farmers, in what was called the Farm Modernisation Scheme, and retirement incentives to non-viable farmers.

These proposals dominated the debate at that time on the merits of Irish accession to the EU. It was argued by those opposed to EU membership that the Mansholt proposals would lead to the decimation of small farmers in Ireland. Against this, it was argued by pro-EU people including the government that the EU policy would merely strengthen the existing Irish policies. In the event both pro-EU and anti-EU arguments proved to be exaggerated, as there was in fact no significant impact of EU structural policy on Irish agriculture. The discrimination among different categories of farmer which was inherent in the Farm Modernisation Scheme was unacceptable politically and was greatly diluted on implementation. And the retirement scheme initially attracted a good response, but this quickly waned as land prices soared and the real value of the benefits shrunk. Furthermore, as the neutered Mansholt plan was being debated, European economic growth was slowing down, aggravated by the energy crisis of 1973 which began an era of growing unemployment. Indeed, the ink was scarcely dry on the decisions regarding the Mansholt plan when the EU did a U-turn under the CAP with the introduction of the Disadvantaged Areas Scheme in 1975. The aim of this scheme, which is still operating, was the very opposite of the Mansholt plan, namely to encourage non-viable farmers to remain in farming in poorer areas.

Structural policy subsequently took a back seat to price policy; in budgetary terms the original intention was to spend about 30 per cent of the CAP budget in guidance or structural policy and 70 per cent on guarantee or price policies. In fact structural policy attracted less than 10 per cent of the total budget in subsequent years.

The EMS experience

The boom up to 1978 laid the foundation for the next crisis in Irish agriculture. Not only were incomes high and rising, but the prospects were also promising. Admittedly, the problem of surplus production was increasing all the time, and sooner or later it would have to be addressed. In response, a *prudent price policy* was implemented after 1977 in the form of a 3 per cent annual reduction in real prices paid to farmers. But this was no immediate threat to the high level of incomes prevailing.

Given these expectations, farmers and finance institutions engaged in the greatest bout of investment and lending ever experienced in the Irish industry. By 1979 the indebtedness of farmers was at record levels. This would not have been a problem if incomes remained high as had been expected. But in 1979 and 1980 incomes collapsed – on average falling by a half and reverting to their pre-EU level. This was caused by exchange rate movements which could not have been anticipated in 1978 and which were unique to Ireland among member states.

In March 1979, the European Monetary System (EMS) was launched with Ireland as one of its members. This radical change in Irish exchange rate policy did not seem to threaten the well-being of agriculture. It was argued that either the Irish inflation rate would have to fall to German levels, in which case high price increases would not be necessary, or the Irish currency would be forced to devalue, in which case green pound price increases would be forthcoming. But the Irish inflation rate did not fall in 1979 and 1980. Nor was it found necessary to devalue the Irish pound within the EMS, as the trade-weighted exchange rate of the Irish pound was maintained by an unexpected revaluation of sterling.

These circumstances pushed Irish farmers into a severe price–cost squeeze. Escalating interest rates, which doubled between 1978 and 1979, compounded the problem. Farmers and bankers, who had borrowed and lent with buoyant expectations, now found themselves with the severest debt problems since the Economic War of the 1930s. Both parties had to compromise to solve the problem, and with the help of recovering incomes most farmers were able to restructure their debt and survive in farming. Yet there is no doubt that the greatest adversity of the first 25 years of Irish agriculture under the CAP was the manner in which exchange rates operated after EMS accession.

The 1980s – milk quotas

The major policy initiative of the 1980s was the imposition of quotas on milk production in 1984. Up to that date dairy surpluses continued to grow, increasing pressure on the CAP budget to unacceptable levels. The prudent price approach was too timid to deal with the problem. Ministers were forced to react, and the choice available to them was to slash prices to reduce surpluses and encourage consumption, or to introduce quotas to restrict production at farm level. Ireland initially resisted the quota approach, arguing that our dairy industry was still underdeveloped and that quotas would stunt its growth. In the end we had to settle for quotas after hard bargaining yielded a 10 per cent bonus in the size of our quota over that of other member states.

Milk quotas are still with us, and it has now been decided to continue them to 2006. Producers with quotas have the advantage of a high price for a restricted amount of production. However, those with little or no quota are frozen out of the industry unless they can afford to pay high prices for the limited quota that becomes available. Furthermore, the Irish and EU dairy industries are rapidly losing world market share as other exporters, such as New Zealand, are free to expand to supply those growing markets.

Table 20.1 shows the strong income recovery after 1980, with real income per family worker in 1996 being nearly three times its pre-EU level. This occurred despite falling real prices and the imposition of milk quotas. Much of the increase is attributable to the 2.5 per cent per annum decrease in the number of family workers over the years. The number of family workers on Irish farms is now less than half of what it was in 1970. At the same time the volume of gross agricultural product grew by about 40 per cent, while interest rates declined. In recent years rapidly increasing direct payments to farmers have been a major boost to income. Prudent prices and milk quotas did not lead to the devastation of farming as was regularly predicted.

Growing pressures for reform

The pace of CAP reform accelerated in the 1990s in response to intensifying pressures. Such pressures had been mainly internal to the EU and were largely expressed through the size of the budget. In 1988 firm budgetary discipline was imposed to curtail the escalating cost of the CAP. This included a ceiling on the guarantee or price support part of the budget: the agriculture ministers and the Commission have been required to operate below this ceiling since then. In addition, a system of stabilisers was introduced which triggered a price reduction in the event of production exceeding a specified ceiling.

External pressures from non-EU agricultural exporters were growing over the years to reinforce the internal pressures. These culminated in 1995 in the Uruguay Round global trade agreement under the GATT, now replaced by the World Trade Organisation (WTO). This brought world agricultural trade under global rules for the first time in history. So after decades of growing protection world traders agreed to set about reversing the process by freeing up international markets.

Two elements of this movement are already in place, in the form of the MacSharry reforms implemented between 1993 and 1995, and the Uruguay Round Trade Agreement (URTA) spanning the years 1995 to 2001. These are discussed in more detail below. Three further elements are on the horizon, namely Agenda 2000 changes to be introduced in the period 2000 to 2005, a second global trade agreement for which negotiations commence before the end of 1999, and EU enlargement to the east, negotiations for which have already begun. All of these initiatives are interlinked as the world gropes towards virtual free trade in the years ahead.

The MacSharry reforms

The stabiliser approach introduced in 1988 proved inadequate to curtail production. Something more radical was called for, and was implemented in the MacSharry reforms. These had three main components:

1 reduced prices for beef and cereal/oilseed/protein crops offset by direct payments to farmers
2 extension of supply control beyond sugar and milk, where it already applied, to beef, sheep and cereal/oilseed/protein crops
3 a set of accompanying measures.

Support prices were cut between 1993 and 1995 by 15 per cent in the case of beef and 29 per cent in the case of cereals. The revenue loss to farmers resulting from these price reductions was offset by compensation paid directly to farmers per head of livestock or per hectare.

Supply control was extended to cereal/oilseed/protein crops and to beef and sheep by capping the direct payments at the level of production prevailing before the reforms were put in place. Any production beyond these levels would be sold at the new lower prices, but without compensation. In addition, in the case of the crops, land set-aside at specified levels was required to qualify for receipt of the compensatory payments, and in the case of livestock extra premiums were paid for low stocking rates.

The accompanying measures consisted of three schemes: one to promote afforestation; a second to encourage early retirement of farmers; and a third as payments for the public good of improving the rural environment.

When MacSharry revealed his proposals in 1991 he was bitterly attacked by the farming organisations. As it happened, farmers experienced substantial windfall gains between 1992 and 1995 because the reduction in support prices agreed in the MacSharry reforms did not cause an immediate reduction in market prices. At the same time, the direct payments were increasing rapidly. As a consequence, farmers' incomes actually rose between 1992 and 1995 (Table 20.1). However, incomes fell by modest amounts in 1997 and 1998.

The evolution of the accompanying measures is also of interest. Their prospective value was impossible to quantify in any meaningful way, because their detailed operation and their uptake were unknown. Nevertheless, the Department of Agriculture, Forestry and Food went on record as saying that they could amount to £55m per year. The budget provision for them in 1999 is £318 million.

The Uruguay Round Trade Agreement (URTA)

As emphasised above, the MacSharry reforms were heavily influenced by the ongoing trade negotiations under the GATT, which is now replaced by the WTO. After eight years of negotiation agreement was finally reached and came into operation in July 1995. It is proceeding on its six-year course to June 2001. The commitments made by all countries under the URTA relate to: (i) reduced domestic support, (ii) increased market access and (iii) reduced export subsidies. However, by tough bargaining the EU succeeded in keeping these commitments to a minimum.

The domestic support conditions will have no impact in the EU up to the end of the agreement period, since the price reductions already made – largely in the MacSharry Reforms – are more than sufficient to meet the required reductions, even though the MacSharry price reductions are fully offset in all member states by direct payments to farmers.

Under market access, existing non-tariff forms of protection were converted to equivalent tariffs to make protection more transparent. This tariffication process resulted in such high tariffs that, even after the required average 36 per cent reduction, they will still be high enough to exclude most products from EU markets. But there is also a minimum access requirement, and this will allow in some extra materials, especially dairy products.

The restriction on export subsidies is the commitment most likely to have an impact, whose precise magnitude will depend on how EU production and consumption evolve up to 2001. The Agenda 2000 agreement will help ease the restriction by reducing prices and the volume of surpluses in beef, cereals and dairy produce.

While the URTA will not have major short-term effects, its real significance is that it has put in place a foundation that will be built upon in future trade agreements. The next trade round talks will begin formally towards the end of 1999. In addition, the EU has opened negotiations for enlargement with six countries, namely Poland, Hungary, the Czech Republic, Slovenia, Estonia and Cyprus, with more to follow later. Further reform of the CAP must be such as to accommodate simultaneously the demands of the EU's trading partners and the accession of the new members.

Towards free trade

This U-turn in the URTA in global agricultural trade policy is not a mere coincidence. Rather it is a reflection of changing economic and political circumstances, which are undermining the traditional political motives for protection. These motives have varied over time and by country, but generally they can be reduced to the following three concerns:

1 supporting farmers' incomes
2 promoting agricultural growth
3 preserving rural society.

The need to support the incomes of poor farmers is not being challenged. The criticism relates to the attempt to do this indirectly by protecting agriculture from competition rather than by the universal practice outside agriculture for dealing with poverty, namely direct income payments. Supporting the income of farmers by maintaining high prices behind agricultural protection is not a very effective approach. It is estimated that under the CAP only about one-third of all transfers to agriculture from consumers and taxpayers combined goes to increase farmers' income. The remainder accrues to upstream/downstream industries, or goes to pay for extra resources employed in farming in response to the high protection, or is offset by depressed market prices brought about by increased production.

Furthermore, maintaining high prices is inequitable in that it benefits producers in proportion to their turnover. This inequity is becoming more evident as farms grow larger. The concentration of production is also undermining the key political concept of the family farm, which has had a powerful influence in sustaining public support for agriculture. There can be little doubt that if agricultural policy, instead of being inherited, had to be constructed today to deal with the problems of the industry, it would be a policy of direct income support for those farmers deemed to be in need of it, namely those incapable of surviving by adapting to the economic and technological forces of change.

In addition to the ineffectiveness and inequity of high-price policies, economists emphasise the waste of such policies which generate excessive surpluses. But a wealthy world that afforded the arms race can readily afford the cost of food surpluses, if that is all that is involved. In rich countries the farmers' share of the consumers' pound spent on all goods and services has declined from around 30 pence at the turn of the century to a mere 3 pence today. Consequently, a relatively large increase in the efficiency of farming would not be of major significance to the well-being of society. The immorality of surplus production is a greater public concern than its cost. The public is being alienated by the focus on excessive food stockpiles which are made to appear all the more incongruous when juxtaposed with pictures of famine. Given these stockpiles, the arguments for agricultural growth have lost any validity they may have had in the past. These arguments have had an economic dimension and a food security dimension. In a developing economy agricultural growth can make a valuable economic contribution, provided it is not being achieved by excessive protection. In developed countries agricultural growth can still benefit individual farmers or a group of farmers, such as Irish farmers within the EU, but it cannot contribute to the overall EU economy if it takes place at heavily subsidised prices. Similarly, the strategic argument for food security was a compelling one in the warring world before and after the Second World War. As memories of such wars recede its appeal has diminished, and the disintegration of the USSR has consolidated this view. Food security today is an important issue for poor countries, but it is not a tenable case for agricultural protection.

If the income and growth props of agricultural protection are being eroded, perhaps the socio-political concern to preserve rural society will survive – and suffice. Certainly up to this point the political influence of farmers around the world has shown remarkable durability. While farm populations continue to decline, the geographic dispersal of the farmer vote and the special arrangements which exist in many countries to favour that vote have enabled farmers to retain disproportionate power. Of the three major trading blocks today – the EU, the US and Japan – only in the EU are there no special arrangements in favour of farmers in the voting system. The US has two Senators per state regardless of the state's population, and the Japanese have the gerrymander of obsolete constituency boundaries which give much more representation per rural vote than per urban vote. For these reasons among others, the change in attitudes towards protection is a slow one. This was evident from the protracted negotiations leading to the URTA.

Trade liberalisation is also being encouraged by events in Eastern Europe. One of the greatest needs of the emerging market economies in these countries is access to markets, including agricultural markets. Agreement was reached early for associate membership between the EU and many of these countries, and now negotiations are under way for full membership. The outcome must be increasing access and therefore more competition for EU farmers.

Conclusion

Commercial farmers will compete in increasingly open markets, while also qualifying to some degree for compensatory payments and payments for the production of public goods. Commodity markets will not always be oversupplied and underpriced. The economic revolution experienced by nearly two-thirds of the world's population in Asia and elsewhere, while now suffering a severe setback, on recovery should bring about a better supply–demand balance and thus ease the adjustment problems of farmers in the new millennium.

Many farmers will continue to seek non-farming sources of income to supplement farm earnings, as so many have successfully done in the past. Continuation of the Celtic Tiger performance along with successful rural development policies will help in this regard. There will remain a number of farmers who fail in farming and fail to find off-farm employment. They will be supported by payments for public goods topped up with general welfare transfers when their incomes fall below the welfare threshold.

Competitiveness embraces the industries upstream and downstream as well as farming itself. The downstream industries have been much criticised over the years for over-reliance on intervention and inadequate efforts to follow market-led strategies. But as a peripheral exporting region with prices well below mainland levels, it was almost inevitable that intervention in Ireland would be attractive in oversupplied markets.

Developments in recent years were encouraging until the eruption of BSE. This not only pushed down demand for beef, but also caused a renationalising of EU markets. The immediate challenge now is to get back to market-led growth as quickly as possible. In all sectors, upstream and downstream, scale of operation has grown, but certainly not at a sufficient pace. In the immediate years ahead we should witness dramatic developments in this area, which are necessary to catch up with and match developments among our competitors.

Part IV
Views of Irish Commissioners

21

European special envoy (1982–85)

RICHARD BURKE

Gaston Thorn, President of the Commission of the European Communities, on a visit to Ireland, was reported as follows in the *Irish Times* (26 February 1983) in regard to Irish media preoccupation with the responsibilities given to me after my return to the Commission:

> The Commission president said that the Irishman had been given special tasks but the argument was now being made that having succeeded in Argentina, Greece and Greenland, Mr Burke should be given new responsibilities. Mr Thorn did not agree. Why should Mr Burke be given other assignments when there was a lot of work to be done sorting out the problems of the Argentines, the Greeks and the Danes? Mr Burke's handling of these assignments were [sic] virtually the only successes of the Commission in the past six months....

There follows, in three sections, a brief account of those responsibilities.

Argentina

I had a particular reason to be grateful to my German colleague Wilhelm Haverkampf for his unstinting support in the Commissions of 1977 to 1985. In the autumn of 1976 we had met for the first time in Dublin, when we were both being targeted by Roy Jenkins for exclusion from the Commission. The latter admitted to me that, in my case, he had been 'used', while the German's predicament had more to do with his successful quest for responsibility for the external relations portfolio. During the Jenkins Commission, Haverkampf had asked me to represent him on several missions to Latin America and in negotiations with the Andean Pact.

My return to Brussels under the Thorn presidency coincided with the Argentine invasion of the Falkland Islands. Prime Minister Margaret Thatcher, speaking to the House of Commons on Saturday, 3 April 1982, outlined the background to the British–Argentine dispute. Britain had resisted Argentine claims to sovereignty over the Falklands and had asserted continuous sovereignty from 1833. Since 1967, successive British governments had held a series of meetings with the Argentinians to discuss the dispute. When I attended the House of Commons debate on Wednesday, 7 April 1982, I had an opportunity of gauging the extent of British hostility to the invasion. The new Foreign Secretary, Francis Pym, who had taken over from Lord Carrington, announced the dispatch of a large task force towards the South Atlantic. Active discussion was under way about measures to be taken by the European Community against Argentina.

My efforts to move on the Argentina question had been seen against the background of the Irish government position. In the words of the *Daily Telegraph* (21 October 1982), my initiatives had

> nothing to do with the views of the Irish government. Even after Dublin had declared itself opposed to economic sanctions against Argentina in May, Mr Burke spoke in favour of them.

The impetus for a new initiative to heal relations between Latin America and the European Community arose from my official visit to Rio de Janeiro and La Paz in October 1982. I was particularly anxious, following on the 1980 visit to Lima, to ensure that Bolivia received financial aid following the restoration of democracy where the EC had 'a good friend' but where the odds against the new administration seemed overwhelming. In my report to Gaston Thorn, I suggested:

> Firstly, that the Commission support a European Parliament move to bolster democracy in Bolivia. There is indeed a real emergency in Bolivia. Bolivian democrats do look to the Community, and, in helping them, we can do much to restore our image, not only in Bolivia and the Andean Pact, but with the entire Latin American public. Secondly, that the Commission should press for a very early signature or an agreement with the Andean Pact countries of Venezuela, Ecuador, Colombia, Peru and Bolivia. Thirdly, in the post-Falklands situation, the EC must take the initiative to capitalise on the pragmatic acceptance by Latin Americans generally, even Argentinians, that we must work together.

My report to Thorn on my meeting with Sr Adolfo Navajas, minister in the Argentine government, stated:

> The minister expressed the predictable feelings of injury and resentment towards the Community, but agreed that, in time, our relations should be fully restored. Interestingly, he seemed to be even

more hostile to alleged Community displacement of Argentine meat in several third country markets through alleged subvention systems. His adviser took a more negative tone, complained about the decision to give emergency aid to the Falklands, and said that while Argentina was friendly towards some states of the Community, she viewed the Community institutionally as hostile. The atmosphere of our meeting, however, was very friendly and we parted with mutual good wishes.

In December 1983, I led the European delegation to Buenos Aires for discussions with the newly installed democratic government and, in particular, with the President and the Foreign Minister. *Europe* (15 December 1983) described the outcome:

> EEC–Argentina: resumption of bilateral relations decided – future examination of concrete possibilities for developing co-operation in all fields of economic life. Brussels (EU) Wednesday, 14 December 1983 – During the inaugural ceremony of the new Argentine President, Mr Paul Ricardo Alfonsin... the Community delegation led my Mr R. Burke held several talks with the Argentine authorities, notably the President and Foreign Minister Mr Dante Caputo. Commissioner Burke has expressed the satisfaction of the Commission on Argentina's return to democracy, the willingness of the Commission to co-operate with Argentina in realising a new start in relations with the Community, and the hope that Argentina would play a new and constructive political role in Latin America and in the world.
>
> The extremely cordial tone in the Argentinians' reception of the delegation shows a new political interest in the European Community. Both sides expressed the desire to explore jointly the possibility of establishing a new framework for permanent consultations and co-operation in all aspects of economic life. To this effect it was agreed:
>
> 1   to intensify contracts through diplomatic channels
> 2   to study ways of reinforcing the Community's presence in Argentina
> 3   to realise in the immediate future a large scale technical mission to Buenos Aires to explore the various possibilities of future co-operation.

The fact that hostility in public opinion had not softened to the same degree as official opinion was brought home vividly to me on the occasion of the installation of President Alfonsin. Earlier I had met Vice-President George Bush for discussions and had even succeeded in getting discussions between him and Commandant Ortega of Nicaragua. Television relayed the inauguration proceedings to the public, who vented their anger as Vice-President Bush paid his respects. Returning along the line he whispered to me 'Sorry friend, you're next'. He was right. When my name was announced the booing erupted again. Calling on skills honed in by-elections in Clashmore, Patrickswell and elsewhere, I succeeded in turning the crowd around to mild applause on my departure from the scene!

By the time I led the Commission delegation to Mexico in December 1984, EC–Latin American relations had greatly improved. My involvement with that continent ceased when the Irish government indicated the ending of my Commission membership. Appointment as Vice-President of the Commission during the Mexico visit was a pleasant coda to two periods in office.

The accession of Spain and Portugal to the EC on 1 January 1986 gave the Commission greatly enhanced advantages in dealing with South America. The EU–Mercosur summit of June 1999 at Rio further enhanced European relations with an area of 200 million inhabitants and, with 1997 exports of $83 billion and imports of $98 billion, forming after NAFTA, EU and Japan the fourth economic area in the world economy.

Greece

In 1959, Greece decided that her future was with the European Economic Community when she chose association with the EEC rather than with the British-inspired alternative EFTA. Her associate relationship with the EEC began on 1 November 1962, this agreement being the first treaty establishing an association between the EEC and a third country. Essentially, the Athens Treaty was a pre-accession arrangement, as may be seen from the Preamble and Article 72 of the association agreement. The agreement established a two-tier transitional period – 12 years for abolition of tariffs, and for a list of products being manufactured in Greece at the time (amounting to 40 per cent of Greek imports) tariffs would be eliminated over 22 years. The member states would extend intra-Community treatment to Greek products much more quickly. The implementation of the association agreement was placed under the supervision of the Council of Association, later added to when a joint Parliamentary committee of 15 members from the European Parliament and Greek Parliament participated in regular meetings of the Joint Committee.

Although a number of difficulties arose in implementing the association agreement, these were on the brink of being resolved when the military coup of 21 April 1967 occurred, leading to the 'freezing' of the association agreement to those parts in current operation.

After a seven-and-a-half-year hiatus, the Greek government of national unity took immediate steps to reactivate the association agreement. The $55 million of unused funds from the first financial protocol was unblocked, and a second financial protocol of 280 million units of account made available over a five-year period ending in 1981. It should be noted that when Greece applied for membership of the EEC many of the problems and difficulties arising were issues that both sides were obliged to resolve in the context of the Athens Treaty. The Commission opinion pointed out that in economic terms, Greece lagged behind the Nine and exhibited structural characteristics that placed limits on its ability to combine homogeneously with the economies of the existing member states. In spite of this, negotiations proceeded apace so that Greece became a full member on 1 January 1981.

In October of that year, PASOK under the leadership of Andreas Papandreou contested the general election with the policy of leaving NATO and the EEC following a referendum. There followed, in March 1982, a memorandum to the Community from the PASOK government, largely inspired by the view that its predecessor had negotiated a thoroughly bad membership deal and that, as a result, Greece's economic problems had been made worse by joining the EEC. (In taking this position they were echoing the British Labour Party's 1975 referendum stance that the Europhile Edward Heath, like Karamanlis later, had conceded too much to the Community.) I did not express a view on the quality of the Greek negotiation, though I discovered in the Commission that during the negotiations, EEC officials were constantly surprised at the manner in which Athens accepted tough Community stances which, it was expected, would be changed under Greek pressure.

In presenting the Greek memorandum, Prime Minister Papandreou found it possible to envisage a Greece in Europe with a new treaty of accession. The Commission took the position that there could be no revision of the Treaty of Accession nor any solution to Greece's problem which involved 'bending' the Treaty of Rome. My objective in producing the Commission response was to get Papandreou 'off the hook' with ideas that were politically and financially realistic, sufficient to secure the Prime Minister's endorsement if he decided to hold a national referendum on Greek membership, which had been promised.

By July 1982, I knew that the omens were good when the Prime Minister claimed credit for the tone of the Commission response, delivered in late June 1982. It helped also that political perception in Athens was that Irish involvement in the search for a solution was a positive one. Ireland, a country with a similar economic profile to Greece, had benefited substantially from the Social Fund and other Community financial instruments. This was made clear by Gregoris Varfis, Under-Secretary of Foreign Affairs, responsible for the EEC portfolio.

The practical result of our initial assessment was to despatch officials of
the Commission in a programme of eleven missions designed to help the
Athens administration cope with its obligations as well as take advantage of
the benefits of EEC membership. The missions were based on a mutual
admission by Athens and Brussels that the Greek administration had up to
then proved itself little able to cope with the realities of EEC membership.
For example, after nearly two years of membership, Greece had introduced
only 20 of the 600 Directives which it was required to adopt under the entry
terms. The missions could examine whether the lapses were due to what the
Greeks admitted was an endemically inert administration, or to more
substantive infrastructural or overtly politically factors. The cost of the
missions, some 500,000 ECU, was a measure of the Community's
commitment to responding to the Greek case, especially when viewed against
the background of financial cutbacks in Brussels. The missions, involving 200
EEC officials over a period of two and a half months, was able to penetrate
the Greek administration on a working level, furnishing information on the
EEC funds including the foreseen integrated Mediterranean programmes, and
practical guidance on how Greece could apply for grants and loans. Receipts
could grow from $150 million (1981) to $700 million (1982) and $1 billion
in 1983. All this would help enormously in making priority decisions in
respect of the 1983–87 five-year plan unveiled later, on 15 November 1982.

By January 1983, the Commission was able to note with satisfaction
Greece's remarkable effort to incorporate Community law into its national
legislation and to implement it in full. Following on the Greek
memorandum, the Commission undertook an analysis of the degree of
implementation of the EEC legislation in Greece – the first time that a study
of this nature had been carried out in a member state. The mission to Athens,
on implementation of EEC legislation, was carried out in November 1982.
My report to the Commission emphasised that the implementation of 25
years of EEC legislation in a new member state required major adjustments in
all sectors of the country's economic and social life and it was clear that while
difficulties remained, the balance sheet was broadly positive. The Greeks had
implemented a 'habilitation law' facilitating the incorporation of Directives
existing before 1 January 1981 into national law. This habilitation would
remain valid until 31 December 1983 for Directives in existence at accession
and until 31 December 1985 for the later ones. The Greeks had covered 50
to 60 per cent of texts for pharmaceuticals, company law, insurance,
technical barriers, transport, environment, consumers, agriculture and rights
of establishment. The remainder, of a more administrative or technical
nature, followed. The result was that the Commission did not open
infringement procedures because of the delays. Two fields were of a political
nature: introduction of the Community VAT system (which I had negotiated

in 1976 as an Irish government minister and, in 1977, introduced as Commissioner for Taxation) and the liberalisation of public supply markets. These other matters included Greek provisions considered incompatible with EEC rules: (a) certain tax discriminations, (b) certain obstacles to exports (the ban on importing diesel engine cars or restrictions on tractors), (c) certain agricultural measures linked to currency controls.

The final mission on longer-term investment issues coincided with my visit to Prime Minister Papandreou and meetings with his foreign, finance and agriculture ministers (the last, Costas Simites, is now Prime Minister of Greece). No major obstacles now remained before the drawing-up of the final Commission position on the Greek memorandum. The *Financial Times* (30 March 1983) noted the political sensitivity of the Commission proposals:

> Although strictly speaking the suggested new regime for Greek membership of the EEC does not change the conditions negotiated before Athens' formal accession in January, 1981, it does imply considerable modification of some of the terms. It therefore risks being branded as a blueprint for a 'two-speed Europe'. The detailed plan for overcoming Greece's EEC membership difficulties is certain to come under close scrutiny by both the Spanish and the Portuguese governments, as its identification of the problem areas in the Greek economy could have a direct impact on the two EEC candidate countries' difficult accession negotiations.

On 11 April 1983, the Greek government approved the European Commission's financial and administrative aid package designed to keep Greece a member of the Ten. The government accepted that our proposals showed a very high degree of comprehension of Greece's problems, and a recognition of the need for decisive action to face them. The statement was issued after my talks with the Prime Minister and members of his cabinet. Armed with the assurance, I now set about the next task of helping Mr Papandreou, at his request, to make a success of the Greek Presidency starting in July 1983.

The Greek Presidency was then only three months away, and the big three – West Germany, France and Britain – were worried about the competence of Greece to handle the task. It was helpful, therefore, when the prime minister invited me to his private residence for discussions. The rest of the Community members had noted Papandreou's frequent refusal to support policies such as the imposition of sanctions on the Soviet Union after its imposition of martial law in Poland. Greece had broken ranks with the EEC ten times more often than any other member state. In March 1983 the Greek government signed an economic and cultural co-operation agreement with the Soviet Union, only informing its EEC colleagues after the event. It also opposed the Reagan proposals on the deployment of medium-range missiles in Europe. In addition, it was important that the country holding the presidency should not at the same time be in fundamental disagreement with the other member states about its own terms of membership.

At our meeting, the Prime Minister asked me directly to advise him on the policies that he should pursue in his term as President of the European Council. I suggested three themes: (i) the necessity of accelerated economic convergence in Europe to avoid the emergence of a two-speed Europe; (ii) the necessity of solving the vexed budget question and the related matters of own resources and reform of the CAP; (iii) policies for dealing with the second industrial revolution – in the electronic, computer and telecommunications industries. (I had spoken for four hours in Dáil Éireann on related questions a decade before.) I was struck by the close attention paid by the Prime Minister. Never before or since did I retain the undivided attention of a head of government in a monologue lasting three-quarters of an hour. My visit to Athens ended with a visit to President Karamanlis, who conferred on me Greece's greatest honour, the Grand-Cross of the Order of the Phoenix.

Greenland

I had not come totally unprepared to the Greenland dossier in March 1982. A year earlier, as an associate fellow of the Harvard University Centre for International Affairs, I had been the guest of the Canadian government on a visit to Western Canada and, in particular, to Yellowknife in the Northern Territories. The local administrative council of 21 members had three Inuit members (as the Eskimos prefer to be called). (In April 1999, Canada acknowledged the specific interests of the Inuit by establishing a separate administrative area called Nunavut.) Two impressions remained with me: (i) the extent and importance of the links between the Canadian, Alaskan and Greenlandic cultures; (ii) the geopolitical importance of Greenland (included under the terms of the Monroe Doctrine) covering the defence of North America, access to the North Atlantic for Soviet warships and nuclear submarines and the necessity of maintaining early warning systems in Greenland's ice-cap against possible missile attacks and as an essential element in NATO defence strategy.

58 million years ago the coasts of Greenland and Scotland were joined together. Greenland is now the largest island in the world, the length of its indented coastline being equal to that of the circumference of the earth at the Equator. Of a total of 2,175,600 square kilometres, 1,833,900 square kilometres consists of an ice sheet of an average depth of 1,500 metres. The

island is populated by 50,000 people of whom 40,000 are Inuit, who are believed to have crossed (4000BC–1000AD) from North America to Northwest Greenland using the islands of the Canadian Arctic as stepping stones. Adam of Bremen, a priest living in Hamburg, recorded in 1070 that King Sven Estridson of Denmark told him of 'a land, discovered by many in that ocean, which is called Vinland' and that beyond Vinland there was 'intolerable ice', an 'awful gulf' where King Harald the Ruthless of Norway had voyaged and seen 'the bounds of the earth grow dark before his eyes' – a reference to the long Arctic night. Apart from early Norse settlers such as Eric the Red, European influence can be dated to the early 18th century with the arrival of Danish missionaries.

Settlement in Greenland is extremely dispersed and largely on the coastal fringe. In the 1970s there were 154 inhabited places, consisting of 19 towns, 117 villages and 18 weather stations and airports. Greenlanders, since integration with Denmark in 1954, have enjoyed equal political rights with Danish citizens and Greenland has been administered by the Greenland ministry in Copenhagen. Unlike the Faroe islands which achieved home rule in 1948, Greenland acceded, as part of Denmark, to the EEC in 1973. Six years later, under the Home Rule Act, No. 577, Greenland achieved a degree of self-government, Denmark retaining responsibility for external relations and currency matters. The Home Rule Act, consisting of 20 sectors in four chapters with a schedule, established an assembly (Landsting) and an administration headed by an executive (Landsstyre). Section 8 (1) enacts that the resident population of Greenland has fundamental rights in respect of natural resources; 8(2) details joint government and Landsstyre interest in exploiting these resources; and 8(3) authorises any member of the Landsstyre to place the matter of government–Landsstyre agreement before the Landsting, enabling the latter to withhold consent. Section 10 places the home rule authorities subject to obligations arising out of treaties and other international rules as, at any time, are binding on the realm. Section 15 enables the government to lay down guidelines for the handling of matters of particular interest to Greenland in the European Community institutions. Finally, Section 18 states that should any doubt arise between the central authorities and the home rule authorities concerning their respective jurisdictions the question shall be laid before a board consisting of two members nominated by those authorities and three judges of the Supreme Court nominated by its president, one of whom shall be nominated as chairman. The judges were given power of decision where the other four disagreed.

In May 1981, the Danish government informed the other member states that, with the agreement of all political parties, it had been decided that an indicative referendum be held before the Landsting would decide to modify Greenland's relations with the European Community. In the hypothesis that, based on the referendum, the Landsting was to request the Danish government to take the measures necessary for Greenland's withdrawal, the Danish government would trigger the official procedures for modification of the Treaties.

Mr Kjeld Olesen, Minister of Foreign Affairs of the Kingdom of Denmark, informed the Council of Ministers on 23 February that the indicative referendum, by 12,615 votes to 11,180, had indicated a decision in favour of withdrawal. Two days later, Prime Minister Jonathan Motzfeldt stated that the Landsting would be requested to institute negotiations for withdrawal to take place on 1 January 1984.

In March 1982, President Thorn asked me to undertake the unprecedented task of effectively halving the territory of the European Community. Preoccupation with the Falklands and Greek memorandum matters meant that it was the summer of 1982 before I got round to thinking about Greenland. The geographical extent of this responsibility was brought home to me on 12 July 1982 when, leaving Athens, I went directly to Greenland, landing at Narsasuaq. I found it impossible to get to the capital, Nuuk, since the place was fog-bound and icebergs prevented an approach by sea. Preliminary negotiations were conducted with the Prime Minister by radio telephone. The only activity possible was a visit to the remains of the dwelling of Eric the Red.

In early September 1982, my second effort to reach Nuuk was more successful. I was met at the steps of the aircraft by the Prime Minister, who drove me to the hotel in his Volkswagen Beetle. Two radio broadcasts and an address to the Landsting were followed widely by the local population. Because of structural differences between the English and Inuit languages, I was amazed at the length of time it took to translate even a simple phrase.

As in the Greek memorandum negotiations, it seems that Irish nationality was a positive in Greenland also. In his public address, Prime Minister Motzfeldt said that:

> I have the greatest confidence in my friend Burke. He understands us – like me, he comes from a small settlement in Europe called Ireland.

In return for a gift of a well-known Irish 12-year-old liquid, the Prime Minister presented me with a book on Inuit life and culture inscribed as follows:

> My friend Burke! Thank you very much for your orientation in our Landsting today. Remember one thing: Greenland is Greenland but we want to have an OCT in our area – remember that! Jonathan.

In the early stages of the discussions on the Treaty of Rome, the French delegation proposed the extensions of the workings of the Common Market to cover the overseas countries and territories with which the member states had a special link. The French initiative led to Part IV of the Treaty of Rome, which, in Annex IV, listed the OCT territories. Denmark was now seeking OCT status for one of its former colonies. Article 131 of the Treaty of Rome sets out the criteria: (i) the territory must be non-European; (ii) it must have special ties with the member state, i.e. it must be a former colony. After the Second World War, Greenland was the only country recognised as a colony by the International Court of Justice in the Hague and, until Greenland became a province of Denmark, Denmark made an annual report to the colonial commission of the United Nations.

It was now necessary to prepare the Commission opinion on Greenland for transmission to the Council of Ministers. This was done in February 1983. The opinion was favourable to the Danish request and indicated that as far as trade in industrial products was concerned, it being understood that the Common Commercial Tariff would no longer apply in Greenland, a free trade area should apply, whereby, for Greenlandic industrial products *vis-à-vis* the Community, all industrial products originated in Greenland would have preferential treatment, giving free access to the Community without any quantitative restrictions, custom duties and charges having equivalent effect. They would, therefore, be subject to rules of origin, and subject to safeguard measures against disturbances on the Community market. As an OCT, Greenland would be able to introduce custom duties and quantitative restrictions on imports of Community products where this would have the effect of promoting its development and industrialisation or would produce budget revenue, but such measures would not be allowed to discriminate among the Ten. Treatment of agricultural products would be more favourable than that granted by the Community or Greenland to third countries, but implementation of this principle would have to be spelled out in any final agreement. In the crucial fisheries sector, there would be a binding agreement allowing Greenland 'optional development' for its fishing fleet while ensuring the continuation of Community fisheries interests in Greenland waters. Financial aid would be periodically determined and added to the OCT appropriations.

Discussions on the Commission proposals in the Council of Ministers took up many monthly meetings in an endeavour to find a balanced solution. This was made difficult by the tension between Greenland's desire to have control over its fish stocks and the Community's desire not to upset the common fisheries policy, negotiated over many years, but only recently secured. Loss of the Community quotas would affect all Community member states with fishing interests in the North Atlantic. (I had signed the NAFO

Treaty for Europe at Ottawa a few years earlier.) The debate in the Council of Ministers on 25 May 1983 took place with Prime Minister Motzfeldt present as a member of the Danish delegation. The *Irish Times* (26 May 1983) described the outcome of that meeting under the title 'Greenlanders oppose paying to leave EEC'. Mr Motzfeldt 'was referring to the entrenched position, particularly of West Germany, on the question of retaining fishing rights for its deep-sea fleet in Greenland waters'.

The European Parliament delivered its opinion on 16 June 1983. The debate was opened by the rapporteur, Mr Janssen van Raay, followed by the Council and the Commission. I paid tribute to the legal affairs committee and to the rapporteur for their outstanding report, adding that the work being done by the Parliament was of tremendous help to the other institutions of the Community.

On 8 February 1984, with my Greek colleague, I advanced proposals in the Commission for a generous severance package for Greenland involving annual payments over five years of 18.5 ECU for the maintenance of fisheries rights, mainly for the West German fleet but also for French and British fleets. The financial arrangements would be reviewed after five years to take account of changing fish stocks and could be extended for a further six years until 2001. I proposed the conclusion of a separate 'fisheries Protocol' to the framework agreement, based on NAFO 1 – Westzone and ICES 14 – Eastzone. These proposals had been preceded by visits to the Foreign Office in London (2 February) and to Mr Genscher in Bonn and to Copenhagen on 7 February 1984.

Finally, the time came to send an arranged message to Greenland. An exchange of telegrams took place between Mr Motzfeldt and myself. My message told Motzfeldt to open the bottle of old Irish whiskey and drink it. Motzfeldt's reply said that the bottle had been opened. The signal to open the bottle was an agreed message to the Greenland prime minister that my former colleague Claude Cheysson, on behalf of the Council, and I had signed the agreement changing Greenland's status within the Community to that of 'overseas territory'. The Prime Minister should have been with us but was snowbound in Greenland. Ratification of the Treaty modifications was to be completed by the lodgement of the necessary instruments with the Italian government by 1 January 1985. By that date, nine of the ten member states had met the deadline, to be followed by the Irish government by 28 January 1985.

═══ 22 ═══

The evolution of economic and
budgetary policy 1973–83

MICHAEL O'KENNEDY

The Community in 1973

When Ireland acceded to the European Economic Community in 1972, the transition from the Common Market of the original six (Belgium, Germany, France, Italy, Luxembourg and Netherlands) to an economic community of nations was well under way. Most member states were effectively at the centre of the geographical and economic market, and obviously stood to gain from the elimination of tariffs and barriers to trade. The political priority of the Treaty of Rome was to bind the former warring nations of Europe together in a multinational economic and trading partnership.

Italy alone of the original six members of the Treaty of Rome was geographically distant from the centre of the Common Market area, and accordingly the EEC needed to develop regional and social policies to support the peripheral economic areas such as the Italian Mezzogiorno to balance the positive impact of the Common Market on the other member states. The CAP was adopted as a common policy applying to all member states, and as such budget funding in respect of it was *ab initio* designated as compulsory. The CAP was a major element in building up the economic cohesion of the new European Economic Community, but this was soon to be further strengthened by the regional and social policies of the Community. Significantly, the funding provided for these and other new policies was 'discretionary' in the sense of not being automatic but requiring agreement by the member states on an annual or multi-annual basis. The budget for these new policies of the European Economic Community, not surprisingly, was greatly underpinned by the more prosperous member states within the new political entity. The 'own resources' of the European Community was based on national contributions, related to GNP, plus 1 per cent of VAT, which was the only common revenue instrument throughout the European Community.

There was always, of course, the political priority of an eventual European Union, but the sequence of development within the new Economic Community was to be the elimination of regional imbalances, leading to economic convergence, leading in turn towards economic and monetary union (EMU) as stepping stones on the way to the ultimate achievement of political union. So when Ireland joined the European Economic Community in 1973 the expectation was that we could benefit from the implementation of these common economic policies, which in turn would enable us to contribute to the realisation of the broader political objectives of the European Community.

It must also be recognised that the first enlargement of the European Community, to include Denmark, Britain and Ireland, was never intended to be the last, and accordingly provision was made in the budget for the funds necessary to underpin further enlargement. The accession of Britain in 1973, and even more dramatically the accession to power of Margaret Thatcher as British prime minister in 1979, introduced a demand for the revision of budget contributions. Prior to that there was certainly no concept of *juste retour* in terms of balancing revenue and contributions of each member state, though there was of course the fundamental *juste retour* of equity among member states in terms of overall market benefits and economic transfers. While Germany and the Netherlands contributed proportionally more than other member states to the budget of the European Community, it is clear that they contributed this from the enhanced resources in their economies from the developing and expanding Common Market.

The budget in 1973

The overall budget of the European Economic Community on our accession in 1973 was about £2.9 billion (5134 m euro), and the contributions of member states was determined by their relative GNP and of course their proportionate share of VAT.

By 1973 Germany and the Netherlands were major net contributors, while at the other end Italy was a major net beneficiary from the budget. However, the benefits to the Federal Republic of Germany and the Netherlands from membership of the European Economic Community far exceeded any net contribution which they made to the budget. It is not surprising then that their commitment to the whole European ideal and the further development and strengthening of the European Community, as it was to become, was firmly rooted in enlightened self-interest allied to equitable sharing of membership obligations. The signals transmitted by this enlightened political leadership to the enterprise sectors in the respective economies were ones of confidence and positive commitment: not surprisingly, German and Dutch entrepreneurs responded accordingly, and the 1960s was a period of sustained growth and expansion in these economies in particular.

The allocation to each member state from the regional fund was broadly appropriate to the state of economic development of that member state. Significantly, shares agreed among the Nine of the new European Economic Community were based not on a proportionate population share-out but rather on a measured share having regard to the relative state of development of each economy. Ireland was allocated 6 per cent of the first regional fund (population 3.5 million) and the Federal Republic was allocated 6.4 per cent (population 61 million). Clearly, Community disbursements were in no way related to size or population. Significantly also a special ex-quota section of the new regional fund was to be reserved for areas of special disadvantage, such as border regions in the European Community, and Ireland's share of this non-quota section – 6 m units of account (6 m euro) – was proportionally in excess of that of other member states.

Soon after accession, the United Kingdom government started to focus on the 'discrepancy' between its contribution to the European budget and its receipts from the funds. Britain's economy was not performing very strongly, and the political attitude to Europe was becoming increasingly negative. In fact, successive British governments were to focus on the narrow ground of budget *juste retour* to the detriment of the huge economic and political potential that could be realised by a country with such unique advantages and experience in international trade, financial markets and technology. This focus became a preoccupation under Margaret Thatcher, and the hope and expectation of enlightened 'Europeans' such as Peter Carrington, Foreign Secretary, and Geoffrey Howe, Chancellor of the Exchequer, were consistently frustrated and blocked by the tunnel-vision and negative attitude of Mrs Thatcher. Even more, the hopes and expectations of the other member states that a vigorous and confident Britain at the centre of European development would establish a new trilateral balance to offset any undue Franco-German dominance have never, to this day, been realised.

By contrast, the vigorous and confident strategy pursued by Ireland since our accession not only has earned the goodwill of our partners in Europe but has encouraged the enterprise sector in Ireland and young entrepreneurs in particular, who see Europe not as a threat against which we must defend our interests but as a great opportunity to explore and develop new commercial outlets and partnerships. The investment in education programme at second and third levels particularly, which had been initiated by Sean Lemass in the 1960s as a precondition to membership of the European Economic Community, was then and is now greatly vindicated and rewarded. New third-level institutions such as the Limerick Institute, now the University of Limerick, and a variety of third-level Regional Colleges of Technology had a specific and identifiable priority – to educate our graduates to 'think European' and to equip them to compete with and beat the élite from other member states.

The emergence of the European Monetary System

In the early 1970s a consensus emerged that Europe itself needed something more than a Common Market, and regional policies were adopted to bring about the cohesion that was required and stability within and across the member states. Accordingly, the exposure of the Community member states to the energy crisis of the late 1970s underlined the need for more effective and co-ordinated action to guard against currency fluctuations. This gave rise in the first instance to bilateral discussions between the representatives of the German and French governments and their central banks. This culminated in the joint Franco-German initiative to replace the old 'snake' with a new framework for exchange rate stability which culminated in the adoption by the member states of the European Monetary System (EMS) at Bremen in July 1979. Significantly, Jim Callaghan as British Prime Minister indicated at the European Council in Bremen that Britain was not, as yet, ready or satisfied to join the system, but as a measure of its intention to do so eventually and of its general goodwill and support for the concept of EMS it requested that sterling should be taken into account in determining the relevant weightings of the member states' currencies in the EMS basket. This was readily agreed to by the other member states. The issue of the British contributions and receipts from the budget was also agreed at Bremen, with provision that the matter could be reviewed again in the light of further studies and information.

Ireland opted for membership of the new system despite the fact that the United Kingdom did not do so. Of course the fact that sterling was floating outside the EMS left open the possibility, even the probability, that sterling would be devalued *vis-à-vis* the EMS, and in view of the very considerable proportion of our exports going to the United Kingdom it was anticipated that we would be at a competitive disadvantage in developing these exports, and in competition with the UK on exports to the other member states. It is significant that the consensus among all the economic commentators and consultants at that time, including those who were actively promoting the new system, was that sterling depreciation *vis-à-vis* EMS was a likely outcome. Accordingly, at the Bremen European Council which I attended with the Taoiseach, Jack Lynch, he negotiated a package of grants and loans (Ortoli facility) with our partners to cushion Ireland against the anticipated depreciation of sterling. Our partners agreed, quite significantly, with our submission that this package should not be renegotiated in the event that the sterling fluctuation was other than anticipated from time to time. The agreement that in any event a break with sterling for the first time since 1826 would be a major adjustment for Ireland, irrespective of the actual currency fluctuation, was received favourably by our partners, which saw our decision as a measure of our confidence in and commitment to the new system even without the participation of the United Kingdom. In the event, the package agreed was in all the circumstances a very satisfactory outcome to our negotiations. Ironically, when the Taoiseach reported to the Dáil on the outcome of the European Council and the arrangements for Ireland's participation in the EMS, he was strongly criticised by spokesmen for the opposition for agreeing to what was alleged to be a totally inadequate package of grants and loans to cushion Ireland against the anticipated downside of our membership of the system.

However, contrary to expectations, after a brief period of sterling depreciation against the EMS currencies it appreciated significantly due to the successful exploration of North Sea oil and, quite unexpectedly, Ireland achieved the dual benefit of a more competitive export regime *vis-à-vis* Britain in addition to retaining the loans and grants that were agreed at Bremen in expectation of our currency becoming stronger than sterling.

The problem of the British contribution

Britain's attitude towards the European Community generally and the new monetary system was sharply in contrast to Ireland's. The Labour government of the day had reservations about the general convergence policies of the European Economic Community, and particularly the development of a monetary system that might diminish in any way the role of sterling as a world currency. None the less, the Callaghan government did not assert in any confrontational manner the minimum demands of the United Kingdom, particularly in relation to the budget balance of contributions and revenue. All this was to change dramatically and abruptly at the Dublin European Council in 1979, presided over by Jack Lynch as Taoiseach. It was Margaret Thatcher's first European Council as Prime Minister, and from the beginning of the meeting she asserted that her priority was to achieve a fair balance between Britain's budget contribution and receipts. She stated that it was clear that the calculation of Britain's budget contribution was grossly unfair, and her opening demand was not only that this calculation be revised downward but also that Britain be reimbursed from the Community budget for the excessive contributions it had already been required to make.

Lest her colleagues did not fully comprehend the message she was conveying, she asserted quite bluntly: 'I want my money back!'. Helmut Schmidt, having listened to her forceful demands, thought it was time to explain to her that the European Community did not work on that basis and addressed her in tones of understanding and explanation:

Margaret, we don't operate here on the basis of the measurement of budget contributions – if we did I would be severely criticised in Germany for the fact that I am prepared to agree to a major net contribution on the part of the Federal Republic of Germany to the Community budget. It is important that each of us take our responsibility not just on behalf of our own government but also as partners in the European Community which enables me to justify to the Bundestag and to the German people generally our huge net contribution to the budget.

Others, notably Giscard d'Estaing, took up the same theme by way of explaining the priorities of the European Community, and the solidarity that was an essential part of it, to Mrs Thatcher. To say she listened would be grossly inaccurate, and her impatient response to the growing consensus around the table was 'But you will have to understand that Britain's contribution is grossly excessive and unfair and I am not prepared to agree to any conclusions here unless I get my money back'. 'But Mrs Thatcher', retorted Helmut Schmidt, 'we cannot reach decisions here in response to one member state only on matters affecting the whole Community. We are certainly prepared to show solidarity with any one colleague in difficulties but not as a precondition to general agreement on matters so fundamental to the European Community at large.' Further contributions and appeals from the other heads of government, far from reassuring Mrs Thatcher, only increased her determination: 'Gentlemen, I don't think you were listening to me or if you were you did not properly understand me. I can only agree to any budget conclusions on the condition that Britain's contribution is greatly reduced as fairness and equity demands and that the excessive contributions we have been making, quite wrongly in my view, must be reimbursed to us as a condition of any further agreement'. Schmidt by this time in exasperation had turned to his newspapers and his final interjection, and the manner and tone of it – 'But Madame, you are the one who has not been listening' – made it clear that there could not be any agreement on the basis of Mrs Thatcher's demands.

Despite those demands from Mrs Thatcher and the risk of a total breakdown, the Taoiseach and the Irish delegation steered the European Council towards conclusions based on certain essential principles – an essential part of the difficulty lay in the manner in which the Community's 'own resources' were regarded. The member states, with the exception of the United Kingdom, accepted that these are taxes or levies collected by the different member states on behalf of the Community. They are not national taxes or revenues but belong wholly to the Community, for which the national government simply acts as a collecting agent. The Irish Presidency underlined the fact that this is a fundamental Community principle. Prime Minister Thatcher, however, on behalf of the United Kingdom took an entirely different view. It regarded the money paid over to the Community as a British contribution, which imposed certain unacceptable disabilities on the British economy.

In the end, when it was clear that these positions could not be reconciled on acceptable terms, the Irish Presidency drew up conclusions based on certain essential principles which received broad acceptance by the Council. These principles were that in any solution:

1   the principles of Community's own resources must be maintained
2   there must be no question of *juste retour*
3   any solution must be financed from the Community budget
4   the VAT ceiling of 1 per cent must not be breached.

It was also agreed that as a general principle the solution that might emerge must preserve existing Community policies intact, and must not operate against the objective of convergence. On that basis the Irish Presidency undertook to continue discussions, particularly with the incoming Italian Presidency, and our objective in those discussions was to achieve a solution that would not damage the Community or seriously affect the vital interests of Ireland.

The media briefing by British sources conveyed the notion that the European Economic Community was now in crisis and presented the Dublin European Council as a disastrous failure. The reality was very different – the disaster would only have occurred had the Irish Presidency been prepared to concede to unacceptable British demands, which would have had long-term and damaging consequences for the European Community in general.

There was no crisis within the Community generally, but rather a solidarity and common purpose based on the principles proposed by the Irish Presidency. A crisis would only have occurred had concessions been proposed by the Irish Presidency that were inconsistent with the basic principles of the European Community and its funding, simply to present the conclusions that were acceptable to the British government. Against this background, what was represented as a failure by British spokespersons was in fact a successful outcome in that it protected the solidarity and principles of the European Community and laid down the guidelines in respect of which the immediate British problem was resolved at the next European Council in Luxembourg.

The British budget question was, regrettably, to dominate the proceedings at the European Council subsequently, and eventually the Commission was given a mandate from the European Council to propose a budget framework for a comprehensive range of new policies appropriate to the deepening and widening of the European Community. The accession of Greece in 1981 and the further enlargement by the accession of Spain and Portugal in 1986 gave added urgency to the Commission mandate. Greece, Spain and Portugal had only recently emerged from a long period of single-party rule, and the need to underpin democracy in each country became a priority with the European Community. With the prospect of enlargement of the Community from six to twelve in just over a decade, clearly the institutional framework of the Community required further examination, and at the European Council in Brussels on 4 and 5 December 1978 a committee that became known as 'the Three Wise Men' had been nominated to consider all aspects of this and to report back to the Council with its recommendations and conclusions. The composition of the Commission and its selection were features of the report eventually produced by the Three Wise Men, which *inter alia* recommended that the practice of appointing two Commissioners from the bigger countries should be discontinued. (The Spierenburg Group Report 1979, which was endorsed by the Three Wise Men in their report later that year, proposed that as adequate portfolios could not be found for 17 Commissioners, the Commission should be composed of one member per country and the President be found within that number.) This was clearly consistent with the need to protect the Commission in the independent discharge of its functions from undue interference or influence from the bigger member states in particular. Fifteen years later, with 15 member states, this issue has still not been resolved but it will clearly have to be addressed if the Commission is to function effectively as a college with collective responsibility.

The role of the Commission

A new Commission was appointed to take up office in January 1981 with Gaston Thorn, former Prime Minister of Luxembourg, as President. The first test of the Commission's independence and of the acceptance of that independence by the member states occurred on the evening of the very first meeting of the new Commission. It had always been a reserved function of the Commission to determine the allocation of portfolios within the college without any intrusion or interference by the heads of government of individual member states. The Commission decided to allocate responsibility for the mandate from the European Council to one Commissioner reporting directly to the President of the Commission. The allocation of this responsibility was the subject of prolonged discussion at the first meeting of the Commission and the demarcation of the relevant responsibilities of the Mandate Commissioner and the Budget Commissioner. I had been appointed as commissioner by the Irish Government and was nominated by the President of the Commission for the mandate portfolio, in addition to the responsibility for personnel and administration within the Commission. The outgoing Budget Commissioner, Christopher F. Tugendhat, was nominated to take responsibility for the budget and the demarcation of the responsibilities between us was the subject of a lengthy discussion at Commission. In the previous Commission, before the mandate responsibility was drawn up, Mr Tugendhat had responsibility for the budget and, like myself, understandably wanted clarification as to our respective responsibilities and the special relationship, if any, between the two portfolios.

At a certain moment during the night Mr Tugendhat absented himself from the Commission meeting, and subsequently Mr Thorn received a message that he was required in his office. He adjourned the meeting of the Commission and each of us withdrew to our respective offices. After approximately half an hour he phoned me in my office and asked me to join him in his office for an urgent and important discussion. When I joined him he was clearly in a highly emotional state and indicated to me that Prime Minister Thatcher had been on the phone to him directly, and at some length, berating him for the diminution of the budget responsibility of Commissioner Tugendhat and challenging what she alleged was a totally unacceptable allocation of the mandate responsibility to me. When I expressed my rejection of this outrageous attempt to interfere with the independence of the Commission he did not in any way demur or disagree. This conveyed the impression to me that he intended to adhere to the proposal originally made when the Commission resumed its meeting. In the event the Commission did resume one hour later, late in the night; clearly the President had taken the opportunity in the interim to consult with other colleagues and notify them of his intentions. However, the issue of how one could propose a range of new instruments and policies in accordance with the mandate from the European Council without having a separate and appropriate budget was conveniently overlooked by Thorn when the Commission meeting resumed, and the other Commissioners were in no mood to prolong the discussions. The independence of the Commission from that moment on was fundamentally undermined, and its authority had been permanently compromised by failing to reject out of hand the unprecedented and totally improper intrusion by Prime Minister Thatcher.

The range of policies drafted by me in response to 'the mandate' were never actually put in place, and it was left to the Delors Commission in the late 1980s to resurrect them and to take a vigorous and independent course of action.

'The mandate' was suffocated at birth and the Commission, which allowed this to happen, was thereafter fatally compromised in its independence and authority. Needless to say, the other reports that had been requested by the European Council, including that of the 'Three Wise Men', never subsequently emerged during the Thorn Presidency.

Institutional procedures

The effective functioning of the Council of Ministers became a major issue with the enlargement of the Community from six to nine in 1973, and subsequently from nine to twelve with the accession of Greece in 1981 and of Spain and Portugal in 1986. In the early days of the European Community the foreign ministers discharged the decision-making function almost exclusively – taking on board the advice from their governments in all relevant areas such as agriculture, social policy, energy policy, industrial policy and, of course, economic and finance policy. In time, of course, the Council met in separate formats as the Agriculture Council, the Ecofin Council, the Energy Council, Social Affairs Council, etc. to deal with the matters immediately relevant to these issues.

The Council in the latter format had already been put in place before we joined the European Community in 1973, but even then the Council of Foreign Ministers continued to deal with matters such as the regional policy of the European Community, the industrial policy of the Community, and many other important and crucial areas for the overall development of the European Community. These included in particular the enlargement negotiations which were, of course, detailed and protracted. In addition, the rationalisation and regulation of the steel industry in Europe became a constant issue at the General Council of Foreign Ministers, consuming a lot of time and energy.

As experts and advisers in these specialised areas attended the Council of Ministers with the national delegations, it happened quite regularly that over 100 people at a time were present in the Council Chamber, and the alternation of officials to advise their ministers on different issues became a regular and disturbing feature of the Council's procedures. In fact, it became clear in the 1970s that the Council was overwhelmed with detail and over-endowed with personnel to the extent that effective and expeditious decision-making became very difficult, if not impossible.

Equally, the 'constant feeding' of 'information' from the various delegations to suit their individual purposes greatly affected, if not undermined, the cohesion of the Council to the extent that by the time the President in Office of the Council and the President of the Commission came to declare the conclusions of the Council's meeting to the assembled media, these already had 'versions' of the discussions at the Council as well as the conclusions arrived at. I recall that at one of my earlier meetings in 1977 I saw these 'briefings' going on in the precincts of the Council Building before we had a private luncheon of the ministers. I deliberately asked at lunch what the established or acceptable procedure for informing the media was, and I clearly recall Gaston Thorn's response: 'It is very simple, Michael – Henri

[Simonet] speaks for all of us as President of the Council – that's of course unless you have got there first!'.

I was aware of the fact that some ministers then and previously at the Council had built up their reputations and courted special favour from the Press by giving 'informal' and non-attributed briefings as a regular practice, and while some of this may have paid dividends in the prominence given to those ministers in the national media in their own countries, it certainly did nothing to strengthen the cohesion and effectiveness of the Council as a whole. In fact, on more than one occasion subsequently I proposed that there should be open access for the media to all Council meetings, other than those that the Council resolved should be held 'in camera'. I still hold that view.

Indeed, I had the same reservations about the closed meetings of the Commission subsequently, and I recall divisive and even violent disagreements between the spokesmen for individual Commissioners, which did great damage to the collegiality of the Commission on numerous occasions. In a strange way, all of this has enhanced the status of the European Parliament as it was, and still is, the only political institution of the European Community or European Union that holds its meetings in public, thereby allowing the Press to reach their own conclusions, as distinct from relying on distorted versions from individual ministers or Commissioners. Significantly, Romano Prodi, the President of the current Commission, has reserved to himself the sole responsibility for communicating Commission decisions henceforth.

However, it has to be said that this breach of solidarity and collective responsibility was not confined to European institutions – more than one senior figure in Irish politics in recent times built up his reputation by establishing a 'special relationship' with the media through informal briefings and leaks on confidential government discussions. I often wondered why the Press were not more questioning of the motives and veracity of those providing this 'service' at national or European level.

Another extremely cumbersome procedure developed about this time – the 'Jumbo Council'. This was a joint meeting of the General Council of Foreign Ministers and of the Council of Ecofin which was always protracted, and by and large inconclusive. When this was enlarged on occasions to have a 'mammoth Jumbo' of Foreign, Finance and Agriculture Ministers, the Council was so overburdened as to collapse under the sheer weight of numbers, and conflicting positions on a variety of unrelated issues.

Due to the growing burden of work at the General Council of Foreign Ministers, it was inevitable that the heads of state and government would have to take a direct hand to expedite decision-making on important issues at European level. Accordingly, at the summit of the heads of state and government in Paris in 1974 it was decided to launch the European Council, comprising the heads of state and government and Foreign Ministers. There was a risk that the Commission might be somewhat side-tracked, if not bypassed, in this innovation – which of course was not provided for in the Treaties at that time – and it is to the credit of the Presidents of the Commission, Francis Xavier Ortoli and subsequently Roy Jenkins, that they insisted on attending these Council meetings, as the Commission had always been represented at the General Council of Ministers. It is a matter of record that both of those committed Europeans played a very significant and consistent role at the European Council subsequently, ensuring particularly that the smaller nations would not be overwhelmed at the European Council by the strength and authority of the heads of state and government from the larger member states such as France, Germany or the United Kingdom. Indeed, it is fair to say that inevitably the heads of government, meeting twice or at most three times a year, did not have the same spontaneous and easy relationships with each other as the Foreign Ministers, who met at least eight times a year formally, apart from the informal 'Gymnich' meetings at least twice a year. The General Council was to that extent much more collegiate and 'communitaire', but it has to be recognised that the European Council introduced a new dynamism and authority which unfortunately were diminishing in the General Council by that time.

Ireland's role

One might well ask whether in all of this Ireland played, or could play, any significant European role, as distinct from that of protecting our own interests at the Council meetings. The answer, emphatically, is 'yes!'. Perhaps this is best illustrated by the fact that the original Lomé Convention between the European Community and the African, Caribbean and Pacific countries was negotiated under the Irish Presidency of Dr Garret FitzGerald in 1974, and renegotiated under my own presidency in 1979. The fact that we had no colonial 'baggage' and, if anything, had a shared experience with the former colonies in the ACP countries gave us an immediate acceptability in the negotiations, which were sometimes protracted and often very passionate.

I recall in my own case that when it became clear that the ACP countries were not ready to conclude during the French Presidency in 1979, I was asked to take over the negotiations two weeks before our presidency. I do not claim to have had any special qualifications personally for the job, beyond that of a commitment to and understanding of the ACP position, but we were able to conclude the difficult renegotiations, which had been frustrated during the French Presidency, within weeks of taking up our responsibility in the presidency of the Council. Incidentally, it is also significant that it was during a subsequent Irish Presidency under Peter Barry that the third Lomé Convention was again renegotiated and concluded.

In addition, the fact that Ireland was the only neutral and non-aligned member state of the Community enabled us to play a very positive and significant role in the political co-operation process. In this context I might mention that during my own presidency in 1979 we achieved agreement among the nine member states for the first time on a common statement in support of Lord Carrington's proposals for the resolution of the Rhodesian conflict, out of which Zimbabwe subsequently emerged. We also achieved agreement which enabled me, as President in Office of the Council, in my address at the United Nations in September 1979 on behalf of the Nine, to mention the PLO for the first time and to assert that it would have to be a party to any Middle-East agreement. Similarly during our presidency we were able to agree a common position at the specially convened UN meeting in Geneva on actions to be taken with our partners elsewhere to deal with the then critical problem of the Vietnamese boat people. In all of this we were excellently served by a very professional and enlightened political directorate in the department of foreign affairs.

It is not surprising, then, that our colleagues often observed: 'If the Irish were not here, we would have to invent them'!

═══════ 23 ═══════

Completing the internal market and competition policy: a personal account

PETER D. SUTHERLAND

Introduction

As with all great political projects, the completion of the internal market, identified by the first Delors Commission as its primary aim, was a deceptively simple one. Both from the economic and political points of view the European Communities (EC) had been in a state of relative stagnation since the creation of the exchange rate mechanism (ERM) and even perhaps since the first oil shock in 1973. A series of reports between 1975 and 1985 had sought to break the political deadlock and to move the integration process forward. The Tindemans report of 1975 and the report of the Three Wise Men in 1979 are examples, but neither was clearly connected with a pragmatic economic goal. Then in February 1984 the European Parliament adopted the draft Treaty on European Union which was the fruit of the initiative of Altiero Spinelli.[1] Following this, the Fontainebleau European Council meeting in June 1984 set up the Dooge Committee as an *ad hoc* committee on institutional reform. At the same meeting Margaret Thatcher, in her tabled statement called 'Europe – the Future', advocated the completion of the Common Market as the major project to be undertaken. Ironically, having regard to her fundamental opposition to greater European unity, this proposal was later effectively to link institutional with economic reform. In fact nobody opposed the idea. In European policy initiative terms, this was a virtually unique circumstance. Furthermore, there were powerful industrial advocates for this new dynamic. Wisse Decker of Philips was prominent among these, and indeed since then he and others from the European Round Table of Industrialists (ERTI) have often claimed, with some justification, that industry was the real driving force for the '1992' project. One way or the other, what is quite clear is that this project started to take shape in late 1984.

In reality, no individual or member state can justifiably claim to have been its sole originator. It was simply a project whose time had come. Of course a customs union had been envisaged in the Treaty of Rome, but the will to actually make it happen had been absent. It had been part of the

Solemn Declaration on European Union signed at Stuttgart on 19 June 1983 by the heads of government and foreign ministers – an event that some commentators claim effectively 'relaunched the Community'.[2] However, in singling out this project from a plethora of others, the main credit clearly must be given to Jacques Delors.

I was nominated by the Irish government in late August 1984 to be a member of the European Commission, which would take up office in January 1985. There had been some discussion before that decision about who might be the most appropriate person to designate. In fact I told Garret FitzGerald when he asked me that either Jim Dooge or Alan Dukes would be a better appointment. When I was nominated I retained my position as attorney general pending the choice of a successor, but immediately began to prepare myself for the task. I thus set about deciding on my cabinet and, even more importantly, considering which Commission portfolio would best enable me to contribute to the work of the Commission.

Allocation of portfolios

I discussed the issue of portfolio with a number of people well versed in EU affairs, and particularly with Andy O'Rourke, Ireland's permanent representative to the EU. In addition I visited Emile Nöel, the secretary general of the Commission, at the Berlaymont in Brussels during September 1984. Emile Nöel's life was devoted to the European venture. Indeed, nobody that I have ever met has known more of its Byzantine workings than he did. Years later, sitting in his small apartment overlooking the Piazza della Signoria in Florence, where he was president of the European University Institute (EUI), we spoke of that early meeting. He told me how convinced he had been that a small country should provide the Commissioner for competition because this would avoid some of the more obvious issues of conflict of interest. My reasoning was different, and perhaps that of a lawyer rather than a politician or an economist. Perhaps more than in any other case, the competition portfolio vested real supranational authority in the Commission. Composed of two elements, anti-trust rules and control of state subsidies, the Directorate for Competition (DG IV) had the means to influence policy in vital industry areas without reference to the Council of Ministers. The authority was already contained in the Treaty of Rome itself rather than in the Commission's right to propose new legislation. As David Allen has pointed out, competition law 'is a symbol, however isolated, of the supranational powers that the Commission aspires to in other areas'.[3]

Even though Emile Nöel always maintained an ostensible distance from the politics of portfolio allocation within the Commission, he certainly helped me more than I expected. In that early discussion in his unobtrusive and chaotic office he was uncharacteristically unambiguous in expressing the view that I should consider the competition portfolio. He said that he would speak about it to Jacques Delors before my first meeting with him, as indeed I believe he did.

In September 1984 I also had dinner with Vicomte Etienne Davignon, the long-serving and legendary Belgian Industry Commissioner who was about to retire from the Commission. Davignon had made an enormous impact during his period as a Commissioner and, ultimately, Vice-President of the Commission. He had first-class political skills although, paradoxically, he had never been an elected politician.

There had been for many years something of a conflict between the Industry Directorate (DG III) and the Competition Directorate. For example, when Commissioner Raymond Vouel was in charge of DG IV he had attacked the proposals for market sharing among synthetic fibre producers advanced by Davignon. There had also been some friction between Davignon and Frans Andriessen, who took over from Vouel in 1981. Notwithstanding this tension, Davignon was quite clear as to the value and potential of DG IV to make a real impact on the development of the EC, not merely from an economic but from a constitutional point of view. He pointed out that if the new Commission was to make the Internal Market its leitmotif, competition policy would have to play a central role. The functioning of a market with free movement of goods and services could only work effectively if the distortions of restrictive practices and of abuses of dominant market positions by undertakings could be controlled. So also with state aids. If governments could protect inefficient enterprises through the use of state funding, then clearly the beneficial effects of a market economy simply would not work to maximise efficiency and innovation. On my return to Dublin I spoke to the Taoiseach, Garret FitzGerald, who was also attracted by the potential of the competition portfolio.

My next task was to secure the portfolio, recognising that the denouement would be at the dreaded 'night of the long knives'. Of all the events in the recurring calendar of Community politics, none was spoken of with more entertaining anecdotes and whispered conspiracy theories than this, the occasion when portfolios are allocated. The nature of the Commission itself made this a complicated exercise. As the President of the Commission (before the Treaty of Amsterdam) was no more than *primus inter pares*, he could not simply designate the portfolios to specified Commissioners. The task was a collective one of the college as a whole. I did not know how forceful Delors would be in this process. While he was clearly the central figure, the possibility of votes and coalitions of interest on who got what was a real one. Stories of past humiliations and triumphs on the issue were recounted with gusto and sometimes with uncharitable relish.

Also, it became clear that others were interested in the competition portfolio and that there might be a contest. I was also conscious and worried about the likely reaction at home. There would be criticism of my appointment as a non-politician, particularly if I were seen to have failed to acquire what was perceived as a substantial role; at that time, the competition portfolio was not understood in Ireland. I decided to try to meet all the members of the incoming Commission with a view to ascertaining their intentions and putting down a marker as to my own. The most important meeting was to be with Jacques Delors.

I met Jacques Delors for the first time over a bilateral lunch at the restaurant Chez Edgar in Paris, which was then the favoured watering-hole of socialist politicians and journalists. We went to a private room and conversed in a mixture of French and English. He talked a great deal about the need for a relaunch of Europe. On the constitutional issues relating to supranational development we were basically in agreement. I suppose that in United Kingdom terms we were both arch-federalists, although we sometimes disagreed later about the areas where supranational powers should be advanced. I found him to be both intense and serious, but extremely likeable. He asked me what portfolio I wanted, and I told him that there were two that were of particular interest to me: development and competition. I mentioned these knowing that in all probability Lorenzo Natali, the senior outgoing Italian Commissioner, would seek and get development. To my consternation, he asked me whether I would I like agriculture. I told him that no Irishman would decline agriculture, and if he wished me to take it I would be honoured, but I also told him that I knew absolutely nothing about the subject. He confirmed that Lord Cockfield was getting the internal market and Lorenzo Natali would be in charge of development policies. As soon as I left him I returned to my hotel and telephoned the Taoiseach with the news. He was, I think, surprised, but said that there could be no question of declining agriculture.

On my return to Ireland, I hastily assembled an extremely effective team from the Department of Agriculture to commence a briefing, but some days later and before this had gone too far I received a call from Delors saying everything had changed. Frans Andriessen, who had initially wanted external affairs, had rejected a divided portfolio in this area as suggested by Delors. He had fallen back on agriculture and Delors proposed to give it to him. This being the case, he asked whether I still wanted competition. I was in fact delighted with this outcome, and even though it was not assured I felt that I was in a reasonably strong position as we approached the fateful meeting, to take place at the Abbaye de Royaumont outside Paris in November.

We met at the Abbaye for a couple of days. During the afternoon of the first day Delors held bilateral confessionals one by one with the new

Commission. The only one absent was Claude Cheysson, who was still serving as foreign minister of France: I was told at the time that he did not believe that the allocation of portfolios could be concluded that day, because this Commission did not yet exist. As a result, perhaps, he was not concerned about being absent. His position, apparently, was that the Commission would only come formally into being in early January and could take binding decisions only then. I met Delors after his meetings with Natali, Cockfield and Andriessen, and he offered to propose competition as my portfolio. He then said that in addition he would like me to also hold the social affairs, health and education portfolio until the Spanish joined the Communities, which could occur, at the earliest, twelve months later. I was delighted by this turn of events, which effectively gave me a double job. I thought it wise to retire early to my room for fear that my position would be damaged by Delors' subsequent negotiations with others. I slept rather badly.

The following morning I rose early on hearing the local church bells at about 7 a.m., and went downstairs to find the debris of the preceding night much in evidence. Empty cognac glasses were everywhere. As nobody appeared to be up, I went out into the grounds and walked down a tree-lined avenue when I saw a figure approach through the early morning mist. It was Jacques Delors. He told me everything had been resolved amicably the previous evening and the portfolios allocated, and in my case everything was as had been agreed. His only concern was whether he could announce the portfolio allocation that day. I strongly urged Delors to arrange an immediate press conference and to announce the agreement on portfolios. Otherwise, I could see the whole delicate compromise falling apart, particularly if Claude Cheysson did not like what he had been given, which was half of the external affairs portfolio (he would share this portfolio with Willy De Clercq). Delors decided to proceed, and a press conference duly took place at 2 p.m.

Towards a single market

When we took up office on 5 January 1985, one of my first press comments focused on air transport and the uniquely anti-competitive cartel run by the national carriers in Europe. I said that I hoped to break it up. Within days I was invited to dinner in the home of former Commissioner Willy Haverkampf, who had continued to reside in Brussels. When I arrived I noticed that there were only three places set. It transpired that the third person was the chief executive of a major European airline. After preliminary pleasantries he rapidly got down to business and unambiguously warned me off any activities in this sector, claiming, spuriously, that air transport was effectively excluded from Art 85 of the Treaty of Rome and that I had no jurisdiction in the matter in any event. The evening ended frostily, but it was an introduction to the sort of pressures with which I was to become familiar in coming years. Talking of a functioning internal market was one thing; bringing it about was quite another.

With the rapid resolution of the issue of portfolios, the new Commissioners had spent some time at that first meeting discussing our priorities for the new year. There has been some debate since about the genesis of '1992' as the date for the completion of the internal market. Jacques Delors, in an article in the *Kangaroo News* (the newsletter of a group of Europarliamentarians) later in the early 1990s, posed the question but did not answer it. Lord Cockfield, in his book *Creating the Single Market*, could not recall precisely where it came from. Pascal Lamy, Delors' chef de cabinet, remembers it being decided by Delors and his cabinet. I believe that it simply emerged at Royaumont following a rather uninformed discussion because no one there knew with any degree of precision how much, or indeed what, legislation would be required to achieve free movement of capital, services, goods and people. Determining eight years as the appropriate time had to be, and was, a wild guess. It proved to be an inspired one.

In fact, as the term of a Commission was four years, the first suggestion was to complete the task by the end of 1988. However, there was a general view that more time would be needed; a period of two terms was proposed, and that brought us effectively to 31 December 1992. And so it was to be. Following Royaumont, at the European Council meeting in Dublin in December 1984, the conclusions included, at Delors' request, a demand to 'the Council in its appropriate formations... to take steps to complete the Internal Market'.

The White Book, as it was known, setting out just under 300 legislative proposals required to complete the internal market, was later sent to the heads of government on 14 June 1985. Lord Cockfield modestly described the Book 'as a programme of immense scope and imagination'. He did not understate its importance (nor his own significant role in putting it together), but he fully deserved the credit subsequently given to him.

From the point of view of my own directorate, this immense undertaking was to be the catalyst for a dramatic advance in competition law and practice. Indeed, the White Book referred to the essential necessity of the rigorous application of competition policy for the effective completion of the Internal Market. As one commentator put it, 'The Internal Market would be an exercise in futility if, at the very moment national barriers to trade were levelled, European companies immediately set about raising them by introducing a new set of commercial barriers to trade and engaging in ingenious forms of anti-competitive behaviour.... [The Commission] proposes to reconcile the irreconcilable by introducing a comprehensive competition policy, granting it the power to appraise all large scale mergers.'[4]

Selecting a cabinet

The selection of a cabinet is vitally important for any Commissioner. This point was emphasised to me by every person who knew the workings of the EC's institutions. Apart from the late Liam Hourican, who was an old friend and collaborator, I had no real ideas about whom to include in my cabinet. Liam had been chef de cabinet for Richard Burke, my predecessor, and was to be invaluable in assisting the process of selection of the team. The cabinet had to include individuals who could effectively cover not merely the portfolios for which I had responsibility but also those of other Commissioners. The process for Commission decision-making on contentious issues usually involved initially a meeting and debate on new proposals by the specialised members of cabinet of all Commissioners. Then their conclusions went for further debate if necessary to the meeting of the chefs de cabinet held under the chairmanship of the secretary-general Emile Nöel on the Monday preceding the Wednesday Commission meeting at which a decision was to be taken. In selecting my team I communicated with all government departments that I thought relevant, and enquired there about possible candidates. I also received a large number of unsolicited indications of interest in a position from a wide range of individuals, many of whom were not Irish and some of whom served in the EC institutions. I decided early that nobody could join the cabinet who did not speak at least one Community language in addition to English. In addition, I sought a specific prior active involvement and expertise in some element of EU affairs. One name mentioned to me was Richard O'Toole of foreign affairs, who at the time was deputy permanent representative in Geneva. He had a formidable reputation and wide experience. This had included working with the International Energy Agency (IEA) in Paris as special assistant to the executive director, and periods on secondment with the French foreign service at the Quai d'Orsay and the Italian foreign service at the Farnesina. He also had served in the Irish Department of Foreign Affairs as first Secretary in the economic division and later in the political division as European correspondent, and knew the EC well. He was about a year younger than I was. We met for dinner for the first time in a Dublin club, and I knew within minutes that he was the man for me. Shortly afterwards I contacted foreign minister Peter Barry and asked for Richard's early release in order to put him on the ground in Brussels to assist in the next stages of my building of the cabinet. I had decided that Liam could not be my chef de cabinet even though this would be hurtful to him, as indeed it was. My reasoning was that whatever way the portfolio was resolved, I would need a chef de cabinet who was familiar with economic and constitutional matters. Neither was Liam's forte. It was typical of the man that when I told him that I intended to appoint Richard O'Toole as chef de cabinet, and offered him the role as deputy chef, he was prepared to accept. It required a really big and generous man to do as he did, but that is what he was. He was to prove to be exceptionally important to me in the period ahead, not merely in his function but as a close and dear friend whose early death shocked and horrified all who knew and loved him.

The other members of the cabinet were as follows. Catherine Day, a Commission official and economist from Dublin, was to handle with consummate skill the most difficult area of my portfolio, control of state aids. Jean Francois Verstrynge, a Belgian, who was later visiting professor of European Law in Harvard, had worked in the cabinet of my predecessor Frans Andriessen and he handled anti-trust matters. He was both courageous and innovative. I asked Eugene Regan to follow agriculture. He had significant experience, being both an economist and a lawyer who, in his varied career – though only 32 years of age – had been chief economist of the Irish Farmers Association and later chief executive of the Meat Exporters Association. David O'Sullivan, another Commission official who, like Catherine Day, was to have a meteoric Commission career, handled social affairs, external relations, development and later relations with the European Parliament. He has recently been appointed chef de cabinet for Romano Prodi. Finally, I asked Delors for the authority to take on an extra cabinet member because of the extent of my responsibilities. This was to be Michel Richonnier, who was something of a visionary. He had written a well-reviewed book presenting future perspectives for Europe in technology, and in the collegiate atmosphere played a role in presenting lateral thinking on a wide range of subjects. Michel and Hywel Jones, a senior official in DG V (social affairs), both worked on my initiative to establish the successful Erasmus student exchange programme launched in late 1985.

Four years later, when I was about to leave the Commission, Roland Gachot, who had long served Emile Nöel, remarked to me that Richard O'Toole was one of the three best chefs de cabinet that he had known in his decades of experience, and that my cabinet as a whole was also one of the best ever. Any minor success I may have achieved was largely due to the team that I had assembled.

Competition policy and the single market

In retrospect, my first Commission meeting in early January 1985 was a watershed in more ways than one. As was the practice, the agenda had been prepared during the preceding days by the specialised cabinet members on their various subjects and then by a meeting of the chefs de cabinet. I had received a written and an oral briefing from Richard O'Toole on each item on the agenda. Shortly after the meeting commenced, however, Delors – without prior warning – said that, as a preliminary matter, he proposed to grant 'the customary habilitations' to Frans Andriessen, the Agriculture Commissioner. I had no idea what a 'habilitation' was, and I felt a particular responsibility to keep a close eye on what happened in such an important portfolio which spent such a large proportion of the Community budget. I said to the President that I did not understand what he meant by 'habilitation', that I had no notice of the matter and would like it put back for a week. Nobody else said anything, although I discovered later that virtually all the new Commissioners were just as mystified as I was. The discussion quite quickly took on an acrimonious tone. Jacques Delors said that this was an absolutely normal delegation of authority to Andriessen to take certain decisions without reference to the Commission as a college, and that it merely followed normal practice. I responded by saying that I did not dispute his explanation but still would like, as a new Commissioner, to look at the issue and be properly informed before proceeding. This was taken badly and I was asked whether I wanted to vote on the issue (the President also said that the previous Commission never had votes, and this would be a bad precedent). I stuck to my guns and we had a vote, which I believe I lost by seven votes to five. Although it may have been a somewhat traumatic beginning to my period as a Commissioner, in retrospect I believe that it was healthy for the Commission to have voted on the issue and it created a good climate for subsequent serious-minded decision-taking, in which voting was quite frequent.

While Jacques Delors (who is a truly historic figure) deserves the main credit for the relaunching of Europe through the '1992' project, I felt he was never entirely at ease with the focus on market economics that it represented. He was not a natural deregulator, and he certainly wanted some balance through social policies. However, he pushed it through and consistently supported Cockfield in the Commission. So did I. Cockfield himself was an unlikely candidate for success. A former tax inspector, his personality on initial contact was distant, and he was without notable political or communication skills. Ironically, Michel Petite, a Frenchman, who worked in his cabinet has described him as 'a cool Cartesian'.[5] However, he took very seriously his responsibilities under the treaties. His logic was inexorable and so was his pursuit of his goal; once he decided on a course he would not be diverted.

As early as his first speech to the European Parliament on 14 January 1985, Jacques Delors was to indicate that he knew that the grand project could not be achieved without institutional reform and, in particular, more majority voting. This reform, to be ultimately attained through the Single

European Act, truly inspired him and was to become one of his two great achievements. (The other was economic and monetary union.) The Single European Act was also to cause Margaret Thatcher some considerable distress. As she had so strongly advocated the completion of the internal market, and it was readily apparent that it could not be achieved without more majority voting, she was caught between a rock and a hard place. She ultimately conceded and signed the Single European Act, something she now claims to regret.

Competition policy, as enshrined in the Treaty of Rome, was never intended simply to endorse and provide the means to enforce the market economy system, but it was and is an essential element in it. There was no absolutism in the regulatory regime proposed by the Treaty, however, and this no doubt reflected the 'social market economy' concept of Ludwig Erhardt that so influenced the drafting of the Treaty of Rome. It was conceded, for example, in Article 92 that regional disadvantage might sometimes justify interventions through state aids that might otherwise be considered distortive and illegal. The provisions sought, however, to apply objectivity and principle to Commission decision-making, but they left considerable discretion to the Commission. An example of the application of the rules to state aid regimes can be found in the case of the International Financial Services Centre (IFSC) in Dublin. When the Irish government applied to me for the essential tax concessions underlying this proposal, there were strong grounds for permitting the scheme. Ireland, as a single regional area, was clearly then disadvantaged in EC terms. The GDP per capita was less than 75 per cent of the current EU average, and unemployment was significantly above the average. In July 1987 the Commission, on my proposal, decided that the 10 per cent rate of corporation tax could be extended to firms whose income was derived from certified international financial services carried on at the Customs House Dock site. The Commission based this exceptional treatment 'not only on the serious economic and social situation in Dublin but also on the development benefits of the project in the overall Irish context'.[6] I believed then, and still believe, that positive intervention can be both necessary and desirable in certain cases, and never felt my proposal to be other than an objective one. This was one of those cases, although I could not at the time imagine the scale of enormous success that the IFSC was ultimately to achieve.

In my opinion, the most important innovative legal step taken in competition policy during my period in office was the first substantive use of Article 90 of the Treaty of Rome to create competition in areas where member states had previously granted exclusive rights to monopolies. This was one of only two areas where the Commission could itself issue a Directive without the agreement of the Council of Ministers. By Directive 88/301/EEC of 16 May 1988, the Commission took its first major step in this area when it required competition in the market for telecommunication terminal equipment. The Directive provided for the abolition of exclusive rights granted in this field by nearly all the member states to their state national telecom companies. This decision was to be the catalyst for one of the great revolutions in the economic affairs of the EU, and when it was taken we all knew that it was the thin end of a very large wedge. Its relevance was that it opened the door for the Commission to drive the liberalisation of markets in areas such as telecommunications, transport and energy, which were generally dominated by state monopolies. This process has in fact transformed the economic environment in Europe and has inevitably led to the wholesale privatisation of public utilities everywhere. The decision itself was bitterly fought in the relevant Commission meeting. A number of member states challenged the decision before the European Court of Justice, but the Court upheld the substance of the Commission's right to act as it had.

The change in the law brought about by the Terminal Equipment case[7] was a striking one. In the earlier Sacchi case,[8] the approach of the Court had been that the state could 'reserve to itself certain sectors of the economy and thus exclude them from competition'. Francoise Blum and Annette Logue, in their book on EC law and state monopolies,[9] concluded that the Terminal Equipment case constituted a turning point that radically altered the law. Monopolies could henceforth be potentially illegal *per se*: 'On the basis of Terminal Equipment all national monopolies at least over products may potentially be contrary to the Treaty insofar as they restrict imports'.

On the other hand, it was particularly noticeable that Commission decisions were generally accepted by governments when they did not involve state enterprise. I do not believe that the issue was essentially one of political ideology. Where public utilities came under threat, the symbiosis between the civil services and the management of the public utilities became apparent. The civil service often nominated the management of public utilities from their own ranks, effectively also providing their boards, so it was not surprising that they often became vigorous defenders of monopoly positions. The prolonged action warfare initiated by DG IV across a range of sectors following the Terminals Directive (including air transport and energy) was highlighted by the increasingly apparent failures and inefficiencies of state-managed European public utilities. It was already evident from the cost reductions in Britain, where liberalisation and privatisation had advanced far more rapidly than elsewhere, that deregulation was essential to achieve structural reform and a more dynamically growing economy in Europe. Ireland, with the exception of the field of air transport, was always a reluctant traveller along the path advancing competition in the areas previously reserved to state monopolies.

From the Single Market to GATT negotiations

My personal involvement with the 1992 single market programme did not conclude when I left the Commission. In July 1992 I was invited by the European Commission to chair an advisory committee to report to the European Council in December 1992 at its meeting in Edinburgh during the British Presidency. The report was intended to help to shape the Commission's objectives regarding the implementation of the internal market for 1993 and beyond, particularly following ratification of the Maastricht Treaties in 1992. The other members of my group were Dr Ernst Albrecht, the former minister and President of Lower Saxony; Christian Babusiaux, director general of competition, consumer affairs and enforcement of France; Sir Brian Corby, president of the Confederation of British Industry; Pauline Green MEP; and Dr Giuseppe Tramontana of Italy. The intention was to encourage greater political commitment to a more effective partnership between the Commission and the member states. As the end of the internal market legislative programme was then in sight, the group was asked to map out the best way to ensure that the full benefits of the internal market were secured in practice.

During the following months, having invited submissions from European associations and interest groups, the committee met regularly and ultimately produced the report that was unveiled at a press conference in Strasbourg on 28 October 1992. The 70-page document contained 38 main recommendations on how EC laws should be implemented effectively at national level. It agreed that there were risks in the debate on subsidiarity, particularly as it could bring about a situation where the implementation of EC laws was so diverse at national level that it endangered the coherent implementation of the internal market.

The British Presidency forcefully pressed for swift action on the report, which was put before the Council of Ministers the week following its initial presentation. The presidency followed this with a consideration of the report at the 10 November Internal Market Council before the discussion at the European Council. The report was generally approved at each level, and the communiqué following Edinburgh expressed general support for its recommendations.

The implications of the largely successful accomplishment of the 1992 programme combined with advances in competition policy cannot be overstated. On the economic level, the process of globalisation that has developed in the 1990s has ordained that Europe had to improve its competitiveness rapidly or suffer serious consequences from import penetration. Therefore the modernisation of the European economy through the development of real competition in all sectors was an absolute requirement for the member states. They in turn had not shown a willingness to confront the thorny political issues that opening up competition would necessarily create. In some respects the Commission was to become a scapegoat for policy initiatives that the national administrations basically accepted as being necessary but were unwilling to advocate publicly. For example, on many occasions ministers told me privately that they accepted elements of competition policy in the area of state aids that they publicly rejected.

In another sense the 1992 project helped globalisation to happen not merely through conditioning European countries to take liberal economic positions in the Uruguay Round, but also in providing examples of how to implement free movement of goods and services through multilateral negotiations in Geneva at the GATT and now the World Trade Organisation. Having been conditioned to market liberalisation, the member states found it possible to agree common positions on the largest and most comprehensive round of trade negotiations ever conducted.

NOTES

1   William Wallace (ed.), *The Dynamics of European Integration*, The Royal Institute of International Affairs, p. 219.
2   Lord Cockfield, *Creating the Single Market*, Wiley, p. 23.
3   Wallace, op. cit.
4   R. Owen and M. Dyner, *Britain in a Europe without Frontiers*, Times Books, p. 112.
5   Charles Grant, *Inside the House that Jacques Built*, Nicholas Brealey, p. 68.
6   17th Report on Competition Policy, p. 181
7   *French Republic v. Commission* 1991 ECR 1223.
8   1974 ECR 409.
9   F. Blum and A. Logue, *State Monopolies under EC Law*, Wiley, p. 2.

24

Reform of the CAP

RAY MACSHARRY

Introduction

I was privileged to have been a member of the European Commission that held office from 1989 to 1992. To have been the Commissioner for Agriculture and Rural Development at that time provided me with a unique opportunity to bring about what I believe will prove to have been a lasting and beneficial change in agriculture and rural development policy; at the same time, the office placed a heavy responsibility on me, not only towards the people who gained their livelihoods from agriculture but also towards other sectors which stood to win or lose as a result of the Commission's actions, notably in the context of international trade negotiations.

Apart from the founding period of the Community, 1989 to 1992 was arguably the most exciting period to have been a member of the Commission. Jacques Delors had already set a series of important challenges for the European Community and wanted to build on the solid achievement of the previous Commission. Putting into practical effect the single market, the initial reform and subsequent development of the structural funds and the new cohesion fund, agreement on Community finances, laying the basis for economic and monetary union through the Maastricht Treaty, German reunification, conclusion of the General Agreement on Tariffs and Trade (GATT) Uruguay round, and the reform of the CAP were all major issues to be tackled.

Agriculture and rural development

As the new member responsible for agriculture, I was to take over from Vice-President Frans Andriessen who had been held in high repute both within the Commission and in the member states and who would be taking responsibility for international trade policy. His task would change from one of discouraging farm imports to advocating freer trade in agriculture. In the division of responsibilities in the new Commission the authority for agricultural trade issues and the corresponding administrative structures remained under the control of myself as the member responsible for agriculture. This was important in enabling me to demonstrate my independence on agricultural issues, while at the same time ensuring a sound working relationship between us, notably in defending the Community's position in the Uruguay Round.

Up to 1989 at least, it had never been expected that Ireland would take the agriculture portfolio in the Commission; its huge dependence on an underdeveloped agriculture, together with a tendency to declare a vital national interest on agricultural issues, would have been among the objections – not openly stated because the question was never on the table, but certainly to the forefront of the thinking of the political decision-takers in Europe – should the question have arisen. Prior to 1989 the member from either the Netherlands or Denmark, both countries with a developed agriculture, was seen as best placed to hold the ring between the competing interests. This had been shown to have been a solid formula: the late Sicco Mansholt of the Netherlands, the founding father of the CAP, who became very unpopular in Ireland in the early 1970s for his proposals to rationalise the policy by reducing drastically the numbers in agriculture, was a very effective Commissioner; so too was the late Finn Gundelach of Denmark – as Minister for Agriculture I had differed with him strongly on milk quotas a decade before, but I recognised him as a tireless defender of agriculture.

Following contacts between certain heads of state towards the end of 1988, decisive support emerged in favour of my appointment as the member responsible for agriculture. For the first time, rural development was added to the title of the portfolio in recognition that my mandate was not limited to supporting the markets but, in parallel to the development of the structural funds, had to be broader and more imaginative in terms of developing rural areas. My views on the importance of rural development coincided with those of Jacques Delors, who would continue to lead the Commission as President. Throughout my period in office I fully shared and supported Delors' ambitious objectives for the Community and his far-seeing vision of a fully integrated Europe. And, despite some differences of view in the latter stages of the agricultural trade negotiations leading up to the Blair House agreement with the United States, I had his full support also in all important decisions.

My extensive background knowledge of agriculture and my ministerial experience meant that I came well equipped for the new job, though the scope of the subject and degree of technical detail to be mastered was formidable. Apart from presentation of proposals to the Commission itself, the Commissioner's mastery of his brief had to be demonstrated both at the monthly meetings of the Council, before ministers always eager to find a response from the Commission to their respective concerns, and also before the European Parliament. I found it enormously helpful to have had practical experience as a member of the Council of Ministers (1977–82 and 1987–88) and of the European Parliament (1984–87). Apart from being well versed in essential Community procedures, I had already met many of the political figures from both institutions with whom I would work as commissioner over the following years.

My interests went wider than agriculture. I was keenly aware from my work as Minister for Finance, especially in the 1987–88 period, of the need for economic reform and budgetary discipline. The decisions taken at the time laid the basis for the subsequent development of the 'Celtic tiger' economy brought about by strict control of public expenditure, increased inward investment, judicious use of transfers of financial resources from the European Community, and social partnership. Conscious of the rapid globalisation of economic activity and of the Community's wider trade interests, I had a strong awareness of the importance of stability in international relations. I was determined that the European Community would be an important player and would profit from what I saw as the inevitable Uruguay Round agreement. This round of trade negotiations – the most comprehensive ever – had been launched at Punta del Este in 1986, and by the beginning of 1989 its content was already beginning to take shape. My experience of the adverse effects of currency instability throughout the 1980s made me a strong advocate of moves towards economic and monetary union, and for a more stable system in Europe which would ultimately lead to a single European currency designed and managed to serve Community objectives and policies, which were often at the mercy of fluctuations in the dollar.

While my period of office tends to be remembered for what have come to be known as the MacSharry reforms – I will come back to this later – I regard what was achieved in two other areas of my portfolio as significant also. The first was the single market, where my responsibility involved preparing and negotiating some 100 Directives, mainly in the difficult areas of veterinary and phytosanitary rules. As I was a strong believer in the single market and fully aware of the damage caused by non-tariff barriers to trade, I am proud of what was achieved to ensure that agriculture would be fully integrated into the single market. The second was in rural development policy, traditionally the 'Cinderella' of the CAP when compared to the work effort and budgetary support given to the markets. Apart from overseeing what was a willing reorganisation of Directorate General VI (Agriculture) in order to equip it not only to prepare rural development initiatives, but also to think 'rural development' as opposed to 'traditional' agricultural structures, the basis was laid for a huge expansion in the resources for rural development under Objective 1 (regions lagging behind, including Ireland, Portugal, Greece and parts of Italy and Spain), and under the specific rural development Objective 5B established as part of the reformed structural funds. There was also the birth of the Community initiative 'LEADER', conceived as a bottom-up initiative designed to provide support to local people to put into effect constructive ideas for the development of their communities. It followed my insistence that a rural development policy without the opportunity for active involvement of local communities was a contradiction in terms. Despite initial scepticism within the Commission, this initiative has proved to be hugely successful, being one of only three initiatives retained by the Commission in its Agenda 2000 proposals for the rationalisation of the structural funds.

The case for reform

I came to Brussels with a firm determination to reorient, if not reform, the Common Agricultural Policy. This was based on my conviction that there was something fundamentally wrong with a system which, on the one hand, cost 30 billion ECU (£21 billion) of taxpayers' money and produced 'mountains' of surplus product, and on the other hand left so many farmers impoverished, and rural areas in continual decline. These were issues with which most of my predecessors had grappled in a piecemeal way, with the result that by 1989 there was an extensive array of corrective measures in place in the markets, and an agricultural socio-structures policy focused mainly on investment aid to encourage greater competitiveness. Despite regular infusions of extra funding, it was becoming more and more difficult on the one hand to prevent the emergence of new surpluses, and on the other hand to prevent farm incomes from falling further behind. The situation was well recognised by senior officials in DG VI, who were supportive of my view that a more radical reform of the policy was needed. When it came to the reform itself, the main opposition was from a combination of powerful farming and agricultural industry interests. My greatest fear was that they would decisively influence the Commission or the Council in the direction of postponement of reform until the outcome of the Uruguay Round was settled, confident in their view that agriculture would emerge unscathed from the international trade negotiations. For many opponents of reform the *status quo* had to prevail, not only to guarantee existing levels of agricultural production but to increase production wherever possible. And, while there would have been some genuine fears among farmers about change, the reality was that the storage and export of millions of tons of cereals, beef and milk products, the distillation of millions of litres of wine and the administration, by producer organisations, of consumption and production subsidies for olive oil, cotton and tobacco was very profitable for many influential business interests.

It was evident to me following the very difficult price negotiations of 1990, carried out against the background of a sharp increase in budgetary costs and falling incomes in agriculture, that the CAP was in serious difficulty both for internal and for external reasons. In domestic terms it depended on continuation of a Franco-German political consensus which might not last forever, and on the continuing goodwill of Parliament which, with an increasing influence over agricultural spending, might not continue to go along with a situation where more that half the Community's overall budget went on agriculture. This was an agriculture incapable of coping with the income problems of farmers and which made little contribution to rural development or to the environment; on the other hand, through its inability to reduce surpluses, the CAP required increasing budgetary resources. On the external side, the policy was the source of continual tension in international relations and there was the real prospect that the GATT would rule against key parts of the CAP support system, notably production subsidies, and possibly also export refunds.

I did not set out to reform of the policy in order to satisfy the numerous opponents of the CAP, notably its external critics. But, as the negotiations on the reform progressed in the Council following the European Parliament's Opinion in December 1991 which was supportive of the approach proposed by the Commission, I saw that the reform could be the key to extricating both the Community and the United States from a dangerous confrontation arising from unresolved trade disputes. The consequences of such conflict would not be limited to agriculture but would affect world trade, with inevitable knock-on effects for global business confidence. The threat of external conflict, in which there could be no winners, was an important argument in favour of reform, although the reform itself was conceived for internal reasons.

Despite its growing defects, I knew that it would be no easy task to get agreement on reforming a policy that had been built up over 30 years and had brought about a remarkable transition in post-war European agriculture from penury to plenty. The question was how to preserve the best features of the policy, while ensuring the necessary adaptations to reflect a changing public opinion which had long forgotten post-war starvation conditions in Europe, and was now more preoccupied with the cost of surpluses, the quality of the product, and damage caused to the environment by intensive agriculture.

Greater competitiveness, brought about by a sharp reduction in prices, had to be at the heart of the reform. This meant re-opening the Franco-German agreement on the common price level for cereals when the CAP was drawn up in 1960. The essence of the agreement had been that Germany would profit from free movement of goods to the benefit of its industry and France would have a system which would provide price support for its farmers and allow its agro-industrial potential in agriculture, especially in cereals, to achieve what it considered to be its rightful share of world markets. As regards the level of common prices, the initial divergence of views reflecting the more competitive low-cost French arable crops sector and the smaller, less productive, high-cost, German family farms had been settled by agreement on the higher German prices, but at the cost of introducing large refunds (subsidies) on exports to third countries, fully financed by the Community. This agreement could last only as long as the export refund system was secure, i.e. no restrictions were imposed on the quantity of exports which attracted refunds or on the overall budget available for refunds.

The international dimensions

On the international front, while the rapid expansion of subsidised cereals exports from the Community – which at one stage reached over 30 million tonnes or about 20 per cent of total production – was a continual source of tension as far as other major world exporters, notably the United States, Canada and Australia were concerned, the refund system itself could at least be defended. But it was the rapid growth of an alternative crop, i.e. oilseeds (sunflower, soya beans), unprotected under the GATT rules but heavily subsidised under the CAP, that led to the most serious conflict. Oilseeds turned out to be the Achilles' heel of the CAP. From the beginning of my mandate, when the first GATT panel ruled that the Community support system was effectively illegal, right through to the end of my term in office when the Blair House agreement with the United States settled the issue, the question of oilseeds was problematic and controversial. And, while gaining international acceptance for the regime arguably required concessions from the Community out of proportion to the sector's economic importance, oilseeds were an issue of capital importance in political terms, especially in France – so much so that they were considered a subject for serious discussion at the level of the European Council. The origin of the problem was that some 30 years earlier import protection levels had been bound by the Community at zero under international trade rules. As Community production had been negligible, and as huge levels of imports were needed in order to supply the Community's beef, pork and poultry sectors, this was not a problem at the time. However, under the impetus of attractive subsidies and new technologies, Community production began to expand rapidly in the 1980s, which led in turn to the regime being challenged internationally by the United States. Unfavourable rulings by the GATT had placed the Community in a situation where it had the choice of, on the one hand, paying compensation to our trading partners and maintaining the regime, or, on the other hand, altering the oilseeds regime to bring it into line with the GATT rules (this was likely to involve a limit on production levels).

There could be no question of paying 'compensation', which would have involved trade concessions by other, possibly non-agricultural, sectors. And, if we were to avoid a series of potentially damaging cases against the Community on other aspects of the CAP, this dispute had to be resolved rapidly: if not as part of the Uruguay Round, then in a parallel agreement. So too would a solution have to be found to a second controversial issue in the animal feed sector, namely the rapidly increasing imports of corn gluten feed from the United States; these imports were essentially a low-priced by-product from industry and, not being subject to import levies, they were rapidly replacing Community cereals whose competitive position in animal feed was becoming seriously eroded.

After a slow start, the Uruguay Round negotiations began to accelerate from 1990 onwards. It had been accepted at the launching of the Round in 1986 that it would involve, for the first time, a comprehensive agreement on agriculture. The Community had, therefore, adopted a position which accepted a reduction in the level of support for agriculture, as well as the tariffication of import levies which in normal trading conditions were set at prohibitive levels. However, the level of reduction (30 per cent) in support offered by the Community, coupled with the adoption of favourable base years designed to minimise concessions, was seen by other countries as grossly insufficient. Furthermore, the Community had initially refused to make any specific commitment on export refunds.

Irrespective of size, isolation is always an uncomfortable position in international trade negotiations. And, if there was any remaining doubt about the support that the Community could rely on to resist more far-reaching proposals on agriculture, this was well and truly dispelled when, at a GATT ministerial meeting of all contracting parties held in Brussels at the end of 1990, apart from lukewarm support from Japan – itself highly protectionist on agriculture – the Community found itself alone. At that meeting some very damaging compromise proposals for the reduction in support for agriculture were put forward by the chairman of the conference, Sweden's Matt Hellstrom, on the basis of work done by Arthur Dunkel, then director general of the GATT. After I had rejected the 'compromise', it became clear to me that the Community's approach was too reactive; it was based on the dangerous assumption that either the overall negotiations would fail on non-agriculture issues, or the Community would be strong enough to refuse concessions which went beyond its own formula on agriculture. The situation required a strategy that would enable the Community to establish a more realistic position such as would tempt our trading partners into seeking a basis for agreement, rather than pursuing a strategy of isolating Europe. This position had to be based on what reform of the CAP could guarantee. Otherwise, the Community would find itself being pushed towards concessions without any assurance that commitments agreed at the international level could be delivered 'on the ground'. This would require my being able to convince the Americans and the Cairns Group, including Australia, New Zealand, Canada and Argentina, that CAP reform involved an effective restraint on production which would in turn create healthier world market conditions, and that it would be counterproductive for them to continue to press their more radical formulae such as a reduction of 80 or 90 per cent in support given to agriculture. The strategy required also that EC ministers be convinced that our trading partners could be brought to accept that compensation to farmers under the newly reformed regimes would not be subject to reduction under GATT rules, and that this assurance would be backed by a 'watertight' peace clause which would prevent the reformed CAP from being challenged in the GATT or in its successor body, the World Trade Organisation.

One of my big fears was the breaking of ranks by individual member states, sometimes with good intentions, which would pass conflicting signals to Arthur Dunkel or to major players such as the United States in relation to the content or timing of a possible change in the Community's offer. This not only would undermine the Commission's position as the Community's negotiator, but would also lead to suspicion and mistrust among individual member states. This meant that, in the interest of Community cohesion, we needed to establish a strategy by which all member states would see CAP reform as the key to resolving what many feared would be an international crisis. At the same time, our trading partners needed to understand that the mammoth task of agreeing on CAP reform meant that it would be out of the question to seek concessions from the Community which would entail any departure from the terms of the reform agreement.

Despite his problems with the North American Free Trade Agreement (NAFTA), which had aroused protectionist fears in the United States, President George Bush succeeded, in the spring of 1992, in getting approval from Congress for the so-called fast-track approach to the Uruguay Round negotiations. This allowed the American administration an important element of flexibility in the overall negotiations. It was essential at that stage to move quickly to establish a consensus between the Community and the United States, which I saw as central to delivering the international protection for the reformed CAP. When this strategy became evident as the negotiations progressed, it was rather simplistically attacked by some agricultural interest groups as 'giving in to the Americans'. The reality was that, unless a successful reform and a linked Uruguay Round negotiation could be agreed within a short time-frame, agriculture would be subject to increasing conflict and instability, and a different reform would sooner or later be forced upon agriculture in much less favourable conditions.

The MacSharry reforms

The CAP reform, which I worked on in the latter stages of 1990 and which was presented in February 1991, had three main objectives:

- to keep intact the common price system, including Community preference as regards imports, and free movement of products within the Community
- to preserve financial solidarity, in other words full Community financing of market measures
- to introduce measures that would guarantee greater price competitiveness and a reduction in surpluses, and would provide farmers with realistic alternatives to increasing food production.

Price competitiveness, and reliance on the market, would be brought about through a sharp reduction in guaranteed prices, notably for cereals (35 per cent), milk (10 per cent) and beef (15 per cent), together with a weakening of intervention guarantees which were to be available only as a last resort. The reduction in surpluses would be guaranteed through linking payment of compensation to farmers for the price reductions to a mandatory reduction in the area devoted to arable crops (set aside at a level of 15 per cent) and to specific quantitative limits established at farm level, in the case of cattle and sheep. The compensation paid to farmers was to operate on the basis of what was to become known as modulation of support, i.e. a deliberate policy to rebalance the support system in favour of smaller producers. This was to be done by limiting the financial guarantees to individual producers beyond certain output levels, exempting small producers from some supply constraints and introducing a new premium for small farmers in the milk sector. The reformed support system was designed also to favour extensive agriculture, for example by fixing maximum stocking rates for cattle. In addition to the changes in the market regimes, which covered 75 per cent of Community agricultural production, including upwards of 85 per cent in Ireland, an attractive package of measures was proposed to accompany the market reforms; these covered special support for agri-environment actions, afforestation, and early retirement of farmers and of farm workers.

In deciding to launch the reform there was a risk that, once proposals entered the negotiation process, some specific aspects would be changed significantly; of greater concern was that some fundamental parts of the policy might be called into question. The Commission remains free to withdraw its proposals at various stages in the negotiations, but in the case of major proposals, once the process starts, this is not a real option. My greatest fear was that the question of part-financing the CAP would become a serious issue, especially since the reformed policy would cost more in budgetary terms as a result of the compensation payable to farmers for the reductions in guaranteed prices. And, while these extra costs could be justified in terms of the benefits to consumers of lower prices and the avoidance of heavy disposal costs in the case of surpluses, there was an initial period when payment of compensation would coincide with running down stocks, thereby driving expenditure up to its legal limit set by the agricultural guideline. In the event, no deviation from my initial approach emerged when the Commission presented its initial discussion paper, 'Reflections on the Common Agricultural Policy', on 1 February 1991 and the detailed reform texts in full in July 1991. In part this was because, once the decision of principle was taken to put forward the reform, the proposals were prepared and presented without delay and confidentiality was largely respected.

The scene was thus set for the Irish Presidency in the second half of 1991 to initiate what proved to be a lengthy and hugely difficult set of negotiations, whose outcome was to have a major impact not only on the CAP but also on the terms on which the agriculture part of the GATT agreement, and in consequence the final Uruguay Round agreement, was eventually concluded in 1994. Reaching agreement on the reform proved immensely more difficult than I had imagined. I had expected that the proposals would have been more widely welcomed, firstly because in political terms they would bring a dramatic shift in the situation where 80 per cent of the expenditure went to 20 per cent of farmers, secondly because there was substantial compensation for farmers through increased direct aid in order to offset the price reductions which were designed to make their product more competitive, and thirdly because there was a very attractive package of accompanying measures with a guaranteed flow of supplementary income to farmers through schemes to support environmentally friendly practices and afforestation and, for those who so wished, to facilitate early retirement.

The initial reaction to the reform proposals was almost universally hostile. This is explained to some extent by member states taking up negotiating positions and in other cases by more widespread opposition of agro-industry and farming organisations. The absence of a balanced debate on the pros and cons of the reform was due also to the silence of those that stood to benefit from the reform, and an unwillingness to explain to farmers that what was on offer to them might not be repeated if the exercise were to fail.

The adverse reaction was all the more disappointing in that, because of the sensitive nature of changes to the CAP, the Commission considered it important to 'test the water' in advance. This was done through the presentation of the 'Reflections' paper in February 1991 setting out the principles guiding the reform and describing the new mechanisms. Apart from objections to modulation of support, the approach had been broadly welcomed.

Following a slow start to the negotiations, when all member states pronounced themselves unable to accept the Commission's proposals, progress began to be made once I convinced the Council that there was no better way to proceed. And, as a result of the intensive efforts of successive Council presidencies, namely Ireland led by Michael O'Kennedy and Portugal led by Arlindo Cunha, the necessary compromises were struck in May 1992. While the record will show that the CAP reform regulations were signed into effect by John Gummer under the UK Presidency, the back-breaking work in terms of finding the final compromise was done by the Portuguese Presidency, with which I worked very closely. The warm relations within the Council and the trust established with the Commission over the previous three years were important also in making the breakthrough. And, while it is invidious to mention names, the old Franco-German alliance in the persons of Henri Nallet from France, a man with a remarkable grasp of his subject and who was prepared to take a strategic view of the place of European agriculture in the world, and Ignaz Kiechle with his tremendous practical knowledge of agriculture and standing in Germany, played an essential part in bringing about the conditions which allowed agreement to be reached in May 1992. Apart from the Portuguese Presidency, the smaller countries played their part too with Ireland's Joe Walsh and my successor as Commissioner, Rene Steichen from Luxembourg, also providing strong backing for the reform.

The European Parliament gave invaluable support to my efforts both in terms of the content and of the timing of its Opinion. Here, in addition to the External Relations Committee led by Belgium's Willie De Clercq, the main driving force came from the German and British members of the agriculture committee. It was Reinhard Bocklett from the European People's Party that, as the agricultural committee's rapporteur for the CAP reform, drove forward relentlessly until he reached his goal of having what must be among the most comprehensive Opinions ever adopted by the Parliament approved on schedule in December 1991. This was all the more vital in that it came at a time when the ministers, after long hesitation, were about to take the decisive step of entering into serious negotiations.

When the final agreement was reached in May 1992 most elements of the reform proposed by the Commission had been accepted; there were substantial reductions in guaranteed prices with cereals reducing by 29 per cent compared to the 35 per cent proposed, and beef prices reducing by 15 per cent as proposed. Substantial compensation to farmers, linked to supply constraints on production, were agreed. The accompanying measures were adopted in full. On the other hand, the Council was unwilling to cut the price of milk by more than 2.5 per cent, to be achieved by a reduction in the butter price of 5 per cent. The proposals for modulation had been weakened to a point where no significant degree of rebalancing in the distribution of income from the CAP occurred. All member states and the principal representative bodies for farmers at European and at national level opposed any worthwhile change in that direction.

Results of reform

The results of the reform were overwhelmingly positive in terms of reduction of surpluses – these reduced dramatically in the following years, especially in the case of cereals (30 million tonnes to 3 million tonnes) – and the boost given to farm incomes, which reached their highest levels in 20 years in the year (1996) after the reform took final effect. I was very pleased with the overall results, not least because I had lived through the 'sweat and blood' of annual price negotiations where it was virtually impossible to reduce prices even by a half a percentage point. The unwillingness of the Council to progress on modulation was a disappointment, though the fundamental change from price support to direct aids will, I believe, boost the case for modulation in the next phase of the negotiations.[1] Some aspects of the decisions by the Council may yet prove to have been short-sighted, especially as, in the years following the reform, farmers in the arable crops sector enjoyed the twin benefits of compensation and exceptionally firm world price levels. Among these are:

- some weakening of the production restraints as a result of the option to calculate penalties on a regional rather than an individual basis
- the complexity brought about as a result of having to design a system for arable crops which calculates compensation down to the level of productivity of very small areas
- refusal of an important new instrument, i.e. the dairy cow premium which was designed as an income support for small farmers but, once introduced, could have been the mechanism through which any enforced changes to the milk quota regime could be carried through later with minimal pain to producers
- the unwillingness to reduce cereals prices by the full 35 per cent, which would have enabled exports to take place without subsidy, and would have benefited the livestock sector further.

I am happy that the Commission has come back to all these issues in its proposals for a further phase in the reform which follows closely the approach adopted in 1992; they include also a sharper cut in the beef price which, regrettably, the financial resources available for compensation did not allow in 1992. These proposals are now being negotiated as part of Agenda 2000.[2]

The Blair House agreement

Once the reform had been agreed in May 1992, it became urgently necessary to conclude on the agriculture part of the GATT agreement and to reach a final settlement of the oilseeds problem. This of necessity meant intensive negotiations with the United States, an exercise which led ultimately to an agreement with the American side in Blair House at the end of 1992. And while the final agreement on the Uruguay Round was not formally adopted by the EC until December 1994, the acknowledged key to the agreement was the progress made at Blair House on agriculture.

The Uruguay Round was the first ever global trade agreement to deal comprehensively with agricultural products, and significant commitments were made to reduce domestic support by 20 per cent over six years, to convert import charges and other restrictions to tariffs and to reduce them by 36 per cent over the same period, and to reduce the volume of subsidised exports by 21 per cent and expenditure on refunds by 36 per cent over six years also. The Community was able to live with the agreement in large part because direct payments under production-limiting programmes were not included in the requirements for reducing support, and the compensatory payments established under CAP reform were exempted under the mechanisms of the agreement. This was expressed by categorising support measures in different-coloured 'boxes' – amber for measures that would have to be reduced, green for measures not subject to reduction, and blue for measures such as compensatory payments linked to production limitations that were not subject to reduction either. A further major benefit for the Community was the agreement on a peace clause which means that measures in conformity with the final agreement on the Uruguay Round are not subject to challenge under the GATT until 2003 at least.

In the run-up to the Blair House agreement I had the benefit of the confidence placed in me by ministers in the Agriculture Council, with whom I enjoyed excellent relations. There was also the willingness of key US negotiators to trust the Community team and their capacity to deliver on the guarantees being provided. As far as agriculture was concerned this came down to myself and, on the US side, Agriculture Secretary Ed Madigan. We were assisted by two very able and compatible officials in the persons of the director general of DG VI, Guy Legras, and the director of the US Department of Agriculture, Joe O'Mara. My colleague Frans Andriessen and US trade representative Carla Hills were fully supportive of our efforts to reach agreement and recognised that if there was to be an agreement between the European Community and the United States, it would have to be worked out between the negotiators on agriculture. The agreement itself was worked through in difficult conditions with endless contacts often leading to stalemate. One of the most difficult issues was oilseeds, and several different formulae were tried until a final agreement was reached at the end of 1992. This provided that, in the Community regime, oilseeds would be treated as an arable crop subject to the same production constraints as cereals, but that the area under cultivation would not be increased. I came to the conclusion in the course of these protracted talks that we could not drive a better bargain. Our negotiating position was further weakened in that, by that stage, a second GATT panel had ruled as illegal certain aspects of the regime as reformed in 1991 and the US was preparing retaliatory measures against Community exports to a value of $1,000 million; besides, earlier US insistence on fixing a production limit for oilseeds supported under the CAP had been resisted.

The question has sometimes been put to me as to whether the Irish dimension was a factor in the ultimate agreement reached in Blair House in the autumn of 1992. Certainly, I had established close relations with Ed Madigan, whose ancestors came from Ireland. The fact that he had the confidence of President George Bush meant that I knew I was dealing with someone who could 'deliver'. Indeed, the question of confidence was the reason for my insistence, not without difficulty, that I must have the necessary assurance that my judgement of what was the right deal for the Community would be fully endorsed by the Commission. Despite the excellent personal relations which developed with our US counterparts and which undoubtedly contributed to the successful outcome, there was never any departure from my primary goal of preserving what we achieved in the reform. I expect that things were no different on the American side.

Future challenges

It was Seamus Sheehy, one of the few commentators to maintain a balanced view of the CAP proposals from their beginning right through to the final settlement, who said that the 'MacSharry' proposals, though by far the most far-reaching in its 30-year existence, were not the first, nor would they be the last, attempt at reform of the CAP. This has been prophetic to the extent that the Commission, as part of the Agenda 2000 proposals, has put forward a further phase of reform. What is important is that this builds on and extends the approach proposed in 1991, and indeed comes back on a number of issues refused by the Council in the agreement of May 1992.

To the extent that the model for the new CAP was set in 1992, the task of finding agreement in the Council should be easier, despite the need to meet the concerns of the three new member states. It is an irony that the agricultural guideline, introduced in 1988 to place an upper limit on expenditure on the CAP linked to growth in gross national product, should prove a blessing to the farm ministers in that it effectively provides an important budgetary margin to allow the next phase of reform to take place in conditions which protect the allocation of funding for the CAP. However, if the level of the guideline, or full financing of market expenditure, were to be called into question as a result of the developing dispute between member states over their contributions to the budget, in the parallel negotiations on Agenda 2000, the reform process would be jeopardised.

The task of securing a satisfactory agreement in the next phase of the international trade negotiations which will begin in December 1999 will be difficult also. This is because of the strong influences in favour of liberalisation of trade and the reduction in support to agriculture. The United States itself, following the adoption of the Federal Agriculture Improvement and Reform (FAIR) Act 1996, has substantially withdrawn from its system of deficiency payments which was accepted in the Uruguay Round agreement as a 'blue box' measure not requiring a reduction in financial support. Furthermore, some of the elements agreed in the framework of the Uruguay Round may not have led to the levels of cutback in production and access to the Community market which our trading partners had expected. To that extent, the formula of further deep cuts in prices and related compensation for farmers as proposed by the Commission will lead to pressure on the Community to do more to ensure production neutrality in the increased aids provided. This reflects the pressure towards decoupling financial support to farmers and production. Greater modulation of support, possibly through setting overall limits on direct payments to individual farms, perhaps on a phased basis, could be an important mechanism in providing reassurance to the other negotiating parties, as well as introducing greater equity into the support system. World price levels and market opportunities, currently depressed by the slow recovery in Japan and in the Far East together with the situation in Russia, will also influence the perspectives and attitudes of our trading partners. Despite all the difficulties, as the 1992 exercise has shown, both the Community and its trading partners have everything to gain by following the gradualist approach already established in the final Uruguay Round agreement, including the continuation of the structures and mechanisms established under that agreement.

CAP reform, especially when followed by adoption of the Commission's latest proposals, should help resolve some of the difficulties arising from the other major challenge now facing the Community, namely enlargement. In the case of price alignment the acceding countries will now be aligning on price levels which should not provide incentives to additional production. To that extent, earlier fears of a build-up of new surpluses and extra costs are likely to be unfounded, and if economic reform in the acceding countries brings the expected results in terms of growth and development, the adjustment problems in agriculture will be greatly eased.

The fundamental challenge which I saw for the CAP in 1989 still remains. This is how to devise a system which, without generating surpluses, ensures that the Community will have security of food supply and stable prices – this is an objective never to be underestimated – and reasonable export prospects for its competitive segment of agriculture. At the same time the policy must make a real contribution to balanced rural development and to safeguarding the environment. Both through specific CAP instruments and through other Community policies and programmes, for example structural funds, environment and research, a sufficient range of opportunities is now available at Community level to ensure that these goals are achieved. With improved prospects of employment through a better trained and educated new generation, there should be further opportunities to bring about the adjustments needed in agriculture. This will result in increased prosperity for rural areas, underpinned by a more competitive and diversified agriculture, coupled with expansion of new business activities, especially in services.

As far as Ireland is concerned, the development of the Community structural funds and the reform of the CAP have brought an unprecedented increase in the transfer of financial resources from the European Union; receipts now account for an estimated £2,332 million, having doubled over the past decade. The growth in average farm income in Ireland, at a rate of 24 per cent over the same period, has been among the highest in the Community. And, while future phases of the structural funds are likely to result in a much reduced level of transfer of resources, the horizontal nature of some of the Community instruments, especially CAP guarantee payments now accounting for some £1,300 million annually, will ensure that Ireland receives a steady flow of resources for many years to come. Globalisation will continue to bring relentless pressure towards greater competitiveness, whether in agriculture, industry or services. Irish agriculture is increasingly integrated into food production structures at European and at world level, a factor which requires the highest international standards of quality at processing and also at primary production levels. This requires an unrelenting effort to modernise, to diversify, and to be able to market successfully high-quality products, which, following the next GATT round trade negotiations, will have to be more competitive than ever. It is clear also that, as the debate on the future financing of the Community has demonstrated, we are entering a new phase where, with a changed political situation following German unification, old certainties no longer apply. This will require a strategic view by Ireland's policy-makers of the future development of Community policies, and of how the exceptional changes brought about in the Irish economy, with substantial support from the Community, can be harnessed to guarantee further sustainable development. Maintaining framework conditions conducive to investment, including strategic support for the development of networks essential to the competitive position of the economy, will be an important priority.

NOTES

1 Under the Agenda 2000 agreement on cereals, a price cut of 15 per cent will be introduced in two equal steps in 2000 and 2001. The monthly increments for cereals are being retained. Premium increases from 54 euros per tonne to 63 euros per tonne will also be introduced in two equal steps in 2000 and 2001.

2 Agreement on Agenda 2000 to date (July 1999) includes a gradual reduction of 20 per cent in the market support price in the beef sector between 2000 and 2002, in two annual decreases of 10 per cent. The price cuts will be supported by an increase in the headage premiums to £400 million, and direct payments will be increased to ensure a fair standard of living for all farmers.

=== 25 ===

Social policy

PÁDRAIG FLYNN

Introduction

Over the 40 years of the life of the European project, we have seen the gradual emergence of what could be called the European social model. This European model is often cast as being in contrast to the American or Japanese social models. It is seen as encompassing the complex and diverse ways in which we organise our lives, our governments and our societies, embracing education and training, health and welfare, social protection, industrial relations, health and safety at work, the pursuit of equality, the fight against racism and discrimination, the attempts to create a fair and integrated society in which the vulnerable have a place. It takes many forms in the different member states and operates through systems steeped in plurality and diversity. But what is the European social policy? What are its values, and does it matter?

European social policy has been developing and changing since the early 1950s, when the idea of a European Community first became a reality. Since that time Europe has been transformed from a group of separate, competing economies into a single economic entity in which the economies of regions and member states have become closely intertwined. We have a single market and a single currency, both extraordinary economic and political achievements. But European society has also been transformed. It has evolved not into a single, harmonised way of life, but into a society with strong common values and a shared attachment to justice and democracy. More importantly, Europe has combined commonality, closeness and participation for its people while continuing to recognise the astonishing diversity of those people's talents, desires, cultures and beliefs.

It was primarily economic and political considerations that dominated the first European Coal and Steel Community Treaty of 1952. The first half of the twentieth century had seen Europe twice devastated by a world war. The cumulative impact of these conflicts was well understood by the six original members of the European Community. When the European Community was created, its founders knew that their most fundamental task was to create a hope of peace and an end to suffering for people in the wake of a terrible war. Given the deep psychological wounds of the conflict and the economic devastation that it caused, it is not surprising that the founding fathers saw economic rather than social integration as their immediate preoccupation. The agreement to pool their coal and steel production was seen as the vital first step in building lasting peace and a hope of prosperity for the next generation.

Even at this stage it was, nevertheless, recognised that economic integration needed some kind of social dimension; however, for many years to come, it was far from clear what that dimension should be. The 1952 Treaty outlined the task of the Community as being to contribute to economic expansion, the growth of employment and a rising standard of living in the member states. There were also provisions enabling the Commission to obtain the information it required to assess how to improve working conditions and living standards for workers, as well as provisions on workers' wages and mobility. In other words, social policy mattered but it was referred to exclusively in the language of economic activity. If Europe needed social policy, it was because it needed a common market. Nevertheless, the seeds of modern European social policy had been sown.

The first period – from the Treaty of Rome to the Single European Act

European social policy was further crystallised in the Treaty of Rome of 1957. The European social fund was established in order to improve employment opportunities for workers in the common market. Member states also agreed on the need 'to promote improved working conditions and an improved standard of living for workers, so as to make possible their harmonisation while the improvement is being maintained' (Article 117). The Treaty denoted areas where the Commission would have the role of promoting close co-operation between member states. These included employment, labour law and working conditions, basic and advanced vocational training, social security, prevention of occupational accidents and diseases, occupational hygiene and the right of association and collective bargaining between employers and workers. The principle of equal pay for equal work between men and women was established in the same Treaty. This was an area of social policy that was to develop considerably through primary and secondary legislation and through landmark decisions of the European Court of Justice. There was provision for paid holiday schemes and for the maintenance of existing equivalents between member states. The Council had the power to assign specific tasks to the Commission for the implementation of certain common measures. Significant progress was made in the area of social security for migrant workers. The Commission was also required to include a

separate chapter on social developments within the Community in its annual
report to the European Parliament.

Social policy had surfaced at European level but remained fragmented and
lacking in any real purpose. In the 1960s, concern shifted to the establishing
of free movement for workers and, to that end, legislation was passed to
encourage the mobility of labour. This was a period of economic growth and
low levels of unemployment. The long post-war boom was not yet over and
people felt that they were enjoying better, richer lives than would ever have
seemed possible in the late 1940s.

The 1970s witnessed something of a shift. Social policy had gained
ground and was now seen as part of the process of European integration. Yet
these were difficult times. The long boom ended when Europe was hit by a
huge recession caused by the quadrupling of oil prices in 1973–74. Recession
brought high levels of unemployment not seen since the 1930s, and Europe
entered a period of protectionism. Member states became inward-looking. To
increase employment, they introduced non-tariff barriers in the hope of
keeping imports down. It was against this background that the Council
adopted its first social action programme at European level in 1974. It had
three aims: the improvement of working and living conditions, participation
of workers in the running of their firms and the achievement of full and
better employment. This social action programme served as the trigger for
legislative initiatives in employment law, equal opportunities, health and
safety at work and the development of the European social fund. During the
mid to late 1970s, some effective pieces of secondary labour legislation were
adopted. Directives were agreed on the protection of employment in the face
of recession, i.e. collective redundancies; on the protection of workers when
undertakings were transferred; on health and safety at work; and on equal
treatment for male and female workers.

The development of social policy at European level remained
overshadowed by a growing and highly ideological debate on the merits of
social welfare and its influence on the economy. The old idea of the deserving
and undeserving poor re-emerged. High taxation was necessary to fund social
welfare systems, and firms felt that they were being forced to pay high social
costs to employ people. Social policy began to be talked about and thought
about at European level but largely in terms of unemployment, to which there
seemed no real solution other than to sit it out and hope for the next recovery.

The second period – from the Single European Act to Maastricht

The main preoccupation of the Single European Act of 1987 was the
completion of a single market by 1992, but it carried implications for the
shaping of European social policy. With its ratification, the nature of social

policy in Europe altered. The emphasis on the single market was followed quickly by pressure for the introduction of a social dimension to counter the effects of stronger cross-border competition and to ensure that the rewards of the new economic order were shared by workers as well as companies.

Article 118a of the Single European Act added a new paragraph to the existing social policy chapter of the EEC Treaty on health and safety at work. The Article said that member states should 'pay particular attention to encouraging improvements, especially in the working environment, as regards the health and safety of workers'. That reference to the working environment was to prove crucial for the development of social policy, for it was used by the Commission to introduce directives with impact on working conditions, for example in the areas of protection for pregnant women and working time.

However, Article 118a was important for further reasons. It introduced for the first time qualified majority voting, as opposed to unanimity among member states. The Article was also evidence of a growing concern that a desirable harmonisation in health and safety regulations could lead to a fall in the national standards of certain progressive member states. It also asked the Council to adopt 'minimum requirements for gradual implementation, having regard to the conditions and technical rules obtaining in each of the member states'. That reference to minimum requirements says that conditions are worth harmonising but it is at the same time important to maintain existing national standards if these are higher. This allowed member states to maintain or to introduce more stringent requirements if they wished, as long as a baseline of harmonisation was achieved. This idea of moving up rather than down was important for the development of social policy and for the spread of the highest values and achievements of the European social model among different national systems.

Article 118b introduced the idea of dialogue between management and labour at European level – a truly European social dialogue. This was something that would some years later, towards the end of 1993, be developed in the agreement on social policy annexed to the Treaty of Maastricht. At this stage the Commission was merely asked to work 'to develop the dialogue between management and labour at European level which could, if the two sides consider it desirable, lead to relations based on agreement'.

These provisions, combined with the introduction of the co-operation procedure which allowed greater input from the European Parliament, ensured the Single European Act's place as a landmark in the development of European social policy. From this point it was clear that the single market had to have a strong social dimension if it was to work well and prove acceptable to the ordinary people of Europe. The late 1980s saw hot debates on the rights of workers. The Community Charter of Fundamental Social

Rights was signed by eleven governments (the UK declining) in October 1989. This was not a legally binding document but it has proved to be the source of a wide range of proposals and legislation in the area of social policy. The Charter was a kind of social policy 'wish list', advocating a minimum standard of social rights for people within the European Community and attempting to achieve a balance between progress on the economic front and what was happening as to how people actually lived and worked.

In 1989 the Commission adopted a second social action programme to implement the objectives of the Social Charter, as it came to be known. The Charter had listed close to 50 actions to be taken at European level, about half of which needed legislation. The second social action programme contained 24 proposals for legislation. Proposals subsequently adopted included the Working Time Directive, the Pregnant Workers' Directive and a series of health and safety measures.

When I became European Commissioner for Employment, Industrial Relations and Social Affairs in January 1993, it was still far from clear how, why and to what extent European institutions, and the Commission in particular, should be involved in social policy. We had the beginnings of a European policy on industrial relations, much of the legislation necessary to complete the single market in place, and a sense that progress in taking forward the second social action programme had been steady but not dramatic. Although my job title gave me responsibility for employment, I found little evidence that this meant a great deal in practical policy terms. Social policy had much more to do with unemployment than it had to do with employment.

At the same time we knew that we were living through the greatest period of political, economic and social change that Europe had known this century. We had seen the fall of the Soviet Union, the break-up of the eastern bloc and the unification of Germany. The single market was developing strongly. Economic and monetary union was on a horizon that was nearer than anyone might have believed possible only two or three years before. At the same time, profound changes were taking place in the structure of the working population. Large numbers of women had entered the labour market and the very nature of jobs had altered with the emergence of new technologies and new approaches to the organisation of work. The population of Europe was ageing; there were changes, too, in the balance of urban and rural living, in family structure and in the patterns of education, leisure and work. Side by side with these forces for change, some familiar problems remained. Despite the growth of the late 1980s, Europe still had stubbornly high rates of unemployment, particularly for young people and women. Unemployment was above all a structural problem for the European economy. It had risen steadily since the early 1970s. At the end of the 1980s, when the economy was going strong, unemployment for the whole of the European Community stood at 12 million. By 1993, after the next, very deep recession, this figure had risen to 17 million. One in two of the unemployed had been out of work for over a year.

My initial reaction to this situation was to reflect. By the middle of that first year of my period of office, all the 47 initiatives announced in the social action programme had been presented by the Commission. Of the 29 that required Council approval, some 16 had been adopted. However, the remaining proposals – some of which were regarded as particularly important – remained blocked. At the same time, the changing socio-economic climate meant that the period of economic growth in which the social action programme had originally been conceived had, by late 1992, given way to a much bleaker economic situation and high and persistent levels of structural unemployment across the Union.

The third period – from Maastricht to Amsterdam

Another important factor soon after entered the equation. The Treaty on European Union (the Maastricht Treaty, as it has become known) entered into force in November 1993. This introduced a number of new possibilities in the social field, notably in the shape of the agreement on social policy, adopted by eleven member states (the exception being the United Kingdom). The agreement stated that the eleven member states 'wish to continue along the path laid down in the 1989 Social Charter' and provided for the adoption by qualified majority of measures in a number of areas that previously required unanimity, such as working conditions and the information and consultation of workers. The agreement was also important in that it set out an enhanced mechanism for the consultation of the social partners in the preparation of proposals, and – for the first time – gave the social partners the option of reaching European-level contractual agreements that could take the place of legislation. In introducing a new basis for action in the field of European social policy, the agreement opened up a new and influential role for the social partners, and the European social dialogue as a whole, in the shaping and making of that policy.

In November 1993 I was able to publish the first results of a period of reflection that lasted most of my first year. The green paper on European social policy (17 November 1993, Green Paper Com (93) 551) was my first major initiative. I wanted to know what ordinary people thought Europe ought to be achieving in the social arena. The Green Paper launched a wide-ranging consultation on the future of European social policy to enable as many organisations and individuals as possible to help to define the future shape of European social policy. I was delighted at the way that grassroots organisations and individuals were given the opportunity to put forward their views before the Commission came forward with concrete policy options. The European-wide debate sparked by the difficulties encountered in the ratification of the Maastricht Treaty brought home a basic truth: the most important views on the relevance of social Europe are the views of European citizens themselves.

The consultative process was a success. We received some 580 written responses, many of which I read for myself. The issues raised by the Green Paper were also widely discussed in a series of conferences held across Europe. The Commission asked the European Foundation of Living and Working Conditions in Dublin to prepare a synthesis of the different responses received to the Green Paper. The Foundation responded with an excellent piece of work that was later published as a volume accompanying the next major social policy initiative at European level – the white paper on European social policy.

In July 1994, the Commission adopted the white paper on European social policy. A year and a half after taking office as Commissioner, I set out the European Union's strategy for the future development of European social policy for the next six years and beyond. One of the key messages that had emerged from our consultation exercise of the year before was that there was something distinctive about the European social model that was not – and is still not – evident in the American or Japanese approach. These models can be broadly defined as a common attachment to a number of shared values such as democracy and individual rights, free collective bargaining, the market economy, equality of opportunity for all. But in the European case, huge importance is also attached to society's duty to provide welfare and solidarity. Indeed, that is arguably the cornerstone, the defining element, of our society.

The white paper set out firmly the belief that this model is valuable, that it should be maintained but that it should also be strengthened and reformed to fit the needs of the modern era. European societies were changing profoundly and would go on changing. The globalisation of world trade and the impact of new technologies on work and individuals were already having profound effects on the way in which people work. Demographic developments and the gradual ageing of our society were having a major impact on the way our society would have to organise itself in the future, with a smaller proportion of the population economically active and higher rates of expenditure on health care and pensions. Moreover, even though there were welcome signs of renewed economic growth in Europe by the middle of 1994, it was clear that our societies and our economies continued to face significant structural problems. There were then 19 million people unemployed across Europe, over half of them for more than one year.

One thing was certain: growth alone would not solve these problems. Meeting the challenges posed by constant change and preserving and developing the European social model required a new approach to social policy. The white paper called, above all, for a new mix, a new complementarity, between social and economic policy. It rejected the view that competitiveness and social progress are mutually antagonistic. It rejected the idea that sustainable growth can be achieved simply by cutting costs and reducing social protection. 'No', said the white paper, 'growth, competitiveness and social progress must go hand in hand.' It is only by investing in people's skills, for example, and in equality of opportunity that you get an adaptable, educated and motivated workforce, the kind of workforce that Europe needs to remain productive.

The white paper did something very important in stimulating this fresh look at the interaction between different social policy measures, employment growth and wealth creation. It said that these must be better integrated and more mutually reinforcing. It also marked the point at which European social policy began to be as much about employment as about unemployment.

The white paper covered three main themes: employment and the fight against unemployment; developing and consolidating the legislative base; and promoting an active society for all. Top priority went to employment and job creation. The need to improve Europe's performance on the jobs front had already been brought to the forefront of political debate with the issuing of the Commission's white paper on growth, competitiveness and employment. This had been presented by President Jacques Delors to the European summit in Brussels at the end of the previous year, 1993. The Delors white paper had carried the basic message that growth alone was not sufficient to bring Europe full employment.

The white paper on social policy took the argument several stages further, stressing the vital need for investment in education and training and highlighting the importance of the European social fund as the major EU instrument of that investment. It set out the basis for the development of a true European labour market. It showed the continuing importance of legislation in a number of areas, but said that in future European social policy would have to be based on a more complex mix of legislative and non-legislative measures in areas such as labour law, health and safety at work, free movement, equality of opportunity between women and men. Finally, it argued for action that encompassed society as a whole, that moved away from the passive labour market policies of the past towards measures that would ensure social and economic integration for all the EU's citizens.

The white paper on social policy proposed a detailed and ambitious action plan at the level of the Union and the member states which was intended to bring about the radical re-design of our entire employment creation systems. The plan itself was presented by the Commission to the Essen European Council in December 1994, some six months after the appearance of the white paper. The European Council agreed the plan, which would see action focusing on five key areas of labour market modernisation: improved employability for people through more access to training and education; increased employment intensity of growth; a drop in non-wage labour costs; more effective and active labour market policies; and specific action in favour of people worst hit by unemployment, particularly young people.

These first two years of my period of office as Commissioner for employment and social policy in the EU were a time of enormous change and intense activity, as Europe essentially abandoned a set of policies that had proved a failure in favour of a whole new stance in relation to our social and employment systems.

It is a process that, far from stopping at the end of 1994, was only starting. In the green paper on the way forward and the white paper that set out the Commission's proposals on what should actually be done at European level and in the member states in the area of social and employment policy, we find all the main ingredients of what has come to be known as the European employment strategy, the Luxembourg process. The seeds of the remarkable political breakthroughs of 1997, 1998 and 1999 were sown in those two vital years of 1993 and 1994. This was the moment when European employment and social policies moved as a single concern to the front rank of political decision-making. This was the moment when the full impact of the evolution of the social dimension, so apparent in the events of the late 1980s, began to be fully understood by Europe's leaders and Europe's people.

That this breakthrough was on its way became clearer with the publication in April 1995 of a new medium-term social action programme for 1995–97 by the Commission. In the course of that year I talked to as many people as I could about just why this new programme was so important and where it was taking us. Essentially, it put the policy-making of the previous three years or so into sharp focus, indicating what specific action was needed at European level in five main areas. These were employment; the consolidation and development of legislation where necessary and appropriate; equal opportunities between women and men; the building of an active society for all; and the need for ongoing reflection and research to back up this new policy approach.

By January the following year, I was able to say that we were on the move, already fulfilling many of the commitments set out in the social action programme. The Commission had seen the adoption by the Council of a number of legislative proposals, including working time and European Works Councils. These Directives signalled real success for the new procedure for European social policy-making set out in the agreement on social policy annexed to the Maastricht Treaty. The agreement reached by the social partners on 14 December 1995 on the reconciliation of family and professional life was a historic landmark.

The fourth period – Amsterdam and the European employment strategy

In 1996 and 1997, the European Commission was sending out a strong message to the Union. The message said that there was no doubt that the EU had under-achieved in the creation of jobs. Our problem was that we had been concentrating – rather passively, it has to be said – on unemployment. What we should have been thinking about was how we could have more employment. We were also anxious to say, however, that the blame for this failure could not be laid at the door of our well-developed social systems. Rather, we had proved too attached to fragmented and inadequate systems of economic management, systems that had proved not up to the task of guiding our increasingly interdependent economies.

EMU was transforming the Union and its capacity to control its destiny. Our employment and social systems needed to keep pace. A new European economic and political order was emerging in which strong social policies would continue to play a major role in support of productivity and growth. Social policies were not there just to help us tackle regional disparities and social exclusion. They were the vital ingredient in maintaining our competitiveness. But this was yet to be fully understood.

Unlike the US, we did not have a single currency. In fact we had 14 separate currencies, and in an increasingly integrated European economy this was causing, if not disaster, then a damaging inertia. Too much of the political focus, especially in social policy, was national. Too little of it was about joint action or co-operative solutions.

In 1997 the European Union and its 15 member states began to focus on a new reality. It was a reality that said that even the most generous social safety nets are cheap if you do not have to use them. They only become expensive when people are failed by the society that they live in. And when balanced with strong, active measures to encourage people into the labour market, generous social systems are a huge asset, a source of motivation and justice and a powerful instrument of successful employment policy.

The new Treaty of Amsterdam, agreed in June 1997, contained a key phrase: 'Member states shall regard promoting employment as a matter of common concern and shall co-ordinate their action in this respect'. This was a massively important step. It showed a real understanding at the highest political level that the real challenge lies in lifting the performance of the EU economy as a whole, expanding output, generating a higher rate of economic growth and, above all, delivering a higher rate of employment. For Europe to succeed, there had to be a fusing of the political, social and economic agendas. The new Treaty of Amsterdam was the sign that this was beginning in earnest.

It had been recognised for some years that EMU was fundamental to the economic success of Europe. What had not been clear until 1997 was that

EMU was also part of a wider, stronger employment strategy at European level. In the wake of the Amsterdam Treaty and the EU jobs summit held by heads of state and government in November 1997, that strategy was launched, making possible real change in European labour markets. Its success has been remarkable. In February 1999, I saw G8 labour ministers in Washington giving the European employment strategy a resounding endorsement: 'We welcome the efforts made within the European Union to develop an integrated and multi-annual employment strategy and look forward to sharing the experience on progress in this field'.

The next period

I have had the privilege to be responsible for European social policy at a time when the EU moved decisively from words to deeds. The European Union is now committed to the creation of jobs for as talented, skilled and diverse a workforce as it is possible to have in the modern world. The strategy is built around four priorities: employability of people, adaptability of businesses and workers, a climate that encourages entrepreneurs, and a culture at work and in wider society of real equality between women and men. The process is irresistible because it is driven by the member states themselves and by their commitment to it. In 1998 they had the opportunity to learn from each other's successes and failures. The emphasis is on winning and sharing the gains of doing so. Those gains look set to increase each year for the foreseeable future.

The European Union has not abandoned the traditional concern that people should have high levels of social protection and support when they need them and that no people, region or country should be left behind in the process of European integration. These are good principles and they have served us well. It is clear that they will continue to serve the European Union as it develops in the 21st century. The European social model has been a productive factor, and it will remain so. We now understand the changes that are needed to meet the new challenges that are constantly coming through in technology, the economy, our whole society and way of life.

The European social model is a fundamental part of Europe's strength and Europe's future. It embraces the diversity that is the European Union of today and tomorrow. It reflects the duality that says that we need strong competition between companies if we are to be a productive, growing economy but we also need strong solidarity with each other as people live in what must be a cohesive and inclusive society. Europe's commitment to social policy is not just a matter of sentiment or social justice. It is equally a matter of productivity. It is European social policy that has made it possible for Europeans to double their living standards over the lifetime of the Union.

Through massive structural change, we have avoided the extremes and cost of social disruption. Our people have not been left to the mercy of the markets. We are one of the strongest, most successful economies in the world and we have the strongest social safety nets in the world.

I am honoured to have played my part in the process that made this possible.

Part V
Present and Future

26

A personal view

JOHN HUME

Membership of the European Union has had a profound impact on our island. However we measure the scale of change, it is clear that things have changed substantially, and for the better. The political, economic, technological and cultural transformations have remodelled life on this island. Though we remain an island, we are no longer an insular society. We have taken our place among the peoples of Europe.

The economic transformations resulting from our membership of the European Union are perhaps the most obvious. Without underestimating the serious problems that persist, the economy has undergone rapid and profound development. There are industries and services that can compete in a global economy. There have been major infrastructural improvements. Most importantly, we are well placed in terms of communications and information technology, thus allowing us to look forward to the 21st century with some confidence.

In cultural terms we have moved from a peripheral and defensive status to be being one of the most culturally vibrant places in the world. Far from being culturally subordinated, we are cultural exporters. We are no longer in anyone else's shadow precisely because of the extent of cultural diversity in the European Union. As a result, the arts in Ireland have a world-wide audience that they have never previously enjoyed. One illuminating example is that Seamus Heaney is the fourth Irish writer to have won the Nobel prize for literature, but he is the first to have spent the vast bulk of his career in Ireland.

Politically too, the European Union has contributed to a tremendous evolution both on this island and in our relations with Britain and the rest of Europe. The old relations of domination and alliances of convenience with our British and European neighbours have been replaced with a more constructive approach. It is clear that, historically speaking, the relationship between the two parts of Ireland, and between Britain and Ireland, has been altered positively by our shared membership of the European Union. Day after day, ministers from Ireland and Britain work together in the EU Council of Ministers while members of the European Parliament from North and South co-operate to promote our mutual interests in the EU. Membership of

the EU has allowed us to address seriously the conflict and to identify the
principles and methods by which it can be resolved.

It is clear that the EU has been a major success story, in terms of
enhancing living standards and of promoting the cause of peace, both on the
European mainland and in these islands. But that is not an excuse for
complacency. There remain many unfulfilled objectives that we must strive
to attain.

We must always remember that the EU, as it is structured at present, is
not an end in itself. It is a framework for achieving common objectives. The
EU is by definition an evolutionary project. It never reaches equilibrium but
instead changes to meet new economic and political realities. It is,
essentially, defined by where it is going, not where it is at. This objective is
to increase the unity and cohesion of Europe.

We have a long way to go before we can guarantee peace and prosperity
for every European. It is therefore equally important to look at the ways in
which the EU will evolve in the next decades.

In essence, there are three broad questions that will be at the centre of the
EU's preoccupations for the foreseeable future. How successful we are in
addressing these questions will determine the ability of the EU to achieve its
objectives. To succeed requires us to take a long-term perspective, to look
beyond the immediate problems and to resist the temptation to focus on
short-term interests.

These three questions are: how do we promote the goal of economic and
social cohesion; how do we adapt EU institutions in order to preserve and
enhance their democratic legitimacy; and how will the EU interact with the
rest of Europe and the world?

The basis of the EU: cohesion

Economic and social cohesion is the fundamental basis for the unity of
Europe. Without it, the EU's political aspirations would not have the force of
attraction that they do. Similarly, the economic and social aspects of
cohesion cannot in practice be separated.

Economic frameworks that wreak havoc on our societies are no more
sustainable than societies that attempt to ignore the demands of economic
and technological advance. In this sense, the challenges of economic and
monetary union, EU budgetary policy, employment and social exclusion are
all different aspects of the same problem – the development of the European
economy in an environment of social justice.

The introduction of the euro at the beginning of 1999 is obviously one of
the landmarks in the construction of European unity. It symbolises and
requires a massive degree of co-operation and co-ordination between the

member states. It will be the most visible external sign of the unity of Europe. The principal task in terms of EMU will therefore be to ensure that the euro will be the currency of the whole of the EU, not just of eleven-fifteenths of the EU.

The other major challenge to the success of EMU is the persistence of high unemployment in the EU. We now know that this is not a transitory problem and that there are structural problems in some parts of the EU economy and labour markets. These structural problems cannot be ignored. It would be morally blind to do so, and politically counterproductive given the negative impact of unemployment and social exclusion on public confidence in politics at all levels, including the European. One of the more positive aspects of the debate on the future of Europe is that this point is well understood by the vast majority of European political leaders. The fundamental political task will be to find practical ways to address the problem.

For too long, professional pessimists have argued that unemployment is a problem that cannot be solved by throwing money at it. The evidence is increasingly pointing to a different answer. It all depends on *how* the money is thrown at the problem. We know, for instance, that one of the major reasons for the success of the Republic in the 1990s has been the vast resources devoted to education and training. On a lesser scale in the North, there is a clear connection between recent growth and the expansion of education and training. It could well be that in the coming decades a virtuous circle can be maintained in which investment in education and training pays off many times over – thus addressing the related problems of unemployment and social exclusion.

We do not have to look far for an example. In both parts of Ireland there are communities that have been excluded from the benefits of economic growth, where high levels of unemployment prevail, educational opportunities are limited and social exclusion advances. Would it not be possible to use EU experience and resources to transform these communities? Can we not build on the European social fund and the developing field of EU educational initiatives to ensure that every EU citizen is prepared for the demands of 21st century labour markets? Can we really afford to write off some sections of our peoples?

Obviously, questions of EU resources must be addressed if the EU is going to engage in active labour market policies on the scale required. The recent agreement on Agenda 2000 is a medium-term solution to the problems of the EU budget for the next few years. To provide a firm long-term basis for EMU, a more comprehensive and extensive budgetary system will be required. It is important that the budgetary argument in future transcends the traditional divide within the EU between net contributors and net beneficiaries. In any case, the likelihood is that nearly all the existing member states will become net contributors in the latter half of the next decade.

It is crucial that we concentrate on principles. First, EMU requires a total commitment to working towards cohesion and the principle of solidarity between the member states and regions of Europe. Cohesion and solidarity in an individual member state mean that regional and social inequalities are, to a greater or lesser extent, compensated for by budgetary policies. Similarly, in one of the classic examples of a monetary union, the USA, federal budgetary policies help to offset regional inequalities. The EU cannot ignore the historical lessons and political realities.

Second, the concept of fairness must be upheld. However, the EU needs to take a broader view of fairness. It cannot be reduced to an equation between contributions and receipts per member state. A broader calculation based on the overall cost–benefit must be employed. For example, it has been shown that ERDF expenditure not only benefits the regions to which it is allocated, but also other regions that have ties of geography or trade. Common sense would suggest that in a single market the development of the poorer regions is also in the interests of the richer ones.

Finally, the resources of the EU must be set at a level sufficient for it to carry out the tasks that are assigned to it. If it is agreed that a particular task should be carried out by the EU, then it must have the resources to carry out that task. This, rather than arguments in the middle of the night about sharing out relatively small sums, should be the basis of budgetary policy.

The institutional dimension

The principal institutions of the EU – the Commission, the Council of Ministers and the European Parliament – represent a major historical advance over the pattern of behaviour prevalent in European politics for centuries until 1945. The recent institutional turmoil should not obscure the fundamental role played by the EU institutions in the development of European integration, and the essential role they will continue to play in the next century.

The continued work of the institutions is absolutely vital. The fundamental characteristic of these institutions is that their very composition upholds the recognition of the diversity of Europe. Every country is represented at every level. All major and many minor shades of political opinion are expressed in the decision-making process. Some critics accuse the EU decision-making procedures of being too cumbersome, but this is a very small price to pay to ensure that the peoples of the EU are represented in the system. A hasty decision by a majority does not carry the same conviction as a perhaps more leisurely decision arrived at by consensus.

It is particularly evident that the institutions have been in a state of evolution. The scope of the powers of the institutions has widened with successive treaties – the Single European Act, the Maastricht Treaty and the Amsterdam Treaty. The balance between the institutions has also gradually changed over time as the democratically elected Parliament extends its powers. There is no reason to think that the process of institutional change and development is not likely to gather pace in the future.

Some trends can be predicted. Of particular importance to us in Ireland, and indeed in the various parts of Great Britain, will be the enhancement of the regional dimension. With new institutions emerging throughout these islands, we will be leaving behind centuries of centralisation. We will be joining the European mainstream where regional structures play a powerful role in European policy-making. We will be adding our weight to the creation of a Europe of the Regions.

The scrutiny role of domestic parliaments is likely to be enhanced. This is already clearly visible in some countries, especially in Northern Europe. But even legislatures such as the House of Commons, which have traditionally neglected their duty to scrutinise the activities of their representatives in the EU Council of Ministers, are beginning to take this role seriously. In the parliamentary democracies of the EU, domestic scrutiny committees will have an increasing role in supervising the EU activities of ministers from their countries. While many legislatures have traditionally allowed the executive some leeway on foreign affairs, it is increasingly obvious that EU policy is no longer foreign policy, given its impact on so many areas of daily life. However, the task of supervising the Council of Ministers as a collective body can only legally and in practice be carried out by the European Parliament.

Above all, the EU needs to ensure that decisions are effectively implemented. It may be necessary to spend a lot of time and effort in arriving at decisions by consensus. But once we do so, implementation must be guaranteed. Indeed, one of the principal underlying reasons for the recent institutional crisis has been the gap between decision-making and the eventual implementation of decisions – itself partly a function of resource problems. To succeed in this respect means that everyone at all levels in the process of decision-making and implementation should accept their responsibilities and recognise the need for accountability.

The long march of the European Parliament through the EU is now irreversible. Traditionally the smaller member states have been sceptical about enhancing the powers of the European Parliament, since their relative weight is much smaller in the Parliament than in the other institutions. But since the Amsterdam Treaty and its major enhancement of the Parliament's powers, the evolution towards a form of joint authority over most EU policies with the Council of Ministers is inexorable. A qualitative leap has been taken. It will be one of the major challenges to the smaller member states and regions in the future EU to ensure that the principle of consensus is maintained as far as possible. Looked at the other way round, it will also be a challenge to the larger states to avoid falling into the trap of old-style power politics and numbers games. The basic EU principle of respect for diversity and the search for consensus will prove its validity in the future as it has done in the past.

The EU and the world

Beyond its borders, the EU faces three major challenges. How does it continue to be a force for peace? How does it end the continuing partition of Europe? How does it relate to the rest of the world and the global economy?

It is beyond doubt that historically the EU has been a force and an inspiration for peace. Old enemies came together and made sure that they could never wage war on one another again. It has helped bring about peace in South Africa. It is a major backer of peace in the Middle East. It has had a profound influence on our own peace process. It has done all this without any military forces of its own.

There has been a wide-ranging debate throughout Europe and in Ireland over the future of Europe's common foreign and security policy. It has revealed many divergences within the EU. Obviously the security environment looks very different in Vienna or London, Dublin or Berlin. From our perspective, it is important to articulate our own vision of peace and security. It is important to recognise that security cannot be reduced to military strategy. It is a far wider issue.

We need to point to the EU's strengths in the field of conflict resolution. We must enhance the peace dimension of security by emphasising conflict prevention. Above all, we must ensure that the EU has the ability to prevent and pre-empt crises. We could make a start by establishing a conflict prevention and resolution department in the European Commission.

One of the most important tasks the EU faces is to play its part in bringing the partition of Europe to an end. Enlargement of the EU to Central and Eastern Europe, and eventually beyond, is an essential objective if we are really to live up to the name of 'European Union'. While we are aware of the genuine difficulties in the enlargement programme, they should not be used as an excuse to keep our fellow Europeans on the wrong side of a new continent-wide divide.

As one of the world's major trading blocs, our relations with the rest of the world and our place in the global economy are vital. The EU is working hard to adapt to the global economy and the information revolution, but there is still much to be done. The remaining hindrances to the European single market and to free movement must be addressed. Common policies and a comprehensive legislative framework for the information society must be put in place. Scientific and technological research must be developed and exploited. The establishment of trans-European networks in transport and communications must be accelerated. These are all essential if the EU is to thrive in the global economy.

At the same time, we have to accept our obligations to the wider world. As one of the principal players in the World Trade Organisation, we must accept our responsibility to create a level playing field in world trade. We also have to work towards a fairer world economic order in which the poorer countries of the world are given the chance to emerge from decades of deprivation and despair. Whatever influence Ireland already commands in this respect can only be enhanced by working through the EU.

It would be short-sighted for Ireland to neglect its privileged relation with North America. It is a recognition of reality rather than any form of imperialism to see that the relationship between the USA and the EU will be a crucial element in the evolution of the world in the 21st century. Given our membership of the EU and our privileged relationship with the USA, we would be remiss if we did not attempt to act as a bridge between the two blocs.

The EU faces a heavy agenda. But we should face it with confidence. The track record is, despite all the problems and setbacks, very positive. We have already surmounted many challenges and disputes. The vision is there. The institutions are there. Ideas and institutions are a very powerful combination that will allow us to fulfil our obligations.

European Movement Council Members, Directors and Chief Executives from 1954 to 1999

Abbott Henry
Adams Michael
Ahern Bertie
Aliaga-Kelly
  Christopher
Archer Liam
Andrews David
Armstrong Lt Col
Arnold Tom
Attley Bill

Barnes Monica
Barrett Liam
Barrett Sylvester
Barrington Ruth
Barrington Tom
Betson Joanna
Blease William
Blake Lorcan
Blood Bindon
Blunden John
Booth Lionel O.
Bradford Roy
Breatnach Padraig
Brennan Peter
Brown Tony
Brugha Ruairi
Bruton John
Byrne Peter
Byrne J.J
Byrne Noreen

Cahill Liam
Candy Ian
Carroll Willie
Cashman Donal

Cassells Peter
Chubb Basil
Clancy P.J.
Clarke Brendan
Cleary Catherine
Clinton Tom
Cluskey Frank
Colley George
Collins Gerard
Conlon Noel
Connellan Liam
Corboy Denis
Costello Declan
Coughlan Aileen
Cox Tom
Coyle Geoffrey
Coyle John
Croke Gabrielle
Crosbie J
Crowley Eric
Curley Joe
Curtin Mary
Cusack Dr

de Rossa Proinsias
Desmond Barry
de Valera Vivien
Devins Mary
Donnelly John
Dooge Jim
Doolan Jim
Dorgan Jim
Dowd Vincent
Dukes Alan
Dunne James
Dunne P. John

Dunne John
Dunne Ruairí
Dwan Frank

Fahy Joe
Farrell Pat
Finlay Mary
Finlay N.
Finnegan Peter
Fitzgerald Alexis
Fitzgerald Frances
FitzGerald Garret
Fitzgerald Rhona
FitzPatrick J.I.
Foley Carmel
Fouere Irwin
Fulton Mary

Gallivan Liz
Gardiner Frances
Garvey Tom
Geraghty Des
Gibson Norman
Gilligan Peter
Gillis Alan
Gordon Raymond
Graham Alan
Greene Juan
Greene Niall

Halligan Brendan
Hannon Camilia
Hardiman Tom
Harmon Carmel
Harney Mary
Hart Joan

Punch Eileen
Purkiss Clive

Quigley Paul
Quinn Gerard
Quinn Ruairí

Rafter Kevin
Rea Joe
Reilly Hugh
Rice Valentine
Rigby-Jones Michael
Robb Harford
Robinson Mary
Rogan Bernard
Roseingrave Tomás

Ross Miceal
Ryan Eoin
Ryan John
Ryan Richie

Scott Dermot
Shanahan John
Shatter Alan
Sheehan Thomas
Sheridan Brian
Smith C.A.
Smith Louis
Spring Dick
Stanford W.B.
Staunton Miles
Stewart Terry

Sutherland Peter
Sutton Mr
Sweetman Michael

Taylor Ann
Thornley David
Tonge Claude
Tynan Ronan

Wafer Brendan
Wall Frank
Walshe Pádraig
White Vivienne
Woods Michael

Yates Michael

Milestones of European integration and Ireland's membership of the Euopean Union

1948	Congress of the Hague
	Organisation for European Economic Co-operation is established
1949	European Movement is established
	Council of Europe is established
	Schumann Declaration calls for common approach to coal and steel production
1950	Treaty of Paris establishes the European Coal and Steel Community
1954	*The Irish Council of the European Movement is established*
	Failure of European Defence Community
1957	The Treaty of Rome establishes the European Economic Community
1959	*The Irish Council of the European Movement is relaunched*
1961	*Ireland, with the UK, Denmark and Norway, applies for membership of the EEC*
1965	*The Anglo Irish Free Trade Agreement is signed*
1966	The Luxembourg Compromise recognises the right of veto where vital national interests arise
1967	*Ireland's application for membership of the EEC is reactivated*
	Ireland joins the General Agreement on Tariffs and Trade (GATT)
1968	General de Gaulle resigns as President of France
1969	*Negotiations on accession begin with Ireland, the UK, Denmark and Norway*
1972	*Treaty of Accession is signed*
	A referendum on membership of the EEC is held; 83 per cent vote in favour
1973	*Ireland, the UK and Denmark join the EEC*
	Oil crisis leads to severe recession in European economies
1974	European Council meetings of heads of government are instituted
	The first Social Action Programme is initiated by the Commission

1975	Treaty of Brussels
	The Regional Fund is established
1977	The European Court of Auditors is established
1979	First direct elections to the European Parliament
	The European Monetary System is established and Ireland joins, breaking the link with sterling
1981	Greece joins the EEC
1983	Spain and Portugal join the EEC
1984	The European Parliament proposes a Treaty on European Union
1985	Jacques Delors is appointed President of a new Commission and announces the 1992 single market project
	The report of the Dooge Committee is published
	An Intergovernmental Conference is established to plan changes to the Treaty
1987	The Single European Act is agreed
	A referendum is held in Ireland on ratification of the Single European Act following Raymond Crotty's court challenge
	The Social Charter is adopted
1990	An Intergovernmental Conference is established to plan further changes to the Treaties
1991	The Maastricht Treaty, providing for a single European currency and greater powers for the European Parliament, is agreed
1992	*A referendum is held in Ireland on the Maastricht Treaty*
	The MacSharry reforms of the CAP are agreed
1993	The Maastricht Treaty is ratified
1995	Austria, Finland and Sweden join the European Union
1996	An Intergovernmental Conference is established to prepare the Union for enlargement
1996	The Amsterdam Treaty is agreed
1998	*A referendum is held in Ireland on the Amsterdam Treaty*
1999	The euro is introduced as a currency on the financial markets
	The Commission resigns following criticism by the European Parliament
	Elections to the European Parliament
	A new Commission is appointed under President Romano Prodi

Glossary

Acquis communitaire	body of Community law
BEUC	European Bureau of Consumers' Associations
BRITE	Basic Research in Industrial Technologies
CCC	Consumer Consultative Committee
CEEP	Confederation of European Employers
CEEPA	Centre for European Economic and Public Affairs
CEMR	Council of European Municipalities and Regions
CERN	European Nuclear Research Organisation
CET	Common External Tariff
CFSP	Common Foreign and Security Policy
COREPER	Committee of Permanent Representatives to the Council of Ministers
COST	Scientific and Technical Co-operation
CREST	Scientific and Technical Research Committee
CSCE	Conference for Security and Co-operation in Europe
CSF	Community Support Framework
CTT	Common Trade Tariff
DG	Directorate General
EAGGF	European Agriculture Guidance and Guarantee Fund
EBRD	European Bank for Reconstruction and Development
EC	European Communities
ECPR	European Consortium of Political Research
ECSA	European Community Studies Association
EEA	European Environmental Agency
EEC	European Economic Community
EFTA	European Free Trade Area
EIB	European Investment Bank
EIB	European Integration Bureau
ELEC	European League for Economic Co-operation
EMBL	European Molecular Biology Research
EMI	European Monetary Institute
EMS	European Monetary System
EMU	European Monetary Union
EOLAS	Irish Science and Technology Agency

EP	European Parliament
EPC	European Political Co-operation
EPP	European People's Party
Erasmus	student exchange programme
ERDF	European Regional Development Fund
ERM	Exchange Rate Mechanism
ERTI	European Round Table of Industrialists
ESA	European Space Agency
ESF	European Social Fund
ESF	European Science Foundation
ESO	The European Southern Observatory
ESPRIT	European Strategic Programme for Research and Development in Information Technology
ESRI	Economic and Social Research Institute
ESRO	European Space Research Organisation
ETUC	European Trade Union Confederation
EUEAP	EU Environmental Action Programme
EUI	European University Institute in Florence
EURAM	European Research in Advanced Materials
EURATOM	European Atomic Energy Community
EUREKA	European Research Co-ordination Agency
GATT	General Agreement on Tariffs and Trade (now WTO)
GNP	Gross National Product
GVA	gross value added
IEA	International Energy Agency
IEA	Institute for European Affairs (set up in 1991)
IEP	Irish pounds
IFIs	international financial institutions
IFSC	International Financial Services Centre
IIRS	Institute for Industrial Research and Standards
INSC	Irish National Science Council
INTERREG	Inter-regional Fund
IULA	International Union of Local Authorities
Jean Monnet	architect of European integration
JRC	Joint Research Centre
KFOR	Kosovo force under UN mandate in Kosovo and Serbia
LEADER	Commission Rural Development Programme
MEP	Member of the European Parliament
Mezzogiorno	term for southern Italy – underdeveloped region
NAFO	North Atlantic Fishing Organisation
NAFTA	North Atlantic Free Trade Area

NBST	National Board for Science and Technology
NESC	National Economic and Social Council
NMRC	National Microelectronics Research Centre
NOW	New Opportunities for Women programme
NUTS	Nomenclature Statistical Territorial Units
NWCI	National Women's Council of Ireland
OCT	Overseas Countries and Territories
OSCE	Organisation for Security and Co-operation in Europe (cf. CSCE)
PfP	Partnership for Peace – associate membership with the NATO alliance
PHARE	technical aid programmes in central and eastern Europe
R&D	research and development
RDO	Regional Development Organisation
RIA	Royal Irish Academy
SFOR	Peace-keeping force under UN mandate in Bosnia.
TACIS	technical aid programmes in the former Soviet states (formerly Commonwealth of Independent States)
TD	Teachta Dála (member of the lower house of the Irish parliament)
TEPSA	Trans European Policy Studies Association
UCLAF	Task Force Co-ordination de la Lutte Antifraude
UNEP	United Nations Environment Programme (set up in 1972)
UNICE	Confederation of European Industry
UNOSOM	peace-keeping force under UN mandate in Somalia in 1994
URTA	Uruguay Round Trade Agreement
WEU	Western European Union (defence alliance)
WTO	World Trade Organisation

Index